Contents

How to use this book

Welcome to your BTEC National Applied Law course.

Your BTEC National Applied Law qualification will give you the opportunity to gain specific knowledge, understanding and skills that are relevant to your chosen subject or area of work. This new BTEC is a great foundation for you to build the skills you need for employment or further study.

You are joining a course that has a 30-year track record of learner success, with the BTEC National widely recognised within the industry and in higher education as the signature vocational qualification. Over 62 per cent of large companies recruit employees with BTEC qualifications and 100,000 BTEC learners apply to UK universities every year.

Choosing to study for a BTEC National Applied Law qualification is a great decision to make for lots of reasons. Working in the legal services sector offers lots of opportunities in a wide variety of roles. Currently it is estimated that around 370,000 people are employed in this sector, which has an estimated value of over £26 billion to the economy. It is a growth area facing up to the challenges of technological change and innovation. Furthermore, a surge in demand for legal guidance and expertise has been predicted as a direct result of the EU referendum.

How your BTEC is structured

Your BTEC National is divided into **mandatory units** (the ones you must do) and **optional units** (the ones you can choose to do). The number of units you need to do and the units you can cover will depend on the type and size of qualification you are doing.

This book covers all the mandatory units – **Units 1 to 3**. The table below shows how each unit in this book maps to the BTEC National Applied Law qualifications.

Unit title	Mandatory	Optional
Unit 1 Dispute Solving in Civil Law	All sizes	
Unit 2 Investigating Aspects of Criminal Law and the Legal System	All sizes	
Unit 3 Applying the Law	Extended Certificate only	
Unit 4 Aspects of Family Law		Extended Certificate only
Unit 5 Consumer Law		Extended Certificate only
Unit 6 Contract Law		Extended Certificate only
Unit 7 Aspects of Tort		Extended Certificate only

Your learning experience

You may not realise it but you are always learning. Your educational and life experiences are constantly shaping you, your ideas, your thinking and how you view and engage with the world around you.

You are the person most responsible for your own learning experience so it is really important that you understand what you are learning, why you are learning it and why it is important both to your course and to your personal development.

Your learning can be seen as a journey with four phases.

Phase 1	Phase 2	Phase 3	Phase 4
You are introduced to a topic or concept and you start to develop an awareness of what learning is required.	You explore the topic or concept through different methods (e.g. research, questioning, analysis, deep thinking, critical evaluation) and form your own understanding.	You apply your knowledge and skills to a task designed to test your understanding.	You reflect on your learning, evaluate your efforts, identify gaps in your knowledge and look for ways to improve.

During each phase, you will use different learning strategies to secure the core knowledge and skills you need. This student book has been written using similar learning principles, strategies and tools. It has been designed to support your learning journey, to give you control over your own learning, and to equip you with the knowledge, understanding and tools that you need to be successful in your future studies or career.

Features of this book

In this student book there are lots of different features. They are there to help you learn about the topics in your course in different ways and understand it from multiple perspectives. Together these features:

- explain what your learning is about
- help you to build your knowledge
- help you understand how to succeed in your assessment
- help you to reflect on and evaluate your learning
- help you to link your learning to the workplace.

In addition, each individual feature has a specific purpose, designed to support important learning strategies. For example, some features will:

- get you to question assumptions around what you are learning
- make you think beyond what you are reading about
- help you make connections across your learning and across units
- draw comparisons between your own learning and real-world workplace environments
- help you to develop some of the important skills that you will need for the workplace, including team work, effective communication and problem solving.

Features that explain what your learning is about

Getting to know your unit

This section introduces the unit and explains how you will be assessed. It gives an overview of what will be covered and will help you to understand why you are doing the things you are asked to do in this unit.

Getting started

This feature appears at the start of every unit and is designed to get you thinking about the unit and what it involves. It will also help you to identify what you may already know about some of the topics in the unit and act as a starting point for understanding the skills and knowledge you will need to develop to complete the unit.

Features that help you to build your knowledge

Research

This asks you to research a topic in greater depth. These features will help to expand your understanding of a topic and develop your research and investigation skills. All of this will be invaluable for your future progression, both professionally and academically.

Key case

In this feature, you will be given the facts of criminal and civil cases which have been dealt with in the courts and you will also be informed of the legal principle – the point of law illustrated by the case. These cases can be referred to in assessments to clarify how the law is applied today.

Discussion

Discussion features encourage you to talk to other students about a topic, working together to increase your understanding of the topic and to understand other people's perspectives on an issue. These features will also help to build your teamworking skills, which will be invaluable in your future professional and academic career.

Key terms

Concise and simple definitions are provided for key words, phrases and concepts, giving you, at a glance, a clear understanding of the key ideas in each unit. Key terms are highlighted in **bold** in the index.

Link

Link features show any links between units or within the same unit, helping you to identify knowledge you have learned elsewhere that will help you to achieve the requirements of the unit. Remember, although your BTEC National is made up of several units, there are common themes that are explored from different perspectives across the whole of your course.

Further reading and resources

This contains a list of other resources - such as books, journals, articles or websites - you can use to expand your knowledge of the unit content. This is a good opportunity for you to take responsibility for your own learning, as well as preparing you for research tasks that you may need to do academically or professionally.

Features connected to your assessment

Your course is made up of mandatory and optional units. There are two different types of mandatory unit:

- externally assessed
- internally assessed.

The features that support you in preparing for assessment are below. But first, what is the difference between these two different types of unit?

Externally assessed units

These units will give you the opportunity to demonstrate your knowledge and understanding, or your skills, in a direct way. For these units, you will complete a task, set directly by Pearson, in controlled conditions. This could take the form of an exam or it could be another type of task. You may have the opportunity to prepare in advance, to research and make notes about a topic that can be used when completing the assessment.

Internally assessed units

Internally assessed units will involve you completing a series of assignments, set and marked by your tutor. The assignments you complete will allow you to demonstrate your learning in a number of different ways, from a written report to a presentation to a video recording and observation statements of you completing a practical task. Whatever the method, you will need to make sure that you have clear evidence of what you achieved and how you did it.

Assessment practice

These features give you the opportunity to practise some of the skills you will need during the unit assessment. They do not fully reflect the actual assessment tasks but will help you to prepare for them.

Plan – Do - Review

You'll also find handy advice on how to plan, complete and evaluate your work after you have completed it. This is designed to get you thinking about the best way to complete your work and to build your skills and experience before doing the actual assessment. These prompt questions are designed to get you started with thinking about how the way you work, as well as understand why you do things.

Getting ready for assessment

This section will help you to prepare for external assessment. It gives practical advice on preparing for and sitting exams or a set task. It provides a series of sample answers for the types of question that you will need to answer in your external assessment, including guidance on the good points of these answers and ways in which they could be improved.

Features to help you reflect on and evaluate your learning

PAUSE POINT Pause points appear after a section of each unit and give you the opportunity to review and reflect upon your own learning. The ability to reflect on your own performance is a key skill that you'll need to develop and use throughout your life, and will be essential whatever your future plans are.

Hint **Extend** These also give you suggestions to help cement your knowledge and indicate other areas you can look at to expand it.

Reflect

These features allow you to reflect on how the knowledge gained in the unit may affect your behaviour in a workplace situation. This will help to place the topic in a professional context, and also help you to review your own conduct and develop your employability skills.

Features that link your learning with the workplace

Scenario

Scenarios throughout the book allow you to apply the learning and knowledge from each unit to a scenario from the workplace or industry. They include questions to help you consider the wider context of a topic. They show how the course content is reflected in the real world and help you to build familiarity with issues you may find in a real-world workplace.

Case study

Case studies are used to allow you to apply the learning and knowledge from the unit to a scenario from the workplace or the industry. Case studies include questions to help you consider the wider context of a topic. This is an opportunity to see how the unit's content is reflected in the real world, and for you to build familiarity with issues you may find in a real-world workplace.

THINK ▶FUTURE

This is a special case study where someone working in the industry talks about the job role they do and the skills they need. This comes with a *Focusing your skills* section, which gives suggestions for how you can begin to develop the employability skills and experiences needed to be successful in a career in your chosen sector. This is an excellent opportunity to help you identify what you could do, inside and outside of your BTEC National studies, to build up your employability skills.

About the authors

Nicholas Price

Nick has considerable experience of teaching and assessing law. He has taught various law courses, including applied law, at a sixth-form college on the south coast. He is an experienced senior examiner with a major exam board. He has contributed to several legal textbooks.

Ann Summerscales

Ann left college with few qualifications, meaning employment options were limited to factory work. However, after getting married and having three sons, she returned to education and gained an LLB, followed by a teaching qualification and later a diploma in management studies. For over 20 years she has pursued a career in teaching at both FE and HE level, and has found it a pleasure and a privilege to contribute to the futures and career aspirations of hundreds of learners in the North West of England. She feels fortunate that all of the work she has undertaken has allowed her to continually research the law and track developments over time, as well as to become a published author.

Richard Wortley

Richard has held a number of examining and assessing roles over the past 25 years. He has taught law at all levels from GCSE to undergraduate and has been a series editor of exam board approved A Level texts. He has developed specifications in law and business for several examination boards and enjoys the challenges of keeping up to date with and writing on his degree subject, law. He retired from management in a large FE college in 2006 to concentrate on examining, specification development, writing and teacher support. When time permits, he enjoys mountain biking near his home in the Yorkshire Dales and following national and international motorsport.

1 Dispute Solving in Civil Law

Getting to know your unit

Assessment
You will be assessed by an external assessment under supervised conditions. The assessment is set and marked by Pearson.

This unit uses the law of negligence to show how claims, such as those resulting from a car crash, are dealt with in English law. Most people assume that an insurance company will deal with these claims. This is not always the case, so you need to know how disputes are settled and how the law can be used to help people.

You will also develop legal skills that will help you in your personal life and career, whether the career is in law or not.

How you will be assessed

This unit is assessed under supervised conditions. You will be provided with a case study a set period of time before the supervised assessment period in order to carry out research.

The supervised assessment period will be explained to you. During this period, you will have to complete a set task, which will be marked externally.

The activities in this book will not form part of the assessment you will have to complete, but will help you develop an understanding of the law so that you can be successful.

As the guidelines for assessment can change, you should refer to the official assessment guidance on the Pearson Qualifications website for the latest definitive guidance.

Grade descriptors

To achieve a grade, you will be expected to demonstrate the following attributes across the essential content of the unit.

To pass this unit:

Learners will demonstrate knowledge and understanding of the civil legal system, the relevant legal personnel and the factors that determine where disputes are heard. They will demonstrate research, referencing and communication skills appropriate to the audience. They will be able to suggest appropriate sources of advice and funding for civil claims. They will demonstrate an understanding of how precedent operates in the courts, and know how to research relevant law and reference sources correctly. They can make some recommendations for actions in the context of negligence claims resulting from interpretation of the legal information provided.

To achieve a distinction:

Learners will be able to critically evaluate, justify and synthesise information relating to negligence claims, their viability and success. They will demonstrate competent legal research and referencing skills and their communication and presentation will be professional and appropriate. They will apply key concepts and legal precedents to real-life scenarios, analyse complex information from different sources and assess its impact and influence on legal decisions. Learners can consider the implications in the context of the legal detail both given and created, making appropriate justified recommendations for necessary actions.

Assessment outcomes

AO1 Demonstrate knowledge and understanding of precedent, the civil justice system and process and the concept of negligence in English civil law, together with legal skills of research and communication.

AO2 Be able to apply knowledge and understanding to examine negligence scenarios and advise clients on the likely outcome of negligence claims, making connections to precedent, courts and appeals, personnel and funding.

AO3 Analyse legal information demonstrating the ability to interpret the potential impact and influence on future cases.

AO4 Evaluate evidence to make informed judgements with appropriate justification, synthesising ideas and evidence from several sources to support arguments.

Getting started

With a partner, discuss what losses you might have if you went down with serious food poisoning after eating badly prepared food in a café. Who could you turn to for help?

Civil dispute resolution

Features of civil law

There are many different ways to classify law. At its simplest, there are two main areas – civil law and criminal law. In Unit 1, you will look at some aspects of the English legal system, with a focus on civil law. If you study law after this course, you may come across other areas of law, such as public law and international law.

Link

Look at Section D of this Unit to find out more about duty of care.

Aim and purpose of civil law

Civil law covers all legal issues, statutes and lawsuits not related to criminal law, including:

- business
- contracts
- estates
- accidents
- negligence
- domestic (family) relations.

The main aim of civil law is to protect people and businesses in our society. The law sets out the rights and duties for businesses and individuals. For example, road users have a duty of care to others on the road. Where there is a road accident, a civil case might be brought by the **claimant** against the person alleged to have caused the accident (the **defendant**) under an area of the **law of tort** called **negligence**.

There is also the possibility of a claim under **contract law**, for example, where goods have been bought but are defective.

Civil law usually seeks to achieve **compensation** for the person who has suffered loss or damage – for example, for repair of a car after a minor car accident. Alternatively, civil law can be used to stop someone doing something that affects another person's rights – for example, to deal with a dispute with a neighbour who regularly practises playing the drums at three o'clock in the morning. A summary of civil law is explained in Table 1.1.

Table 1.1: Summary of basic points about civil law

Civil law	Brief explanation
Purpose	If a civil wrong is committed and the party at fault is found to be liable, the purpose of the case is to find a solution or remedy for the injured party.
Outcome and remedies	The outcome for the injured party is usually compensation or, where compensation is insufficient, a court order such as an injunction to stop the defendant continuing the activity.

Key terms

Claimant – the person or organisation complaining that they have suffered loss or damage.

Defendant – the person alleged to have caused the loss or damage.

Law of tort – part of the civil law dealing with civil wrongs, such as negligence and nuisance.

Negligence – a failure to act or acting in a way not expected of a reasonable person.

Contract law – part of the civil law protecting people and businesses who have made agreements – for example, about buying and selling goods and services.

Compensation – a sum of money paid to someone (a claimant) who has successfully brought a case against someone else (a defendant).

▸ **Table 1.1:** *Continued*

Civil law	Brief explanation
Taking the case to court	The decision to take the matter to court is made by the individual who wishes to make a claim that cannot be settled in any other way such as by negotiation.
Parties to an action	The two sides in a civil action are the claimant (who is making a complaint against the other party to show that they are liable for injury, damage or death) and the defendant (who will argue that they are not at fault).
Standard of proof	In a civil case, the decision is made on a 'balance of probabilities'. In other words, to make a decision against the defendant the judge has to be over 50 per cent sure that they are liable.
Case names for current and past cases	Civil cases are referred to by the surname or business name of the claimant and that of the defendant – for example, Paris v Stepney Borough Council (1951).
Terminology	Words such as 'sue', 'liable', 'not liable' and 'remedies' relate to civil law.
Courts	If the parties cannot agree to an out-of-court settlement, a trial will take place in either the County Court or the High Court.
Examples of areas of civil law	Areas of civil law include negligence in the law of tort and contract law.

Standard and burden of proof in civil cases

Link

You will look at criminal law in Unit 2.

In every civil case, evidence is needed that shows why the claimant should win their case. The standard of proof is the level of certainty with which the claimant's case must be proved. In civil cases, the **balance of probabilities** is used. This is a lower standard than in criminal cases, which must be proved beyond reasonable doubt.

The **burden of proof** sets out who has to prove their case to the required standard. In civil cases, this is the claimant.

Key terms

Balance of probabilities – the standard of proof in civil cases that means that the judge must be more than 50 per cent sure that the defendant is liable.

Burden of proof – in civil cases, the claimant must prove their case on the balance of probabilities.

Courts of first instance – the courts that hear the initial trials of cases (either the County Court or the High Court).

Doctrine of precedent – once a point of law has been decided in a particular case, that statement of the law must be applied in all future cases containing the same material facts.

Discussion

Why do you think that there are different standards of proof in civil and criminal cases? Do you think that there should be any difference between the two standards?

Make a list of the points your group discusses and see whether your views change by the end of the course.

PAUSE POINT What is the difference between the burden of proof and the standard of proof?

Hint Think about how a legal case might be proved.

Extend Do you think the burden of proof should be higher in civil cases? What arguments are there for and against this suggestion?

Structure and jurisdiction of the English civil courts

There are only two civil courts in which a case may be started:

- a County Court
- the High Court

Civil court hierarchy

There is a hierarchy of courts in England so that there is a clear route from the initial trial of a case to the final appeal. This is very important for the **doctrine of precedent** that you will study in Section C of this unit.

Civil courts of first instance

The court that hears the initial trial of a case is either the County Court or the High Court. As these are the only courts that hear an initial trial, they are known as **courts of first instance**.

Whether a case begins in the County Court or the High Court depends on the complexity of the case and the amount of money being claimed. For example, less complex cases and those seeking smaller amounts of money are heard by lower-ranking judges in the County Court. Figure 1.1 shows how cases are allocated to a relevant court.

High Court
Claim above £100,000 or personal injuries above £50,000

County Court Multi-track
Any claim not in fast track or small claims track

County Court Fast-Track
Claims up to £25,000 and personal injuries up to £50,000

County Court Small Claims Track
Claims up to £10,000 or personal injuries up to £1000

Figure 1.1: Diagram of the civil court structure – courts of first instance

Cases in the County Court may be heard by a **District judge** or a **Circuit judge**. District judges are full-time judges who deal with the majority of cases in the County Courts. There are also deputy District judges who are appointed on a part-time basis. Circuit judges are more senior, and usually have served either part-time as **recorders** on criminal cases or full-time as District judges on civil cases. Some judges **sit** part-time after they have retired and are then known as deputy Circuit judges.

Cases in the High Court are heard by High Court judges. The High Court is divided into three divisions for administrative purposes and to enable the High Court judges to become specialists in a particular area of law.

Key terms

District judge – a full-time judge who deals with the majority of cases in the County Courts.

Circuit judge – a more senior judge to a District judge.

Recorders – a judge who may sit in both Crown and County Courts, but most start by sitting in the Crown Court. The appointment is part-time, perhaps for 20–30 days per year, and is the first step on the ladder of judicial appointments.

Sit – to hold a session at court or perform an act that is judicial in nature.

- **Queen's Bench division** – this division's main work is hearing cases involving contract and tort cases in which the amount claimed is over £100,000, or personal injuries where the damages are likely to exceeded £50,000. It also has several specialist areas of work with separate courts:
  - Commercial Court, which deals with matters such as banking and insurance law. These cases are often dealt with by the judge considering paperwork and written submissions rather than a formal trial.
  - Mercantile Court, which deals with commercial and business disputes.
  - Admiralty Court, which deals with shipping matters, such as claims for damages caused by collisions at sea. The judges are helped by shipping experts (assessors from Masters of Trinity House).
  - Technology and Construction Court, which deals with cases involving technical knowledge about construction, engineering or computing.
  - Administrative Court, which reviews decisions made by people or bodies, such as local authorities and regulatory bodies. This is often dealt with through a process known as judicial review.
- **Chancery division** – this division deals with disputes about matters such as land, wills and **insolvency**. There is also a separate specialist court within the Chancery division, called the Companies Court. It handles cases relating to the insolvency of companies.
- **Family division** – this division deals with some aspects of divorce, children's welfare and medical treatment. Most family law matters are dealt with in Family Law Courts rather than the High Court Family division.

Key terms

Insolvency – when an individual or business cannot pay its debts. It is usually accompanied by having more liabilities than assets.

Appellate courts – courts that hear appeals from first-instance decisions.

Link

The Family division is explored in greater detail in Unit 4.

Civil courts of appeal

If the result of the case in the High Court or the County Court is considered incorrect, by either the claimant or the defendant, there may be an appeal. The case is passed on to one of the **appellate courts**.

The appeal routes can be seen in Figures 1.2 and 1.3.

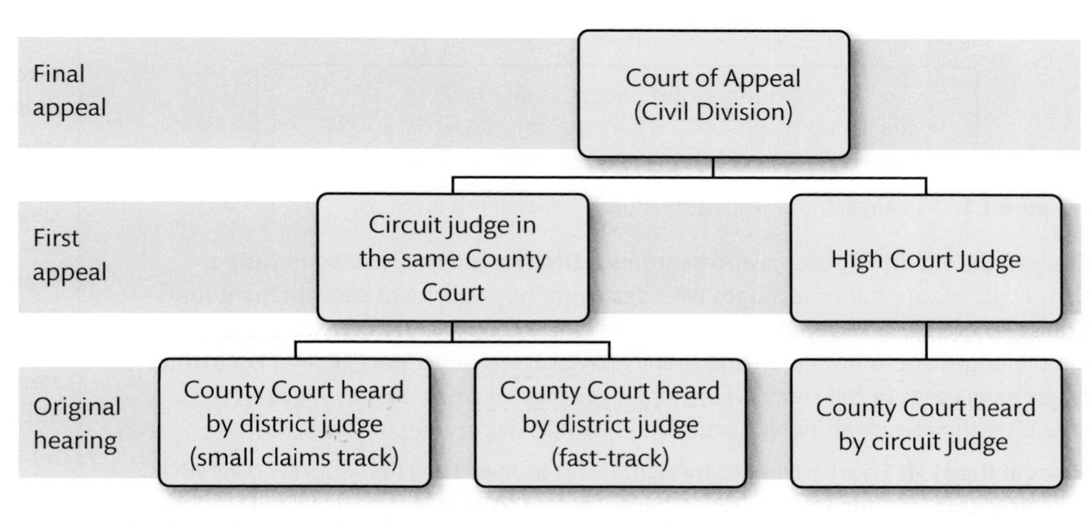

Figure 1.2: Appeal structure from small claims and fast-track cases in the County Court

High Court or County Court multi-track case → Court of Appeal (Civil Division) → Supreme Court

▶ **Figure 1.3:** Appeal structure from multi-track cases in the County Court and from the High Court

The appeal structure may seem quite complex, but it is designed to be efficient and cost effective for the parties involved in the cases and for the Courts Service.

How to appeal

An appeal is requested by filing an appeal notice within 21 days after the date of the decision of the lower court. Usually, permission is required for appeals. Permission will not be given unless the appeal is likely to succeed. For almost all appeals, the appeal court will allow an appeal only where the decision of the lower court was wrong or unjust because of serious irregularities in the lower court. This restriction shows confidence in all judges, but a willingness to admit that sometimes mistakes are made. There are relatively few appeals each year, as shown in Table 1.2.

▶ **Table 1.2:** Appeal cases 2009–13

Year	Supreme Court	Court of Appeal Civil Division	Court of Appeal Criminal Division
2009	49	1275	7195
2010	51	1225	7250
2011	63	1297	7475
2012	71	1190	7610
2013	76	1154	6851

PAUSE POINT List the different courts in the hierarchy.

Hint Start with the Supreme Court and work downwards.

Extend Write a brief statement about what each court does.

Role of judges in civil cases

A wide range of cases can be taken to court. There might be a dispute about damage to goods or recovery of a debt or a large personal injury claim. These claims could be between individuals or involve small or large businesses.

Civil cases are heard in open court, which means that the public are allowed to come to the court to listen to the hearing. There are also hearings in the judge's private room from which the public are excluded. These hearings might be about when or which documents or witnesses will be needed in the trial. You will often read about court cases in newspapers or see references to them on the Internet. Such media reports of previous cases can be useful but are not guaranteed to be accurate enough for judges to use in court when looking at the case before them. Law reports will be looked at in more detail in section C of this unit.

Discussion

Find a current civil case in the news, for example a road accident or hospital error. Follow ithe case week by week by keeping extracts from newspapers or articles from reliable websites.

▶ A civil court room

Most civil disputes do not end up in a trial in court. Many are dealt with through one of the alternative dispute resolution methods, which you will look at later in the unit.

Where a case does go to court, the aim is to make the process as simple and efficient as possible. Judges in civil cases do not have the power to imprison a losing party. There are usually no juries in civil cases (with rare exceptions). The judge hears the case alone and decides the outcome by finding facts from the evidence given, applying the relevant law to those facts and then giving a reasoned judgment. There may also be an argument about what the law is.

The court hearing

Before any hearing, and particularly before a trial, the judge reads the relevant case papers to become familiar with the dispute, the evidence and the relevant law. The judge also has an important role in case management. This includes:

- encouraging the parties to cooperate with each other in the conduct of the case
- helping the parties to agree to a settlement of the case
- encouraging the parties to use an appropriate alternative dispute resolution procedure
- controlling the progress of the case.

Where there is a trial, the judge keeps control in court and makes sure that witnesses can be cross-examined to ensure that their evidence is as reliable as possible. This makes sure that the case is presented as fully and fairly as possible. During the case, the judge may feel that a point needs more explanation and will ask questions. The judge also decides on all matters of procedure that may arise during a hearing.

Sometimes the parties will have agreed the relevant facts. If they have, it is not necessary for the judge to hear any oral evidence from the parties or witnesses. The judge will have to decide how to apply the law to the facts agreed.

Judgment

When the law has been applied, the judge makes a decision in the form of a judgment. The judgment sets out a reasoned argument based on the relevant law. Judgments are presented in writing so that a decision is available to the parties and to other interested persons. This is very important, as these decisions form the basis of much of the law by setting **judicial precedent**. Judicial precedent is considered in detail in section C of this unit.

The part of the decision that the parties are particularly interested in is the order made at the end of the judgment. This is often a statement of the sum of money to be paid by one party to another. It could also be an order about arrangements for visits to see children by one party in a divorce or an order to prevent activities taking place through an injunction. The task of the judge to is to decide on the appropriate outcome, and to agree the precise terms and wording of any order made.

Costs

After the judgment has been made and any order agreed, the judge must deal with the matter of **costs**. These may amount to a large sum of money. The judge's role is to ensure that the amount claimed for costs is fair. Costs are likely to include the fees of any lawyers, court fees paid out by the parties, fees of expert witnesses, earnings lost, and travelling and other expenses incurred by the parties and their witnesses.

While the general rule is that the unsuccessful party will have to pay the successful party's costs, the judge may decide, for example, that the unsuccessful party should pay only a proportion of the successful party's costs, or that each party should pay their own costs.

The trial process can be quite worrying for the people involved, as a court is not a place with which many people are familiar. To help with this and to keep costs down, there is a small claims track in the County Court which is less formal, quicker and cheaper than a full trial.

The small claims track is for cases involving less than £10,000, or, where personal injuries are involved, the likely award of damages is less than £1000. Here, the judge acts as an **arbitrator** between the parties, in a much less formal manner than a trial. The hearing takes place in a private room rather than in a court room.

Key terms

Judicial precedent – the system whereby a judge must follow the decision made in previous cases where the facts are the same as those in the present case.

Costs – the expenses of the winning party that are usually ordered to be paid by the losing party.

Arbitrator – an impartial person who makes a decision on a dispute by means of arbitration. This is an alternative to a court hearing to settle a dispute.

Can you list the various roles that a judge takes in the course of a case? Can you put them in order of importance?

Hint List all the points you can think of. Consider the start, middle and end of a trial.

Extend Decide which of these are general aspects of a judge's role, which are preparatory to a trial and which relate to the trial itself.

Alternatives to the courts in civil dispute resolution

Alternative dispute resolution (ADR) refers to ways of resolving disputes that do not involve going to court. ADR has been encouraged by the government for many years, as it is cheaper, simpler and more easily accessed by the general public. Businesses have also been encouraged to use ADR for the additional reason that disputes are resolved in private. Most businesses are keen to avoid bad publicity that might arise as a result of a court case involving allegations about their poor-quality goods, service or treatment of their employees.

ADR processes and regulations are improved regularly, as can be seen in the Alternative Dispute Resolution for Consumer Disputes (Amendment) Regulations 2015 and the increased encouragement to use online dispute resolution.

Types of ADR

There are several types of ADR that you will need to know about:

- arbitration
- mediation
- ombudsmen.
- conciliation
- negotiation

Key terms

Arbitration – a service that provides an impartial referee to settle disputes.

Conciliation – a process where an impartial expert (known as a conciliator) encourages the two sides to come to an agreement between themselves.

Mediation – a process that focuses on working on the relationship between the parties involved.

Arbitration

Arbitration uses an independent arbitrator instead of a judge. The arbitrator may be agreed by the parties in dispute. Often, an expert in the area of work that is in dispute is chosen. For example, a dispute about building work may be settled by an arbitrator recommended by the Royal Institute of British Architects (RIBA).

Arbitration is usually based on the paper evidence provided, rather than evidence from witnesses in person. The decision the arbitrator makes is legally binding. You cannot start a civil claim in the courts later if you do not agree with the arbitrator's decision. However, you can go to court later to enforce the decision if that has not been carried out.

Some arbitration schemes are free. Where fees are payable, it is usually still cheaper than going to court.

Conciliation

Conciliation involves an independent person helping to make a settlement between the parties in dispute. Conciliators play an active role and make suggestions about how to resolve the dispute. Conciliation is often offered first in consumer cases to attempt to settle disputes about goods bought.

Mediation

Mediation focuses on working on the parties' relationship and is completely voluntary and confidential. An independent, impartial person helps the parties to reach a solution to the dispute that is acceptable to both. Mediation is common in family matters where the relationship between the parties is sensitive, especially where children are involved.

Mediators do not make judgments or decide the outcome of the dispute. They try to help the parties understand the issues and see the options for resolving the dispute. This is done by asking questions that help to uncover their problems and the best way to solve them. The mediator can talk to both sides separately or together.

There is a list of local mediators who provide members of the public and businesses with a simple, low-cost method of resolving a wide range of civil disputes out of court. Their fees, if agreed through the government website, are fixed based on the amount being claimed, as shown in Table 1.3.

Table 1.3: The cost of mediation

Amount you are claiming	Fees per party	Length of session
£5,000 or less*	£50 + VAT	1 hour
	£100 + VAT	2 hours
£5,000 to £15,000	£300 + VAT	3 hours
£15,000 to £50,000**	£425 + VAT	4 hours

* The mediator/mediation provider should agree in advance whether this should be dealt with in one or two hours. For the one-hour rate, the option is available to settle over the telephone if appropriate, and if the parties agree.

** If the claim is for more than £50,000, the fees will need to be agreed with the organisation providing the mediation.

Negotiation

Negotiation is a direct discussion between two parties to find a solution to their dispute. This is often conducted between the parties themselves. However, once solicitors are involved, they will continue trying to negotiate a settlement even while the case is with the court. Negotiation through solicitors is more expensive than negotiating directly with each other.

Ombudsmen

An **ombudsman** is a person who investigates complaints about organisations. They may be able to help resolve a complaint without going to court. There are different ombudsmen for different industries, such as the Financial Ombudsman Service for the financial sector. You can use the Ombudsman Association to find the right person for a complaint. Ombudsmen are independent, free of charge and unbiased. In most cases, a party must complain first to the organisation with which they are in dispute, before making a complaint to the ombudsman.

Investigations by an ombudsman can take a long time. If they find that a complaint is justified, they will recommend what the organisation should do to put things right. An ombudsman cannot force an organisation to go along with their recommendations, but organisations almost always do.

Research

Find out about mediators in your local area. A good starting point would be to look here: **https://civilmediation.justice.gov.uk**

Key terms

Negotiation – a direct discussion between two disputing parties, with the aim of finding a solution.

Ombudsman – a person who investigates complaints about organisations.

Adversarial process – a process of setting out two conflicting positions for judgment.

Discussion

You bought a new, expensive mobile phone two months ago. The battery no longer holds its charge. The shop you bought it from tells you to contact the manufacturer. When you do, the manufacturer tells you to get the shop to replace it.

The shop states you must have abused the phone or used an incorrect charger.

Discuss in a small groups whether you would rather go to court or use a form of ADR. Think about the advantages and disadvantages of your decision.

Comparison of ADR methods with each other and with civil courts

The civil justice procedure has been criticised for its cost, duration, complexity, lack of accessibility and use of an **adversarial process**. Civil cases often face delays and legal terminology, rules and procedures all add to the complexity. Going to court may require legal representation, which can be very expensive. Not everyone can afford to take a legal issue to court and therefore some people are denied access to justice. The fact that cases have a winner and a loser and use an adversarial process drives the parties in dispute further apart, whereas ADR tries to bring them closer together. Some of the strengths and weaknesses of ADR are outlined in Table 1.4.

Table 1.4: Advantages and disadvantages of using ADR

Advantages of ADR	Disadvantages of ADR
Quicker and cheaper, as many ADR procedures do not need legal representation. ADR also attracts less publicity.	There can be a lack of legal expertise.
ADR procedure is less formal than in courts and less complicated, leading to a less stressful experience for the parties.	There is a lack of certainty, as each case is settled on its own merits.
ADR schemes are carried out by people with specialist knowledge related to the area of dispute.	Decisions can be difficult to enforce.
ADR aims to provide a solution that keeps both parties satisfied.	The dispute may still end up being resolved in court.

Research

Think about each type of ADR. Do some research on each of the following bullet points in relation to each type of ADR. Discuss your findings as a group.

- Cost of using the type of ADR
- Time for the process to be completed
- Privacy of the process
- Are appeals available against an unsatisfactory decision?
- How formal are the proceedings?
- Is legal representation allowed or needed?
- How easy is it to access the type of ADR?
- How appropriate is ADR for the type of dispute?

Link

Legal sources, and delegated legislation will be covered in more detail in Unit 2.

Legal skills

Legal skills include general skills that are transferable to many careers. There are communication skills that lawyers, in particular, require to do their job. There are also specific skills that relate to finding law relevant to the problem that the client has posed to the lawyer - researching and referencing legal information.

Researching and referencing legal information

You will always be required to justify your arguments. In law, this is done by stating the relevant law and where it comes from. This stated law can then be applied to the facts of the case or the point you are making by showing how it demonstrates the point.

The law is found in decided cases and Acts of **Parliament** (also known as statutes) and in forms of delegated legislation.

Key terms

Parliament – the body authorised to make laws. In the UK, Parliament consists of the elected House of Commons, the appointed House of Lords and the Queen all acting together.

Precedent – a legal case that establishes a principle or rule, used by the court when deciding later similar cases.

Decided cases

The judgments made in previously decided cases form the **precedent** of your argument. These cases are found in law reports, which are discussed in more detail later in this unit.

Acts of Parliament

Acts of Parliament are much easier to reference as they can be found on the government website, but it is not always easy to find the exact part you are looking for. An Act of Parliament creates a new law or changes an existing law.

Access to Justice Act 1999

1999 CHAPTER 22

An Act to establish the Legal Services Commission, the Community Legal Services and the Criminal Defence Services; to amend the law of legal aid in Scotland; to make further provision about legal services; to make provision about appeals, courts, judges and court proceedings; to amend the law about magistrates and magistrates' courts; and to make provision about immunity from action and costs and indemnities for certain officials exercising judicial functions.

[27th July 1999]

Be it enacted by the Queen's most Excellent Majesty, by and with the advice and consent of the Lords Spiritual and Temporal, and Commons, in this present Parliament assembled, and by the authority of the same, as follows:–

An example of an Act of Parliament

An Act of Parliament is known by its title and then the relevant section number(s) and subsection if appropriate.

This might appear as follows:

Theft Act 1968 Section 1 subsections 1 and 2

1 Basic definition of theft.

(1) A person is guilty of theft if he dishonestly appropriates property belonging to another with the intention of permanently depriving the other of it; and 'thief' and 'steal' shall be construed accordingly.

(2) It is immaterial whether the appropriation is made with a view to gain, or is made for the thief's own benefit.

This would be written as: 'Theft Act 1968 s1(1) and (2)'.

Methods of appropriate professional communication

Discussion

How important do you think it is to communicate well as a lawyer? What are the reasons for good communication? What might happen if communication is not good or is to the wrong person? Summarise your findings and share them with other groups.

As a lawyer, you have to communicate with:

- clients
- other lawyers and colleagues
- the courts.

▶ It is essential that lawyers can communicate clearly to offer ideas and advice to their clients. Consider what other information they may need to communicate effectively.

Clients

Before any communication starts, you need to remember that there is total **confidentiality** between you and your client. Usually a lawyer will have to ask permission to carry on discussions with the client with someone else present. This should be the case if you do work experience with a solicitor.

Key term

Confidentiality – keeping information private.

Communication with your clients is a two-way process. The first things to do are to listen and to read instructions and documents carefully. Remember that your client is likely to be in unfamiliar surroundings and might be anxious. Having listened and read, you need to ask relevant questions. At first, these questions might be quite general, but your knowledge and understanding of the general area of law in question should allow you to collect more information. You are likely to have more questions when you have reflected on what you have learned and researched the specific areas of law involved. This requires an eye for detail and precision in what you do.

When you communicate with clients, whether by talking to them or in writing, you need to use language that is appropriate. Your client may not understand legal terms, so you will have to be able to explain them clearly and accurately.

Solicitors and barristers communicate with each other often, and so communicate with each other in a way that recognises their professional status. However, barristers often meet or have to draft letters to the solicitor's client, so they, too, will need to be aware of communication issues with the client.

Key terms

Solicitor – a member of the legal profession regulated by the Law Society who is qualified to deal with all legal matters. A solicitor may also instruct barristers and represent clients in some courts.

Barrister – a member of the legal profession regulated by the Bar Council. Barristers specialise in particular areas of law and act as advocates, draft court and legal documents and are sources of advice.

Other lawyers

When you work with other lawyers, you may be dealing with another **solicitor** who is acting for the other party to the case (or other parties if there is more than one involved). Alternatively, you may deal with a **barrister** who will work on your case on behalf of your client.

In addition to the expectation that other lawyers will be familiar with legal terminology, there are some important things to be aware of when communicating with other lawyers.

- Communications 'without prejudice'

Such communications are usually made at the beginning of a document such as a letter or an email, but possibly at a meeting. To be 'without prejudice' means the documents are not admissible in evidence, as they are aimed at settling a dispute.

- Communications between solicitors and barristers

A solicitor briefs or instructs a barrister (who is known as 'counsel'). The barrister is sent instructions (when asked to give an opinion on a case) or a brief (if the barrister is to appear in court). Instructions are always headed with details of the court and parties followed by a heading showing what counsel is instructed to do. See Figure 1.4 for an example. Examples of other communications can easily be found online.

The instructions or brief should include:

- who is instructing or briefing the barrister
- on behalf of whom they are instructed or briefed
- other parties to the case
- the background to the case
- the nature of the dispute or case
- a list of relevant events, in date order
- important dates and deadlines
- what the barrister is being asked to do – for example, give an opinion as to the law, draft some legal documents and appear at court
- copies of relevant documents such as court papers, correspondence, contracts or details of losses or injuries

Barristers will reply with an opinion as requested or appear at court at the correct place and time. They might suggest a meeting with the client or the solicitor to discuss the case further. This is known as a 'conference with counsel'.

Barristers do not discuss fees directly with the instructing solicitor or client. This is always done through their barrister's clerk, who will deal with all such administrative matters.

IN THE HIGH COURT

BRISTOL DISTRICT REGISTRY

JAMES TAYLOR (claimant) v John Smith (respondent)

INSTRUCTIONS TO COUNSEL TO DRAFT DEFENCE AND COUNTERCLAIM

Instructing Solicitors are instructed by ABC Plc Insurance Company to represent their insured driver John Smith of 47 Blodwyn Close, Alderley Edge, Cheshire, who is the defendant in these proceedings.

Proceedings have been commenced by Mr James Taylor of 143 Acacia Avenue, Wilmslow, Cheshire against Mr Smith. Mr Taylor is represented by solicitors on the instructions of his insurers DEF plc.

Background to the case

Mr Taylor alleges that he was returning on foot from an evening out with friends at The Farmers Arms on 14 June 2015. Mr Taylor claims that as he was crossing South Oak Lane, Wilmslow he was hit by Mr Smith's car and suffered a number of injuries. Mr Taylor had spent the evening meeting friends at a local public house but states that he was sober and that his actions in crossing the road where not affected by any alcohol consumed. He is seeking compensation for these injuries and together with loss of earnings for the period until he returned to work on 10 October 2015. He claims that Mr Smith was driving too fast and not paying proper attention to him as a pedestrian who was crossing the road.
In his statement Mr Smith states that he was observing the 30 mph speed limit, and had slowed down near the junction with Acacia Avenue when he saw someone on the pavement unsteady on his feet, whom he now believes to be Mr Taylor. Mr Taylor suddenly stepped off the pavement and emerged from between two parked cars into the road. Mr Smith braked hard and swerved to attempt to avoid Mr Taylor. Unfortunately, the car hit Mr Taylor with a glancing blow. In swerving to avoid Mr Taylor, he hit a parked car (a claim from the owner of that car has been settled by the insurance company).

Mr Smith is very shocked at what happened. He was only 17 years old at the time and had passed his driving test two months previously. His car was written off even though there was relatively minor damage. The car cost him £995 and was purchased one month prior to the accident. His insurance premium was £2,000. His insurers have paid him £500 for the value of the written off car.

The police report showed no drink or drugs in Mr Smith's body at the time of the accident.

Mr Smith was not prosecuted for any offence relating to the accident.

Attached are:

(1) copy summons and statement of claim relating to the proceedings commenced by Mr Taylor

(2) Mr Smith's detailed statement of the events of that night

(3) copy police report relating to the traffic accident that occurred on 14 June 2015 at 11.35 p.m.

(4) a bundle of papers including correspondence relating to the case and attempts to settle the claim.

Counsel is instructed to prepare a defence and counterclaim in this matter.

LOWE AND COMPANY
SOLICITORS FOR THE DEFENDANT

Date 8 September 2016

Figure 1.4: Example of instructions to counsel

The courts

Communicating with the courts begins with the completion of the correct forms and paying a fee. When doing this in person, it is essential to be polite. Remember that you may need the help of the court staff at some later stage – for example, in urgently contacting a judge to obtain a court order or in getting a favourable time for a court hearing.

When appearing in court, you must be appropriately dressed for the type of hearing. This would include a barrister wearing a wig or a gown in certain circumstances. If a lawyer does not comply with this, traditionally, the judge would say 'I cannot hear you Mr… '. This is not an invitation to speak more clearly or loudly (although speaking clearly and projecting your voice is important). It is an indication that the judge considers the lawyer to have broken the professional dress code and so the case cannot proceed until this is corrected.

You need to be respectful of the judge, magistrates and other court officials.

A lawyer's regular appearance before a judge or magistrate often results in a good relationship between them, which may even be amusing, within the limits of the case and the surroundings.

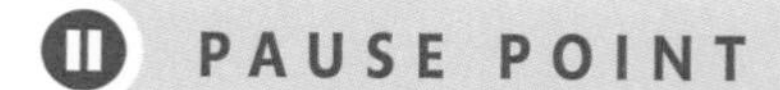

Make a list with a brief explanation of each method of dispute resolution.

Hint Start with a trial at court and then think of alternatives.

Extend Which methods seem to be promoted by the department of justice today? Why might they be promoting certain forms of dispute resolution?

Assessment practice 1.1 A01

The prospect of online dispute resolution (ODR) is becoming a reality. Create a presentation showing the advantages and disadvantages of ODR for dealing with consumer complaints.

Choose a consumer dispute, such as a tablet computer that you have bought failing after one week's use.

Compare ODR with existing methods of dispute resolution through the courts and other ADR methods.

Research and discuss in a small group the advantages and disadvantages of online resolution compared with the methods you have studied. Look for articles such as 'Online dispute resolution platform now operational', 18 February 2016, at **www.out-law.com/en/articles**

Plan

- What is the task? What is my research being asked to address?
- Are there any areas of the task that I think I may struggle with?
- Do I need clarification on anything?
- What resources do I need to complete the task? How can I get access to them?

Do

- I need to spend time planning my approach to the task.
- I need to make connections between what I am researching and the task and identify the important information.
- I need to identify when I have gone wrong and adjust my thinking to get myself back on course.

Review

- I can explain what the task was and how I approached it.
- I can explain what skills I employed and which new ones I have developed.
- I can explain what I have learned about methods of dispute resolution and why it is important.

Enforcement of civil law

Sources of advice

If you have a legal problem, you need to consider where best to go for legal advice. You could use one or more of the many sources available, including:

- solicitors
- barristers
- Citizens Advice Bureau
- Law Centres
- insurance companies
- the Internet.

With the range of options available to help you in a civil case, you may not be sure where to start. You might be worried about receiving a large bill from a legal adviser. It might, therefore, be a good idea to talk to someone who can give you general advice about the possibilities in advance.

There are a number of ways you can get help to make your decision. If you have a local Law Centre or Citizens Advice Bureau, this would be a good place to start. You may also see firms of solicitors offering a free initial interview or a fixed-fee interview. This should help you decide whether it is worth taking your case further.

Solicitors

Solicitors are the main legal professionals who have direct contact with the public. Within a firm of solicitors, you are likely to deal with different solicitors for different types of work. Some firms do not undertake certain areas of work, as they prefer to specialise in other areas. Some firms include a solicitor who speaks a language other than English, to ensure that they can communicate without the need for a translator. Some legal advisers are also members of accreditation schemes. This means that they have been assessed as having special competence in a particular area of law.

Research

Look at the details of all the accreditation schemes and other aspects of solicitors on the Law Society website at **www.lawsociety.org.uk**. How well do you think they work to inform and reassure the public? Write a sentence or two on each to help you learn and understand the material.

Solicitors work in many different areas of law and offer many different services. Solicitors are confidential advisers providing expert legal advice and assistance in a range of situations. The work undertaken by solicitors includes:

- personal matters, such as buying and selling a house, preparing a will or dealing with the estate of someone who has died
- protecting the rights of individuals, so that they are treated fairly by public or private bodies
- making and defending claims arising from negligence, which results in personal injuries or other losses
- helping businesses with legal issues.

Solicitors are often supported by paralegals, who carry out some types of legal work even though they have not qualified as solicitors or barristers. This can involve advising and assisting with the law in the same way that a solicitor advises and assists clients. Paralegals are often specialists in a particular area of law such as conveyancing or wills.

Barristers

Barristers are highly trained professionals dealing with the vast majority of serious and high-profile court cases. They are also a source of specialist legal knowledge on the law and the drafting of court and other legal documents. They are independent, objective and trained to advise clients on the strengths and weaknesses of their case.

Solicitors have good working relationships with barristers and turn to barristers for legal advice or to represent a client in court, particularly in complex cases. Members of the public have a right to choose who should represent them in court and they often choose a barrister briefed by their solicitor. Solicitors are likely to be able to identify the most suitable barrister to deal with a given case. Assuming that the barrister identified is available and that there are no conflicts of interest, they are under a duty to take on a case offered to them. This is known as the **'cab rank' rule**.

Key term

Cab rank rule – if a barrister is available for a case and has no conflict of interest, they are required to take on the case.

Since 2004, members of the public can contact a barrister directly, rather than through a solicitor. However, this facility has not been used to any great extent, as individuals usually find it difficult to describe their requirements precisely.

Contact with barristers is through their clerks, who deal with all administrative matters on their behalf. Barristers are self-employed but commonly work in groups of offices known as chambers. Not all barristers practise in chambers. Some work for Law Centres or government agencies, and some large national and international business organisations employ barristers for their specialist legal knowledge.

Some senior barristers become Queen's Counsel (known as QCs). They do this by making an application (a process known as 'taking silk'). Achieving silk is seen as a mark of outstanding ability. QCs are usually instructed in very serious or complex cases, but can only appear in court when accompanied by a junior (a barrister who is not a QC). Most senior judges once practised as QCs.

Research

Investigate how to become a solicitor, barrister or paralegal.

PAUSE POINT What are the main differences between solicitors and barristers?

Hint Consider their roles, qualification and training.

Extend What are the advantages and disadvantages of having the two separate roles of solicitor and barrister?

Citizens Advice

Citizens Advice is an independent advice charity that provides free, confidential and impartial advice. Their goal is to help everyone find a way forward, whatever problem they face.

You can find more detail at **https://www.citizensadvice.org.uk/about-us/introduction-to-the-citizens-advice-service/**

Law Centres

The first Law Centres opened in the early 1970s. Their purpose is to work within their communities to defend the legal rights of local people. They specialise in social welfare law, have an in-depth knowledge of the issues communities face and are a source of help and advice. They offer legal advice, casework and representation to individuals and groups, and some Law Centres have other areas of expertise. Law Centres use this knowledge, for example, to help people save their homes, keep their jobs and protect their families. They are independent and operate on a not-for-profit basis.

Research

More details can be found at **http://www.lawcentres.org.uk/**

Insurance companies

Many insurance companies offer legal expenses insurance. This is often an optional feature of a household or car insurance policy. It usually involves the company instructing a solicitor on a client's behalf when they make a claim under the policy.

The Internet

The Internet has plenty of advice on legal matters. The difficulty is in ensuring that the advice is accurate and that the website is giving advice based on English law rather than, for example, US law. A useful site is **http://www.lawsociety.org.uk**

Table 1.5 summarises the advantages and disadvantages of each type of source of legal advice.

Table 1.5: Advantages and disadvantages of sources of legal advice

Source of advice	Advantages	Disadvantages
Solicitors	• Professional • Easy to access • Confidential • Properly regulated and insured concerning poor work such as delay, mistakes or overcharging	• Can be expensive • Local firm may not specialise in the area you need
Barristers	• Professional • Specialist • Confidential • Properly regulated and insured concerning poor work such as delay, mistakes or overcharging	• Can be expensive • Access usually through your solicitor • Not always local
Citizens Advice	• Free • Wide range of advice available • Relatively local • Get quick advice ready for the next step (if necessary)	• May not be able to do more than suggest going to a solicitor
Law Centres	• Cheap or free • Experts in their field of work • Often open at convenient times	• Under pressure for funding • Relatively few exist (about 50) • Not necessarily local
Insurance companies	• Easy to access • Can specialise in particular types of claims, such as classic cars	• Client must pay a premium for the policy, whether they use it or not • Dealt with at a distance • Sometimes limited range of cases dealt with
Internet	• Instant availability • Wide range of information available • Free	• Not necessarily based on law in England and Wales (law in Scotland is sometimes different, with a different system in place). • Not necessarily accurate • Sometimes incomplete unless the user signs up and pays

Sources of funding

Going to court can be very expensive. Court fees are payable in addition to lawyers' fees, and financial help is not always available. This section looks at how someone might be able to pay for their legal work.

Some of the most common forms of funding a case are:

- own resources
- insurance
- state funding
- conditional fees
- trade union membership
- Citizens Advice Bureaux
- pro bono.

Own resources

Sir James Mathew, an Irish judge at the turn of the 20th century, is said to have joked that justice in England is open to all, 'like the Ritz Hotel'! He meant that you can always pay for your legal services yourself, but you must have the money to do so.

The Solicitors Regulation Authority states: 'When you use a lawyer or firm that we regulate, they must make their fees as transparent [clear] as possible. Charges vary between lawyers and different law firms so you should shop around to find the best one for you.'

Insurance

Legal expenses insurance is designed to cover the costs of legal advice and/or the costs of bringing or defending a court case. Where it is linked to a car insurance policy, it usually only covers legal expenses in negligence cases as a result of using the car. With someone's household insurance policy, the legal work covered includes taking or defending legal proceedings arising from a number of different areas. Typically included are: claims arising from ownership of the insured home; employment; death; personal injuries; personal contracts for the purchase of goods or services.

The insurer will not help you pursue or defend a claim unless there is a 'reasonable chance of success'. See the Scenario below for an example.

Scenario

Mr and Mrs W had a problem when a skip company would not remove a skip from their driveway. The skip had been ordered by a contractor who had subsequently stopped working on their property. The contractor would not arrange for the skip company to remove it and Mr and Mrs W would not pay for the skip hire as they had not ordered the skip.

Mr and Mrs W had legal expenses insurance extension to their home and contents insurance at a cost of about £20 per year. They contacted their insurance company who used a firm of solicitors several hundred miles from the house. All dealings with the solicitor were by phone, post and email. The skip was removed and Mr and Mrs W had to pay nothing.

With the information given, the solicitor's initial assessment was that they had a reasonable prospect of success. Had they not given accurate information to the insurance company and solicitor, they would have had to pay the solicitor's fees estimated at £4,000 and expenses of £500. The charging rate for the solicitor who did the work was £223 per hour (in 2013).

How well did this work as a way of resolving the dispute?

Consider these questions to help you.

1. What other sources of advice might Mr and Mrs W have considered in this situation?
2. List the sources and their advantages and disadvantages.
3. Do you think that the skip company would have had to get legal advice?
4. Would the skip company have been better advised to move the skip when asked rather than spend money on solicitors?
5. What would you have done if you were Mr or Mrs W or the skip company?

State funding

State funding (paid for by the government) of legal cases is available through legal aid. The cost of legal aid has grown enormously over the years and governments have tried to reduce the cost to the state. The result is that there are great restrictions as to what legal aid is available.

Civil legal aid helps pay for legal services regarding problems such as housing, debt and family matters. Where no financial support is available, clients might have to make a conditional fee arrangement. You will look at this in the next section.

To qualify for legal aid, a client must meet certain financial conditions. In some cases, legal aid is free. In other cases, the client must make a contribution. There are different types of civil legal aid, including:

- Legal Help and Family Help – advice on rights and options and help with negotiating and drawing up agreements.
- Help at Court – this is where someone speaks on the client's behalf at court.

- Family Mediation – helps the client to come to an agreement in a family dispute after a relationship has broken down, but without going to court. It can help to resolve problems involving children, money and the family home.

Legal aid services can be provided only by organisations that have a contract with the Legal Aid Agency. Those with contracts include solicitors, Law Centres and some Citizens Advice offices. If legal aid is available, the logo is usually displayed at the establishment providing it.

PAUSE POINT Do you think that it is right that there are limits on the availability of legal aid?

Hint Look for newspaper, magazine and UK Internet sites for articles about the availability of legal aid.

Extend What areas of law would you make a priority for legal aid?

Conditional fees

A conditional fee arrangement (CFA) is sometimes known as a 'no win, no fee' agreement. It is where a solicitor and client agree to share the financial risk of taking the case. The agreement is that part – or sometimes all – of the solicitor's fees will be payable by the client only if the client wins their case.

If the case is lost, the client will pay a reduced fee or no solicitor's fees. However, this does not include expenses – only fees. The losing party will also have to pay the winner's costs.

In practice, this means that the solicitor will charge a fee that is higher than usual when the client's action is successful. This sounds unfair, but costs are generally awarded in court to the successful party, so at least a good proportion of the bill will be recovered – assuming that the losing party has the means to pay. Overall, the result is that a successful claim for damages may not result in receipt of the full amount of the award.

The risks and cost involved have the effect that it encourages settlement of claims rather than **litigation**. Despite this, the NHS Litigation Authority's figures for 2013/14 show that claimant legal costs amounted to 22 per cent of the £1.2 billion expenditure on clinical negligence claims. Defence costs accounted for 8 per cent (£92.5 million) of spending.

Key term

Litigation – the process of taking a case to a court of law so that a judgment can be made.

Discussion

In pairs, discuss whether the points listed below are advantages or disadvantages of conditional fee arrangements (CFAs). Can you explain your decision?

- CFAs help the public gain access to justice.
- CFAs have the costs linked to outcome.
- If 'after the event' insurance is taken, you do not have to pay winner's costs.
- A CFA may encourage early settlement of the case.
- Usually, costs are paid by the loser.
- Solicitors with a CFA work harder to win a case.
- The other party must be told if you have a CFA.
- The other party must be told of any risk analysis your solicitor does to work out possible success fees.
- Free solicitors' advice is available.
- Solicitors are reluctant to take difficult cases because of the risk of losing and of not being paid.
- The client has to pay the cost of 'after the event' insurance.

Trade union membership

Trade unions often provide legal services for their members in industry-related cases, such as employment issues or industrial accident claims.

Trade unions provide these services to members for free. You will find some examples of these services at **http://www.gmb.org.uk/unionline**

Citizens Advice

The Citizens Advice service provides advice on many issues such as employment, consumer complaints, and landlord and tenant disputes. Most queries are dealt with face to face or by telephone, but an increasing number by email or webchat. All the services are free but you will have to pay standard rate for any phone calls you make to them.

Research

Check out where your local Citizens Advice office is situated and how it is funded. What services does it provide?

Solicitors and barristers often support Citizens Advice by doing *pro bono* work (see below).

Pro bono

Key term

Pro bono – 'for the public good'.

In legal funding, ***pro bono*** refers to solicitors and barristers doing legal work free of charge. Typically, it involves lawyers and law students working on a voluntary basis for people who need legal assistance but who are not in a financial position to get proper support. You can also find groups who aim to increase knowledge and awareness of the law, particularly to young people.

Research

Look at university law school, the Law Society and the Bar Council websites under '*pro bono* activities'. What do they do? Compare them with each other. At which university would you consider studying law?

PAUSE POINT Now that you have studied the methods of funding legal cases, consider how people decide which methods to use.

Hint What are the advantages and disadvantages of each method?

Extend Do you know someone who has been involved in a civil case? How did they fund it? How much did it cost? What was their experience of the legal process?

The cost of taking legal action

The cost of taking a case to court can be enormous. This is reflected in the encouragement to consider alternative methods of resolving a dispute. You should consider four main areas before embarking on a court case:

- court costs
- legal representation costs
- awarding of costs against the unsuccessful party
- hidden costs, loss of reputation and enforcement of award.

Court costs

This cost is represented by the fees charged by the Courts Service for starting a case and continuing to other stages in the procedure to trial. Court fees for money claims are straightforward; they are based on the amount of money claimed. There is a reduction in the fee if the claim is made using the Money Claim Online (MCOL) procedure. For example, for a debt of £800, the fee to start proceedings in 2016 was £70. For a debt for £250,000, the fee was £10,000. You can explore these fees at the Courts Service website (**https://www.gov.uk/government/organisations/hm-courts-and-tribunals-service**).

Legal representation costs

Solicitors generally calculate their charges based on an hourly rate, but sometimes they charge a fixed fee. The Solicitors Regulation Authority sets out principles that solicitors should follow so that their fees are as clear as possible. Charges vary between lawyers and different law firms. Generally, fees are higher in London and major cities, as overhead costs (such as rent) are higher. The amount a court will require a losing party to pay the winning party is reflected in the assessment of costs at the end of a case.

Discussion

Using the Internet, carry out research on fees charged by solicitors. Do they charge fixed fees for anything?

Share the information you have found with a partner. Discuss whether you think the fees are high and why they might need to be at the rate they are.

Reflect

Do the solicitor's fees seem reasonable?

Awarding costs against the unsuccessful party

The losing party is usually expected to pay the costs of the winning party. Costs are often agreed as part of any negotiated settlement. If they cannot be agreed, there can be a court procedure known as a detailed assessment of costs. This can be a long and costly process in itself. A bill of costs is prepared by the successful party and served on the other party. The bill of costs is a detailed analysis of all the costs in a case. This is usually prepared by a specialist laywer called a 'law costs draftsperson'. Some large firms of solicitors will employ a person who is a specialist in this work. Other firms may use an independent individual who will carry out this task for a fee .

Hidden costs, loss of reputation and enforcement of award

There may be other 'hidden' costs associated with going to court. Even if you are successful, you may find it difficult to get the losing party to pay the amount the court awards plus costs. Not everybody will be covered by insurance or have the means to pay what is owed. Some individuals and companies will declare insolvency and a party claiming costs from them might get only a small proportion of what they are owed back. Even if there are **assets** available, it can be difficult and costly to get hold of them or even find them. In addition to this, taking legal action is very stressful and time consuming and so can be costly to a person's well-being and work-life balance.

Key term

Asset – something of value owned by someone.

Reflect

Think about the effect taking a case to court might have on you. Would you be anxious? Worried that you might not win? Not sure whether to settle the claim **so as** to end the matter?

PAUSE POINT The cost of going to court can be expensive. What are some of the different costs involved?

Hint Do not limit your answer to just financial costs.

Extend To what extent do you think going to court is a last resort?

Assessment practice 1.2

A01 A02

The provided material for your external test might be something like the case set out below. If that is the case, you might have a few hours to prepare for the test and you might be allowed to take a limited number of notes with you. The case below is quite complicated, so you need to look at all the terms involved and make sure that you know what each means and the context in which they are used. A number of words and phrases have been listed. Prepare a table of the words and phrases and explain (or outline) what each term means. Note that not every term listed appears in this book. That could be the case with your actual external test. See: **http://cases.iclr.co.uk/Subscr/search.aspx?path=WLR%20Dailies/wlrd2016/wlrd2016-372**

Queen's Bench Division

Surrey and others v Barnet and Chase Farm Hospitals NHS Trust

[2016] EWHC 1598 (QB)

2016 May 25, 26; July 1 Foskett J

Costs – Detailed assessment – Conditional fee agreement – Claimant changing funding from legal aid to conditional fee agreement prior to legislative changes – Claimant's solicitor failing to inform claimant of loss of 10 per cent uplift as consequence of changed funding – Bill of costs including success fee and after the event insurance premiums – Whether costs reasonably incurred – Whether solicitor's advice relevant to reasonableness of decision to change funding – Proper approach to assessing reasonableness of decision to change funding

Appearances:

Benjamin Williams QC and Robert Marven (instructed by Irwin Mitchell LLP) for the claimants.

Alexander Hutton QC (instructed by Acumension Ltd, Manchester) for the defendant.

Plan

- What am I required to do?
- Are there any areas of the task I may struggle with?
- I need to be confident that I know what each term means.

Do

- I need to look up unfamiliar terms.
- I need to make connections between what I am researching and the task and identify the important information in order to advise clients correctly.

Review

- I can confidently look at a case, pull out the relevant information and apply knowledge and understanding to negligence scenarios.
- I can explain what skills I employed and which new ones I have developed.

C How precedent works

▶ Law reports are records of cases where the judge's decision sets a precedent.

Precedent

Judicial precedent, sometimes referred to as case law, is the system whereby judges follow the decisions made in previous cases where the facts are the same. The doctrine (guideline) of judicial precedent requires the application of the principle ***stare decisis***. This is a Latin expression that means 'to stand by the decided decision'. It is based on the idea that if law is to be just and fair, it must be certain. Two identical cases should have the same outcome for the same reasons.

Much of civil law comes from decided cases and can be found in precedents. Precedents are the statements of what the law is and lawyers, and students, use them as authorities to justify their arguments about what the law is and how it applies to a particular situation.

Judicial precedent has a number of important features that are needed to ensure that the doctrine works effectively:

- hierarchy of courts
- *ratio decidendi* and *obiter dicta*
- law reporting of decisions
- following precedent:
  - powers of the appeal courts
  - binding precedents
  - persuasive precedents
  - avoiding binding precedents.

Hierarchy of courts

It is essential to have a defined court structure in order for precedent to work. The general principle is that the decisions of a court at one level must be followed by courts of the same or lower levels. The hierarchy of the courts is shown in Figure 1.5.

Key terms

Judicial precedent – the system whereby a judge must follow the decision made in previous cases where the facts are the same as those in the present case.

Stare decisis – a Latin term meaning 'to stand by the decision'. It is the central principal of the doctrine of judicial precedent.

Binding precedent – decisions of the Court of Appeal and the Supreme Court that must be followed by courts of the same or lower level.

Precedents set in the Supreme Court and the Court of Appeal are **binding precedents** on courts of the same or lower level. However, there are two important exceptions. The first is that the Supreme Court may not follow its previous decisions. The second is that the Court of Appeal may, in certain situations, refuse to follow one of its previous decisions.

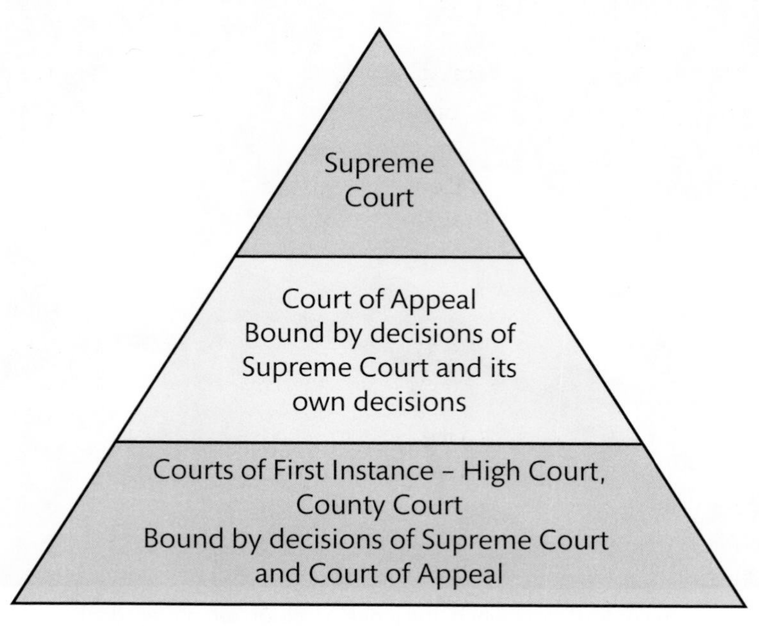

▶ **Figure 1.5:** Diagram of civil court hierarchy

Key terms

Practice Statement – forms part of the judicial rules that courts must follow.

Per incuriam – a Latin term meaning 'through a lack of care'. In legal terms, this is where a decision of the court is made that fails to apply a relevant statute or ignores a binding precedent.

The Supreme Court

The Supreme Court is the highest authority in the interpretation of law. Therefore, if it was not allowed to depart from its own previous decisions, the only way that any changes to a Supreme Court decision could be made would be by an Act of Parliament. That would require a change to the law and could be a very drawn-out process.

The House of Lords (whose judicial function has now passed to the Supreme Court) was bound by its own previous decisions until 1966, when the Lord Chancellor, Lord Gardiner, announced a change of practice. This was done in a **Practice Statement**. The 1966 Practice Statement stated that although the House of Lords would treat its decisions as normally binding, it would 'depart from these when it appeared right to do so'. However, this right has been used very rarely since then, so that certainty in law remains.

The Court of Appeal

The Court of Appeal must follow the decisions of the Supreme Court, even if the appeal court judges think that the law is incorrect. Only the Supreme Court (or an Act of Parliament) can change a decision made by the Supreme Court.

However, the case of Young v Bristol Aeroplane Co (1944) listed the following circumstances where the Court of Appeal could refuse to follow one of its own decisions.

- There are two conflicting decisions of the Court of Appeal. It can then choose one of the decisions (which becomes the precedent) and the other is discarded.
- The decision of the Court of Appeal conflicts with a later Supreme Court decision. The Supreme Court decision is the correct precedent and the Court of Appeal decision is discarded.
- The Court of Appeal decision was decided ***per incuriam***, that is, without taking into account a relevant precedent from either the Supreme Court, the Court of Appeal, a relevant Act of Parliament or delegated legislation made under an Act of Parliament.

Other courts

These do not set binding precedents and so their decisions do not have to be followed.

Ratio decidendi and *obiter dicta*

Not every statement the judge makes in a case can form a precedent. There are two parts to a decision:

- the ***ratio decidendi*** (the legal reason for the decision) forms a binding precedent
- the ***obiter dicta*** (a judge's opinions about the judgment) are only persuasive precedents and do not have to be followed by same-ranked or lower-ranked courts.

For example, in the famous case of Donoghue v Stevenson (1932), the *ratio decidendi* was that manufacturers owe a duty of care to the ultimate consumers of their products.

Key terms

Ratio decidendi – a Latin term meaning 'reason for deciding'. It means the rule of law on which the judge's decision is based.

Obiter dicta (singular ***obiter dictum***) – a Latin term meaning 'words said aside'. A judge's opinion in their judgment that is not essential to the decision and is therefore not legally binding.

Key case

Donoghue v Stevenson (1932)

Facts

Mrs Donoghue went to have an ice cream float in a café. The contents of a bottle of ginger beer made by Stevenson were in the float. Mrs Donoghue consumed some of the ice cream float. When she poured out the rest of the bottle, she found a half-decomposed snail in the remains in the bottle. The bottle was opaque, so she could not have seen the snail before the float was poured. She claimed damages for shock and a stomach upset. The drink had been bought for her by a friend, so she had no contract with either the café or the manufacturer.

Legal principle – manufacturers owe a duty of care to the ultimate consumers of their products.

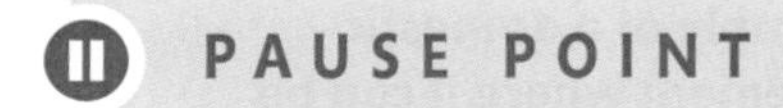

When can the Supreme Court and the Court of Appeal depart from their previous decisions?

Look at the 1966 Practice Statement and the case of Young v Bristol Aeroplane Co (1944).

Do you think judges should be able to change the law on appeal?

Law reporting of decisions

A law report is a record of the judge's decision that sets a precedent. It is important to remember that few cases set a precedent. Law reports are only published when the case sets out a new principle of law, makes a change to the law or clarifies an aspect of the existing law. About 2500 new law reports are published each year. A transcript (or record) of the case is always available for the parties involved to study to see whether there have been mistakes that may form the basis of an appeal. The transcripts are made (for a fee) from the audio recordings of the trial.

Before 1865, barristers attended hearings and published reports of cases, often under their own name. Some early reports were very unreliable as they reflected what the barrister hoped the outcome of the case would be rather than what actually was said or argued. However, the establishment of the Incorporated Council of Law Reporting (ICLR), which publishes the Official Law Reports, provided the accuracy needed.

Law reporting today is precise and accurate. Law reports incorporate the full judgment given by the court, together with a summary of the case known as the headnote or a summary report. Case summaries are much shorter, less formal and are produced more quickly.

Research

Research law reports by accessing a suitable UK web link such as **http://www.iclr.co.uk/learning-zone/law-report/**. In this particular article, you will see that 13 headings are set out.

List each heading and make a note about each one so that you understand how a law report works.

Avoiding binding precedents

Sometimes a judge wishes to avoid a precedent. There are a number ways that precedents are avoided:

- distinguishing
- overruling
- disapproving
- reversing.

Distinguishing

Distinguishing is where an earlier case is not used as an authority because the facts in the present case are different from those in the original precedent. An example of this can be seen in the cases of Balfour v Balfour (1919) and Merritt v Merritt (1970), which you will study again in Unit 6.

Key term

Distinguishing – where the judge finds that the case being heard contains different material facts from the facts in the precedent. The judge can then come to a different conclusion.

Overruling – when the court decides that a precedent is incorrect and should no longer be considered good law.

Key case

Balfour v Balfour (1919)

Facts

Mr and Mrs Balfour were living happily together. They made an agreement about payment of a regular sum to Mrs Balfour while the husband worked abroad.

Legal principle – the case is an example of a domestic arrangement where it can be presumed that legal intention does not exist.

Key case

Merritt v Merritt (1970)

Facts

This case differed from Balfour v Balfour as the husband and wife were separated when they made the agreement about payment of a regular sum.

Legal principle – the presumption of no legal intention in domestic agreements was rebutted and the agreement was legally enforceable.

Overruling

A precedent is **overruled** when the court decides that it is incorrect and should no longer be considered good law. The effect is that the overruled precedent ceases to exist.

An example of this was seen in Pepper v Hart (1993). This decision overruled the decision in Davis v Johnson (1978), which said that Hansard (the record of what is said in Parliament) could not be consulted. This is also an example of the 1966 Practice Statement being used.

Key case

Pepper v Hart (1993)

Facts

Malvern College ran a scheme where staff were entitled to have their children educated at the school. The Inland Revenue tried to tax this benefit based on the Finance Act 1976. The Special Commissioners, charged with assessing tax, disagreed with the High Court of Justice and Court of Appeal, so the case went to the House of Lords.

Legal principle - Hansard (the record of what is said in Parliament) could be consulted when trying to decide what certain words in an Act of Parliament meant.

Key term

Explaining - where a judge sets out an interpretation of an earlier decision before applying it or distinguishing it.

Disapproving - where the court decides that a precedent is not a relevant one, and believes the precedent should not be good law.

Reversing - where a higher court changes (reverses) the decision in the previous court.

Often the judge **explains** a precedent before distinguishing or overruling it. This makes it clear, particularly for any further appeal of the case, the reasoning behind their decision.

When the precedent is distinguished or overruled, a new precedent is created that states the law from that moment. The new precedent must be followed rather than the old one. This is one reason why law reports and case summaries are essential to keep up to date with precedents.

Disapproving

A precedent is **disapproved** when an appeal court thinks that a precedent that has been suggested by one of the barristers in the case is relevant. The court decides that it is not relevant but goes on to make the point that the court believes that the precedent should not be good law. This is an opinion of what might happen in future cases which relate directly to the point in question.

Reversing

Reversing takes place where a higher court changes (reverses) the decision of a court of the same or a lower level. The key thing is that the changed decision relates to the same case. An example of this is Gillick v West Norfolk and Wisbech AHA (1986) where the House of Lords (now Supreme Court) reversed the decision of the Court of Appeal.

How to research, find and interpret case law

Today, law reports can be full-text law reports, which incorporate the full judgment given by the court, together with a summary of the case known as the headnote or a summary report. Case summaries are much shorter and less formal, but are produced more quickly. Newspapers such as *The Times* often have case summaries, as do professional journals. Case extracts in this book are usually based on case summaries. You can read more about this at **http://www.iclr.co.uk/learning-zone/law-report/**

Advantages and disadvantages of the doctrine of precedent

The distinction between making law and applying it is not so clear cut. Judges have discretion through the system of judicial precedent to make new and original precedents. You can see that from cases such as Gillick v West Norfolk and Wisbech AHA (1986) where judges were able to adapt the law to current social values. Table 1.6 shows the advantages and disadvantages of judicial precedent.

Research

Look up the case of Gillick v West Norfolk and Wisbech AHA (1986). List the arguments in favour of the approach taken by the House of Lords and the decision that they reversed in the Court of Appeal.

▶ **Table 1.6:** Advantages and disadvantages of judicial precedent

Advantages	Disadvantages
Certainty – by looking at precedents used, lawyers can have some indication as to how a case will be decided.	There are so many previously decided cases that it can be difficult to find the most appropriate precedent.
Flexibility – allows the application of the law to be adapted to modern cases and changes in society.	The *ratio decidendi* can be difficult to extract when several judges have given judgment.
Precise – the use of similar cases can mean that the application can be precise as use of the precedent over the years builds up on variations of the facts.	The system is too rigid and a poor precedent may take several years to be amended in a higher court capable of overruling it.
Time saving – the judge has a set of guidelines and uses the decisions made by superior judges.	Although like cases should be treated alike, different judges can use different reasons for distinguishing a case on the facts – this brings in some uncertainty.

Reflect

Consider the advantages and disadvantages of the doctrine of precedent listed in Table 1.6. Expand on these, giving examples and thinking of other advantages and disadvantages.

List the key points about the doctrine of precedent.

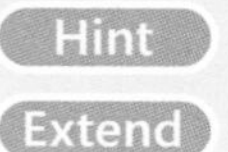

Hint Look at the difference between binding and persuasive precedent.

Extend How effective is the doctrine of precedent? Does it just create more appeals?

Assessment practice 1.3 A03

Where a judge is looking at previous decisions, they may find a binding precedent. They can try to get around a precedent that is binding by distinguishing the present case from the precedent. The judge might also be able to state that the precedent was made *per incuriam*.

1 Outline the meaning of the terms binding precedent, distinguishing a precedent and *per incuriam*. Where possible, use decided cases to illustrate your answer.

2 Analyse how well the system of precedent works.

Plan

- I need to be sure what each term means.
- I need to understand how the system of precedent works.

Do

- I need to make arguments for and against the system of precedent.

Review

- I can evaluate the system of precedent.
- I can write my answers in clear terms.

D Application of the law of negligence

Duty of care

The law of negligence is concerned with a person's claim when they have been injured or their property has been damaged by another. Negligence needs proof of fault on the part of the person who caused the damage or injury. There are three elements to negligence:

1. A duty of care must be owed by the defendant to the claimant.
2. That duty must have been broken through a failure to reach the required standard of care.
3. The broken duty must have caused the damage or injury.

All three elements must be proved for there to be liability in negligence (see Figure 1.6). If they are proved, then the victim can claim compensation, known as 'damages'.

Historical introduction

The law of negligence started to be developed in the case of Blyth v Birmingham Waterworks Co (1856). The modern law of negligence about a duty of care came in the famous case of Donoghue v Stevenson (1932). The facts of that case have been set out in section C earlier in this unit. In Donoghue, Lord Atkin set the test for when a person would owe a duty to another. He said:

> 'You must take reasonable care to avoid acts or omissions which you can reasonably foresee would be likely to injure your neighbour.'

He went on to explain this by saying:

> 'Who then, in law, is my neighbour? Persons who are so closely and directly affected by my act that I ought reasonably to have them in my contemplation as being affected when I am directing my mind to the acts or omissions in question.'

This case established a broad principle when a duty of care was owed and that there was general liability in negligence.

This principle has been further developed by the 3-stage test in the case of Caparo Industries v Dickman and others (1990).

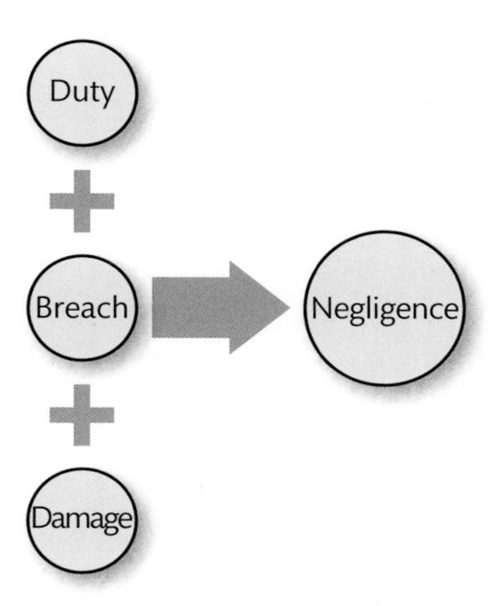

▶ **Figure 1.6:** Negligence essentials

3-stage test

The 3-stage test is the modern test used in new negligence claims to establish when a duty of care is owed.

1. Is there a sufficiently close (or proximate) relationship between the claimant and the defendant?
2. Could a reasonable person see that some damage or harm is foreseeable to someone in the claimant's position?
3. Is it fair, just and reasonable to impose a duty of care?

All three parts of the test must be present if a legal duty of care is to be owed by the defendant to the claimant.

Proximity

This part of the test requires proximity in either space and time, or in the relationship between the claimant and the defendant.

With respect to space and time, the idea is that no duty is owed to someone who was not present at the act that supposedly caused the loss or injury. As the law of negligence developed, there was usually no claim allowed by someone who was in a safe place at the time of the incident or who had not witnessed or been involved in the incident. An example this is the case of Bourhill v Young (1943).

Key case

Bourhill v Young (1943)

Facts

Mrs Bourhill was getting off a tram when she heard a car and motorbike crash a short distance away. She rushed over to see what had happened. She suffered shock and a miscarriage as a result. No duty was owed to her by the person who caused the crash, as she had been in a safe place at the time of the crash and had had no reason to go and look at the gory aftermath of the crash.

Legal principle – there must usually be a connection in space and time for someone who suffers injury as a result of an incident to be able to claim.

In the later case of King v Phillips (1953), a mother was upstairs in her house. She heard her six-year-old child, who was playing on the pavement on his tricycle, scream. She could not see her child, but saw his tricycle under the wheels of a car that had been turning round. She suffered shock despite the fact that the child was unhurt. Her claim failed.

More recently, the case of McLoughlin v O'Brian (1983) provided some help to claimants for shock who were not witnesses to an incident, but who could reasonably be foreseen to be seriously affected by the aftermath of the incident.

Key case

McLoughlin v O'Brian (1983)

Facts

Mrs McLoughlin's husband and three of her children were involved in a car crash with a lorry. One of the children was killed on impact. An ambulance took the injured to hospital. On being told of the crash, Mrs McLoughlin went immediately to the hospital. She saw her family suffering before they had been treated and cleaned up. As a result, she suffered severe shock, depression and a personality change. Her action in going to the hospital was what any reasonable person would expect to happen.

Legal principle – proximity by relationship was demonstrated in this case, even though the actual incident was not witnessed by Mrs McLoughlin.

This was followed in the case of Galli-Atkinson v Seghal (2003), where Mrs Galli-Atkinson's 16-year-old daughter was killed when a car mounted the pavement as she walked along. The mother came upon the scene, witnessed a police cordon at the scene of the accident and was told of her daughter's death. She later saw the daughter's injuries at the mortuary and suffered psychiatric injuries herself. The visit to the mortuary was part of the incident and her claim succeeded as there was sufficient proximity as a result of the relationship.

Foreseeability

This part of the test deals with the idea that it should be reasonably foreseeable that the defendant's actions are ones that can be expected to cause loss or damage to anyone in the claimant's position. If you were to apply the test to Donoghue v Stevenson (1932), you would conclude that it is reasonably foreseeable that anyone drinking contaminated liquid is likely to become ill.

An example of this can be seen in the case of Kent v Griffiths (2000).

Key case

Kent v Griffiths (2000)

Facts

The claimant, an asthmatic, had waited a long time for an ambulance to arrive after a 999 call. The wait was much longer than normal. There were no good reasons for the delay. She stopped breathing before she got to hospital. The court decided that an individual patient who had called for an ambulance could be owed a duty of care by the ambulance service.

Legal principle – it is reasonably foreseeable that the unnecessary delay could result in injury to the patient for whom the ambulance had been called.

Fair, just and reasonable

This is part of the updating of the principle in Donoghue v Stevenson. It brings in a public policy test as to whether there should be a duty of care owed or not. In general, this part of the test protects public servants such as the police and fire service, who are doing their work, from fear of a case against them or their employer. It is also used to prevent the opening of the floodgates of litigation (many cases in the same sort of area). It does not mean that all public servants are always protected, as we have seen in Kent v Griffiths.

PAUSE POINT Think how the doctrine of precedent applies to the negligence cases you have just studied.

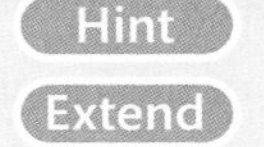

Hint Consider the significance of the dates of the cases you have studied in this section.

Extend Consider the courts that were involved and whether the precedents used were *obiter dicta* or *ratio decidendi*.

Scenario

Asif fitted a hoist for his mother, Kamala, who was a wheelchair user so that she could get in and out of bed without much help. He did not check the strength of the joist in the ceiling. The first time Kamala tried to use the hoist on her own, she was lifted part way and then the joist broke, bringing the ceiling and heavy hoist on top of her.

Apply the 3-stage test to determine if Asif owes a duty of care to Kamala.

Breach of duty

Objective standard

Once it has been shown that a duty of care is owed, the next stage is to prove that the duty of care has been broken. This occurs when the defendant fails to reach the required standard of care that a reasonable person would do while performing the task competently. In this way, the standard of care expected is objective.

Negligence can result from either an act or a failure to act. This can be seen from the famous definition of Baron Alderson in the case of Blyth v Birmingham Waterworks Co (1856) as 'failing to do something which the reasonable person would do or doing something which the reasonable person would not do'.

The reasonable person test

The reasonable person is described as one who takes a degree of care that is sensible given the risk involved. An example can be seen in the case of Wells v Cooper (1958).

Key case

Wells v Cooper (1958)

Facts

While trying to close the door in a strong wind, the door handle came away and the claimant was injured after falling down the steps outside the defendant's door. The handle had been fitted by the houseowner, who was not a professional carpenter or builder, but who was reasonably competent at DIY jobs.

Legal principle – the appropriate standard was met, as the houseowner should be judged against the standards of a reasonably competent contractor, standards that Cooper had met.

Special characteristics of the defendant

The law looks at different types of defendant in terms of whether they are a reasonable person. These categories are:

- professionals
- learners
- children (under 18 years old).

Professionals

To prove breach of a duty of care, it must be shown that the professional's conduct fell below the standard of a reasonably competent professional in the same area of expertise. For example, a surgeon must reach the standard of a reasonably competent surgeon.

Sometimes, a profession accepts more than one way of performing a task. In that situation, any accepted way of performing the task is reasonable. This can be seen in the case of Bolam v Friern Hospital Management Committee (1957).

Key case

Bolam v Friern Hospital Management Committee (1957)

Facts

Mr Bolam was a voluntary patient at a mental health hospital. He agreed to have electric shock treatment. He was not given any muscle relaxant and his body was not restrained. He suffered serious injuries as a result of the violent movement of his body.

Legal principle – the duty had not been breached because the doctor reached the standard required by medical opinion, even though there were different medical opinions on how the treatment should be carried out.

Where no one knows that an outcome is possible, then there is no breach of duty, as the reasonable person cannot be expected to take precautions against unknown risks. This can be seen in the case of Roe v Minister of Health (1954).

Key case

Roe v Minister of Health (1954)

Facts

The claimants had been given an anaesthetic for minor operations, but became paralysed because the anaesthetic had been contaminated with sterilising fluid during storage. Following hospital procedure, the anaesthetic was stored in glass containers, which were immersed in sterilising fluid. It was later discovered that tiny cracks were present in the containers but these cracks could only be seen with a microscope.

Legal principle – there was no breach of duty because the risk was not foreseeable.

Learners

The standard of care of someone learning a skill or profession is that of a reasonably competent person with that skill or of that profession. The law can be seen in the case of Nettleship v Weston (1971).

Key case

Nettleship v Weston (1971)

Facts

Mr Nettleship gave a friend's wife, Mrs Weston, driving lessons. He was an experienced driver and he made sure to check her insurance before accompanying her. On her third lesson, she crashed into a lamp post and he was injured. The court decided that a learner driver is responsible and owes a duty of care to people in the car and on or near the highway.

Legal principle – the standard of care expected of a learner driver is that of the reasonably competent driver.

Discussion

Would you be angry if a driver who had just knocked you down and injured you said 'It is my first driving lesson so I am not legally responsible for your injuries'?

List the points you have made and see how they relate to the standard of care the law expects.

Children

The standard expected of young people is determined by comparing the care taken with that of an ordinary young person of the same age. This can be seen from the case of Mullin v Richards (1998).

Key case

Mullin v Richards (1998)

Facts

Mullin and Richards were friends at school. They were hitting each other's plastic rulers as though in a sword fight. One of the rulers snapped and a fragment of plastic entered Mullin's eye, causing her to become effectively blind in that eye. Richards was only expected to meet the standard of a reasonable 15 year old, not that of a reasonable adult. She was found not to be in breach of duty.

Legal principle – a young person is judged by the standard of other young people of the same age.

Research

Have a look at a transcript of the case at **http://www.bailii.org/ew/cases/EWCA/Civ/1997/2662.html**

There are a number of complications in the actual case, but consider how long it has taken to be resolved since the incident happened. What do you think the effect might have been over that period of time for all involved? Link this back to the hidden costs of going to law discussed above.

 **PAUSE POINT** What are the differences in the types of reasonable person test?

List the different categories of the reasonable person test and a case for each that illustrates the principles.

Extend What are the arguments against distinguishing between the types of test?

Factors that affect the standard of care required

The risk factors that affect the standard of care required are those that the reasonable person would take into account and cause them to modify their behaviour. If the behaviour was not modified, then it is more likely the duty had been breached. The reasonable person takes precautions against likely risks, but does not take precautions against every eventuality. For example, there is a risk that debris from an aircraft or a meteor could hit your house and injure you while you sleep. It is unlikely that you have taken precautions against that risk by strengthening the roof of the house.

There are the following categories of risk factor to consider:

- special characteristics of the claimant
- the risk of harm
- social utility
- taking of precautions.

Special characteristics of the claimant

When the reasonable person knows that someone else to whom they owe a duty is at greater risk than the ordinary person, the reasonable person takes more care. For example, if you are walking to the shops with a two-year-old child, you would, as a reasonable person, hold their hand tightly while crossing a busy road.

This higher standard of care can be seen in the case of Paris v Stepney Borough Council (1951).

Key case

Paris v Stepney Borough Council (1951)

Facts

Mr Paris had been injured at war, which resulted in near total blindness in one eye. He now worked for Stepney Council as a mechanic. The council knew of his eyesight problems. They did not provide him with goggles when he worked, and a splinter of metal from a vehicle he was working on entered his good eye. He lost sight in that eye too.

Legal principle – a breach of duty occurred here, as the employer knew that the claimant was at more risk of serious injury as a result of his existing condition and required a higher standard of care.

The risk of harm

The general principle is that the greater the risk, the more care must be taken if there is not to be a breach of duty. On the other hand, if the risk is minimal, the reasonable person does not need to take precautions. Compare the cases of Bolton v Stone (1951) and Miller v Jackson (1977).

Key case

Bolton v Stone (1951)

Facts

Miss Stone was hit by a ball that had been hit out of a cricket ground. The ground was protected by a 2-metre-high fence beyond the boundary line. The evidence was that the ball had been hit out of the ground on about six occasions in the past 30 years. The distance from the wicket was nearly 100 metres.

Legal principle – there was no breach of duty as the risk of the ball going out of the ground was very small and reasonable precautions had been taken.

Key case

Miller v Jackson (1977)

Facts

A new housing estate was built on land next to a cricket ground. The club erected a fence more than 5 metres high, to prevent balls landing in the gardens of the new houses. Despite this, in two years, 15 balls had gone out of the ground landing in the gardens of the houses and, on one occasion, breaking a window in the house.

Legal principle – there were regular incidents of the ball leaving the ground and affecting the public, so adequate precautions had not been taken.

The reasonable person would take more precautions in the case of Miller v Jackson (1977), and so would breach their duty if the ball caused damage or injury to someone in the houses or their gardens behind the ground.

Social utility

This is concerned with the benefits to society of taking the risk. This usually involves an emergency situation where normal precautions are minimised for the greater good. This can be seen in the case of Watt v Hertfordshire County Council (1954). In that case, Lord Denning said 'the saving of life or limb justifies taking considerable risk'.

Key case

Watt v Hertfordshire County Council (1954)

Facts

A woman was trapped under a heavy vehicle not far from the fire station. The fire service sent an ordinary lorry with a jack and the firemen on the back of it, rather than the specialist vehicle as that was being used elsewhere. On the way to rescue the woman, the jack slipped. One of the firemen was injured.

Legal principle – breach of duty is less likely to occur when the damage occurs in dealing with an emergency.

Taking precautions

The reasonable person does everything in their power to prevent damage. They do not, however, take all possible precautions if they are excessive in relation to the risk. This is similar to the cricket club cases considered for the risk of harm. Another good example of this is the case of Latimer v AEC (1953).

Key case

Latimer v AEC (1953)

Facts

Very heavy rain flooded the factory where Mr Latimer worked. The company did their best to clean up the slippery water and oil film from the floor. They used brushes and all the sawdust and sand they had, and put up warning signs. However, when Mr Latimer came on shift he slipped and was injured. The company took every step that reasonably could have been taken except shutting the factory. Shutting the factory was not a reasonable action in the circumstances. Therefore, the company had not breached its duty of care.

Legal principle – the reasonable person does not have to totally eliminate a risk – only to do as much as the reasonable person would do in the circumstances.

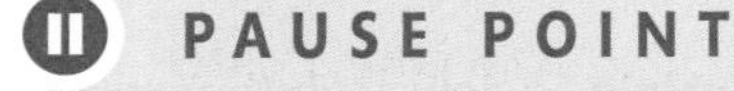

Think about how the risk factors affect the standard of a reasonable person.

Hint: Does it make it easier or harder to be found to have broken your duty of care?

Extend: Does the law on this point lead to confusion?

Damage

The third element of negligence is that the breach of duty must have caused the damage, whether it is injury or loss. There are two parts to damage: **causation** and **remoteness of damage.** Both parts have to be proved in order for a negligence claim to succeed.

Key terms

Causation – the breach of duty of care has caused the injury ot loss. This is factual causation.

Remoteness of damage – the test to determine whether the injury or loss was reasonably foreseeable. This is legal causation.

'But for' test – a test to establish causation – 'but for' the defendant's act or omission, the injury or loss would not have occurred.

Factual causation

Factual causation is demonstrated through the **'but for' test**. The test determines whether, 'but for' the defendant's act or omission, the injury or loss would have occurred? If yes, the defendant is not liable. If no, the defendant is liable.

The test can be seen in the case of Barnett v Chelsea and Kensington Hospital Management Committee (1969).

Key case

Barnett v Chelsea and Kensington Hospital Management Committee (1969)

Facts

Three night-watchmen went to a hospital A & E department, complaining of vomiting after drinking tea. The duty doctor, who did not come to examine the men, recommended that they go home and see their own doctors. One of the men went home and died a few hours later from arsenic poisoning. It was claimed that the doctor owed a duty of care and, by not examining Mr Barnett, had broken that duty of care. However, the evidence showed that by the time Mr Barnett had gone to the hospital, there was nothing that could have been done to save his life. Therefore, his death was not caused by the doctor's breach of duty of care, as it could not be said that 'but for' the doctor's failure to examine him, he would not have died.

Legal principle – there is no liability in negligence if there is no factual causation.

Similarly, there is no factual causation where there is an intervening event that becomes the factual causation in an incident. The intervening act breaks the chain of causation. For example, if someone was injured as a passenger in a car that crashed as a result of the driver's negligence, the driver would be liable for those injuries, such as a broken arm. If the ambulance taking the person to hospital then crashed and they were killed, there would be a new act that caused the death. You could argue that they would not have been killed but for the initial car crash, but the real cause of death is the ambulance crash. Figure 1.7 shows the chain of causation of a new act intervening.

This can be seen in Knightly v Johns (1982).

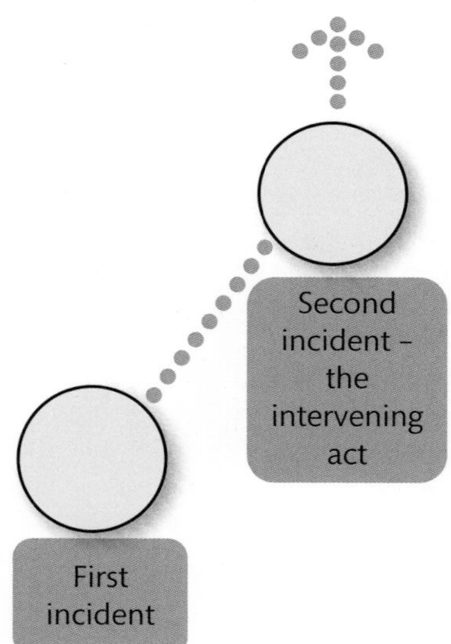

Figure 1.7: New act intervening

Key case

Knightly v Johns (1982)

Facts

Mr Johns caused a crash on a dangerous bend in a road tunnel in Birmingham. The police inspector at the scene should have closed the tunnel to traffic but forgot to do so. He therefore ordered Officer Knightley to ride back on his motorbike, against the flow of traffic, in order to do so. As he did so, Officer Knightley was involved in a separate crash and was injured. The second accident broke the chain of causation, as it was a new act intervening, so Mr Johns was not liable for the injuries to Officer Knightley.

Legal principle – a new act intervening breaks the chain of causation.

Remoteness of damage

Once factual causation has been proved, there is still no liability unless the damage is reasonably foreseeable. Reasonable forseeablility is the test for remoteness of damage. This part of the test establishes exactly what losses are the responsibility of the defendant. The question of compensation is then a separate matter and will be dealt with later in this unit.

Reasonable foreseeability

The idea of reasonable foreseeability is that the reasonable person could foresee the type of damage that occurred.

The main test for remoteness of damage is that the damage must be reasonably foreseeable. This principle comes from the case of The Wagon Mound (1961).

Key case

The Wagon Mound (1961)

Facts

Fuel oil had been negligently spilled from the defendant's ship into the sea in Sydney harbour. The wind and tide carried the oil spill towards the claimant's wharf. The claimant was carrying out welding repairs to another ship. Two days later, the oil caught fire due to the sparks and hot metal coming from the welding. The fire spread on the oil to the claimant's wharf and burned it down. It was decided that although damage done to the wharf by oil being spilled was reasonably foreseeable, fire damage was not reasonably foreseeable and therefore was too remote to give rise to liability.

Legal principle – the test for remoteness of damage as the damage must be reasonably foreseeable.

The type of damage caused

As long as the type of damage is foreseeable, the actual form of the damage can be extreme. This can be seen in the case of Bradford v Robinson Rentals (1967).

Key case

Bradford v Robinson Rentals (1967)

Facts

The claimant was sent by his employer to drive a long distance to exchange an old van for a new vehicle during extremely cold weather conditions. Neither of the vehicles he drove were heated and, as a result, the claimant suffered frostbite. Although frostbite is rare, injury through cold exposure could be foreseen in this case.

Legal principle – if the type of damage is reasonably foreseeable, it does not matter if the damage suffered is rare or extreme.

Research

Research the case of Hughes v Lord Advocate (1963), which also considered an extreme form of damage.

Could the reasonable person foresee the injury caused in this case? Consider the idea of duty and breach, which would also have had to be proved in the case.

The 'thin skull' rule

The 'thin skull' rule deals with the idea that everyone and everything is different in a case. This means that if a person injures someone in a car crash, it does not matter, in the eyes of the law, whether the victim has a particular sensitivity to injury. You have seen this with respect to known medical problems in Paris v Stepney Borough Council

(1951) and the standard of care required. In terms of reasonably foreseeable damage, the principle extends to pre-existing conditions, as seen in the case of Smith v Leech Brain (1962).

Key case

Smith v Leech Brain (1962)

Facts

A man was burned on the lip by molten metal. The man had an existing pre-cancerous condition. The burn eventually brought about the onset of full cancer and the man died. The company was liable to compensate for his death, as they had to take their victim as they found him.

Legal principle – in negligence, you take your victim as you find them.

Unknown to science

You have already seen that there is no breach where no one knows that an outcome is possible, as the reasonable person cannot be expected to take precautions against unknown risks. Similarly, damage is not reasonably foreseeable if the accident occurred as a result of a totally unknown type of event. This can be seen in the case of Doughty v Turner Ltd (1964).

Key case

Doughty v Turner Ltd (1964)

Facts

The cover on a cauldron of exceedingly hot molten sodium cyanide was accidentally knocked into the cauldron. The claimant worker was injured when, a short time after the cover was knocked into the cauldron, the cauldron erupted like a volcano exploding. Scientific knowledge at the time was that there might be a small splash, not a violent explosion.

Legal principle – the claim failed. The defendant employer owed a duty of care in respect only of a foreseeable risk: that of splashing of the liquid if the cover fell into it, not for the unknown violent consequences.

Key terms

Damages – money as compensation for loss or injuries caused to the claimant payable by the defendant.

Damages

The aim of awarding damages in negligence

Damages are for the value of the goods destroyed or for their repair to the condition they were in before the incident. The general aim of **damages** in negligence is to put the successful claimant in the same position as they would have been in if the negligence had not occurred.

Special damages

Special damages are losses that can be calculated at the time of the trial. Pecuniary losses are financial losses such as lost wages. This includes a loss of salary to date, damage to property and expenses such as travelling to hospital for appointments as a result of an accident.

General damages

General damages are all other forms of financial compensation.There are two elements to general damages:

- damages for the effects of the injury - pain, suffering and loss of amenity
- damages for future financial loss - loss of future earnings and the effect of loss of expectation of life.

As a person must take their victim as they find them, the amount will vary with the claimant in each case. Scarring of my face is almost certainly going to end up with a smaller sum than scarring the face of an actor or model who cannot work in the same roles as before.

Pain, suffering and loss of amenity

Pain and suffering is very difficult to calculate. Every case is different. The amount will vary with the individual but will take into account medical reports and other evidence in court. The test is subjective (based on personal feelings or opinions) and the court will assess the claimant's past and future position as at the date of trial.

Loss of amenity is the reduction in the ability to perform everyday tasks. It can include all manner of interference with hobbies and pastimes, loss of a skill and an impact on sex life, as well as everyday tasks such as getting dressed.

The distinction between damages for loss of amenity and damages for pain and suffering can be seen in the example of someone in a coma. Clearly, there is a total loss of amenity, as the victim can do nothing. However, little or nothing would be awarded for pain and suffering since the claimant has no subjective awareness of pain and suffering.

A claimant is not compensated for the physical injury itself. The compensation is for the loss suffered as a result of that injury, such as not being to reach full earnings potential. The amount is calculated from awards in comparable cases that have been decided by the courts.

Loss of earnings

Claims for loss of earnings are common in personal injury claims and can be very large and very complicated. If you are a 17-year old student who can never work as a result of your injury, then how would you assess your loss of future earnings? Would it be different if you already earned a great deal of money from running a website or as a musician?

Therefore, calculating loss of earnings also depends on all the evidence. It also depends on whether the incident has affected the claimant's life expectancy. Consider the case of Pickett v British Rail Engineering Ltd (1980), where the claimant, aged 51, inhaled asbestos at work, causing mesothelioma. Evidence at trial was that his life expectancy was one year. The court decided that future loss of earnings should be assessed on the basis that, without the disease caused by the asbestos, he would have been expected to work until 65 years old, so loss of future earnings would be based on 14 years' earnings, not one year's.

On top of that, the court has to take into account things such as pensions and pension rights, tax and benefits.

Future medical expenses

In some cases, the impact of an injury is such that the claimant requires professional nursing care and future medical treatment. In claims arising from severe brain injury, this may be the biggest element of the claim. All the court can do is estimate the cost of this and include it in the award.

Mitigation of loss

Every claimant is required to **mitigate their loss**. This means that claimants are required to take reasonable action to keep their losses to a minimum and defendants cannot be forced to pay for avoidable losses. For example, if you were involved a car crash, you may have to hire a car while yours was repaired. The person who hit your car would

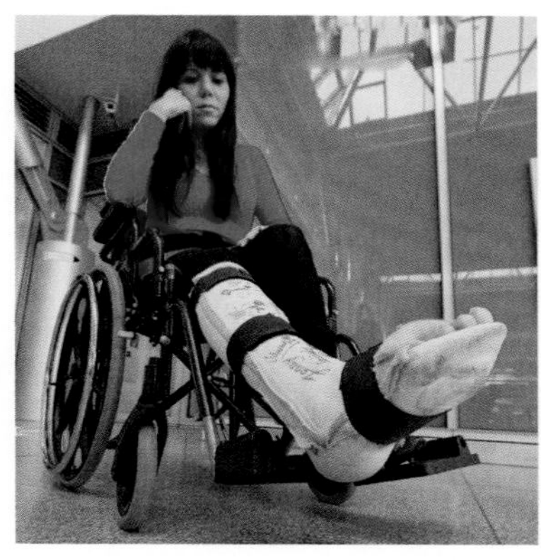

▶ Victims of injury may be entitled to claim damages for the effect on their day-to-day life

Key terms

Loss of amenity - the reduction in the ability of a person to perform everyday tasks.

Mitigate their loss - the requirement that claimants should take reasonable action to keep their losses to a minimum.

Research

Look at recent guidance for personal injury claims at **http://www.lawsociety.org.uk/for-the-public/common-legal-issues/personal-injury-claim/** Reflect on how the guidance for personal injury claims has been considered through this unit.

expect you to hire a replacement car equivalent to the cost of the car that you owned. This means that you could not rent a Ferrari at the other driver's expense. However, if you had been driving a Ferrari, then that would have been a reasonable expense.

Contributory negligence

The principle of **contributory negligence** is that if a claimant has contributed to the losses, then a proportion of the damages will be lost. The proportion lost depends on the amount to which the claimant's own acts are negligent. This can be seen in the case of Sayers v Harlow Council (1958).

Key case

Sayers v Harlow Urban District Council (1958)

Facts

Mrs Sayers used a public toilet in Harlow. Unfortunately, she could not then get out as the lock was faulty. To try to get out, she decided to climb over the partition and into the next cubicle. She balanced on the toilet roll holder but it rotated and she fell and was injured. The court decided that she had contributed to her fall by her own negligence. She lost 25 per cent of her damages because of contributory negligence.

Legal principle - a proportional amount of the damages can be lost if the claimant contributed to their damage or loss.

Key terms

Contributory negligence - where the claimant in a negligence case has made a contribution to their own injuries by their actions.

Annuity - a fixed sum of money paid to someone each year, typically for the rest of their life.

Contingencies - a future event or circumstance which is possible but cannot be predicted with certainty.

The Law Reform (Contributory Negligence) Act 1945 sets out the law. The court is given guidance so that it can reduce damages 'to such extent as the court thinks just and equitable having regard to the claimant's share in the responsibility for the damage'. This means that every case depends on the evidence and all relevant circumstances. There are occasions where the court can find 100 per cent contributory negligence.

There are some general guidelines. For example, not wearing a seat belt does not cause an accident, but it can contribute to the extent of the injury.

A similar principle could apply where a person knowingly allows themselves to be driven in a car with a drunk or drugged driver.

Payment of damages

Damages are paid either in a lump sum or through a structured settlement.

Lump sum

All special damages and most general damages are paid as a lump sum. The only possible problem for a claimant is that the defendant may not have enough money to pay the damages if they are not insured. For very large amounts of damages, it may be better for both parties to organise payment through the use of a structured settlement.

Structured settlement

A structured settlement is a type of settlement usually used in accident and medical negligence claims as an alternative to the payment of a lump sum by the defendant to the claimant. There are often three parts to a structured settlement:

1. a lump-sum payment to cover costs and expenses met by the claimant before settlement of the case. (This would include medical and legal costs up to the date of the settlement of the claim - in other words, the special damages.)
2. a series of regular monthly payments, usually paid through an **annuity**, as part of the general damages. (This usually lasts for the lifetime of the claimant and is designed to meet future care costs and loss of earnings.)
3. a further lump sum to cover **contingencies** that may not be met by the general damages annuity payments.

If you had the choice, would you take £500,000 now or £60,000 a year for life? That is a typical choice between a structured settlement and a lump sum payment. How would you (or those caring for you) decide?

Hint Research some case studies such as those you can find in the newspapers or online.

Extend Advice may be given to you on this. Do you think that insurance companies prefer to make structured settlements in large personal injury cases? What is in it for them?

Burden of proof and *res ipsa loquitur*

Burden of proof in negligence cases

You have learned that the claimant must prove their case on a balance of probabilities. This standard means that the court must be satisfied that the event in question is more likely to have occurred than not. However, the burden of proof shifts to the defendant if the principle of ***res ipsa loquitur*** applies.

Key term

Res ipsa loquitur – a Latin term meaning 'things speak for themselves'.

Res ipsa loquitur

As a legal expression, *res ipsa loquitur* means that it is presumed that the incident was the result of a negligent act or omission, so that the defendant then has to show they were not negligent. There are three parts to the test to see whether the incident can be considered one where *res ipsa loquitur* applies:

- the thing that caused the damage was under the sole control of the defendant
- the incident is one that would not have happened unless someone had been negligent
- there is no other obvious reason as to why the incident occurred.

One of the leading cases is the case of Scott v London & St Katherine Docks Co (1865).

Key case

Scott v London & St. Katherine Docks Co (1865)

Facts

A customs officer was passing a warehouse and six sacks of sugar fell from a crane onto him. The crane and sacks of sugar were under the sole control of the warehouse. It was agreed that sacks of sugar do not fall from cranes unless someone has been negligent and there is no other obvious reason as to why such an incident should have occurred.

Legal principle – as the defendant could not give any explanation as to why he was not negligent, he was liable in negligence.

Other examples include the case of Byrne v Boadle (1863), where a barrel fell from the upstairs floor of a building, and Mahon v Osborne (1939), where a surgeon sewed up his patient, leaving some swabs inside him.

The fact that *res ipsa loquitur* applies does not necessarily mean that the defendant is liable in negligence. All it means is that the defendant has to show, on the balance of probabilities, that they were not negligent. In the cases that you have looked at so far, it would be very difficult for the claimant to show how the accident happened. It is likely that none of the claimants would remember anything about the event.

In the case in Pearson v North West Gas Board (1968), a gas board was able to show how the incident happened and that it had not been negligent.

Key case

Pearson v North West Gas Board (1968)

Facts

The gas main outside Mr and Mrs Pearson's house exploded, killing Mr Pearson and destroying the house. The gas board was able to show it had not been negligent, as it had taken all reasonable precautions to prevent gas leaks and, if they occurred, to stop the leak safely. It showed that there had been particularly cold weather and this caused the ground to freeze and then buckle during the thaw. This natural event caused the pipe to fracture. The gas board owed a duty of care to Mr and Mrs Pearson but had not broken that duty as having regular inspections and 24-hour emergency call-out teams was a sufficient standard of care.

Legal principle – *res ipsa loquitur* applied and the defendant could show that it had not been negligent.

PAUSE POINT Research the cases of Byrne v Boadle (1863) and Mahon v Osborne (1939) and apply the test for *res ipsa loquitur* to them.

Hint Find the facts of these cases and apply the rules of *res ipsa loquitur* to the facts.

Extend Search news reports for articles such as 'surgeon removes wrong kidney' or 'mother given wrong baby' and decide whether *res ipsa loquitur* applies in the cases you find as a result of your research.

Assessment practice 1.4

A04

Stephen, a keen cook, had been invited to try out Paul's expensive new kitchen. Stephen decided this was a good opportunity to use his blow torch to finish off a special meal he was going to create. Stephen did not check the blow torch, which he had not used for several months.

Stephen turned on the blow torch and tried to light it. As he did so, the gas canister on the blow torch came off and burst into flames, destroying the kitchen.

Paul suffered burns which took much longer than usual to heal, as he had a skin complaint that made healing difficult. Fumes from the fire spread to the house next door and damaged a valuable painting that was hung on the wall. Experts were amazed that the painting had been damaged. Close examination showed that it had been created with a unique mix of materials that had never been seen before. When the mix was tested later, it was found to be liable to react to fumes such as those that had been created in the incident.

You are working for a law firm and have been asked to assess this case to decide whether there has been negligence or not. You need to prove both factual causation and remoteness of damage for damage to be established. Use case authority to prove your points, and write a note evaluating the legal position so that the client, Paul, can understand the law involved.

Plan

- What is the task? What is my research being asked to address?
- Are there any areas of the task that I think I may struggle with?
- Do I need clarification on anything?
- What resources do I need to complete the task? How can I get access to them?
- What areas of law are involved? What are the relevant cases I will have to explain?

Do

- I need to make connections between what I am researching and the task and identify the important information.
- I need to list the cases that help me to make my arguments.
- I need to identify when I have gone wrong and adjust my thinking to get myself back on course.

Review

- I can explain what the task was and how I approached it.
- I can explain what skills I employed and which new ones I have developed.
- I can explain what I have learned about the law of negligence and why it is important.

Getting ready for assessment

This section has been written to help you to do your best when you take the external examination. Read through it carefully and ask your tutor if there is anything you are not sure about.

About the test

Ahead of your supervised assessment you will be issued with Part A of your assessment, which contains material for the completion of the preparatory work for the set task.

- Before the preparation time, make sure that you have reviewed the entire specification and made sure that any areas you do not understand fully are explained to you again.
- Make sure that you know the main terms and ideas as you will, realistically, be able to use your permitted notes only for details that you find difficult to get precisely correct or are confused about. You will not have time in the set assessment to look through your notes for basic details.
- Read all of Part A carefully.
- Highlight or underline key words. Look for the areas of law involved. Consider what questions might arise as a result of your exploration of the material in Part A.
- You will have time beforehand to complete independent research around this. Make sure that you put time aside in your diary for this well in advance.
- You will be allowed to make your own prepared notes to support you during the supervised assessment. Your teacher will tell you the amount of time you have and the length and format of notes you can take.
- Tutors cannot give you any support with respect to the notes and the work must be completed independently.
- Decide with your tutors on where you will carry out this preparatory work so that you are not disturbed and have access to suitable materials.
- Get together everything you might need as directed by your teacher.
- As the guidelines for assessment can change, you should refer to the official assessment guidance on the Pearson Qualifications website for the latest definitive guidance.

Preparing for the test

This unit is assessed under supervised conditions. Pearson sets and marks the tasks. As mentioned, you will be provided with a case study prior to a supervised assessment period in order to carry out research.

The external assessment will last a set period of time and must be completed in one session.

You will need to respond to a number of tasks, which will vary in each assessment.

- Always make a plan for your answer before you start writing. Sketch this out so that you can refer to it throughout – remember to include an introduction and a conclusion and think about the key points you want to mention in your answer, and make sure to use supporting evidence from your notes. On this plan, think about setting yourself some timeframes so that you make sure you have time to cover everything you want to – and, importantly, to write the conclusion!
- Try to keep your answer as focused on your key points as possible. If you find your answer drifting away from that main point, refer back to your plan.
- Make sure that you understand everything being asked of you in the activity instructions. It might help to underline or highlight the key terms in the instructions so that you can be sure your answer is clear and focused on exactly what you have been asked to do.

Make sure that you arrive in good time for your test and that you leave yourself enough time at the end to check through your work. Listen to, and read carefully, any instructions you are given. Marks are often lost through not reading instructions properly and misunderstanding what you are being asked to do. There are some key terms that may appear in your assessment. Understanding what these words mean will help you to understand what you are being asked to do.

Command word	Definition – what it is asking you to do
Analysis	Learners present the outcome of methodical and detailed examination either: • breaking down a theme, topic or situation in order to interpret and study the interrelationships between the parts and/or • of information or data to interpret and study key trends and interrelationships.
Application	The bringing together in order to establish some relationship or connection, as in the application of a rule or principle to a case or fact. Learners indicate the main features or purpose of something by recognising it and/or being able to discern and understand facts or qualities. They then make connections and relate to examples to show what is meant or what might result in a specific context.
Evaluation	Learners' work draws on varied information, themes or concepts to consider aspects, such as: • strengths or weaknesses • advantages or disadvantages • alternative actions • relevance or significance. Learners' inquiries should lead to a supported judgement showing relationship to its context. This will often be in a conclusion.
Explanation	Gives clear details and reasons and/or evidence to support an opinion, view or argument. It could show how conclusions are drawn (arrived at). Learners are able to show that they comprehend the origins, functions and objectives of a subject, and its suitability for purpose.
Outline	A summary or overview or a brief description of something.
Prepare a presentation	Prepare the materials for a visual presentation.
Research	Learners carry out their own research into primary sources of law.
Solicitor's letter	Formal letter containing legal information but written appropriately for a non-lawyer.
Summary for the file or file note	Brief but comprehensive synopsis of a legal case, written by solicitors, containing detailed research relevant to the case.

Sample answers

Look at the sample questions that follow and the tips on how to answer them well.

Worked example

Set task brief

- You must research the information in the case referenced below.
- You will carry out secondary research on the law, legal process, courts and personnel relevant to this case.
- In Part B you will be asked to apply your research to a new case scenario.
- You will be allowed to take notes to support you during the supervised assessment.
- You are expected to spend time on this research.
- Set task information – case material

Here is a summary of the case of Orchard v Lee (2009).

Mrs Orchard was working as a lunchtime assistant supervisor at a school. She was with another supervisor and walking outside in an area where the children regularly ran around playing.

The defendant is a 13-year-old boy who, when giving evidence, described the incident:

'I was running, playing a game of tag with my friend. I did not really think I was breaking a rule, it did not occur to me that I was. I collided with Mrs Orchard. I was running across the courtyard. I had seen her but thought I wouldn't go near her. I turned round to look at my friend and then the back of my head collided with Mrs Orchard's head. I was running backwards for a moment, I cannot say how many paces, and that led to the collision.'

The County Court rejected Mrs Orchard's claim for damages in negligence against the boy. She then appealed that decision.

Underline the key words in the text to research further to check that you fully understand the meaning.

Make a list of areas of law you have studied in Unit 1 that are relevant to the information.

Search for other key cases that may help you to deal with a similar scenario.

What the underlined words might trigger

The case – A decided case, presumably taken from a law report – how does law reporting work? Who is involved in a case? What is their role?

The defendant – He is being sued by the claimant – Mrs Orchard.

Evidence – Why is the boy giving evidence? Look at burden and standard of proof.

County Court – What sort of cases are heard in the County Court? Why might this case be heard in the County Court?

Claim for damages – What are damages and how are they calculated?

Negligence – I know that three things must be proved for negligence – duty, breach and damage. What are the cases, the authority, that demonstrate this? Do I know the key cases – if not – into my notes! What similar cases are there? – need to research this and make notes!

Appealed – Where does an appeal from the County Court go?

Part B of your assessment will be held under supervised conditions. You will be provided with further information relating to the subject of your preparatory work for Part A.

Worked example

What are the trigger words and possible forms of communication needed?

Look at 'Key words typically used in assessment' that can be found in the unit specification. What have I been told by my tutors on that? Make sure I use any specific format asked for in the external assessment!

How much do I know? What areas do I need notes on to have confidence that I will get the law and its application correct?

There are two activities. You will have a set time to complete the activities and will be told how many marks each is worth.

Read all the information provided.

Part B Set Task Information

You are a new trainee at the solicitor's firm of Stabler and Benson, in Birmingham. You are sitting in with a solicitor who specialises in personal accident claims. You have been asked to take notes and help prepare the client's case. Given the clients tardiness in instructing the firm, the solicitor has left you to do this as he is anxious to start proceedings immediately. He has rushed to the court to ensure proceedings are commenced in time.

The client is Endof, a well-known and previously very successful rapper, real name Dwayne Forrest. He lives in one of a small group of five large houses with gated access to the public road. The gates are controlled by permanent security guards and all the neighbours are very wealthy.

About two and a half years ago, Endof was walking along the pavement approaching his house when he saw one of his neighbours, 15-year-old Julian Lands, trying to do tricks on a skateboard. Endof stopped to watch and Julian sped towards him shouting, 'Look at this!' Endof clapped his first effort and then asked him if he could do it again while jumping over him, while he (Endof) was crouched down. Julian spectacularly failed to achieve this and crashed into Endof.

Endof was seriously injured and had to cancel a world tour. Since then, his career has struggled to gain any momentum and he is likely to have to sell his house. He also can no longer drive so will have to sell his collection of exotic cars for which he was famous.

Endof has left with you his medical reports to date and financial records from his agent and manager showing his decline in earnings following the accident.

Julian (and his family) have refused to accept any responsibility for the incident, claiming Endof stood up just as Julian was approaching. Another neighbour, Sasha Duval, has made a statement about what she recalls of the incident, which she saw as she was driving out of her property.

You must complete ALL activities.

Refer to your notes for preparatory work completed in **Part A**.

Instructions for learners

Read the set task information carefully.

You must plan your time accordingly and be prepared to submit all the required evidence.

You will need to refer to any preparatory work from **Part A** to complete the set task in **Part B**.

You will complete this set task under supervision and your work will be kept securely during any breaks taken.

You must work independently throughout the supervised assessment period and must not share your work with other learners.

Outcomes for submission

You will need to submit two documents on completion of the supervised assessment period:

- summary for the solicitor's file
- a draft brief to counsel to prepare the statement of claim in proceedings against Julian for damages.

You must also fully complete an authentication sheet; you do not need to submit any prepared notes with the final outcomes to Pearson.

SET TASK

You must complete ALL activities.

You will need to refer to the additional task information given on the following pages and the notes of any preparatory work completed in **Part A**.

Activity 1

Prepare, for your supervisor, a summary for the file of your client, Endof.

This summary should include:

- an explanation of the law relating to Endof's claim
- how the law applies to his case, using appropriate precedents
- how his claim might be challenged
- an evaluation of the likelihood of success in this case, with a justified conclusion
- an indication of how damages might be assessed.

Activity 2

- Draft a detailed solicitor's letter to your client explaining the law before you brief counsel to prepare the statement of claim in proceedings against Julian for damages and an opinion on the merits of Endof's claim.
- Indicate the court in which you expect to commence proceedings.

Included in the brief to Counsel will be:

The statement of the client, Endof

The statement of Sacha Duval (neighbour)

Endof's medical reports to date

Endof's financial records from his agent and manager showing his decline in earnings following the accident.

Activity 1 Answer:

This will be a civil claim based on the law of negligence. The point of taking a claim will be to claim damages. It might be possible to deal with a claim out of court by negotiating with the person who caused the injury but if the negotiation is not successful the case will have to go to court. Which court will deal with the case will depend on the amount of damages being claimed.

A claim of negligence requires three things to be proved. Firstly a duty of care has to be shown which proves a legal relationship between the parties. According to the case of Caparo v Dickman a duty of care requires a relationship, foreseeability of some harm and the duty needs to be fair, just and reasonable. In this case there is a relationship as Julian and Endof were neighbours, it is foreseeable or possible that there might be an accident and injury and it is fair.

The second part of a negligence claim is breach of duty. This means that if a person falls below the standard of the reasonable person when they caused the injury they will be liable. The court will consider factors such as the likelihood of injury happening and whether the person causing the injury is a learner. A relevant case is Bolton v Stone. In that case a woman was hit by a cricket ball when walking in the street outside a cricket ground. The court decided that the cricket club had taken all precautions and the woman lost. The court would decide if Julian had breached a duty of care and I think he would have.

The third part of negligence is damage. It has to be shown that Julian caused the injury to Endof and that there is nothing to break the chain of causation. The injury has to be reasonably foreseeable according to the Wagon Mound case.

If all three parts are proved negligence is present and damages can be claimed. I think that Julian is negligent.

Julian could argue a defence that Endof agreed to suffer the injuries. This is known as the defence of consent. The defence is a complete defence and if successful the claim of negligence will be defeated. Here, Endof asked Julian if he could do it again whilst jumping over him. This could be evidence of Endof agreeing to risk the injury. The court will again decide if Endof consented to his injuries. I think he did and he will lose the case.

If Endof is successful he could claim damages. The aim of the award of damages is to put the claimant (Endof) back in the position he was in before the accident. Damages can be special or general. Special damages are amounts that can be calculated specifically. They include loss of earnings and specific medical costs such as private physiotherapy up to the date of the court case. General damages are amounts for the future. They include loss of future earnings, future medical expenses, pain and suffering and loss of amenity. This means that the injured person cannot do something after the accident that they could do before. Damages can be claimed as long as they are not too remote. In this case Endof's loss of earnings would not be too remote but the loss of money from the sale of the exotic cars is likely to be too remote and not recoverable.

One of the first things that will have to be looked at is whether Julian and possibly his parents are worth suing and whether they have the money or insurance to cover accidents such as this. This should be investigated before any court action is taken.

Activity 2 answer:

Outline

Our client Endof, an internationally well-known rapper, was badly injured by a 15–year–old skateboarder who was showing off his tricks on the pavement near their houses. According to our client's statement he was injured when the skateboarder sped towards him shouting, 'look at this!' Our client applauded the first effort but was then injured when the skateboarder attempted to jump over him while he crouched down. He spectacularly failed to achieve this and crashed into our client. This account is supported by the evidence of a passing neighbour whose statement is attached. The skateboarder denies our client's account and suggests our client encouraged him to make the jump and stood up as he jumped causing the injuries to himself.

Negotiations to arrive at a settlement have failed and our client is forced to take court action to recover damages. As can be seen from the medical reports serious long–term injuries have been suffered by our client. It can also be seen that our client has suffered a considerable loss of earnings and is being forced to sell his collection of valuable cars.

Counsel is requested to:

Advise on the merits of Endof's claim;

Advise on the merits of any possible defence that may be argued by the skateboarder;

Advise on the amount of damages that could be claimed by our client;

Advise on the court in which a claim should be issued;

Draft a statement of claim for issuing in court.

Comments on activity answers

Assessment focus 1	Selection and understanding of legal principles relevant to context
Assessment focus 2	Application of legal principles and research to data provided
Assessment focus 3	Analysis of legal authorities, principles and concepts
Assessment focus 4	Presentation and structure

Activity 1 Answer:

Firstly a duty of care has to be shown which proves a legal relationship between the parties. According to the case of Caparo v Dickman a duty of care requires a relationship, foreseeability of some harm and it needs to be fair, just and reasonable. In this case there is a relationship as Julian and Endof were neighbours, it is foreseeable or possible that there might be an accident and injury and the duty is fair.

This only provides basic information of the three parts of the Caparo test. The assertion (not application) made in the answer is that a duty of care is owed. As the Caparo test has not been explained and with no reference to authority, the answer is in band 1 for Assessment Foci 1, 2 and 3 at this stage.

The second part of a negligence claim is breach of duty. This means that if a person falls below the standard of the reasonable person when they caused the injury they will be liable. The court will consider factors such as the likelihood of injury happening and whether the person causing the injury is a learner. A relevant case is Bolton v Stone. In that case a woman was hit by a cricket ball when walking in the street outside a cricket ground. The court decided that the cricket club had taken all precautions and the woman lost. The court would decide if Julian had breached a duty of care and I think he would have.

This part of the test for negligence is a little better. There is reference to authority, Bolton v Stone. Unfortunately the explanation of the principle in the case is weak and does not relate it to the standard of care required of the reasonable man if there is not to be a breach of duty. The law is stated vaguely and needs precision to be improved. Again there is little, if any, application. The answer is in band 1 for Assessment Foci 1 and 3 at this stage. This might just be raised to band 2 for Assessment Focus 2.

The third part of negligence is damage. It has to be shown that Julian caused the injury to Endof and that there is nothing to break the chain of causation. The injury has to be reasonably foreseeable according to the Wagon Mound case.

The answer demonstrates an understanding of the concept of damage, but does not expand on this. An explanation of Wagon Mound would improve this. There is no application.

If all three parts are proved negligence is present and damages can be claimed. I think that Julian is negligent.

Answer needs to make a reasoned decision at this point.

Julian could argue a defence that Endof agreed to suffer the injuries. This is known as the defence of consent. The defence is a complete defence and if successful the claim of negligence will be defeated. Here, Endof asked Julian if he could do it again whilst jumping over him. This could be evidence of Endof agreeing to risk the injury. The court will again decide if Endof consented to his injuries. I think he did and he will lose the case.

The idea of consent needs to be considered here in the context of contributory negligence. This has not been developed and will gain little credit.

If Endof is successful he could claim damages. The aim of the award of damages is to put the claimant (Endof) back in the position he was in before the accident. Damages can be special or general. Special damages are amounts that can be calculated specifically. They include loss of earnings and specific medical costs such as private physiotherapy up to the date of the court case. General damages are amounts for the future. They include loss of future earnings, future medical expenses, pain and suffering and loss of amenity. This means that the injured person cannot do something after the accident that they could do before.

This explanation of damages is quite good. This is into band 3 of assessment focus 1 – there is little authority available and the general principles use correct terminology with some examples.

Damages can be claimed as long as they are not too remote.

In this case Endof's loss of earnings would not be too remote but the loss of money from the sale of the exotic cars is likely to be too remote and not recoverable.

Back to basics – there needs to some explanation of what this means and how it can be applied.

Assertion only about the earnings. The point about the sale of the cars seems to be based on no evidence – there is no mention that the sale is at a loss. Little creditworthy here.

One of the first things that will have to be looked at is whether Julian and possibly his parents are worth suing and whether they have the money or insurance to cover accidents such as this. This should be investigated before any court action is taken.

Good point about the financial implications. Perhaps it could also be pointed out that Endof is apparently still reasonably wealthy, but the file note should remind the solicitor to get some financial details before a large bill is run up that will not be paid!

Activity 2 Answer:

This is not set out as one might expect. (See sample instructions to counsel in Figure 1.4).

This is assessment focus 4 band 1 at present.

While proceedings are not fully under way, we do know the case is more likely to be complex and high value, so is likely to be heard in the High Court. This would be a band 4 response to the assessment focus 2 for this part.

Overall

The answers are just about in band 2 for assessment foci 1, 2 and 3 with assessment focus 4 being in band 1.

Further reading and resources

Newspapers with law sections – for example, *The Times*, which has regular law reports and a law section once a week.

Websites

- **https://www.gov.uk/browse/justice/rights**
- **http://www.legislation.gov.uk/**
- **https://www.gov.uk/government/organisations/hm-courts-and-tribunals-service**
- **https://www.citizensadvice.org.uk/**
- **http://www.iclr.co.uk/**
- **http://www.newlawjournal.co.uk/**
- **https://www.lawsociety.org.uk/**
- **http://www.barcouncil.org.uk/**
- **http://www.cilex.org.uk/**

Investigating Aspects of Criminal Law and the Legal System

2

Getting to know your unit

Assessment
This unit is internally assessed using a series of assignments set by your tutor.

In this unit you will develop the skills to investigate and research how laws are made both inside and outside Parliament. There is a particular emphasis on investigating how criminal laws relating to non-fatal offences are applied and how the criminal justice system works.

How you will be assessed

This unit will be assessed by assignments set and marked by your tutor. You will need to work independently on your assignments, so it will be important to be well prepared. Collect all your notes, research and material from class activities in a folder and make use of the unit specification and assignment brief to help plan your approach to this unit and in planning your time. You will find it helpful to create a glossary of legal terms and terms that relate to the assignments in this unit. You will need to practise the higher-level skills required for Merit and Distinction grades so that you can develop the points you make in an assignment to make rational judgements and valid conclusions. This unit contains useful information and activities to help you prepare for your assignments. The recommended assessment approach for this unit is two assignments, to include the suggested criteria.

The assignments set by your tutor will consist of a number of tasks designed to meet the criteria in the table below. They are likely to include written assignments but could also be activities such as:

- case studies where you make decisions about the application of relevant law and provide legal advice
- magazine articles considering the roles of those involved in the criminal justice system
- presentations to illustrate how ideas for change can develop into new laws and practices.

Assessment criteria

This table shows what you must do in order to achieve a **Pass**, **Merit** or **Distinction**, and where you can find activities to help you.

Pass	Merit	Distinction
Learning aim A Explore how statutory rules are made and interpreted.		
A.P1 Choose a statute to research, then explain the influences that impacted on its progress into law. **Assessment practice 2.1**	**A.M1** Analyse the effect of influences and interpretation on Parliament's law-making. **Assessment practice 2.1**	**AB.D1** Present an evaluation of the law-making processes both inside and outside Parliament. **Assessment practice 2.1**
A.P2 Explain the rules of statutory interpretation using given case studies. **Assessment practice 2.1**		
Learning aim B Examine how legislation is made outside Parliament.		
B.P3 Apply the various forms of delegated legislation and their controls in given case studies. **Assessment practice 2.1**	**B.M2** Analyse the effectiveness of the controls on delegated legislation. **Assessment practice 2.1**	
B.P4 Research, select and explain examples of EU regulations, directives and decisions. **Assessment practice 2.1**	**B.M3** Assess the impact of EU laws on the UK and the resolution of any conflicts, using actual recent examples. **Assessment practice 2.1**	
Learning aim C Explore the various legal personnel involved in a criminal trial.		
C.P5 Using given case studies of criminal trials in different courts, explain the roles of both the lay and legal personnel involved. **Assessment practice 2.2**	**C.M4** Demonstrate work-related skills with confidence and proficiency to meet objectives in different situations. **Assessment practice 2.2**	**C.D2** Evaluate the impact of using lay people in the criminal justice trial process as opposed to legal personnel, providing a justified conclusion. **Assessment practice 2.2**
C.P6 Explain the advice and representation available in given criminal case studies. **Assessment practice 2.2**		
Learning aim D Apply the key elements of crime and sentencing in non-fatal offence case studies.		
D.P7 Explain, using given case studies, the elements of non-fatal offences. **Assessment practice 2.3**	**D.M5** Analyse and apply the current law on specific non-fatal offences to given case studies to determine the charges and possible sentences in these situations. **Assessment practice 2.3**	**D.D3** Evaluate the current law on non-fatal offences against the person and related current sentencing trends. **Assessment practice 2.3**
D.P8 Discuss the aims of sentencing and the types of sentence for specific offences in given case studies. **Assessment practice 2.3**		

Getting started

In groups, think of some laws that you would like to change or introduce. What are the reasons for your choices? How would you go about bringing about the change in those laws?

Also, imagine that you have been charged with a criminal offence. Who would you go to for advice about what to do next? Do you have to pay for this advice? What happens if the case goes to court? What could happen to you if you are found guilty?

A Explore how statutory rules are made and interpreted

Legal skills

Researching legal information

In law, you will always be required to justify your arguments by stating what the law is and where it comes from. This stated law can then be applied to the facts of the case or the point you are making by showing how it demonstrates the point.

There are three main official sources of legal information for you to research and to refer to in your work:

- Acts of **Parliament** – made in Parliament. Laws made in Parliament are called **legislation or statutes**, and a single law is called an Act of Parliament.
- Delegated legislation – made by local authorities, and others who have been given the power to do so.
- Decided cases – made by judges. This is called judicial precedent and was covered in Unit 1.

> **Key term**
>
> **Parliament** – the body authorised to make laws. In the UK, Parliament consists of the elected House of Commons, the appointed House of Lords and the Queen all acting together. Scotland has its own elected Parliament to make laws that apply only to Scotland.
>
> **Legislation/statutes** – a set of laws suggested by government and made by Parliament.

You will not be expected to quote EU law (also covered in this unit) in your work as this has mostly been incorporated into UK law. The United Kingdom consists of England, Wales, Scotland and Northern Ireland. Scotland and Northern Ireland have their own legal systems so the laws that you will be covering in this course are those that apply in England and Wales.

Online versions of Acts now may include a set of explanatory notes, which set out the reasons for the passing of the Act and what it is designed to achieve. These notes have not been debated or approved in Parliament so are not to be regarded as official as the Act itself. They do, however, help to give an insight into the background behind the Act.

> **Research**
>
> Most universities have guides as to how you should reference statutes, statutory instruments and cases.
>
> An example is **http://portal.solent.ac.uk/library/help/factsheets/resources/referencing-law-oscola.pdf?t=1471441246250**
>
> Use this link to reference the following:
>
> - Riot Compensation Act 2016
> - Registration of Births, Deaths, Marriages and Civil Partnerships (Fees) Regulations 2014
> - R v Miller (1983).

How to read an Act of Parliament

Figure 2.1 shows the first page of an Act of Parliament, with some explanations of its various elements.

The official and short title. As it is called an Act it has passed through all the stages in the Houses of Commons and Lords and has received Royal Assent. As such it has become part of the law of the land.
The chapter number shows that it is the eight Act to be passed in 2016.

This is the long title, which can be used as an intrinsic aid for statutory interpretation

Riot Compensation Act 2016

2016 CHAPTER 8

An Act to repeal the Riot (Damages) Act 1886 and make provision about types of claims, procedures, decision-making and limits on awards payable in relation to a new compensation scheme for property damaged, destroyed or stolen in the course of riots.

This is the date the law received the Royal Assent

[23rd March 2016]

Be it enacted by the Queen's most Excellent Majesty, by and with the advice and consent of the Lords Spiritual and Temporal, and Commons, in this present Parliament assembled, and by the authority of the same, as follows:–

This paragraph again shows that the Act went through all the stages in Parliament

Claims for compensationE+W

1Claims for compensation for riot damage etc

(1) Where–

(a) a person's property has been damaged, destroyed or stolen in the course of a riot,

(b) the property is property in respect of which a claim may be made under this subsection (see section 2(1)), and

(c) the property was not insured, or was not adequately insured, for the damage, destruction or theft, the person may claim compensation from the appropriate local policing body.

This is the start of the Act. As you can see it is divided into sections - this extract is part of section 1 - subsections - this extract has two subsections - and sub subsections - this extract has three sub subsections.

(2) Where–

(a) a person's property has been damaged, destroyed or stolen in the course of a riot,

(b) the property is property in respect of which a claim may be made under this subsection (see section 2(2)), and

(c) an insurance company has (to any extent) met a claim by the person under a policy of insurance in respect of the damage, destruction or theft, the insurance company may claim compensation from the appropriate local policing body.

There are a total of 12 sections in this Act, which is quite short for an Act. It will have been drafted by specialist Parliamentary draftspeople.

10 Repeal of Riot (Damages) Act 1886 and consequential amendments etc

(1) The Riot (Damages) Act 1886 is repealed.

The previous relevant law has been replaced by this new law and so is no longer of any effect.

11 Regulations

(1) Regulations under this Act are to be made by statutory instrument.

(3) A statutory instrument containing regulations described in subsection (2)(a) or (b) may not be made unless a draft of the instrument has been laid before each House of Parliament and approved by a resolution of each House.

This section allows the relevant Secretary of State or government minister to make regulations or delegated legislation to fill in some detail.
Subsection 3 requires there to have been an affirmative resolution in Parliament for the approval of the regulation.

12 Commencement, extent and short title

(1) Sections 1 to 10 and the Schedule come into force on whatever day or days the Secretary of State by regulations appoints.

(2) This section and section 11 come into force on the day on which this Act is passed.

(3) This Act extends to England and Wales.

(4) This Act may be cited as the Riot Compensation Act 2016.

The last section in an Act shows:
- when the Act comes into force - this Act will come into force partly in the future and partly on 23 March 2016. A search will have to be made for a statutory instrument that brings the Act into force
- which countries of the UK it applies to, and
- the short title.

Figure 2.1: The introduction page of an Act of Parliament

Finding appropriate and reliable sources

There are so many laws in the UK that a lawyer cannot be expected to know every single one. To give an idea of how many laws are made each year, the BBC reported in 2011 that 3506 laws were introduced in the UK in 2010. It would be impossible for a single person to keep fully up to date with every law passed each year.

Therefore, one of the skills a lawyer develops is how to research the law. The lawyer can then decide from reading the legislation and the judgments from any relevant cases what the law is and how to advise the client.

Lawyers should only fully rely on official sources when researching the law. A lawyer can rely on the accuracy of information at legislation.gov.uk, the government's website gov.uk, official bodies' reports such as those from the Law Commission and certain authorised series of law reports.

However, there are many other unofficial sources of information. If a lawyer was to use an unofficial source, they might have to check the accuracy of the statement. These sources may include textbooks, newspapers and Internet articles. You should certainly not wholly rely on Wikipedia, Wikilaw or social media comments as being authoritative sources of information.

Referencing sources in your work

There is no minimum number of sources you should use to achieve the best grade but it is important to accurately reference the sources you have used in your work because:

- it shows the relevant legal authority to support your work
- it allows the reader to find the sources you have used
- it helps you to avoid suggestions of plagiarism as you are showing where you have used other people's work
- it shows a range of research and a variety of sources you have used to complete your work
- it shows you have used reliable and trustworthy resources.

Your bibliography will be made up of all the sources you used in your work. Place the bibliography at the end of your work after the main text. In law work, bibliographies should include a separate list for each category, such as legislation, cases, government publications, books and journal articles. List items alphabetically within each category. Different sources of legal information should be set out in specific ways:

- Refer to an Act of Parliament by its short title and date (the year), for example Riot Compensation Act 2016. If you refer to a particular section of the Act, use 's' or 'ss' and the number or numbers.
- Refer to a Statutory Instrument by its full name, number and year.
- When referring to cases try to use the same series of law reports throughout.

Discussion

When you are writing your coursework, you may do some or all of the following. In groups, discuss whether you would need to give a reference for:

- your own opinion about a law or a case – whether it is good or bad or whether it works or not
- the results of your own survey
- a paragraph of text from a book, statute or law report
- a diagram or photograph that you did not take
- a fact that is commonly known
- something you know you have seen somewhere but you cannot find the source
- your own opinion about a whole topic.

Using, interpreting and applying information from sources and authorities

Before your assessment on this unit, your teacher will give you a variety of case studies or scenarios that will allow you to apply the rules of law to the scenario and to analyse whether the law works or not. Looking at these case studies or scenarios will allow you to understand what rules can apply to a situation and how they can apply.

You should explain plainly what the relevant law is and give clear advice on a course of action or whether the client is guilty of a criminal offence. For example, if the law is contained in an Act of Parliament, your client will not want you to just copy and paste a whole Act into your work. They will not understand it or how it applies to them. They will just need to be referred to the relevant section or part of the instrument that applies to their case and how it applies to their situation.

Similarly, if the law is contained in a law report, the client will not want to be given the whole report to read because, again, they will not understand it or its context. They will want you to select relevant parts of the judgment and explain clearly how it applies to their case and, from this, the likely outcome of their case.

Presenting information verbally and in writing

Verbally

Presenting information verbally could include advising your client at a police station, in the office or at court. This could also include making a presentation to others in your firm or to a wider audience who may or may not have legal knowledge. The same applies if you address a court or a judge.

Here are some useful tips for presenting verbal information:

- Prepare what you intend to say.
- Use PowerPoint slides or similar to support your presentation but do not overload each slide with text. Make sure that you use a large enough font size for your audience to easily read.
- Check whether there is a time limit and any PowerPoint slide limitations.
- Make sure that you have an introduction on what you will cover, a middle section on the main content and a conclusion to wrap up what you have said.
- Explain key terms.
- Avoid repetition.
- Use pictures or graphics to illustrate your presentation but make sure that you do not make the slides too flashy, or your audience will be distracted.
- Do not just read everything that is on the slide – your audience can do this for themselves. You should use the slides to support what you have to say.
- Rehearse your presentation in front of a small group or a single person. Their feedback will be useful.

In writing

If you are writing to other lawyers, a third party or your client, all written communication should be informative and formal. This means that you use appropriate legal terms and avoid being overfamiliar.

- If you are writing to your client with information and advice about a case it should still be formal, setting out the relevant law that applies, and giving your client clear advice on what to do next.
- If you are writing a witness statement, it should be written in the first person – for example 'As I was walking down the street I saw…'. It should clearly set out what the witness saw or heard as this account may later be required as evidence in court. It should not contain any speculation of what might have been or what the witness thought they saw or heard.

Reflect

Your client Mr Jones tells you he is owed £3,000 for building work he has carried out at Mr Smith's property. Mr Smith has not complained about the quality of the work but is refusing to pay. Mr Jones has contacted him a number of times but has still not received any money. On the last occasion, he told Mr Smith that he would be contacting his solicitor about recovering the payment.

Draft a formal letter to Mr Smith demanding payment and threatening court proceedings if payment is not made.

- If you are writing a file note it will be read by other people in your firm, but not your client. It can be informal, can be written in the third person and can contain your views on the credibility of the witness. It should set out the relevant rules of law, how those laws apply to the charges, whether you see any possible defence and your views on the strength of the case generally.

Research

Visit **www.legislation.gov.uk** and choose an Act of Parliament from the past year.

Look at the explanatory notes section. Can you work out from reading this why the Act was introduced? Was it introduced because it was an idea of the government, a pressure group or the media? (Note: not all Acts have this section.) Can you work out what the Act is trying to do?

Influences on Parliament

Parliament can either make a new law or change an existing law. A reason for a new law may be because of a national or international event. For example, since the September 11 attacks in 2001 there have been a number of new laws introduced to deal with the threat of terrorism. A reason for change to existing laws could be that current laws do not cover new situations or developments. For example, there have been suggestions to introduce new laws to deal with online bullying and virtual harassment – issues that did not exist ten years ago.

Key term

Government – the political party with the largest number of seats in the House of Commons. The government is responsible for the day-to-day running of the country.

Most ideas for new laws come from the **government**, as they have been elected to govern the country for a period of time to carry out the agenda they put forward before the election. It is very difficult for an individual member of the public to bring about a new law, as they have no direct link with Parliament. However, there are certain ways in which a member of the public can contribute to a change in the law.

Pressure groups

Pressure groups are groups of people who have similar ideas and campaign for changes in the law. They try to influence government and Parliament to legislate on matters of interest to them. They can range from just a few people to large groups with hundreds of thousands of members. They may use lots of different methods in their campaigns such as petitions, marches, demonstrations, strikes or a publicity campaign with advertising.

The main types of pressure group are:

- sectional – promote the interests of their members
- cause groups – promote an idea or belief
- insider groups – are influential and have access to government ministers, officials and law-makers
- outsider groups – are not influential and do not have access to law-makers.

A demonstration/march/strike against climate change

Research

Find an example of each of the four main types of pressure group. For each group, find its aims and how it tries to influence others on its views.

- How successful is each group? Have any laws been introduced as a result of its influence?
- Can you think of reasons for its success or failure?

Table 2.1 shows the advantages and disadvantages that pressure groups have as influencers of legislation.

Table 2.1: Advantages and disadvantages of pressure groups as an influence on legislation

Advantages	Disadvantages
They can raise public awareness of an issue.	They may be biased in favour of their cause and not be able to consider alternative views.
Large groups can have huge memberships, which politicians will not want to upset.	Outsider groups may be prepared to resort to violence or criminal actions to promote their cause.
They have considerable detailed knowledge of their interest.	Supporters of the pressure group may represent only a small proportion of the population.

Research

Research the Snowdrop campaign from 1996 and answer the following questions.

- Why was the campaign group formed?
- Which type of pressure group was it?
- What did they campaign for?
- Were they successful?
- What happened to the group at the end of their campaign?

Law Commission

The Law Commission is an independent body set up by the Law Commissions Act 1965. Its role is to keep the law of England and Wales under review and recommend reform where needed. In particular, it focuses on the **codification** of existing law and the **repeal of obsolete law**. The Law Commission Act 2009 amended the previous Act so that the government must explain the reasons why they have not implemented Law Commission proposals.

It has five full-time Law Commissioners, who are experienced lawyers each responsible for a specific area of law, and its chairperson is a High Court judge. The Law Commission mainly investigates areas of law that are referred to it by government and that are not politically sensitive. However, it can also decide itself to investigate an area of law.

An investigation will research the current law and a working paper is produced with suggestions for reform. This working paper will be circulated to lawyers interested in the issue asking for their comments. A period of consultation will follow with anyone interested in that area of law. Following the consultation, a final report will be issued together with a **bill**. The government will then decide whether to introduce the bill into Parliament.

Key terms

Codification – putting all the law on a topic into one new law. The Law Commission has suggested that there should be a code for all criminal offences.

Repeal of obsolete law – the removal of an old, out-of-date law.

Bill – the name given to a draft Act as it goes through the stages in Parliament.

Research

Visit **www.lawcom.gov.uk** and find the following:

- an area of law that has been changed as a direct result of a Law Commission report and its recommendations.
- an example of a Law Commission report that has not yet been acted on by government or Parliament.
- what projects the Law Commission currently working on?

Discussion

In small groups, discuss whether the following are advantages or disadvantages of the Law Commission as an influence on legislation. Give reasons for your decisions.

- Its Commissioners have considerable legal expertise and experience.
- The government does not have to consult the Law Commission on any proposal it wants to introduce.
- It is independent and unbiased.
- Its investigations are thorough and recommendations are well informed.
- Many of its recommendations (about one third) are not acted on.
- A draft bill will accompany its report.

Media

The media is a wide term that covers the ways in which information is reported. Traditionally it covers TV, radio, newspapers and magazines. More recently it includes information on the Internet and especially social media. All of these forms of media can inform the public, represent public opinion and help form public opinion. There is a strong link between pressure groups and the use of media, and increasingly law-makers in Parliament use social media to inform and encourage engagement and the expression of views.

Sometimes traditional media can run a campaign to attempt to change the law. A famous example was the successful campaign by the *News of the World* to name and shame paedophiles following the murder of Sarah Payne. This pressure forced Parliament to introduce the Criminal Justice Act 2003, allowing parents, guardians and carers to enquire with police about suspicious individuals.

Sometimes media pressure and campaigns can combine with other influences to bring about a change in law. The same Criminal Justice Act 2003 introduced a reform to the **double jeopardy rule**, which allows a suspect to be retried for an offence of which they had previously been acquitted if there was strong new evidence available. This change was brought about due to media campaigns following the trial of the suspected killers of Stephen Lawrence. An inquiry led to a Law Commission investigation and recommendation that the law should be changed.

Key term

Double jeopardy rule – allows suspects to be retried for an offence if there is new evidence available.

Table 2.2 shows the advantages and disadvantages of the media as an influence on Parliament.

Scenario

▸ A pit bull terrier was considered a dangerous dog

Six-year-old Rucksana Khan was playing in a park near her home in Bradford when she was attacked by a pit bull terrier and taken to hospital with severe head and chest injuries. Her case was featured heavily in the media, along with other dog attacks on ten other people. This prompted the Home Secretary to introduce a bill promising to rid the country of these dangerous dogs. Because of the press coverage there was no consultation with animal charities, breeders or experts in the field. The Dangerous Dogs Act 1991 was swiftly introduced and placed restrictions on four different types of dog traditionally bred for fighting, though there was little or no evidence that any other than pit bulls had been involved in attacks. The restricted types were listed as pit bull terriers, Japanese Tosa, Fila Braziliero and Dogo Argentino. An offence was created for an owner to be prosecuted if they allowed their dog to be dangerously out of control.

When cases under the Act came to court, judges found difficulty interpreting the Act. The use of the word 'type' (which should have been breed) and attempts to convict owners who were allowing other adults or children to exercise their dogs in public were two issues the judges found. Parliament had to pass an amending Act in 1997 to deal with these and other issues, which should have been dealt with before the first Act was passed.

1. Why was the Dangerous Dogs Act 1991 swiftly introduced?
2. What were found to be the problems with the Act?
3. How could these problems have been avoided?
4. Why did Parliament have to pass an amending Act to deal with the problems?

Table 2.2: Advantages and disadvantages of the media as an influence on Parliament

Advantages	Disadvantages
Issues of concern are raised through traditional media or online petitions. The government may then introduce proposals into Parliament.	Some traditional media sources are not neutral or impartial and people can express strong or unlawful views on social media.
The media can lead and bring about public awareness and concern, which are essential for the government to consider reform. Ultimately, the government is answerable to the electorate.	Traditional media are businesses and may run a campaign to sell copies and expand readership rather than inform.

Discussion

In groups, think of a new law or a change in the law that you would like to be introduced.

- Which of these three influences (pressure groups, Law Commission or the media) would you think would be best suited to pressure government and Parliament to introduce your suggested change?
- Why did you choose this influence?

Share your ideas with other groups.

The law-making procedure in Parliament

Parliament consists of the **House of Commons**, the **House of Lords** and the **monarchy** all acting together to make laws. The House of Commons is elected every five years by a **general election**. The members of the House of Lords are **life peers**, but there are 92 members who are **hereditary peers**. There are also 26 bishops of the Church of England, known as the Lords Spiritual.

The Houses of Parliament

Separation of powers

According to the French philosopher, Montesquieu, an ideal state should be divided in to three separate areas: the **legislature**, the **executive** and the **judiciary** . Each of these areas should have its own separate function.

In theory, each of these three areas should remain separate from each other. They should be balanced against each other and be able to check and limit the power of the others. The UK does not strictly follow the theory of the separation of powers, as much of the law is made by the executive through **delegated legislation** and by judges through judicial precedent.

Key terms

House of Commons – the elected chamber of Parliament. The government is formed from the party having the majority of seats in this House.

House of Lords – the second House of Parliament consisting of hereditary peers and life peers. The House can revise or amend legislation that has been passed to it by the House of Commons.

Monarchy – the king or queen.

General election – held every five years when the electorate have the chance to vote for the MP to represent them in parliament.

Life peers – people who have been given the title of 'Lord' or 'Lady', but only for their lifetime.

Hereditary peers – men who have been given a title such as 'Lord', which can be passed down to their heirs.

Legislature – its role is to make law. In the UK, this is carried out by Parliament.

Executive – its role is to administer the law when it has been made and to govern the country day to day. In the UK, this is carried out by the government.

Judiciary – judges who apply the law in cases in court.

Delegated legislation – law made outside Parliament, but with Parliament's approval.

Link

See Unit 1 for more detail on judicial precedent.

Key terms

Parliamentary sovereignty – the concept that Parliament is the highest legal authority in the UK.

Constitution – the laws and rules the UK is governed by. The UK constitution is contained in some Acts of Parliament, court judgments and some authorised writings.

Green Paper – a report of policy proposals for discussion.

White Paper – a report with plans for a new law.

Parliamentary sovereignty

Parliamentary sovereignty is a theory and an important principle of the UK **constitution**. It makes Parliament the highest legal authority in the UK so that it can make any law or end any law it chooses. Generally, the courts cannot overrule any law passed by Parliament, and future Parliaments can change laws passed by previous Parliaments.

Over the years, the UK Parliament has passed laws that limit the theory and application of parliamentary sovereignty. They include:

- the devolution (or transferring) of law-making power to bodies such as the Scottish Parliament and Welsh Assembly
- the Human Rights Act 1998, which says that any law passed by Parliament must be interpreted and given effect, so far as possible, in acordance with the European Convention on Human Rights (ECHR). This means that the ECHR is superior to the UK Parliament. If Parliament wishes to pass a law against the ECHR, the government minister proposing the law must give a certificate of incompatibility and reasons for the need for the law.
- the UK's entry to the European Union in (EU) 1973, which made EU laws superior to national laws. This means that any law passed by the EU has to be brought into force in the UK. However, in view of the referendum vote in June 2016 to leave the EU, this might not be the case in future.

One view is that these laws do not completely affect the principle of parliamentary sovereignty, because, in theory at least, Parliament could repeal any of the laws implementing these changes. It remains to be seen how the UK Parliament will deal with the decision to exit the EU, although it can be said that by leaving the EU, the UK Parliament will be fully regaining its sovereignty.

Research

- Find an example of a recent Green Paper. Have the proposals within this document been introduced in a bill into Parliament?
- Find an example of a recent White Paper. Have the proposals within this document become law?

Pre-legislative stages

Often, the government will have specific ideas for new laws, which they may have included within their election manifesto. They will introduce these ideas directly into Parliament without any previous consultation. Sometimes they will wish to consult different groups before introducing a proposal into Parliament by publishing a **Green Paper**. The government will ask for feedback to their ideas in this paper, which they may include in their bill. After receiving these responses they may then publish a **White Paper**, which sets out their firm plans for a new law. The draft bill will usually be based on these plans.

Once a bill has completed all the stages, it becomes an Act and then is part of the law. A bill may be a public bill, a private members' bill or a private bill, as detailed in Table 2.3.

Table 2.3: Types of bill

Type of bill	Description
Public bill	Introduced by the government and will affect everyone in the country when it comes into force.
Private members' bill	Introduced by a single MP. Very few of these bills are passed unless they have government support. They will often be about moral issues. The most famous private members' bill led to the Abortion Act 1967.
Private bill	Usually promoted by an organisation, such as a local authority or private company, to give themselves specific powers. Private bills only change the law as it applies to that organisation or company, rather than the general public.
Hybrid bill	A mix of a public and a private bill. The changes to the law proposed by a hybrid bill are likely to affect the general public as they will often concern major construction projects.
Money bill	A bill relating to taxation and generally introduced after the budget. Money bills have to be introduced into the House of Commons. The House of Lords cannot amend them and they can receive Royal Assent even if they have not been passed by the Lords.

The legislative stages

A bill will often be introduced into the House of Commons where the following procedure will take place (see also Figure 2.2):

- First reading - the bill is announced by the government minister responsible or the promoter of the bill. A date will be set for the next reading. There is no debate or vote.
- Second reading - there will be a debate on the general idea behind the bill. A vote will be taken on whether the bill should go ahead. If a bill passes this stage, it will generally become a law.
- Committee stage - a committee of 16-50 MPs will consider the bill clause by clause and line by line. Amendments can be made at this stage.
- Report stage - the committee report back to the House on their discussions and suggested amendments.
- Third reading - there may be another general debate on the proposals in the bill and another vote may be taken on the bill as a whole or the amendments.
- If the bill and its amendments are accepted, it will be passed to the House of Lords for a similar process to take place. At the end of their discussions, it will be returned to the Commons.
- 'Ping-pong' stage - if amendments are made by the Lords, they will be considered by the Commons. The amendments may be accepted in which case the bill passes for Royal Assent or they may lead to further discussion or debate. This stage is formally known as 'Lords Amendment Considered'.
- Royal Assent - the bill is signed by the monarch and then becomes an Act. It comes into force on midnight of the day the Act is signed, unless otherwise stated.

An Act can be brought into force immediately or at some later date. It can be brought into force as a whole or in parts.

Table 2.4 shows the advantages and disadvantages of making laws in Parliament.

Table 2.4: Advantages and disadvantages of making laws in Parliament

Advantages	Disadvantages
There are several opportunities for debate, checking and amendment of the original proposals at various stages of the process. The House of Lords is particularly effective in checking government proposals that have passed through the House of Commons as many peers are independent of the government and have considerable expertise in a range of topics.	The government is in charge of the timetable of debates in the House of Commons and is likely to win most debates for laws introduced by it. This control also means that few private members' bills are likely to become law. Government can use the Parliament Acts 1911 and 1949 to force a law through, even if the House of Lords objects to it.
Laws are made by elected MPs who can put forward the views of the people that elected them.	There are many stages a bill has to go through so the process can take many months. This may not be appropriate if a law needs to be made quickly.
Laws can be made in different ways. Government bills are introduced to fit election promises. Private members' bills can be introduced to deal with topics that government may not have thought of or may be unwilling to deal with, such as moral issues.	Neither the monarch nor the House of Lords is elected. Royal Assent is considered by some as an unnecessary formality (though in practice it takes little time to be given). In the House of Commons, MPs are usually persuaded to vote with their party rather than in accordance with the wishes of their constituents.
Money bills have to be introduced in the House of Commons and the House of Lords can only delay the passing of money bills for a short time.	Acts are often drafted using language and structure that is difficult for the ordinary person to understand. It is not common practice for Parliament to consolidate all the laws on a topic. Therefore, several Acts will have to be read together to understand what the law on a certain topic is. It is also difficult to find when an Act comes into force. Much of the work of the Supreme Court is taken up with interpreting the meaning of Acts of Parliament. If it is found there are problems with the language within an Act, it can only be changed by a later Act.

First reading – the bill is announced by the government minister responsible or the promoter of the bill. A date will be set for the next reading. There is no debate or vote.

Second reading – there will be a debate on the general idea behind the bill. A vote will be taken on whether the bill should proceed. If a bill passes this stage, it will generally become a law.

Committee stage – a committee of 16-50 MPs will consider the bill clause by clause and line by line. Amendments can be made at this stage.

Report stage – the committee reports back to the House on their discussions and suggested amendments.

Third reading – there may be another general debate on the proposals in the bill and another vote may be taken on the bill as a whole or the amendments.

If the bill and its amendments are accepted, it will be passed to the House of Lords for a similar process to take place. At the end of their discussions, it will be returned to the Commons.

'Ping-pong' stage – if amendments are made by the Lords, they will be considered by the Commons. The amendments may be accepted in which case the bill passes for Royal Assent or they may lead to further discussion or debate. This stage is formally known as 'Lords Amendment Considered'.

Royal Assent – the bill is signed by the monarch and then becomes an Act. It can come into force either immediately or at some future date.

Figure 2.2: The legislative process starting in either the House of Commons or House of Lords

What are some of the reasons for introducing a new Act of Parliament?

Choose an Act of Parliament made in the last three years and read its introductory notes. What were the reasons for introducing the Act?

Extend

Identify the different groups and influences who may have been involved in introducing the legislation.

How statutes are interpreted by the courts

Statutes are interpreted when judges give a meaning to the words of a statute (an Act) when dealing with a case in court. Judges use four main principles when interpreting statute:

- the literal rule
- the golden rule
- the mischief rule
- the purposive approach.

The literal rule

The literal rule of statutory interpretation should be the first rule that judges apply. Under this rule, the words of the Act are read word for word and are interpreted by using the accepted meaning of the language. The judge may use a dictionary from the time the Act was passed to help find the meaning. The words will be applied without the judge seeking to make sense of the whole statute.

An example of this rule is the case of London and North East Railway v Berriman (1946).

Key case

London and North East Railway v Berriman (1946)

Facts

Mr Berriman worked on the railways and he was killed while oiling the track. No look-out had been provided. According to the relevant law, compensation was payable to the family if a worker died while 'relaying or repairing' the track. Using the literal rule, oiling was considered as maintenance work and did not come into either of these categories.

Legal principle – this result was unfair and harsh but according to the literal meaning of 'relaying or repairing', Mr Berriman's widow was not entitled to compensation.

Research

Look up the case of Fisher v Bell (1961). In this case, the judge used the literal rule to interpret the statute.

- What decision did the judge come to using this rule?
- What change in the law had to be made as a result of the judge's decision in this case?

Table 2.5 shows the advantages and disadvantages of the literal rule.

Table 2.5: Advantages and disadvantages of the literal rule of statutory interpretation

Advantages	Disadvantages
Parliamentary sovereignty is respected and the role of judges is to apply the law made by Parliament.	If there is more than one possible meaning to a word, this rule will not help.
Decisions using this rule can show problems with the law and Parliament can later pass an amending law.	It assumes that the drafting of the Act is perfect.
	Its use can lead to absurd and unfair results.

The golden rule

The golden rule of statutory interpretation is an extension of the literal rule. It allows the judge to look beyond the literal rule if the use of that rule would lead to an absurd judgment. This rule has both a narrow and a broad approach.

The narrow approach is used when a word has more than one meaning. This was illustrated in R v Allan (1872).

Key case

R v Allen (1872)

Facts

The defendant was charged with bigamy under s57 of the Offences Against the Person Act 1861. The section stated 'whosoever being married, shall marry any other person during the lifetime of the former husband or wife is guilty of an offence'. Using a literal interpretation of the words, the offence would be impossible to commit, as family law will not recognise a second marriage while the first is still in existence, and an attempt to marry while already married would not be a valid marriage. The court used the golden rule and decided that the word 'marry' should be given the meaning of 'going through a ceremony of marriage' and found the defendant guilty.

Legal principle - where a word or phrase is capable of more than one literal meaning, the narrow application of the golden rule allows the judge to select a meaning that avoids the absurdity.

The broad approach is used when a word has only one meaning but applying it would cause an absurdity. In this case, the court will modify the meaning of the word to avoid the absurdity. This was illustrated in Adler v George (1964).

Key case

Adler v George (1964)

Facts

The Official Secrets Act 1920 made it an offence to obstruct a member of the armed forces when in the vicinity of a prohibited place. The defendant was actually inside the airbase as opposed to within the vicinity of it. The court used the golden rule to find him guilty as otherwise it would result in an absurdity.

Legal principle -where there is only one literal meaning of a word or phrase in an Act of Parliament, but that meaning would result in an absurdity, the court can apply a broad approach to avoid the absurdity.

Table 2.6 looks at some of the advantages and disadvantages of the golden rule.

Table 2.6: Advantages and disadvantages of the golden rule

Advantages	Disadvantages
It prevents absurd or unjust judgments that can result from use of the literal rule.	There is no definition of what an absurd result is. This means the use of this rule is unpredictable, which makes it difficult for lawyers to advise their clients appropriately.

Table 2.6: *Continued*

Advantages	Disadvantages
It is more likely than the literal rule to produce a result that was intended by Parliament.	It can be seen as undemocratic as power is given to judges to decide when and how to use the rule.
It allows the court to choose the most appropriate meaning of the words in an Act and parliamentary sovereignty is maintained.	It has been described as a 'feeble parachute' because although it allows judges to escape from the literal rule, they are still limited in what they can do.

Research

Look up the case of Re Sigsworth (1935). The judges used the golden rule to interpret the statute.

- What decision did they come to using this rule?
- Why did the court use the golden rule and not the literal rule?

The mischief rule

The mischief rule was formed in Heydon's Case (1584). It allows the court to look at the former law in order to discover what 'mischief' the Act was designed to remedy. It is best explained in the case of Smith v Hughes (1960).

Key case

Smith v Hughes (1960)

Facts

The defendants were prostitutes who had been charged under the Street Offences Act 1959. This made it an offence to solicit in a street or public place. The prostitutes were soliciting from a private house, behind windows or on a balcony above the street.

The court used the mischief rule to decide that the activities of the women were within the mischief the Act was aimed at, even though using a literal interpretation of the words 'in a street or public place' they were not guilty. In this case the mischief aimed at by the Act was of men being solicited and the women were guilty.

The lead judge in this case, Lord Parker, said in his judgment 'everybody knows this is an Act designed to clean up the streets'. This was his view of the mischief or problem. It was not specifically stated as such in the Act.

Legal principle – when using this rule to interpret an Act the judge will focus on what they think Parliament was trying to put right in the law, not on the literal meaning of the words used.

Table 2.7 looks at the advantages and disadvantages of the mischief rule.

Table 2.7: Advantages and disadvantages of the mischief rule

Advantages	Disadvantages
It is flexible allowing the law to be applied as Parliament intended.	It is undemocratic by giving too much power to unelected judges. In some cases, judges have updated law, which is the role of Parliament.
Its use avoids absurd and unjust outcomes.	It is not always easy to identify the mischief that Parliament intended to remedy.
It was approved by the Law Commission in 1969 over the literal and golden rules.	It is out of date as it was established in the 16th century. The purposive approach is more appropriate to use now.

Research

Look up the case of Elliott v Grey (1960). The court used the mischief rule to interpret the statute.

- What statute was involved in the case?
- What was the mischief aimed at by the Act and what decision did the judge come to using the mischief rule?

The purposive approach

The purposive approach to statutory interpretation comes from the approach of the European Court of Justice. It looks for the purpose of the legislation as a whole and is an extension of the mischief rule. It is a more flexible approach than the other rules, giving judges greater scope to develop the law in line with what they think Parliament's intention was in introducing it.

As a result of the case of Pepper v Hart (1993), judges can now look at Hansard (the official record of Parliamentary debates) to help them decide Parliament's intentions.

Key case

Jones v Tower Boot Company (1997)

Facts

The court had to decide whether the physical and verbal abuse of a young black worker by his workmates fell within 'the course of employment' under s32 of the Race Relations Act 1976. If it did, the employer would be liable to pay compensation to Jones. The employer argued that the actions fell outside the course of the workmates' employment, because such behaviour was not part of their job and they were not liable. The Court of Appeal, using the purposive approach to interpret the Act, decided that Parliament's intention when enacting the Race Relations Act was to eliminate discrimination in the workplace and this would not be achieved by applying a narrow construction to the wording. The result was that the employers were liable to pay compensation.

Legal principle – when using this rule to interpret an Act, the judge will focus on establishing the purpose of the whole law that Parliament was trying to achieve, not on the literal meaning of the words used.

Research

Look up the case of Cutter v Eagle Star (1998). The court used the purposive approach to interpret the Road Traffic Act 1988.

- What was the purpose of the Act?
- What meaning did the court give the words of the Act?

Table 2.8 looks at the advantages and disadvantages of the purposive approach.

Table 2.8: Advantages and disadvantages of the purposive approach

Advantages	Disadvantages
It follows the approach used by judges in EU courts. However, this may be considered less of an advantage now in view of the referendum vote in June 2016.	It is undemocratic by giving too much power to unelected judges.

▶ **Table 2.8:** *Continued*

Advantages	Disadvantages
It is flexible allowing the law to be applied as Parliament intended.	In some cases, judges have updated law based on public policy reasons, rather than the words of an Act. This is the role of Parliament, not judges.
Its use avoids absurd and unjust outcomes.	

PAUSE POINT Produce a table detailing the four rules or approaches to statutory interpretation.

Hint Include an outline of the meaning of each rule or approach and a case example showing how the rule works in a case.

Extend Why is it necessary to have these four rules or approaches?

B Examine how legislation is made outside Parliament

Delegated legislation

Delegated legislation is law made by a person or body other than Parliament, but with the authority of Parliament. That authority is usually laid down in a 'parent' Act of Parliament, known as an **enabling Act**. This creates the framework of the law and then delegates power to others to make more detailed law.

Key term

Enabling Act - an Act that gives power to a government minister to make a piece of delegated legislation.

There are three types of delegated legislation:

- Orders in Council
- statutory instruments
- by-laws.

Orders in Council

An Order in Council is a type of legislation made in the name of the Queen. The Queen and the Privy Council have the authority to make Orders in Council. The Privy Council is made up of the Prime Minister, other leading members (or former members) of government and selected other appointees. Orders in Council allow laws to be made without going through Parliament.

Orders in Council can be made on a range of matters, especially:

- giving legal effect to European Directives
- transferring responsibility between government departments - for example, when the Ministry of Justice was created, the powers of the previous Department of Constitutional Affairs and some of the powers of the Home Office were transferred to this new department
- bringing Acts (or parts of Acts) of Parliament into force
- dealing with emergencies when Parliament is not sitting
- dealing with regulatory matters - for example, the Constitutional Reform Act 2005 allows the Privy Council to alter the number of judges in the High Court, Court of Appeal and Supreme Court
- dealing with other types of law - for example, in 2003, an Order in Council was used to alter the Misuse of Drugs Act 1971 so as to make cannabis a class C drug. Five years later, the government decided that it had been a mistake to downgrade cannabis and another Order in Council was issued changing cannabis back to a class B drug.

Research

Look up recent Orders in Council on the Privy Council website at **https://privycouncil.independent.gov.uk**.

- Make a note of two recent Orders that were made.
- How many members are there of the Privy Council?
- Who have been the three most recent members sworn in?

Statutory instruments

Statutory instruments are rules and regulations made by government ministers who are given authority to make laws in areas under their responsibility. For example, the Secretary of State for Work and Pensions can make regulations on work-related matters, such as the minimum wage and workplace pensions, while the Secretary of State for Transport can deal with road traffic regulations.

Statutory instruments can be very short, such as making the annual change to the minimum wage. However, other statutory instruments may be very long with detailed rules that were too complicated to include in an Act of Parliament.

Statutory instruments are a major way of making law, with as many as 3000 made each year.

Research

Look at the latest regulation setting the minimum wage (the National Minimum Wage (Amendment) Regulations 2016).

- Which government minister made these regulations?
- What was the name of the enabling Act under which the regulations were made?
- What is the amount of the minimum wage that was set for the next year?
- What is the amount of the living wage that was set?

By-laws

These can be made by local authorities to cover matters within their own area. For example, a county council can pass laws affecting the whole county while a city or town council can only make by-laws for its city or town. Many local by-laws will involve traffic control, such as parking restrictions. Other by-laws may be for matters such as banning the drinking of alcohol in certain streets or banning dogs from public beaches at certain times of the year.

By-laws can also be made by public companies and organisations. For example, railway companies can ban smoking in stations and the National Trust can ban dogs or horses from parts of their properties.

Controls on delegated legislation

Delegated legislation is often made by non-elected bodies. As there are so many people with the power to make delegated legislation, it is important that there should be some control. Control can be exercised by Parliament and by the courts.

Parliamentary controls

Parliament has the initial control over what powers are delegated. For example, an Act will state which government minister can make regulations. It will also state the type of laws to be made and whether they can be made for the whole country or only for certain places. The Act can also set out whether the government department must consult other people before making the regulations.

The parent Act will set out how the delegated legislation must be made, who it can be made by and any procedures, such as consultation, that must be followed. If these procedures are not followed, the delegated legislation can be challenged.

Parliament also retains control over the delegated legislation as it can repeal the powers in the enabling Act at any time. If it does this, then the right to make delegated legislation will stop.

After an Act has been passed, there will need to be checks to make sure that delegated powers are not being used incorrectly. Parliament has the following ways of checking on delegated legislation:

- affirmative resolution
- negative resolution
- super-affirmative resolution procedure
- questions in Parliament
- scrutiny committees.

Affirmative resolutions

Some statutory instruments are subject to an affirmative resolution. This means that the statutory instrument will not become law unless specifically approved by Parliament. The need for an affirmative resolution will be set out in the enabling Act. One of the disadvantages of this procedure is that Parliament cannot amend the statutory instrument; it can only be approved, annulled or withdrawn by the government minister.

Negative resolutions

Many statutory instruments will be subject to a negative resolution, which means that the relevant statutory instrument will be law unless rejected by Parliament within 40 days. The main disadvantage with this procedure is that, with as many as 3000 statutory instruments made each year, there is not enough time to look at them all.

Super-affirmative resolution procedure

This procedure is available if delegated legislation has been made under the authority of the Legislative and Regulatory Reform Act 2006, where Parliament is given greater control. The Act gives ministers very wide powers to amend Acts of Parliament (which only Parliament itself can normally do under the principle of parliamentary sovereignty).

Questions in Parliament

Each government minister is responsible to Parliament for the work of their department, so they can be questioned by MPs and Lords in Parliament on their work. This can include questions about proposed regulations they intend to make.

Scrutiny Committees

The Delegated Powers Scrutiny Committee is appointed by the House of Lords to consider whether parts of any bills going through Parliament delegate legislative power incorrectly. It reports its findings to the House of Lords before the Committee stage of the bill.

The Joint Select Committee on Statutory Instruments, otherwise known the Scrutiny Committee, can also perform checks. This committee reviews all statutory instruments and, where necessary, draws the attention of both Houses of Parliament to points that need further consideration. The review is a technical one and not based on policy. The main grounds for referring a statutory instrument back to the Houses of Parliament are that:

- it imposes a tax or charge – only an elected body has a right to impose a tax
- it appears to have a retrospective effect that was not provided for by the enabling Act
- it appears to have gone beyond the powers given under the enabling Act
- it makes an unusual or unexpected use of delegated powers
- it is unclear or defective in some way.

The Scrutiny Committee can only report back its findings; it has no power to alter any statutory instrument.

Control by the courts

Ultra vires is a phrase that means 'beyond the powers'. If a person acts beyond their power, that is said to be *ultra vires*. For example, in the case of R v Home Secretary, ex parte Fire Brigades Union (1995), changes made by the Home Secretary to the Criminal Injuries Compensation Scheme were decided to have gone beyond the delegated powers given to him in the Criminal Justice Act 1988.

Key terms

Affirmative resolution – a statutory instrument will not become law unless approved by Parliament.

Negative resolution – a statutory instrument will become law unless Parliament rejects it within 40 days.

Ultra vires – a Latin term meaning 'beyond the powers'. This means that it goes beyond the powers given by Parliament in the enabling Act. If delegated legislation is ruled by the court to be *ultra vires*, it is void and of no effect.

Produce some notes detailing the three main types of delegated legislation. Which of the checks in Parliament is the most effective? Why do you think it is the most effective method of checking?

Hint Include how each type is made, by whom, the authority that gives the power to make the legislation and who it affects.

Extend Evaluate why it is necessary to have delegated legislation.

Key case

R v Home Secretary, ex parte Fire Brigades Union (1995)

Facts

The Criminal Justice Act 1988 provided a new statutory scheme paying compensation for criminal injuries. However, the government decided to change an existing tariff-based scheme using the royal prerogative. This alternative scheme would save money by awarding less compensation. A trade union sought judicial review of the decision of the Home Secretary not to bring into force the statutory scheme.

The House of Lords decided that the government minister had gone beyond the delegated powers given to him in the Criminal Justice Act 1988 and that his action was *ultra vires*.

Legal principle - government ministers can only act in accordance with the powers given to them by Acts of Parliament.

An unreasonable decision can also be ruled to be *ultra vires*. This is often known as 'Wednesbury unreasonableness' after the case of Associated Provincial Picture Houses v Wednesbury Corporation (1948). An example is R (Rogers) v Swindon NHS Primary Care Trust (2006) when a woman with breast cancer was prescribed the non-approved drug Herceptin. Her NHS Trust refused to provide her with the drug as it said her case was not exceptional, though it did provide the drug for some patients in its area. This decision was decided to be unreasonable and *ultra vires*.

Procedural *ultra vires* is concerned with whether the correct procedure in the enabling Act was followed. If the correct procedure is not followed, the delegated legislation can be declared *ultra vires* and void. An example is the Aylesbury Mushroom case of 1972 when an order against mushroom growers was *ultra vires* because it did not allow for consultation as required by the parent Act.

Substantive *ultra vires* considers whether the content of the delegated legislation goes beyond the limits set out in the parent Act. An example is Attorney General v Fulham Corporation 1921. An Act gave the Corporation the power to provide public clothes-washing facilities. The Corporation set up a commercial laundry, which included the washing of residents' clothes. This was *ultra vires* as the Corporation did not have the power to set up a laundry.

Reflect

- Who is likely to bring a court action for judicial review of a piece of delegated legislation?
- Why is it necessary to have a system of judicial review?
- What is the effect of a successful challenge of judicial review?

Table 2.9 looks at the advantages and disadvantages of delegated legislation.

Table 2.9: Advantages and disadvantages of delegated legislation

Advantages	Disadvantages
It saves time as it does not have to go through Parliament. This is good in the case of emergencies.	Laws made by government ministers (part of the executive) goes against the principle of separation of powers.
Those with specialist knowledge can help draft or contribute to the legislation.	There is little publicity given to the making of any form of delegated legislation. As with primary legislation, the wording is not easy to follow and may need judicial interpretation.

▶ **Table 2.9:** *Continued*

Advantages	Disadvantages
There is some form of parliamentary control.	Judicial review is expensive and time consuming. There is limited parliamentary control through the negative resolution procedure.
It is democratic as government ministers and local authorities making by-laws are elected.	It may not be democratic as Parliament does not debate much delegated legislation. It may be drafted by unelected civil servants in government departments.

The European legislative process and its institutions

The United Kingdom joined what was then the European Economic Community in 1973. The EEC subsequently became the European Union (EU) in 1993. When the UK joined, it agreed to adopt all past and future EU law.

The most recent reorganisation of the EU was in 2009 by the Treaty of Lisbon. There are now two treaties setting out its rules. These are:

- the Treaty on European Union (TEU)
- the Treaty on the Functioning of the European Union (TFEU).

Despite the referendum vote in June 2016 to leave the EU, the UK remains a member of the EU and it continues to recognise all EU law-making institutions and to apply and enforce EU law.

The institutions of the European Union

The main law-making institutions are:

- the Council of the European Union
- the European Commission
- the European Parliament
- the European Court of Justice.

Council of the European Union

The government of each Member State of the EU sends a representative to the Council. The Foreign Minister is usually the main representative, but Member States are free to send any of its ministers to Council meetings. The minister responsible for the discussion topic will attend the meetings of the Council. For example, the Minister for Agriculture will attend when the issue to be discussed involves agriculture.

Twice a year, the heads of government (for example, the Prime Minister for the UK) meet in the European Council or 'Summit' to discuss broad matters of policy. The Member States take it in turn to act as the President of the Council for a six-month period.

The Council is the main decision-making body of the EU. Voting in the Council is on a weighted basis, which means that each country has a number of votes roughly in proportion to the size of its population. When the heads of Member States meet, their decisions are made on the basis of unanimity.

European Commission

This body consists of 28 Commissioners, one from each Member State. Each Commissioner leads a department with special responsibility for one area of European Union policy, such as economic affairs, agriculture or the environment.

The Commission as a whole has several functions:

- to act impartially
- to propose policies and present drafts of laws to the Council
- to be responsible for the administration of the EU
- to act as a 'guardian' of the treaties. (It ensures that treaty provisions and other measures adopted by the Union are properly implemented. If a Member State does not introduce European Union law within its own country, the Commission has a duty to intervene and, if necessary, refer the matter to the Court of Justice of the European Union.)

European Parliament

The European Parliament has no direct law-making power. Its main function is to discuss proposals put forward by the Commission. It also passes laws proposed by the Commission in conjunction with the Council. Its members are directly elected in elections that take place every five years.

Within the European Parliament, the members form political groups with those of the same political views. It has standing committees that discuss proposals made by the European Commission, which then report to the full European Parliament for debate. Decisions made by the European Parliament are not binding.

European Court of Justice

The function of the European Court of Justice is set out in Art 19 on TEU, which states that the Court must 'ensure that in the interpretation and application of the Treaty the law is observed'. The Court sits in Luxembourg and has 28 judges, one from each Member State. For a full court, 15 judges will sit, but the European Court of Justice also sits in chambers of five judges or three judges.

The Court is helped by 11 Advocates General, who hold office for six years. Each case is assigned to an Advocate

General whose task is to research all the legal points on cases submitted to the European Court of Justice.

The Court's task is to ensure that the law is applied in the same way in all Member States. It does this by:

- hearing cases to decide whether Member States have fulfilled their obligations – the European Commission usually starts these actions.
- hearing references under Art 267 TFEU from national courts for preliminary rulings on a point of EU law – this is a very important function as rulings made by the European Court of Justice are binding on courts in all Member States, ensuring that the law is uniform throughout the EU.

This means that the Supreme Court in the UK must refer questions of EU law to the European Court of Justice. However, the Court of Appeal and lower courts do not have to refer questions of this type. They have a choice to either refer the case or decide the case without any referral.

When a reference is made, the European Court of Justice makes a preliminary ruling on the point of law but it does not actually decide the case. The case then returns to the original court for it to apply the ruling to the facts in the case. Cases are presented on paper and lawyers are required to present their arguments in written form.

The deliberations of the judges are secret and, where necessary, the decision will be made by a majority vote. However, when the judgment is delivered in written form, all the judges who formed part of the panel sign it.

The European Court of Justice is not bound by its previous decisions. It prefers the purposive approach to interpretation.

European sources of law

There are primary and secondary sources of law. The main primary sources are the **treaties**, particularly the Treaty on European Union. Secondary sources are legislation passed by the institutions of the EU under Art 267 TFEU.

Treaties

As a result of s2(1) of the European Communities Act 1972, all treaties signed by the UK's head of government become part of English law automatically. This section states that:

> All such rights, powers, liabilities, obligations and restrictions from time to time created or arising by or under the treaties and all such remedies and procedures from time to time provided for by or under the treaties, as in accordance with the treaties are without further enactment to be given legal effect or used in the United Kingdom, shall be recognised and available in law and be enforced, allowed and followed accordingly.

Direct effect

Direct effect not only makes EU law part of UK law but also allows a person to rely on it. This means that a person can argue a right given by EU law in English courts.

The case that established this rule was Van Duyn v Home Office (1974) when the Court of Justice decided that a person was entitled to rely on Art 39 (now Art 45 TFEU) giving the right of freedom of movement. The Article had direct effect and conferred rights on individuals, which could be enforced not only in the Court of Justice, but also in national courts.

This means that citizens of the United Kingdom are entitled to rely on the rights in the treaties, even though English law may not have specifically given those rights. This is clearly illustrated by the case of Macarthys Ltd v Smith (1980).

Key terms

Treaties – a formal agreement, made between countries, that becomes law in all the signatory countries. The Treaty of Rome was made in 1957 and set out the rules and procedures for the EEC, which became the EU.

Direct effect – treaties and regulations automatically become law in the member countries and individuals in the member countries can rely on them as authority for their case.

Key case

Macarthys Ltd v Smith (1980)

Facts

Wendy Smith's employers paid her less than her male predecessor for exactly the same job. As the employer did not employ the two people at the same time, there was no breach of English domestic law. However, Wendy Smith was able to claim that the company that employed her was in breach of Art 141 of the Treaty of Rome 1957 (now Art 157 of the TFEU) over equal pay for men and women, and the Court of Justice confirmed this claim.

Legal principle – Wendy Smith was able to use the principle of direct effect to rely on EU law in her claim.

Secondary legislation - regulations

Under Article 288 of the TFEU, the EU has the power to issue regulations, which are binding in every respect and directly applicable in each Member State. This means that regulations, like treaties, have direct effect and can be relied on by a person in a UK court. They automatically become law in each Member State, which do not have to pass their own laws to give effect to them. This point was tested in Re Tachographs: Commission v UK (1979).

Key case

Re Tachographs: Commission v United Kingdom (1979)

Facts

The EU issued a regulation requiring mechanical recording equipment to be installed in lorries. The UK Government decided not to implement the regulation, but to leave it to lorry owners to decide whether or not to install such equipment. When the matter was referred to the Court of Justice, it was held that Member States had no discretion in the case of regulations.

Legal principle - the wording of Article 288 was explicit, which meant that regulations were automatically law in all Member States and the UK had to enforce the installation of tachographs.

A Member State cannot pick and choose which regulations to implement. As a result, regulations make sure that laws are the same across all Member States.

Secondary legislation - directives

Article 288 of the TFEU gives power to the EU to issue directives. They are different from regulations because each Member State is free to decide how best to introduce a law to comply with the directive. This means that laws are consistent across the EU. Directives have been introduced in areas such as employment, health and safety, and consumer law.

Article 288 says that directives 'bind any Member State to which they are addressed as to the result to be achieved, while leaving to domestic agencies a competence as to form and means'. In the UK, directives have been introduced by Acts of Parliament such as the Consumer Protection Act 1987 or by statutory instruments such as the Working Time Regulations 1998.

If a Member State has failed to introduce its own law to give effect to a directive, as a result of the decision in Francovich v Italian Republic (1991), it may be required to pay compensation to a person who has lost money as a result of the failure.

Key case

Francovich v Italian Republic (1991)

Facts

Italy failed to bring into force an EU Directive requiring the state to pay compensation to workers whose employers had gone into liquidation. The claimant lost wages when his employers went into liquidation and he sued the state. The European Court of Justice decided that the state was liable to the claimant.

Legal principle -an EU state could be liable to pay compensation to a person who suffered loss because of the Member State's failure to introduce an EU directive into their national law.

The importance of rulings of the Court of Justice

Direct effect has been a very important concept for the effectiveness of EU law. If the Court of Justice had not developed this concept, citizens of Member States would not have been able to enforce the rights given to them.

In particular, where a government has not implemented a directive, the rights of individuals in many important areas, especially employment law and discrimination, would have been lost. The rulings of the Court of Justice have allowed individuals to rely on EU law in claims against their state, and have forced governments to implement EU law more fully.

Conflict between European law and national law

As a result of various Court of Justice decisions, EU law takes precedence over each Member State's own law. In Costa v ENEL (1964), the Court of Justice said: 'the Member States have limited their sovereign rights, within limited fields, and have thus created a body of law which binds both their nationals and themselves'.

The effect of European law on the sovereignty of Parliament

When they joined the EU, all Member States transferred their sovereign legal rights to the EU. No Member State can rely on its own law when it is in conflict with EU law. This principle has been in effect since the UK joined the EU in 1973 and was one of the main concerns of the Brexit campaigners in the 2016 referendum to leave the EU. While the UK remains a member of the EU, the EU has supremacy over UK law.

Scenario

Instead of using television service Sky, which had the sole rights to screen the Premier League in the UK, a Portsmouth pub owner Ms Karen Murphy used the Greek station Nova's coverage in her pub, which was cheaper than the equivalent Sky package. She paid £800 a year for a Greek decoder, saying she 'couldn't afford' Sky's charge of £700 a month.

The Premier League took legal action against her and she was fined £8,000 for dishonest reception of a television channel. She appealed against her conviction to the High Court, who decided that a matter of EU law was involved. They referred the case to the European Court of Justice for a ruling.

The European Court ruled that the EU free movement of services and competition rules prohibited clauses and laws that prevent viewers in one EU Member State from importing satellite decoder devices from another Member State in order to watch the services of a foreign broadcaster. In this case, the rules infringed Article 101 of the TFEU and live matches were not protected by copyright. Therefore, Ms Murphy was not in breach of the Premier League rules.

However, it also ruled that the opening sequences, the anthem, some pre-recorded highlights and graphics were separate and could be covered by copyright rules and could be charged for.

The case was referred back to the High Court where it was conceded that Ms Murphy's appeal against her conviction must be allowed and she and other pub owners, both in the UK and throughout the EU, could show live football matches from foreign providers.

1. What principle of EU law was involved in this case?
2. Why was the case referred to the European Court of Justice by the High Court?
3. Why did the European Court of Justice refer the case back to the High Court?
4. What was the effect of the eventual decision of the High Court on other publicans in the UK?
5. What was the effect of the decision of the European Court of Justice on bar and restaurant owners throughout the EU?

Assessment practice 2.1

A.P1 A.P2 A.M1 AB.D1 B.P3 B.P4 B.M2 B.M3

1 The local Neighbourhood Action Group knows that you have received some legal training. They ask you to prepare a set of notes for discussion at their next meeting. Your notes have to cover:
- the introduction of statutory law and the reasons for its introduction
- how statutes are interpreted in court
- the different forms of delegated legislation and how this form of law making can be controlled
- the different forms of EU law.

2 For each of these different forms of law, you decide that the best way to explain them to the group is to use actual examples. You need to carry out the following research:
- Choose a recently introduced Act of Parliament and discover the reasons for its introduction and how it was debated through the Parliamentary process.
- Explain each form of statutory interpretation – the literal, golden and mischief rules and the purposive approach, and use a case example to illustrate each rule and approach.
- Choose one example each of a statutory instrument, an Order in Council and a by-law and explain their effect. You will also need to show how each could be controlled.
- Choose one example each of an EU Regulation, Directive and Decision and explain their effects.

3 You know that there is a lot of material to cover, but you are told that you do not have to cover judicial precedent as this topic was covered by a part-time judge at the previous meeting.

In addition, the group ask for a written report that they can take away with them that covers the following:
- an analysis of the effect on parliamentary law-making of influences and statutory interpretation
- an analysis of the effectiveness of the controls on delegated legislation, an assessment of the impact of EU laws on the UK and the resolution of any conflicts between these two forms of law
- an evaluation of the law-making process in the UK both inside and outside Parliament.

Plan
- I need to choose which statutes and forms of EU law I will explain.
- I need to know where I can access information about these statutes.
- I need to use my notes from class and discuss any difficulties with my tutor.

Do
- I need to plan my time effectively to cover all of the material.
- I need to first produce my set of notes for the group, making sure that I present these notes clearly and using correct legal terminology.
- I need to make a plan for the structure of the report.

Review
- I can explain how statutory law is made and how it is interpreted in courts.
- I can evaluate the different forms of law-making processes.
- I can select different statutes and talk about their key points.

Explore the various legal personnel involved in a criminal trial

In England and Wales, there are two main types of lawyer – barristers and solicitors – who are jointly referred to as 'the legal profession'. In addition, **legal executives** and **paralegals** work for solicitors and may be involved in a criminal case.

Key terms

Legal executives – legal executives have a legal qualification and carry out similar work to solicitors, but usually specialise in a specific area such as litigation or conveyancing. They often work for, and may do much of the same work as, solicitors.

Paralegals – members of solicitor's staff who have completed some legal training but are not qualified as a solicitor or legal executive.

Link

Look back at Unit 1 to read about the legal profession in civil law. This unit focuses on criminal law.

The legal profession

Solicitors

Most solicitors work in a private practice. In criminal cases, they may be able to act for a person charged with a criminal offence. Some solicitors are employed by the Crown Prosecution Service (CPS) and deal solely with the prosecution of offences.

Defence work

A solicitor working for a private practice will either be employed by a firm or be a partner in a firm. The firm may also employ legal executives and/or paralegals to help the solicitor in the preparation of the case.

Everyone who is arrested and detained by the police has the right to free, independent legal advice, paid for by the state and available at any time. A solicitor's first contact with a client may be at a police station to give advice.

If a person has been charged with a serious offence the solicitor can help to apply for legal representation, which pays for initial preparation and, later, for representation in court either by a solicitor and/or barrister. If a solicitor has a Certificate of Advocacy, they may be able to present the case in the Crown Court.

If the case is less serious and is heard in the magistrates' court, a solicitor can represent the defendant and be paid privately. A solicitor will charge an hourly rate for their work.

Prosecution work

Solicitors working for the CPS will be required to advise the police on the offence with which to charge a suspect and whether there is enough evidence to form a charge. Once the charge has been made, the CPS advise the police if more evidence is needed and, when the case comes to court, they will conduct the case. If the case is heard in the magistrates' court, a solicitor will present it. If the case is heard in the Crown Court, the CPS will usually instruct a barrister to conduct the case on their behalf.

Barristers

Key term

Bar – the collective name for practising barristers.

Barristers practise at the **Bar** and, unlike solicitors, are self-employed. They usually work from a set of chambers where they can share administrative expenses with other barristers. They usually charge a fixed amount depending on the complexity and length of the case in court.

A barrister can advise before trial and will carry out advocacy in court. Barristers have full rights of audience, which means that they can appear in all courts including the magistrates' court, the Crown Court or the appeal courts.

Normally, barristers operate the 'cab rank' rule, which means they cannot turn down a case if it is within the area of law they deal with and they are available. Senior barristers can become a Queen's Counsel (QC) .

Crown Court trials take place before a jury and all the evidence, both written and spoken, will be put before them to allow them to decide on the defendant's guilt or innocence. During a trial a barrister will:

- make an opening statement outlining their case
- examine witnesses appearing for their side

- cross examine witnesses appearing for the opposing side
- at the end of the evidence, make a closing speech summarising their case
- if acting for a defendant who has been found guilty, make a plea in mitigation to the judge.

After the trial, if the defendant is found guilty, the barrister may advise the defendant on the prospects of an appeal against their conviction and/or sentence. If an appeal is made, the barrister can argue the appeal in the appeal court.

Legal executives

Legal executives work in solicitors' firms. They have separate qualifications from solicitors. They can help in the preparation of the case by researching relevant law or taking witness statements. They can assist the solicitor in court and, if they hold a Criminal Proceedings Certificate, can apply for bail for the defendant in the magistrates' court.

Paralegals

Paralegals also work in solicitors' firms. They have separate qualifications from legal executives. They help in the preparation of the case by researching relevant law or taking witness statements. They can assist the solicitor in court but cannot carry out any advocacy.

Regulation and complaints against legal professionals

If a defendant wants to complain about the service provided by a lawyer in a criminal case, there are several options available. These include:

- They can appeal to a higher court. If the lawyer did not do a good enough job of presenting the case and the defendant is found guilty, an appeal can be launched. The appeal court will first make a decision about whether there is an arguable claim before hearing the detailed arguments about the case. They will not usually hear new evidence but will concentrate on the fairness of the conviction. Legal representation may be available to pay for the cost of an appeal.
- If the defendant has lost money as a result of poor practice, it may be possible to sue for negligence. As a result of the case of Hall v Simons (2000), it is possible to sue a barrister or solicitor for their negligent handling of a case.
- The defendant may complain to the **Legal Ombudsman**. This organisation is independent of the legal professions and will investigate if the client has received an unsatisfactory service from their lawyer. If this is found, the lawyer can be ordered to make an apology.
- If the defendant thinks that the solicitor has mishandled the case, a complaint can be made to the Solicitors Regulation Authority for an investigation. If the handling of the case has been poor or the solicitor has been dishonest, the solicitor can be charged with **professional misconduct** and the case can be referred to the Solicitor's Disciplinary Tribunal. A hearing can take place and if the solicitor is found guilty, this tribunal has the power to fine, reprimand, suspend or strike off the solicitor so that they can no longer practise.
- If the defendant thinks the barrister has mishandled their case, a complaint can be made to the Bar Standards Board who can discipline the barrister for breach of the Bar's Code of Conduct. The barrister can be required to attend before the Disciplinary Tribunal of the Council of the Inns of Court, who have the power to suspend or disbar the barrister.

Key terms

Legal Ombudsman – an independent and impartial scheme set up to help resolve complaints about lawyers and claims management companies in England and Wales. A client's complaint can be investigated and compensation may be awarded if the complaint is upheld.

Professional misconduct – breaking the rules of the solicitor's profession.

Financing advice and representation in a criminal trial

The Legal Aid, Sentencing and Punishment of Offenders Act 2012 states that criminal legal aid is administered by the Ministry of Justice. To do this, the Ministry makes contracts with solicitors and barristers to provide criminal legal services paid from government funds.

Legal advice at the police station

Advice is available at any time to anyone detained in a police station who requests advice. This advice can be given over the telephone or by a lawyer attending in person. An adviser should have a Certificate of Accreditation, which is a certificate of competence to act.

Funding for legal representation

The Legal Representation scheme pays for the solicitor's fees for the preparation of the case before trial and for advocacy by a solicitor or barrister in trial. Lawyers are paid a fixed fee depending on the charge, not the complexity of the case. In order to receive legal representation, the defendant has to qualify under a means test and an 'interests of justice' test.

Means testing

The defendant's income and value of their assets have to be given. If their income and assets are above certain limits, they may have to pay a contribution to their legal fees. There will be no contribution for those on low incomes.

In magistrates' court cases, the levels are very low, which means that many adults do not qualify for legal representation. In the Crown Court, legal representation is more readily available. If a defendant is found guilty, they may have to pay a contribution if they have sufficient funds. If a defendant is found not guilty, any contributions paid will normally be refunded.

Interests of justice

A defendant will only have legal representation if they can show that they meet at least one of the five 'interests of justice' factors.

1. If found guilty, the defendant would be likely to lose their liberty or livelihood or suffer serious damage to their reputation.
2. The case involves considering a point of law.
3. The defendant is unable to understand the proceedings in court or to state their own case.
4. The case may involve the tracing, interviewing or expert cross-examination of witnesses.
5. It is in the interests of another person, perhaps the victim, that the defendant is represented (such as in a sexual assault case).

Complete a job description for a solicitor, barrister, legal executive or judge.

Hint Think about where they work and what they do in both civil and criminal cases.

Extend Depending on the job description chosen, investigate the qualification and training requirements.

Lay people

Lay people are involved in the criminal justice process as **magistrates** and **jurors**.

Magistrates

Selection and appointment

Local advertisements are placed with the aim of achieving a panel that is representative of the area, with a balance of occupations, ages, gender and social groups.

Candidates will be interviewed and a local advisory committee, which is made up of current or former magistrates, will submit names of suitable candidates to the Lord Chief Justice, who will then appoint new magistrates from this list. Once appointed, magistrates may continue to sit until the age of 70.

Lay magistrates do not have to have any qualifications in law but they must:

- be aged between 18 and 65 on appointment
- live or work in or near the local justice area to which they are allocated
- commit to sitting at least 26 half days each year
- take the oath of allegiance.

Restrictions on appointment include:

- people with serious criminal convictions or undischarged bankrupts
- people whose work is incompatible, such as police officers, traffic wardens and members of the armed forces
- being a relative of someone working in the local criminal justice system
- those with hearing impairment or an infirmity who cannot carry out the duty. However those with a disability, including blindness, are encouraged to apply.

Reflect

Looking at the qualifications needed to become a lay magistrate, who do you think are the most likely group of people to be selected and appointed?

Compare your thoughts with the breakdown of those currently serving. You will find figures of judicial statistics (including lay magistrates) on the Courts and Tribunals Judiciary website

Training

The training of lay magistrates is carried out by a court legal adviser and overseen by the Judicial College.

The areas of training are:

- managing yourself – this focuses on self-management in preparing for court, conduct in court and ongoing learning
- working as a team member – this focuses on decision-making as decisions in magistrates' courts have to be unanimous
- making judicial decisions – this focuses on impartial decision-making
- managing judicial decision-making – this is for the chair of a bench and focuses on working with the legal adviser, managing the court and ensuring effective, impartial decision-making.

New magistrates have to complete:

- introductory training – which covers understanding the organisation of the bench, administration of the court and the roles and responsibilities of those involved in the magistrates' court
- core training – which provides new magistrates the opportunity to acquire and develop the key skills, knowledge and understanding required of a competent magistrate

Key terms

Lay people – non-legally qualified people who decide the guilt or innocence of those on trial in the criminal courts.

Magistrates – are trained and work regularly in the lowest criminal court deciding the guilt or innocence of accused persons and punishments for those found guilty.

Jurors – members of the public who sit in the Crown Court hearing cases against accused persons who have pleaded not guilty. They decide guilt or innocence.

- activities – which involves observations of court sittings and visits to prisons or probation offices.

After completing their training, a new magistrate will sit as a 'winger' to hear cases as a panel of three. The chair (who sits in the middle) is an experienced magistrate. During the first two years, a new magistrate will continue to receive training and have a mentor who reviews their progress.

Role of lay magistrates in criminal cases

Ninety-seven per cent of all criminal cases are dealt with in the magistrates' court. They deal with preliminary matters in the remaining 3 per cent, such as deciding whether to remand the accused in custody, or to grant, bail. If bail is granted they can decide on any conditions to impose.

Before criminal trials, magistrates attend:

- early administrative hearings
- remand hearings
- bail applications
- transfer proceedings where serious criminal cases are sent to the Crown Court for trial.

During a criminal trial, magistrates will:

- listen to the evidence from the prosecution and defence
- listen to any addresses on the law and closing speeches from advocates or defendants in person
- decide the verdict – they must reach a unanimous decision. They can take advice from their legal adviser on the law and their powers.
- decide the sentence for those they find guilty
- hear appeals in the Crown Court from cases originally heard in the magistrates' court on a panel with a judge.

Table 2.10 looks at the advantages and disadvantages of the use of lay magistrates.

Table 2.10: Advantages and disadvantages of the use of lay magistrates

Advantages	Disadvantages
Magistrates are a cheap system of justice. It would be expensive to replace them with legally qualified judges.	Magistrates may be biased towards prosecution.
Magistrates are chosen from people living or working local to their courts.	Magistrates are less likely to have knowledge of the local area as court closures mean there is less local justice.
Persons appointed are from a wide section of the community.	Magistrates today are likely to be unrepresentative of the local area as mostly mature, well-educated persons are appointed.
There are few appeals against conviction and sentences.	There may be inconsistencies between different benches and areas, especially in sentencing.
Magistrates have the benefit of a qualified legal adviser.	Magistrates lack legal knowledge and may rely too much on their legal adviser.
There is a training programme and support for newly appointed magistrates and ongoing training on changes in the law.	Training quality may be variable or insufficient.

Juries

Qualification and disqualification

The Juries Act 1974 sets the criteria that you must meet to be able to sit on a jury. Jurors must:

- be aged 18–75
- be registered on the current electoral roll
- have lived in the UK for at least five years since their 13th birthday
- not be disqualified due to a previous conviction of a serious offence or a mental disorder.

Restrictions on appointment include:

- excusals – a person who has problems that make it very difficult for them to do their jury service may ask to be excused or for their period of service to be put back to a later date, for example, due to pregnancy, holiday, exams or job commitments
- lack of capacity – such as those who cannot understand sufficient English, or suffer deafness or blindness.

Selection of juries

A pool of jurors will be randomly selected by the Central Summoning Bureau and required to attend court on a certain date. At court, another random selection of 15 from the pool will be chosen for each trial. After this, a further random selection from the 15 by the court clerk will choose the final panel of 12 jurors. The panel is then sworn in to give a true verdict according to the evidence.

The whole jury can be challenged by the defence (called a challenge to the array) on the grounds that it is unrepresentative. An individual juror can be challenged if there is a valid reason why that juror should not serve on the jury – no reason has to be given to the juror when this occurs. The vetting of individual jurors or the whole panel can only be done in cases of terrorism or involving national security and with the **Attorney General's** permission.

Role of juries in criminal cases

A jury is used at the Crown Court when the defendant pleads 'not guilty'. The trial is presided over by a judge who oversees the swearing in of the jury. The judge decides points of law and the jury decides the facts. The jury is independent from the judge and the judge cannot direct the jury to find a defendant guilty. The following process is followed in a criminal case.

- Evidence is presented by the prosecution followed by the defence.
- Legal representatives for the prosecution and defence can make closing speeches summing up the case for their side.
- The judge will sum up the law and evidence.
- The jury retires (leaves the court) for a secret discussion on the case. They will be instructed to first reach a unanimous (united) decision. If, after a minimum time of 2 hours and 15 minutes they have not been able to reach such a decision, they can be directed to reach a majority verdict.
- The decision is announced in open court by the **foreperson**. No reasons are given for their decision. The jury has no influence on the sentence if the defendant is found guilty.

How do juries reach their verdict?

Because of the Contempt of Court Act 1981, no one can enter the jury room while discussions are taking place. The Act also forbids jurors from telling the media anything about their discussions, and the media reporting anything from a discussion. Jury members must not disclose details about the case to anyone who is not a fellow juror.

Key terms

Attorney General – an MP and the government's chief law officer. They represent the government in any court cases. They are also responsible for ensuring that the criminal court procedure works correctly.

Foreperson – the first task the jury are directed to do when they leave court to deliberate the verdict is to elect one of their number to lead the discussion. This foreperson will then announce the verdict of the jury when the jury return to court.

Table 2.11 lists the advantages and disadvantages of the use of juries in criminal cases.

Table 2.11: Advantages and disadvantages of the use of juries in criminal cases

Advantages	Disadvantages
Juries are not bound by past decisions and can make their decisions based on fairness.	The jury may reach a verdict that could be considered unjust.
The jury is independent of the judge and parties in the case.	The jury may be biased against the defendant.
Secrecy of the jury room allows free discussion.	What is discussed in the jury room cannot be investigated.
There is public confidence in the system of jury trial.	Juries may not understand the language in court, legal procedure or what is required of them.
Trial in open court means open justice where all evidence and issues are considered.	Juries may not understand complicated evidence (especially in fraud trials).
	Jury members could be affected and upset by the evidence they hear.
	Jury members could use Internet research, make inappropriate use of social media or be affected by media coverage of the trial.

PAUSE POINT As a group, change your classroom into firstly a magistrates' court, then into a Crown Court. Assign each class member a role and ask them to explain their role.

Hint Download a courtroom plan from the Internet or base your plan on a court visit.

Extend Ask your tutor to obtain a script for a mock trial and perform that case.

Judiciary

All judges have a legal qualification and experience of practice as a solicitor or barrister. Lawyers may be appointed as either an inferior- or superior-level judge.

Inferior-level judges are:

- district judges – hearing criminal cases in the magistrates' court
- recorders – part-time judges sitting in the Crown Court
- circuit judges – full-time judges hearing cases in the Crown Court.

Superior-level judges are:

- High Court judges – hearing serious cases in the Crown Court and sitting on appeals in the Court of Appeal
- Lord Justices of Appeal – hearing appeals in the Court of Appeal
- Supreme Court Justices – hearing appeals in the Supreme Court.

The role of judges in criminal cases

In magistrates' courts

A district judge will sit alone and hear summary and some **'either way' cases**.

- If the defendant pleads guilty, the judge will hear from the prosecution the facts of the case and a plea in mitigation by the defendant. The judge will sentence the defendant.
- If the defendant pleads not guilty, there will be a trial before the single judge. The prosecution will give their case, followed by the defence. The judge will decide the verdict and give reasons for the decision. If the judge decides the defendant is guilty, a sentence will be given. If the judge decides the defendant is not guilty, the defendant will be freed.

Key term

Either way cases – cases that can be tried in either the magistrates' court or the Crown Court.

In the Crown Court

Recorders, circuit judges and High Court judges all hear cases in the Crown Court.

- If the defendant pleads guilty, the trial judge will hear from the prosecution on the facts of the case and a **plea in mitigation** by the defendant. The judge may also hear reports from the **National Probation Service** and from victims on the impact of the offence on them. The judge will then issue a sentence to the defendant.
- If the defendant pleads not guilty, there will be a trial before a judge and a jury. The judge will firstly oversee the swearing in of the jury. The prosecution sets out its case, with witnesses, followed by the defence. During the trial, the judge may be required to rule on legal issues, such as the trial procedure or the evidence to be heard. The prosecution and defence can make closing speeches to the jury. The judge will then sum up the relevant law and evidence to the jury. The jury will go to the jury room to decide on the verdict. If the jury decides the defendant is guilty, it will be the judge who will sentence (taking into account any reports or plea in mitigation). If the jury finds the defendant not guilty, the defendant will be freed.

Key term

Plea in mitigation – made by the defence solicitor or barrister after the defendant is found or pleads guilty. Reasons are put forward why a lower sentence should be imposed.

National Probation Service – the body responsible for dealing with offenders who have had non-custodial sentences imposed on them.

Appeals in the Crown Court

A judge and two lay magistrates can hear appeals against conviction and/or sentence from a trial in the magistrates' court. The court can either dismiss the appeal or grant it and set the conviction aside.

Appeals in the Queen's Bench Division (Divisional Court)

Two judges will sit to hear:

- appeals against conviction only on a point of law from the magistrates' court
- appeals against conviction only on a point of law from the Crown Court.

The hearing consists only of legal arguments. The court will rule on the law and can either dismiss the appeal or grant it to return the case to the trial court.

Appeals in the Court of Appeal (Criminal Division)

Three judges will sit in this court to hear:

- an appeal by the defendant against sentence – if the defendant pleaded guilty in the Crown Court and receives (in their view) a very harsh sentence, an appeal can be made against the sentence. The court can either uphold the original sentence, or increase or decrease the sentence in severity.
- an appeal by the defendant against conviction and/or sentence – if the defendant pleaded not guilty in the Crown Court but is found guilty, an appeal can be made against the conviction. It will have to be based on either an irregularity in the trial procedure or on the judge misdirecting the jury when summing up the law. The hearing consists of legal arguments. However, the court can occasionally hear new evidence. The court can dismiss the appeal or grant it to either order a new trial or order the defendant's conviction to be set aside. The defendant can appeal against the sentence as well as the conviction.
- an appeal by the prosecution against a very light sentence – this appeal can only be made by the Attorney General under s36 of the Criminal Justice Act 1988 if it is felt that the trial judge has ordered a very light sentence on the convicted defendant. The Court of Appeal can either dismiss the appeal or grant it to impose a different sentence on the defendant.

Appeals in the Supreme Court

Five Justices will normally hear an appeal. The appeal can only be by the defendant against conviction based on the judge misdirecting the jury when summing up the law. The hearing consists only of legal arguments. The court can either dismiss the appeal or grant it and either order a new trial or order the defendant's conviction to be set aside.

Assessment practice 2.2

C.P5 C.P6 C.M4 C.D2

You are working for BFG Lawyers. One day, Gemma contacts you and tells you, in a panic, that she has been charged with actual bodily harm (ABH) under s47 Offences Against the Person Act 1861. You tell her that this is a serious offence with a maximum five years imprisonment. You also tell her it is an 'either way' offence.

She wants you to explain what this means and what choices she has as to where her trial can take place. You are asked to explain the differences between trial before magistrates and jury.

Gemma has never been in trouble before and wants to know whether she should represent herself in court or whether she should have a lawyer to represent her. You offer to explain and compare and contrast the roles of the different lawyers in criminal trials. She does not know the trial procedure or the role of judges or magistrates, so you offer to explain and compare and contrast their roles too. Gemma also wants to know, if she decides to use a lawyer, how she could pay for a lawyer to represent her. You offer to explain and compare and contrast the different methods of paying for lawyers in criminal cases.

You arrange to see Gemma the next day and prepare some notes for the meeting for Gemma to take away with her.

At the meeting Gemma asks why non-legally qualified people are used in the criminal justice system, as opposed to using just lawyers. You promise to write a report to her evaluating the impact of using lay people as opposed to lawyers.

Plan

- I need to identify each point that Gemma needs explaining.

Do

- I need to write clear notes for Gemma that explain each of her queries.
- I need to be able to evaluate each of Gemma's queries in an unbiased way, presenting only facts.

Review

- I can explain the different types of trial.
- I can explain the different methods available to pay for a lawyer.
- I can evaluate the role of lawyers in criminal trials.

D Apply the key elements of crime and sentencing in non-fatal offence case studies

Key terms

Actus reus – the guilty act part of a crime.

Mens rea – the guilty mind part of the crime.

In many crimes, there are two parts that the prosecution must prove to show that the defendant is guilty. The parts are known as the ***actus reus*** and the ***mens rea***. The *actus reus* is the physical part of the crime – what the defendant has done or failed to do. The *mens rea* is the mental element of the crime – what the defendant is thinking when the *actus reus* is committed.

Elements of a crime

Every crime has its own *actus reus* and *mens rea*. This will usually be set out in the statute that makes the action a crime. For battery, the *actus reus* is applying unlawful force to another person. The *mens rea* is intending to apply the unlawful force or being reckless as to whether force is applied.

The *actus reus*

The *actus reus* is the physical part of a crime. It can be:

- an act
- a failure to act (an omission)
- a state of affairs.

For some crimes, the *actus reus* must have an act or omission and a consequence. In the non-fatal offences, the consequence is the injury caused to the victim. For example, for the offence of assault occasioning actual bodily harm (s47 of the Offences Against the Person Act 1861), there must be the threat or the use of force and there must be a consequence of 'actual bodily harm' – an injury to the victim. This could be a broken nose or broken finger that needs medical attention.

Voluntary nature of *actus reus*

The act or omission must be voluntary on the part of the defendant. If the defendant has no control over their actions, they have not committed the *actus reus*. In the case of Hill v Baxter (1958), where a driver caused harm, the court gave examples where a driver of a vehicle could not be said to be driving voluntarily. These included where drivers lost control because they were stung by bees, struck on the head by a stone or had a heart attack. Another example of an involuntary act is where the defendant hits another person due to a reflex action or a muscle spasm over which they have no control.

The rule of having control over your actions is an essential part of a crime because it shows fault by the defendant. Where there is no fault, the defendant is not usually liable.

Omissions as *actus reus*

In some cases, it is possible that a failure to act (an omission) is the *actus reus* of a crime. An Act of Parliament can create liability for an omission, such as the driving offences of failing to report a road traffic accident or failing to provide a specimen of breath. For non-statutory offences, an omission can amount to the *actus reus* where there is a duty to act. A duty can arise:

- when imposed by a contract, such as a contract of employment – this is shown in the case of R v Pittwood (1902)

Key case

R v Pittwood (1902)

Facts

A railway-crossing keeper failed to shut the gates. A person crossing the line was struck and killed by a train.

Legal principle – the keeper was guilty of manslaughter as he had failed to perform his contract of employment properly.

- because of a relationship, such as parent and child – this is shown in the case of R v Gibbins and Proctor (1918)

Key case

R v Gibbins and Proctor (1918)

Facts

A child's guardians failed to feed their child. The child died of starvation.

Legal principle – they were guilty of murder as they both owed the child a duty to take care of it.

- when taken on voluntarily, as in the case of R v Stone and Dobinson (1977)

Key case

R v Stone and Dobinson (1977)

Facts

The defendants agreed to look after Stone's sister who was suffering from anorexia. They were barely able to look after themselves due to mental health problems. The defendants tried to get medical help for the sister but failed. Eventually she died from neglect. The defendants were found guilty of gross negligence manslaughter. They had assumed a duty of care towards Stone's sister but failed in that duty leading to the victim's death.

Legal principle – A person can be guilty of a crime by omission if they accept a duty to care for another person and fail to complete that duty.

- when imposed by an official position, as in the case of R v Dytham (1979)

Key case

R v Dytham (1979)

Facts

A police officer witnessed a violent attack, but took no steps to intervene or summon help. Instead, he drove away from the scene.

Legal principle – the officer was guilty of failing to perform his public duty. The court's view was that a police officer, unlike a private individual, owes a duty of care to all of society.

- when the defendant has set in motion a chain of events and failed to deal with them – this is shown in the case of R v Miller (1983).

Key case

R v Miller (1983)

Facts

A squatter started a fire by leaving his cigarette burning when he fell asleep. When he realised this, he left the room and went to sleep in another room. He did not attempt to put out the fire or summon help.

Legal principle – he was guilty of arson because of his failure to deal with the situation or call for help.

Key term

Chain of causation – an unbroken link in the *actus reus* from the initial act or omission to the end result – the victim's death or injury.

Causation

There must be a direct link from the defendant's conduct to the consequence (the end result – usually an injury or death). This is known as the **chain of causation**. Where a consequence must be proved, the prosecution has to show that:

- the defendant's conduct was the factual cause of that consequence
- the defendant's conduct was in law the cause of that consequence
- there was no intervening act which broke the chain of causation.

Factual cause

The defendant can only be guilty if the consequence would not have happened 'but for' his actions. The case of R v Pagett (1983) demonstrates this principle.

Key case

R v Pagett (1983)

Facts

The defendant used his pregnant girlfriend as a shield as he shot at armed policemen. The police fired back and the girlfriend was killed.

Legal principle – Pagett was convicted of his girlfriend's manslaughter as she would not have died 'but for' him using her as a shield in the gun battle.

Link

See Unit 1 for more detail on the 'but for' test in negligence.

Cause in law

There may be more than one person whose act may have contributed to the consequence. The defendant can be guilty even though their conduct was not the only cause of the consequence. The rule is that the defendant's conduct must be more than a 'minimal' cause, but it need not be a substantial cause. The case of R v Smith (1959) applied the cause in law rule.

Key case

R v Smith (1959)

Facts

Two soldiers, the defendant and the victim, had a fight and one was stabbed. The victim was carried to a medical centre by other soldiers, but was dropped on the way. At the medical centre, the staff gave him artificial respiration by pressing on his chest. This made the injury worse and he died. Had the proper treatment been given, his chance of recovering would have been as high as 75 per cent.

Legal principle – the defendant was still guilty of his murder as the stab wound was the main cause of the death.

The defendant must also take the victim as they find them. This is known as the 'thin skull rule'. It means that if the victim has something unusual about their physical or mental state that makes an injury more serious, the defendant is liable for the more serious injury. This is shown in the case of R v Blaue (1975).

Link

See Unit 1 for more details of the 'eggshell skull' rule in negligence.

Key case

R v Blaue (1975)

Facts

A young woman was stabbed by the defendant. At hospital, she was told she needed a blood transfusion to save her life. The woman refused to have one as she was a Jehovah's Witness and her religion forbade blood transfusions. She died and the defendant was convicted of her manslaughter.

Legal principle – the defendant was still guilty because he had to take his victim as he found her including her religious beliefs.

Key term

Novus actus interveniens – an intervening event which will break the chain of causation.

Intervening acts

If there is an intervening act (a ***novus actus interveniens***), this may break the chain of causation and the defendant will not be guilty. This was considered in the case of R v Roberts (1971).

Key case

R v Roberts (1971)

Facts

The defendant made sexual advances to a woman to whom he was giving a lift. To escape, she jumped out of the moving car at 30 miles per hour, suffering concussion, cuts and bruises. The defendant argued that her injuries were caused by her own actions and this amounted to a break in the chain of causation.

Legal principle – the court decided that what she did was a reasonable response and the chain of causation was not broken.

However, if there is an unreasonable response or the victim does something completely unexpected, the chain of causation will be broken by this *novus actus*, as decided in the case of R v Williams and Davis (1992).

Key case

R v Williams and Davis (1992)

Facts

The victim, who was a hitchhiker, jumped out of a moving car and was killed by other traffic. The prosecution alleged that the driver and his friend attempted to rob the victim but this could not be proved.

Legal principle – it was decided that the victim's response was unreasonable to any possible threat and this broke the chain of causation.

Mens rea

Mens rea is the mental or thinking part of an offence. Each offence has its own *mens rea* to be proved by the prosecution.

Intention

The highest level of *mens rea* is intention. In other words, it is a deliberate act. The defendant's motive or reason for doing the act is not relevant. It may be argued that the defendant did not fully intend the consequence.A model direction to be given to juries when considering whether the defendant had indirect intent was given in R v Woollin (1998).

Key case

R v Woollin (1998)

Facts

The defendant threw his 3-month-old baby towards his pram, which was against a wall 3 or 4 feet away. The baby suffered head injuries and died. The defendant argued that he intended to stop the baby crying, not to kill it.

Legal principle – the House of Lords confirmed that if the jury were satisfied the consequence (the death) was a virtual certainty and the defendant realised this, then he intended the death.

Recklessness

This is a lower level of *mens rea* than intention. Recklessness is the taking of an unjustifiable risk. It has to be proved that the defendant realised the risk, but decided to take it anyway. This is known as subjective recklessness and comes from R v Cunningham (1957).

Key case

R v Cunningham (1957)

Facts

The defendant tore a gas meter from the wall of an empty house in order to steal the money in it. This caused gas to seep into the house next door, where a woman was affected by it. The defendant was charged under s23 of the Offences Against the Person Act 1861 of maliciously administering a noxious substance.

Legal principle – the court decided that 'maliciously' meant that in order to have the necessary *mens rea*, the defendant must either intend the consequence or realise that there was a risk of the consequence happening and decide to take that risk. Cunningham was not guilty as he did not realise the risk of gas escaping into the adjacent house. He had not intended to cause the harm, nor had he taken a risk he knew about.

 **PAUSE POINT** How can a jury decide what the defendant was thinking at the time of the alleged offence?

Hint Would the time of the offence, arrest, interview or court appearance be relevant?

Extend What are they going to take into account to help them decide what the defendant was thinking?

Coincidence of *actus reus* and *mens rea*

In order for an offence to take place, both the *actus reus* and the *mens rea* must be present at the same time. This is shown in the case of Thabo Meli v R (1954).

Key case

Thabo Meli v R (1954)

Facts

The defendants decided to get the victim drunk and kill him. They took him to a hut, gave him a lot of alcohol and hit him over the head. Thinking he was dead, they dragged him out into the open and left him. He later died of exposure. The defendants argued that when the victim died of exposure they did not have the *mens rea* as they thought he had already died.

Legal principle – it was decided that where there is a continuing act for the *actus reus* and while that act is still going on, the defendant has the necessary *mens rea*, then the two do coincide and, as in this case, the defendant is guilty.

Strict liability

Offences of strict liability are those, usually imposed by statute, where the defendant is guilty because they did the *actus reus*. There is no need to prove any *mens rea*. This can seem unfair as the defendant will be guilty even though they had no intention of committing any offence. An example of this is the case of Harrow London Borough Council v Shah (1999).

Key case

Harrow London Borough Council v Shah (1999)

Facts

The defendants owned a newsagent's shop and sold lottery tickets. They trained and instructed their staff not to sell tickets to underage children and put up notices in the shop. A member of staff sold a ticket to an underage child.

Legal principle – they were guilty of the offence despite all the precautions they had taken as the offence was committed when the ticket was sold.

A problem with strict liability arises when the Act that sets the offence does not specify whether or not mens rea is required. In this situation, a judge will presume that a criminal offence requires mens rea. This was the decision made in the case of Sweet v Parsley (1970).

Key case

Sweet v Parsley (1970)

Facts

The defendant rented out her farmhouse to students. The police found cannabis at the farmhouse and the defendant was charged with 'being concerned in the management of premises used for the purpose of smoking cannabis resin'. The defendant did not know that cannabis was being smoked there and all dealings with the students were via managing agents.

Legal principle – it was decided that she was not guilty as the court presumed that this offence required *mens rea*.

Justification for strict liability

The main justification for strict liability offences is that they help to protect society by promoting greater care over matters of public safety. They encourage higher standards of hygiene in processing and selling food, and in protecting vulnerable members of society. They allow a business to be prosecuted and they help to make sure that businesses are run properly.

They are easier to enforce as there is no need for the prosecution to prove *mens rea*. As a result, defendants are more likely to plead guilty. Penalties are often minor (usually a fine) and the fact that the defendant is not blameworthy can be taken into account when sentencing. Finally, most strict liability offences are not considered truly criminal.

Arguments against strict liability

The main argument against the idea of strict liability is that it makes people who are not blameworthy guilty. Even those who have taken all possible care will be found guilty and can be punished as seen in the case of Harrow London Borough Council v Shah (1999).

Are strict liability offences fair, such as that in Harrow London Borough Council v Shah (1999)?

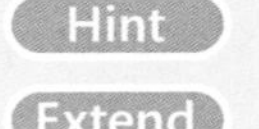

What punishment do you think should be imposed on a person such as Mr Shah?

Extend What is the justification for having strict liability offences?

Non-fatal offences

Non-fatal offences are defined as:

- common assault
- actual bodily harm
- grievous bodily harm
- grievous bodily harm with intent.

Common assault

Common assault is the lowest level of offence against the person. There are two types of common assault:

- **assault**
- **battery**.

The prosecution will choose which of these offences is appropriate, depending on the facts. They are not defined in any Act of Parliament but it is stated in s39 Criminal Justice Act 1988 that assault and battery are both **summary offences**.

Actus reus of assault

The *actus reus* of an assault requires an action or words which causes the victim to fear immediate and unlawful personal violence against them. There has to be an action or words by the defendant – an omission or failure to act is not sufficient. There will be no physical contact between the parties. An assault can be carried out in different ways:

- by words
- silent phone calls – although the phone calls do not have to be silent. If words said on the phone cause the victim fear this can amount to an assault
- stalking
- sending letters – this could now include other written ways of communication such as text messages, emails and the use of social media
- looking at the victim
- frightening the victim through a joke.

Key terms

Assault – the defendant must intentionally or subjectively recklessly cause another person to fear immediate unlawful personal violence.

Battery – the defendant intentionally or, subjectively recklessly, applies unlawful force to another. The injury suffered will be minor not needing medical attention such as a minor cut, a graze or a bruise.

Summary offences – the lowest level offence. They can only be tried in the magistrates' court and have a maximum penalty of six months imprisonment and/or a fine of £5,000.

Mens rea of assault

The *mens rea* of an assault must be either an intention to cause the victim to fear immediate and unlawful personal violence, or recklessness as to whether such fear is caused. To be reckless, the defendant must realise the risk that their acts and/or words could cause another to fear unlawful personal violence.

Actus reus of battery

The *actus reus* of a battery requires there to be some force that causes minor injury. It can be applied either directly or indirectly.

- Direct application of force is where the defendant actually touches the victim.
- Indirect application of force is where the defendant causes unlawful force to be applied to the victim, even though they do not personally touch the victim.

Some cases involve both direct and indirect application of force, as shown in the case of Haystead v DPP (2000).

Key case

Haystead v DPP (2000)

Facts

The defendant and his girlfriend had an argument and he punched her. This was direct application of force. At the time, she was holding their baby and as a result of the punch she dropped the baby causing it to bang its head. This was indirect application of force.

Legal principle – the defendant was convicted of two charges of battery.

Mens rea of battery

The *mens rea* for battery must be either an intention to apply unlawful physical force, or recklessness that the force will be applied. As with assault, the recklessness is subjective, so that the defendant must realise the risk of unlawful physical contact and take that risk.

Actual bodily harm

Actual bodily harm is an offence under s47 of the Offences Against the Person Act 1861.

Actus reus of actual bodily harm

This is a more serious form of assault or battery. Actual bodily harm has been defined as causing 'any hurt or injury calculated to interfere with the health or comfort' of the victim. This includes injuries such as cuts and bruises, a broken nose or finger, loss of hair, loss of consciousness or any other injury that needs medical attention.

It also includes psychiatric or mental injury, more than 'mere emotions such as fear, distress or panic'. Because of the age of the Offences Against the Person Act 1861, modern developments have meant that judicial interpretation has been required to apply the offences to modern life. The sending of letters in R v Constanza (1997) caused the victim to fear harm and it was decided that this amounted to the offence of actual bodily harm. It is only because of judicial development in cases such as this that 'bodily harm' can now be interpreted to include psychiatric illness. If the judges had not interpreted the injury in this way the law would have failed to protect victims. However, it would be much more satisfactory if the law was re-written and made clearer.

Mens rea of actual bodily harm

This is for common assault only. The defendant must either intend or be reckless to:

- cause the victim to fear the application of immediate unlawful force which amounts to actual bodily harm
- apply unlawful force which amounts to actual bodily harm.

Actual bodily harm has the same *mens rea* as an assault or battery. It does not require the defendant to intend or even realise that there is a risk of any injury. This appears unfair and unjust. Several reports have called for the reform of non-fatal offences based on this injustice.

Grievous bodily harm

Grievous bodily harm is an offence under s20 of the Offences Against the Person Act 1861. The offence can be committed by either a wound or by inflicting grievous bodily harm with or without a weapon. The prosecution must choose the correct version of the offence depending on the injuries suffered by the victim.

A wound means a cut or a break in the continuity of the whole skin. A cut of internal skin, such as in the cheek, is sufficient, but internal bleeding where there is no external cut of the skin is not a wound.

It can be considered unjust that a person who causes a small cut can be charged with the more serious offence of s20 instead of the offence of actual bodily harm under s47. This is because s20 refers to 'wound or grievous bodily harm', yet clearly there are different levels of wound and many of them do not amount to grievous bodily harm.

Grievous bodily harm means the infliction of internal injuries. Severe bruising may be grievous bodily harm where the victim is a young child or a frail elderly person, as shown in the case of R v Bollom (2003).

Key case

R v Bollom (2003)

Facts

The defendant had caused severe bruising to a 17-month-old child.

Legal principle – the Court of Appeal decided that this amounted to grievous bodily harm to this victim, even if it would not have amounted to the same injuries if inflicted on an adult.

Inflicting a disease can also amount to grievous bodily harm, as shown in R v Dica (2004).

Key case

R v Dica (2004)

Facts

The defendant had sex with two women knowing that he was HIV positive. Both women contracted HIV.

Legal principle – the defendant was convicted of causing grievous bodily harm under s20.

Serious psychiatric injury can also be grievous bodily harm. In the case of R v Burstow (1997), the stalking of the victim causing psychiatric injury could amount to grievous bodily harm. As with the case of R v Constanza (1997), the judges had not interpreted the injury from the arguably outdated Offences Against the Person Act 1861.

Actus Reus of grievous bodily harm

Actus reus of grievous bodily harm is causing serious internal injury to the victim.

Mens rea of grievous bodily harm

For the *mens rea*, the defendant must intend to cause another person some harm or be subjectively reckless as to whether the person suffers some harm.

Grievous bodily harm with intent

Grievous bodily harm with intent is an offence under s18 of the Offences Against the Person Act 1861. It is a more serious offence than s20 of the Act due to the *mens rea* of the offence - the intent.

Actus reus of grievous bodily harm with intent

This offence is committed by wounding or causing grievous bodily harm to another person. The meanings of wounding and grievous bodily harm are the same as for s20.

Mens rea of grievous bodily harm with intent

Grievous bodily harm with intent is a specific intent offence. This means that intent only has to be proved to either:

- wound
- cause grievous bodily harm
- resist or prevent the lawful apprehension or detention of any person.

Recklessness is not sufficient for this offence.

The operation of s18 can be unfair as someone who intends to resist arrest can be charged with s18 even though they only caused a small wound to the victim. This means that such a defendant can be guilty of the same offence as a defendant who intended to cause serious harm and did in fact cause very severe injuries.

Aims of sentencing

Whenever a person pleads guilty, or is found guilty of an offence, the court must decide what sentence should be given. Each offence has a maximum sentence and a judge or magistrate can impose a sentence up to the maximum. However, magistrates can only impose a maximum of 6 months' imprisonment for one offence (or 12 months' for two) and a maximum fine of £10,000. Judges in the Crown Court can impose up to the maximum for the offence.

Purpose of sentencing

When a judge or magistrate has to impose a sentence, they will also have to decide what they are trying to achieve by the punishment they give. Section 142 of the Criminal Justice Act 2003 sets out the aims of sentencing for adults. A court must have regard to:

- the punishment of offenders, also known as **retribution**
- the reduction of crime (including its reduction by **deterrence**)
- the reform and **rehabilitation** of offenders
- the protection of the public
- the making of **reparation** by offenders to persons affected by their offences.

In addition, **denunciation** of a person's criminal activity is also recognised as an aim of sentencing.

Key terms

Retribution - a form of revenge; a severe sentence is imposed for committing a serious offence.

Deterrence - a sentence that discourages others from committing the same or similar offences.

Rehabilitation - helping offenders to deal with their problems and avoid committing future offences.

Reparation - giving something back to the victim or society.

Denunciation - public disapproval of committing an offence.

Retribution

Retribution means that the offender deserves punishment for breaking the law. It does not try to reduce crime or alter the offender's future behaviour, although the offender may receive treatment or some education while in prison. A judge using this aim is only concerned with the offence that was committed and making sure that the sentence given is proportionate to the offence.

 **PAUSE POINT** Produce a table detailing the five non-fatal offences

Hint Include the *actus reus*, how the offence can be committed, the type of injuries suffered and the *mens rea*.

Extend Research an example of each offence from news articles.

Retribution is based on the idea that every offence has a certain tariff or level of sentencing and guidelines are set for most offences. Judges have to follow these guidelines and should not normally give a lower sentence than the set minimum.

Reducing crime and deterrence

Reducing crime is achieved by detaining the offender so that they cannot commit further crimes.

Individual deterrence tries to make sure that the offender does not reoffend because of fear of future punishment. Severe penalties such as a prison sentence, a suspended sentence or a heavy fine can be imposed to deter an offender from committing future crimes. However, prison does not appear to deter offenders as nearly 60 per cent of short-term adult prisoners reoffend shortly after release.

General deterrence is aimed at preventing other potential offenders from committing the same or similar crimes by making an example of the offender. However, the value of this aim is doubtful, as potential offenders are rarely deterred by severe sentences passed on others. General deterrence conflicts with retribution as an offender is sentenced at a higher level than the standard tariff for the offence.

Reform and rehabilitation

This aim is to reform the offender and rehabilitate them back into society in the hope that their behaviour will be altered and they will not offend in the future.

Reform is very important for young offenders, but it is also used for some adult offenders. The court will be given information about the defendant's background, usually through a pre-sentence report prepared by the probation service, and can consider other factors such as job prospects, training courses, lifestyle changes or medical issues.

Protection of the public

The public have to be protected from dangerous offenders and life imprisonment or long terms of imprisonment are given to those who commit murder or violent or serious offences.

Other ways in which the public can be protected are by disqualifying dangerous drivers or imposing exclusion or curfew orders to prevent the offender from going somewhere at a time where they are likely to commit an offence.

Reparation

Reparation is aimed at compensating the victim by ordering the offender to pay money to the victim or to return stolen property. The sentencing of supervised unpaid work as part of a **community order** is also seen as reparation.

Denunciation

Denunciation is where society shows its disapproval of criminal activity. A sentence should indicate to the offender and to others that certain types of behaviour are not acceptable. It shows that justice is being done.

For example, the severe penalties imposed on drink drivers have helped to change society's opinion of this behaviour. The same condemnation of driving while using a phone is being addressed at present.

Key term

Community order – a non-custodial punishment. It can take a number of forms including community work, treatment for an addiction or a curfew.

Reflect

- Which of these sentencing aims do you think is the most effective?
- Which is the least effective?

Factors involved in sentencing

In addition to the general aims of sentencing, the judge or magistrates will consider any individual **aggravating factors** that should increase the sentence or **mitigating factors** that should reduce the sentence.

Aggravating factors could include:

- pleading not guilty
- previous convictions
- the offender being on bail when the offence was committed
- any racial or religious hostility shown
- the offender being part of a group, particularly if they were leading the group
- the victim being vulnerable, such as a young child or an elderly person
- the crime being planned.

Mitigating factors could include:

- cooperating with the police or pleading guilty
- any physical or mental illness
- having no previous convictions
- evidence of genuine remorse, such as offering compensation or returning stolen goods.

Key terms

Aggravating factors – count against the defendant and are likely to result in a higher sentence being imposed by the court.

Mitigating factors – count for the defendant and are likely to result in a lower sentence being imposed by the court.

Custodial sentences – a sentence of imprisonment for a fixed period of time or for an undefined period.

Types of sentence

Custody

Custodial sentences are the most serious punishments a court can impose and can range from weeks to life imprisonment. They are meant to be used only for serious offences. The Criminal Justice Act 2003 says that the court must not pass a custodial sentence unless it is of the opinion that the offence was so serious that neither a fine alone nor a community sentence can be justified.

Types of custody include:

- a mandatory life sentence – this is the only sentence a judge can impose when sentencing a defendant found guilty of murder. The judge has to set the minimum number of years' imprisonment that the offender must serve. This is known as the 'tariff' period. The defendant can then be released on licence. Provided they remain on good behaviour, they will not have to serve any further period of imprisonment. If, however, they reoffend, they can be recalled to prison.
- a discretionary life sentence – this is where the maximum sentence for the offence is life imprisonment, but the judge does not have to impose it.
- a fixed-term sentence – this is where the offender is sentenced to a set number of months or years in custody. A prisoner will not usually serve the whole of this sentence, as they will be automatically released on licence after they have served half of the sentence.
- a suspended sentence – a prison sentence will not take effect immediately. A period of suspension up to two years will be fixed. If, during this time, no further offences are committed, the prison sentence will not be served. However, if offences are committed, the prison sentence is 'activated' and the offender will serve that sentence together with any sentence for the new offence. A suspended sentence should only be given where the offence is so serious that an immediate custodial sentence is appropriate, but there are exceptional circumstances that justify suspending the sentence. It gives the offender one last chance to avoid prison.

Community orders

Community orders were created by the Criminal Justice Act 2003. The court can combine one or more of the following requirements it thinks necessary:

- unpaid work
- an activity or a prohibited activity
- a programme, such as a training programme
- a curfew
- exclusion from an area
- a residence requirement (to live at a certain place)
- mental health treatment
- drug rehabilitation
- alcohol treatment
- a supervision order
- to spend time at an attendance centre (only if the offender is aged under 25).

Fines

Fines are the most common way of sentencing in the magistrates' court. The maximum fine in that court used to be £5,000 but, from March 2015, for certain serious offences such as the manufacture, import and sale of realistic imitation firearms, the maximum fine is unlimited. The Crown Court has the power to impose fines of an unlimited amount for each offence.

Discharges

A discharge can be either:

- conditional – where it is thought that no further punishment is necessary, the court discharges an offender on the condition that no further offence is committed during a set period up to three years. If an offence is committed within this time, another sentence can be imposed, as well as a penalty for the new offence.
- absolute – this means that no penalty or condition is imposed following a conviction for a very minor or technical offence.

Research

In small groups, find five criminal cases that have been reported in a national or local newspaper, or from an online report. Make sure they are cases dealt with in England or Wales. Discuss the following questions in your group.

- What was the crime?
- If the defendant was found guilty, what sentence was imposed?
- Was the sentence fair in each case?.

Assessment practice 2.3

D.P7 D.P8 D.M5 D.D3

You have recently started to work in the criminal litigation department of Legal Eagle solicitors.

Winston calls you to tell you that he was waiting to be served in a long queue in a kebab shop last Friday night. Duane was in front of him. Winston was in a hurry and became a little angry about the slow service. When the queue moved forward a little, Duane did not move as he was talking on his phone. This annoyed Winston who pushed Duane in the back, causing him to fall on to Agnes, an elderly lady. Agnes was knocked over and suffered a broken hip. Duane was unhurt. Winston immediately called an ambulance and gave all possible help to Agnes before she was taken to hospital. Winston tells you he has never been in trouble before. The police have suggested that Winston could be charged with a criminal offence. Winston wants to know what offence he could be charged with, especially as he says he never touched Agnes. Winston also wants to know what matters will be taken into account by the court if he is found guilty and the possible sentence he could receive.

You arrange to see Winston the next day and prepare some notes for the meeting.

At the meeting Winston tells you he is interested in social sciences. He wants to know more about the working of non-fatal offences in general and the current sentencing trends. You promise to research these matters and write a report for him evaluating the current law on non-fatal offences against the person and current sentencing trends.

Plan

- I need to identify which offences Winston may be charged with, and what their penalties are.
- I need to research current sentencing trends for non-fatal offences and where to find this information.

Do

- I need to be able to explain clearly each offence and the sentence it carries to Winston.
- I need to evaluate how non-fatal offences against the person are currently being sentenced.

Review

- I can identify which offences may apply to this particular case.
- I can talk about how non-fatal offences against the person are currently sentenced.

THINK FUTURE

Gavin Capper

Barrister

After I qualified as a solicitor I worked as a police station and magistrates' court advocate before working my way up to more complicated Crown Court work. This included meeting with clients and providing initial advice, applying for legal aid, taking part in conferences with counsel (barristers), carrying out casework, which could include obtaining witness statements and expert reports, drafting bail applications and advising on appeals. As an advocate I represented defendants in court for many different types of offence.

However, I always had it in my heart that I wanted to be a barrister and specialise as an advocate. So, after two years working as a solicitor, I contacted the Bar Council who informed me that I could transfer to the Bar. Due to my advocacy experience I was able to apply for exemption from pupillage, which is the standard qualifying requirement for barristers. I therefore applied to the Bar Council, providing references and a certificate of good standing. I was granted an exemption from pupillage and was called to the Bar at Middle Temple in 2015. Initially, I found my role did not change significantly. However, I have recently been undertaking a much greater variety of work, including representing both prosecution and defence. I also undertake some civil cases in the county court.

I enjoy the pressure of the work as a barrister and not having to conduct the initial interviewing and client care aspects carried out by solicitors. The skills needed by a barrister include communication (as all trials are conducted orally in court), self-confidence and the ability to think and work under pressure. In jury trials in the Crown Court, an important skill is listening to, and being able to react to, the evidence being heard. Another important requirement is the ability to take in a huge amount of information and reformulate this for the purpose of presenting your case.

As a self-employed barrister I work, and am paid, as and when I receive an instruction (also known as a brief), with payment coming at the end of a case. It is not unusual to receive a brief the day before a trial, so I often have to study the evidence and relevant law into the early hours. It is also not unusual to have a number of different cases running at the same time, so I have to be organised. Being instructed so late, I often find that I am not as fully in control of all the evidence as I would like, which means I have to think creatively.

As a solicitor you are generally a contracted employee and paid monthly. You can work long hours, including being on call 24/7 at police stations, but generally you have more time to prepare a case for a hearing and you have more control over your case. A solicitor has more of a relationship with their client and will spend more time with them, taking instructions and generally dealing with the case as well as, in some circumstances, representing them in court.

Applying the Law 3

Getting to know your unit

Assessment
You will be assessed by an external assessment under supervised conditions. The assessment is set and marked by Pearson.

Legal professionals apply criminal law on a daily basis to individual cases. The task provided for external assessment will allow you to identify and explain the law relevant to given scenarios. You will then analyse, evaluate and apply the law in order to advise the parties involved.

How you will be assessed

This unit is assessed under supervised conditions. You will be provided with a case study a set period of time before the supervised assessment period in order to carry out research.

The supervised assessment period will be explained to you. During this period, you will have to complete a set task, which will be marked externally.

The activities in this book will not form part of the assessment you will have to complete, but will help you develop an understanding of the law so that you can be successful.

As the guidelines for assessment can change, you should refer to the official assessment guidance on the Pearson Qualifications website for the latest definitive guidance.

Grade descriptors

To achieve a grade, you will be expected to demonstrate the following attributes across the essential content of the unit.

To pass this unit:

Learners will demonstrate knowledge and understanding of homicide and property offences, together with an understanding of the powers of the police. They will be able to suggest appropriate sources of advice and funding for civil claims. They will demonstrate an understanding of how the law works in relation to these offences, and know how to research relevant law and reference sources correctly. They will understand police powers of arrest, detention, search interviews and samples. They can make some recommendations for actions in the context of homicide and property offences resulting from interpretation of the legal information provided.

To achieve a distinction:

Learners will be able to critically evaluate and synthesise information relating to homicide and property criminal claims, their viability and success. They can apply key concepts and legal precedents to real-life scenarios, analyse complex information from different sources and assess its impact and influence on legal decisions. Learners can consider the implications in the context of the legal detail both given and created, making appropriate justified recommendations for necessary actions.

Assessment outcomes

AO1 Demonstrate knowledge and understanding of both homicide and offences against property together with the law relating to police procedure using legal terminology.

AO2 Apply the laws relating to both homicide and offences against property together with the law relating to police procedure, using legal terminology and relevant case law and statute law to illustrate points made and make connections.

AO3 Analyse the law relating to homicide, property offences and police procedure, demonstrating the ability to interpret the potential impact, outcome and influence on future cases.

AO4 Evaluate evidence to make informed judgements with appropriate justification, synthesising ideas and evidence from several sources to support arguments.

Getting started

In pairs, create a table with three columns. In column one, list any facts you know about criminal law. Column two is for any terminology you are aware of which relates to criminal law or procedure and column three is for definitions of the terminology.

A The laws relating to homicide: murder and voluntary manslaughter

Types of fatal offence

The purpose of criminal law is to define what is and what is not acceptable behaviour in society. Criminal law sets boundaries on both the behaviour of people and on the ways that the criminal justice system operates. For example, the police are given the power to investigate crime, but can only make arrests based on reasonable suspicion. The courts try to sentence offenders, but only when it has been proved beyond reasonable doubt that they have committed an offence.

Criminal law is a fascinating subject and although the law relating to, for example, **fatal offences** applies equally to all such cases, each case is unique with a different set of people, personalities and circumstances. The legal professionals apply the law to cases heard in court fairly and objectively, but you will find that many cases can be disturbing and upsetting. It is important to recognise how cases can lead to devastating consequences for those involved, which makes fair decisions all the more important.

Key terms

Fatal offence – such an offence involves the death of a person.

Homicide – the killing of a human being.

You may be familiar with the word **homicide**, having heard it on television or at the cinema. Many learners think that it is American terminology and has no place in the English legal system. However, the Homicide Act 1957 has affected the law of England and Wales for many years. The offences that fall into the category of unlawful homicide are murder, voluntary and involuntary manslaughter – these are all fatal offences where a person causes the death of another.

It may seem strange to have the category of unlawful homicide, but in some circumstances homicide can be lawful, such as:

- killing another person but using reasonable force in self-defence
- during war time where the objective is to destroy the enemy
- where, in the interests of justice, force is used to make a lawful arrest
- in some countries, carrying out a lawful death sentence.

PAUSE POINT — Produce a diagram showing the potential consequences of both lawful and unlawful homicide.

Hint — Explain legal procedure and sentencing relating to fatal offences.

Extend — Think about the purpose of punishing offenders and whether sentencing powers are adequate.

Murder

There is no definition of murder in any Act of Parliament. The definition comes from the **common law** and in particular from Sir Edward Coke in 1797. His definition is written in very old-fashioned language:

> Murder is when a man of sound memory and of the age of discretion, unlawfully killeth within any county of the realm any reasonable creature in *rerum natura*, under the King's peace, with malice aforethought, either expressed or implied by the law, so as the party wounded, or hurt, etc., die of the wound, or hurt, etc., within a year and a day after the same.

This definition is broken down in Table 3.1.

Key terms

Common law – law developed by judicial decisions.

Human being – in the instance of murder, a human being is a person who is born and capable of breathing, a person who is not classed as legally brain dead.

Transferred malice – the intent to kill in one offence can be transferred to another. For example, if A intends to shoot B but misses, killing C instead, his intent is transferred to the victim (C) and so A will still be liable for the death.

Table 3.1: Common law definition of murder

Term	Definition
When a man	This refers to either a man or woman.
of sound memory	The person must not be classed as legally insane.
age of discretion	A child under the age of 10 is classed as incapable of fully understanding the nature of criminal wrongs.
within any county	This aspect of the definition is now wider as murder committed by a British citizen outside the UK may be tried in England, as may a murder committed on a British aircraft or on a foreign aircraft coming to the UK.
reasonable creature in *rerum naturana*	The victim must be a living, breathing human being.
under the King's peace	Whether the reigning monarch is a King or Queen, this excludes enemy soldiers killed in the course of war.
with malice aforethought	This means that at the time of the killing, the accused intended to kill (expressed malice) or intended to commit grievous bodily harm (implied malice). The term does not require pre-planning or an evil motive.
within a year and a day	This part of the definition was abolished in 1996 mainly due to advances in medical treatment where victims could remain alive on life support machines.

Reflect

Think back to Unit 2 and to the meaning of *actus reus* and *mens rea*. Highlight the words in the definition of murder in Table 3.1 that relate to *actus reus* and *mens rea*.

Actus reus of murder

The *actus reus* element of murder is any action or conduct which causes death. This element must cause the death of a **human being**. Although this sounds reasonably straightforward, it has led to some lengthy discussion about unborn children. A baby still in the womb cannot be a victim of murder as it is not classed as a person 'in being' that is capable of existing independently of its mother. Cases such as R v Poulton (1832) and R v Enoch (1833) established that the child had to be fully expelled from the womb and be alive to have an existence independent of the mother.

The following case shows how the doctrine of **transferred malice** could not be applied as the foetus could not be classed as a human being at the time of the attack.

Key case

Attorney General's Reference (No. 3 of 1994) (1997)

Facts

The defendant stabbed his girlfriend, who was five and half months pregnant. She recovered from the wound but seven weeks later the child was born prematurely and died after four months. Evidence showed that the stab wound had penetrated the child while still in the womb and that this was the cause of death. The defendant was charged with the murder of the child but was acquitted as the judge decided that the case was not homicide. The Court of Appeal concluded that the trial judge was wrong and that a murder conviction was possible using the principle of transferred malice. On further appeal to the House of Lords, it was decided that, at most, manslaughter was possible.

Legal principle - transferred malice was not applicable as the transferee had to be in existence at the time when the defendant formed mental intent.

As mentioned previously, a murder victim must be a human being and therefore a person who is already dead cannot be a victim. However, the legal definition of death has changed over time due to medical advancements. Originally, death was said to occur when the heartbeat and breathing stop. In cases involving life support machines, the courts have favoured the medical tests for brain death.

Key terms

Factual causation - the principle that the action of the defendant caused harm.

Legal causation - the examination of an action to see if it contributed to harm.

Proving causation for murder

When a person is accused of murder, the prosecution must establish a link between their actions or conduct and the death of the victim. The jury will then decide whether the accused caused the death of the victim. The jury must be satisfied that the actions of the accused are the factual and legal cause of death.

Factual causation is sometimes referred to as the 'but for' test. In other words - 'but for' the defendant's action, harm would not have occurred. The classic case to establish this point is R v White (1910).

Link

See Unit 2 for more detail on causation.

Key case

R v White (1910)

Facts

The defendant put poison into his mothers' drink intending to kill her and inherit her money. Later, his mother was found dead on the sofa and though she had drunk some of the drink, medical evidence found that she had died of a heart attack. The defendant had not used enough poison for a fatal dose. The defendant had *mens rea* and had performed the *actus reus* but this did not cause death. The defendant was convicted of attempted murder.

Legal principle - causation must be proved in a murder case.

Legal causation examines the action of the defendant and whether it contributed to the death. If the defendant's action speeds up the death of the victim, such as a doctor giving excessive pain relief to a terminally ill patient, this could be seen as a cause of death, but the jury may not find legal causation. The culpable (or blameworthy) act of the defendant does not have to be the only cause of death – other factors could have contributed to it.

The 'thin skull' rule means the accused must take the victim as the accused finds them and that even if the victim is particularly susceptible to physical or psychological injury, this cannot excuse the defendant. Furthermore, this principle has been extended to cover the victim's mental condition or religious beliefs.

Link

See Unit 1 for more detail on the 'thin skull' rule.

Key term

Intervening event – an event that breaks the chain of causation, sometimes referred to as *'novus actus interveniens'*.

Intervening events and acts may break the chain of causation (see Figure 3.1). The following case provides an example of the chain of causation being broken.

Key case

R v Jordan (1956)

Facts

The victim had been stabbed and died eight days later. The defendant was convicted of murder but appealed. New evidence showed that the cause of death was an injection given after the victim had previously shown signs of intolerance to the medication. The medical treatment was described as 'palpably wrong' and the conviction was quashed as this poor treatment broke the chain of causation.

Legal principle – a new intervening event can break the chain of causation.

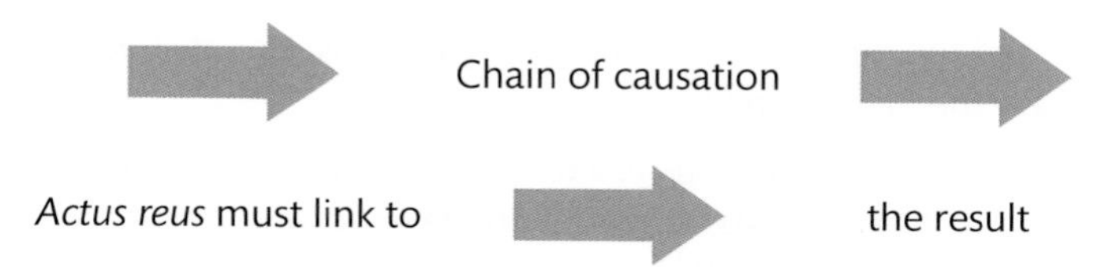

▶ **Figure 3.1:** The chain of causation must not be broken; it must link the defendant's action to the outcome or result

The following case illustrates the chain of causation. The victim's religious beliefs did not break the chain as the defendant had to 'take his victim as he found her', which is the application of the 'thin skull' rule.

Key case

R v Blaue (1975)

Facts

The defendant stabbed a girl four times because she refused to have sex with him. She was admitted to hospital where she was informed that a blood transfusion could save her life. She refused to give consent for the transfusion to take place based on religious grounds and died a few hours later. The defendant argued that her actions broke the chain of causation but this was rejected.

Legal principle – this case illustrates the 'thin skull' rule.

Mens rea of murder

The offence of murder requires proof of the intention to kill or the intention to cause grievous bodily harm. *Mens rea* relates to the state of mind of the defendant at the time of causing death, and is different to the motive, which relates to the reason for a course of action. For example, a woman agrees to pay a contract killer to murder her husband. The contract killer buys a gun, finds the victim and shoots him. The *mens rea* is the intention to kill, but the motive is that they did it for money.

Malice aforethought means intention; an intention to kill may be expressed through words and threats or implied by conduct. For example, buying and loading a gun could indicate an intention to kill. There are two types of intention - direct and indirect (which is sometimes referred to as oblique) intent.

Direct intent means that the defendant had a purpose or desire to cause death. **Indirect** or **oblique intent** is more complicated. The defendant states that they did not intend to cause death, but in fact believed that death was very probable as a consequence of their action.

The following case shows that the defendant must foresee death or serious harm as a virtual certainty for indirect intent to apply.

Key terms

Direct intent - the purpose or desire to cause harm.

Indirect (or oblique) intent - a defendant states that they did not intend to cause death but in fact believed that death was virtually certain.

Law Commission - a statutory, independent body created to review the law in England and Wales.

Key case

R v Woollin (1998)

Facts

The defendant killed his three-month-old son by throwing him against a wall and fracturing his skull. The defendant claimed his actions were unintended. The defendant had picked up the baby and shook him as he was choking, then, in frustration, he threw the baby towards a pram. The trial judge directed the jury that they might infer intention if they thought the defendant appreciated his acts posed a substantial risk of harm. The defendant was convicted of murder but appealed on grounds that the jury were misdirected. The House of Lords accepted the appeal and reduced the conviction to manslaughter.

Legal principle - indirect intent is based on the defendant at the time of the offence believing that death was virtually certain.

Criticisms of the current law and proposals for reform

The **Law Commission** reviews the law to ensure that it is fit for purpose. Its aim is to create a system where the law is fair, modern, simple and cost effective. The Law Commission referred to the law related to unlawful homicide as a 'mess' and in a report published in 2006 'Murder, Manslaughter and Infanticide' they put forward several recommendations for reform.

Some of the criticisms were as follows.

- There is no clear definition of murder, as it has developed from common law.
- Some of the terminology is confusing because it is so old-fashioned.
- Advice given to juries on intention has changed often and has become confusing.
- Cases vary in detail and the current law can be inflexible when dealing with these differences, for example there is little discretion between someone intending grievous bodily harm and a serial killer.
- Self-defence is problematic: the force used to defend yourself must be reasonable, but there is no definitive line for what counts as an 'overreaction'.

The Law Commission recommended a new act to replace the Homicide Act 1957 with clear definitions of offences and defences. The new Act would offer clarity and the offences would be easier to understand, as shown in the Table 3.2. However, this recommended Act was not passed and so did not replace the Homicide Act.

Table 3.2: Definition and sentences for murder recommended by the Law Commission

Offence	Definition	Sentence
First degree murder	• Killing intentionally • Killing when there was an intention to do serious injury with an awareness of the risk of death	Mandatory life sentence
Second degree murder	• Killing when the offender intended serious injury • Killing when the offender intended some injury, fear or risk and was aware of a serious risk of death • Killing when there is a **partial defence** to murder	Discretionary life maximum penalty
Manslaughter	• Killing through gross negligence • Killing as a result of a criminal act with an intention to cause injury or an awareness of a serious risk of causing injury	Discretionary life maximum penalty

Key term

Partial defence – this type of defence will not lead to an acquittal (escaping any liability or punishment). Partial defences only apply to a murder charge and reduce the charge to voluntary manslaughter.

When the courts have tried a defendant on a charge of murder, the jury decides the verdict based on the facts of the case (see Figure 3.2). If the verdict is guilty, the judge will pass sentence. For murder, the sentence is a mandatory life sentence. The judge will set a minimum term to be served depending on the circumstances of the case and the age of the defendant, which may be a whole life term or

- 30 years
- 25 years
- 15 years
- 12 years (if defendant is under 18 at the time of the offence).

Murder = *Actus reus* – causing death,
Mens rea – intention either direct or oblique

Voluntary manslaughter = *Actus reus* – causing death,
Mens rea – intention mitigated by loss of control

Involuntary manslaughter = *Actus reus* – causing death,
Mens rea – gross negligence, recklessness or intention to commit another crime

Figure 3.2: Criminal liability for all offences, other than strict and absolute liability offences, requires proof of *actus reus* and *mens rea*

Research

Examine the factors determining the minimum term contained on **http://www.cps.gov.uk/legal/s_to_u/sentencing_and_dangerous_offenders/index.html#a14**

Using newspapers and/or news websites, find three cases where a life sentence has been given.

- Try to find evidence of the *actus reus*, *mens rea* and causation from the facts of the case. Do you think the sentence matches the offence committed?

Voluntary manslaughter

Voluntary manslaughter as a partial defence to murder

Manslaughter refers to all unlawful homicides that are not classed as murder. There are two categories - voluntary and involuntary manslaughter. Unlike murder, a manslaughter charge does not carry a compulsory life sentence. The judge will decide whether this is needed depending on the circumstances of the case. Voluntary manslaughter may be used as a partial defence to murder.

To be charged with voluntary manslaughter the defendant must have committed the *actus reus*, have *mens rea* and there must be a **causal link** between the defendant's act and the death. However, there will be **mitigating circumstances** that mean the charge of murder is reduced to voluntary manslaughter.

These mitigating circumstances form partial defences to a murder charge. A partial defence can only be applied to murder, and the aim of a partial defence is to reduce the charge to manslaughter. There are three partial defences to murder:

- **loss of control**
- **diminished responsibility**
- killing in pursuance of (following) a suicide pact.

We will look at loss of control and diminished responsibility in the next sections.

Key terms

Manslaughter - a homicide that is not classed as murder. There are two categories of manslaughter - voluntary and involuntary.

Causal link - the same principle as causation, there must be a link between the *actus reus* and the result.

Mitigating circumstances - conditions of the case that do not excuse the action of the defendant, but may be considered with regard to reducing a charge from murder to manslaughter.

Loss of control - the *mens rea* of the defendant is influenced by fear or an abnormality of mental functioning.

Diminished responsibility - a plea where an abnormality of the mind is used as an explanation for the defendant's actions.

Loss of control

Before the introduction of the Coroners and Justice Act 2009, loss of control as a partial defence to voluntary manslaughter was referred to as 'provocation'. It was defined by s3 of the Homicide Act 1957 as follows:

> Where on a charge of murder there is evidence on which the jury can find that the person charged was provoked (whether by things done or by things said or by both together) to lose his self-control, the question whether the provocation was enough to make a reasonable person do as they did shall be left to be determined by the jury; and in determining that question the jury shall take into account everything both done and said according to the effect which, in their opinion, it would have on a reasonable person.

This definition included two tests:

- a subjective test - was the actual defendant provoked enough to lose self-control?
- an objective test - would the reasonable person have been provoked enough to lose control and do as the defendant did?

Over the years, the law of provocation developed through case law. The requirement for provocation was that the loss of control must be 'sudden and temporary', established in the case of R v Duffy (1949).

Later developments introduced the reasonable person test, which examined if a reasonable person in the same situation would have carried out the defendant's actions. In DPP v Camplin (1978), the age of the defendant was a relevant factor in applying the objective test.

Key case

DPP v Camplin (1978)

Facts

The defendant, a 15-year-old boy, had been raped by a middle-aged man who then laughed at the boy. The boy lost control and hit the man over the head with a chapati pan, causing death. The trial judge instructed the jury to consider how a reasonable man would have reacted to the provocation and the boy appealed against his conviction. The Court of Appeal stated that the jury should have considered the reaction of a reasonable 15-year-old.

Legal principle – some characteristics of the accused can be attributed to the reasonable person.

Other characteristics could relate to the defendant's physical or psychological state, to the defendant's history or to the circumstances of the provocation. Eventually, the jury was directed away from applying the reasonable person test and concentrated more on what could reasonably be expected of the defendant.

The law relating to provocation had become unclear and was criticised as provocation had a very wide meaning. Critics also claimed that anger was given a higher status than other emotions such as fear or desperation. They also claimed that the defence requiring the loss of control to be sudden and temporary excluded some defendants and was gender biased. This was addressed in the case of R v Ahluwalia (1992).

Key case

R v Ahluwalia (1992)

Facts

The defendant had an arranged marriage with her husband and he had been violent towards her for many years. He had assaulted and threatened her on many occasions and one night he stated that unless she paid a bill the next day, he would beat her up. Later, when he was asleep she poured petrol over him and set him alight. He suffered severe burns and died six days later. The defendant was convicted of murder but appealed on grounds of diminished responsibility and provocation. The Court of Appeal rejected provocation but ordered a retrial based on diminished responsibility, where she was convicted of manslaughter.

Legal principle – provocation had to be sudden and temporary and did not allow for so called 'slow burn' cases where a person reacts, not to any particular act or incident, but acts in desperation after cumulative years of abuse. The law was changed in 2009.

PAUSE POINT Create a spider diagram showing the factors that you think should be considered as mitigating factors for a charge of murder to be reduced to voluntary manslaughter. How would the legal system be perceived if mitigating factors were never taken into account?

Hint You could find examples of how other countries operate in a way that you would consider as unfair by looking at some of the case studies on the Amnesty International website.

Extend Think about the disadvantages of legal systems that retain the death penalty.

The burden of proof

If the jury finds sufficient evidence, they must assume that the defence is satisfied unless the prosecution provides beyond reasonable doubt to the contrary.

The following case shows how s55 Coroners and Justice Act 2009 is applied in court.

Link

See Unit 1 for an explanation of the burden of proof in civil law.

Key case

R v Clinton (2012)

Facts

The defendant and his wife were on medication for depression caused by stress. They agreed that they would benefit from a trial separation. The defendant was struggling to cope and showed signs of being suicidal. His wife told him she was having an affair. He asked her to meet with him so that they could tell the children together. He had arranged for the children to be elsewhere and when she arrived he beat her and strangled her, causing her death. He was convicted of murder and appealed on grounds that the trial judge had not allowed loss of control as infidelity should be disregarded as a qualifying trigger. His appeal was successful – it was decided the defence should have been put before the jury.

Legal principle – where other factors count as a qualifying trigger, sexual infidelity can be taken into account to assess whether the things said or done amounted to a circumstance of extremely grave character and gave the defendant a justifiable sense of being wronged.

How is the law applied for loss of control

The new partial defence of loss of control amends the previous defence of provocation. Loss of control need not be sudden and temporary, but there has to be a qualifying trigger. Table 3.3 summarises the partial defence and notes some of the differences between provocation and loss of control.

Table 3.3: Summary of loss of control

What needs to be proved?	Effects of the 2009 Act	Points to be considered
Was there a loss of control?	Requirement of 'sudden and temporary' has been dropped. This is wider than the law on provocation.	If there has been a significant time delay, the judge may decide whether or not the defence is available.
Was it triggered by fear of serious violence?	Subjective element – the actual defendant must have feared serious violence from the victim or another person.	Sexual infidelity alone and revenge cannot be classed as triggers. This is narrower than the defence of provocation.
Was it triggered by things said and/ or done giving the defendant a sense of being seriously wronged?	The defence is narrower than provocation as two new tests have been included (subjective test and objective test).	

Table 3.3: *Continued*

What needs to be proved?	Effects of the 2009 Act	Points to be considered
Would a person of the same age and sex and with a normal degree of tolerance have reacted in the circumstances in the same way?	Similar to provocation but the objective test is narrower – only sex and age are taken into account.	If the jury consider a reasonable person would have lost control but would not have reacted in the same way, then the defence is lost.

Diminished responsibility

The partial defence of diminished responsibility was introduced by s2 of the Homicide Act 1957 and was defined as:

> A person who kills or is party to the killing of another is not to be convicted of murder if they were suffering from such abnormality of mind as substantially impaired his mental responsibility for his acts and omissions in doing or being party to a killing.

Abnormality of the mind was for the jury to decide but depended on medical evidence. Such a condition was defined as arising from 'a condition of arrested or retarded development of mind or any inherent causes or induced by disease or injury'. This has led to a wide range of medical conditions, both physical and psychological, being a basis for a plea of diminished responsibility. The defendant's ability must have been substantially impaired and this gave the jury some discretion when deciding whether the partial defence is applicable.

However, the Law Commission's 2008 report titled 'Murder, Manslaughter and Infanticide' stated that the partial defence of provocation was too confusing, as it mixed case law with statutes. The Law Commission also noted that the partial defence of diminished responsibility was out of date and was failing to keep up with medical developments.

Section 52 of the Coroners and Justice Act 2009 replaced the definition of diminished responsibility. The defendant must now be able to demonstrate an abnormality of mental functioning which arose from a recognised medical condition and substantially impaired the defendant's ability to either:

- understand the nature of their conduct
- form a rational judgement
- exercise self-control.

The abnormality of mental functioning must provide an explanation for the defendant's acts and omissions in doing or being a party to the killing.

This is a clearer and more modern definition of diminished responsibility. By requiring a recognised medical condition has allowed for changes in medical knowledge where the classification lists may be amended. Table 3.4 breaks down the definition from the Coroners and Justice Act 2009.

Table 3.4: Definition of diminished responsibility from the Coroners and Justice Act 2009

Term	Definition
abnormality of mental functioning	A state of mind so different from that of ordinary human beings that a reasonable person would identify it as abnormal.
a recognised medical condition	The jury is not bound to accept medical evidence but the act stresses the importance of expert psychiatric evidence. Classified lists of recognised medical conditions can be found in the World Health Organisation's International Classification of Diseases.
substantially impaired	The jury decides on the definition of 'substantial'.
provides an explanation for	There must be some causal link between the defendant's abnormality and the killing. However, the abnormality does not need to be the sole cause. The defence will not be successful if the defendant's abnormality made no difference to their behaviour.

Research

Find the legal definition of 'insanity' so that you can compare and contrast the factors required and the consequences of each plea.

Diminished responsibility and intoxication

It can be confusing for a jury to decide whether diminished responsibility is relevant to a case when the defendant has a relevant condition but was also intoxicated. They must consider whether the mental impairment had an impact on the killing or if it was just intoxication. Intoxication alone through either drugs or alcohol is not a defence to murder.

Generally, if the defendant establishes that their abnormality of mind or medical condition substantially impaired their mental responsibility for their act of killing the victim, then, even if they were intoxicated, the jury should find them guilty of manslaughter rather than murder. The courts followed this in cases such as R v Dietschmann (2003), R v Hendy (2006) and R v Robson (2006). The jury are likely to consider the following.

- Does the defendant have an abnormality of mind?
- Did it arise from a recognised medical condition?
- Did it impair their ability substantially to understand the nature of their conduct or form a rational judgement?
- Did it affect their exercise of self-control?
- Was the abnormality a significant factor in the killing of the victim?

The answers to these questions would influence the decision to convict of murder or manslaughter.

Some cases have acknowledged that where intoxication is involuntary as a result of addiction (for example, alcohol dependency syndrome), this could be classed as diminished responsibility due to the effect on the brain. The Court of Appeal considered this issue in R v Wood (2008) and R v Stewart (2009). They concluded that addiction could be a source of an abnormality of mental functioning but that the nature, extent and seriousness of the addiction had to be considered.

The abnormality of mind must be linked to a recognised medical condition but must also substantially impair the defendant's responsibility for their actions, as illustrated in the following case.

▶ Should a defendant who is intoxicated be allowed to use this fact in his defence?

Key case

R v Lloyd (1966)

Facts

Medical evidence showed that the defendant suffered from reactive recurrent depressions and that his mental responsibility was impaired by the abnormality but not to a substantial degree. The defendant had strangled his wife. The defendant was convicted of murder.

Legal principle - substantial impairment was to be interpreted in a common-sense way as more than trivial.

A difficulty arises when it is unclear as to whether the substantial impairment has been caused by an abnormality of mind or by intoxication. This was a question for the jury in the following case.

Key case

R v Egan (1992)

Facts

The defendant entered an elderly lady's house at night after drinking heavily, attacking and killing her. He had a mental condition which was classed as an abnormality of mind. The issue was whether the abnormality of mind had impaired his responsibility for his actions or whether it was the abnormality of mind in conjunction with the alcohol he had consumed. The defendant was convicted of murder.

Legal principle – the defence of diminished responsibility is lost if the jury believe that but for the voluntary consumption of alcohol the defendant would not have killed the victim.

Alcohol dependence can be classed as a disease causing an abnormality of mind when the drinking is involuntary and the defendant lacks self-control. In the following case, the drinking was deemed to be voluntary.

Key case

R v Tandy (1989)

Facts

The defendant was an alcoholic who, after drinking a bottle of vodka, strangled her 11-year-old daughter. The defendant took the first drink of the day voluntarily and so the drinking for the whole day is classed as voluntary and diminished responsibility would not apply. She was convicted of murder.

Legal principle – alcoholism could be classed as a disease inducing abnormality of the mind, but only if it caused a gross impairment of judgement and the drinking was involuntary due to the addiction.

The burden of proof

The burden of proof is on the defendant; in most other defences, the defendant has to raise the defence and then it is up to the prosecution to disprove it.

Suicide pacts

This remains as a partial defence from s4 of the Homicide Act 1957. A murder charge is reduced to manslaughter where the survivor of a joint suicide pact took part in the killing of another person in the suicide pact or was a party to that killing.

Infanticide

Section 1 of the Infanticide Act 1938 has been amended by s57 of the Coroners and Justice Act 2009. Rather than being a partial defence or even a concealed partial defence, infanticide is an offence in its own right. This offence will only apply to the mother of her own child where she has caused the death of the child by a wilful act or an omission. The child must be under the age of 12 months and it must be proved that at the time of the killing her mind was disturbed by reason of not having fully recovered from giving birth. The offence is dealt with and punished in the same way as manslaughter.

Create a flowchart to show how a murder charge can be reduced to voluntary manslaughter.

Hint You could refer to the specific sections of the Homicide Act and the Coroners and Justice Act.

Extend Think about the difficulties the jury may have in ascertaining the state of mind of the defendant - sanity, loss of control and diminished responsibility.

Victims

The latest figures taken from the Office for National Statistics, including the offences of murder, manslaughter, corporate manslaughter and infanticide, show that around two-thirds of victims were male and one-third female. Females were shown to be more likely to be acquainted with the principal suspect. The relationship between the principal suspect and victims over the age of 16 is shown in Table 3.5.

Table 3.5: Findings from analyses based on the Homicide Index recorded by the Home Office covering different aspects of homicide (for year ending March 2015)

Relationship	Male victims	Female victims
Killed by partners or ex-partners	6%	44%
Killed by friends or acquaintances	32%	8%
Killed by strangers	31%	12%
	331 offences	186 offences

Using your numeracy skills, you will have noted that the figures in the columns don't add up to 100 per cent. This is because victims under the age of 16 are not taken into account in this table. The police recorded a total of 518 homicides, which represented a decrease of just over 1 per cent on the previous year.

The findings from the cases involving those under 16 were that 65 per cent were acquainted with the principal suspect, who was generally a parent or step-parent, and for some victims a principal suspect had not been identified.

The circumstances of the homicides are noted in the Office for National Statistics findings and approximately half resulted from an argument, a revenge attack or a loss of temper. Around 7 per cent were said to result from irrational acts and around 4 per cent were related to acts of theft or gain. In 17 per cent of cases, the circumstances could not be ascertained.

Discussion

There was an increase in violent crime in 2016. One potential explanation for this was an increase in the reporting and recording of **domestic violence and abuse** cases. Think about:

- ways of reducing this type of crime
- ways of reducing crime in general.

Key term

Domestic violence and abuse - the government definition is 'any incident or pattern of incidents of controlling, coercive or threatening behaviour, violence or abuse between those aged 16 or over who are, or have been, intimate partners or family members regardless of gender or sexuality'.

Criticisms of the current law and proposals for reform

The Coroners and Justice Act 2009 has made significant reforms in relation to loss of control and diminished responsibility, but critics argue that some problems still remain. These are:

- for loss of control - the factor of sexual infidelity cannot be a qualifying trigger but can be taken into account - this produces a grey area to be clarified through further case law decisions.
- for diminished responsibility - the burden of proof is on the defendant, which goes against the principle of 'innocent until proven guilty'.

Scenario

SummerScales for Justice is a local law firm dealing with criminal law and you have approached the firm requesting a summer placement. Mrs Summerscales is one of the senior partners, who has set you a task to assess your ability before offering a placement.

She wants you to apply the law to the following case.

The case concerns Mr X. He found out that his son's drug dealer had threatened that the son would 'get a slap' if he tried to buy drugs from any other dealer. Mr X took a razor and a shotgun, and went to the dealer's house. He then inflicted serious injuries on the dealer using the razor and then as he left, Mr X fired the shotgun. The cause of death established in court was that the shot had hit a wire fence and particles from the fence had ricocheted and killed the dealer.

1. Identify which offences apply to this case and explain your reasoning.
2. Explain *actus reus* and then determine the *actus reus* in this case.
3. Explain *mens rea* and then determine the *mens rea* in this case.
4. Explain causation and determine whether there is a link between Mr X's action and the death.
5. Identify and explain any relevant partial defences.
6. Apply any of the relevant tests for the partial defence(s) to the actual case.
7. What is the likely charge for Mr X? Explain why.
8. What are the consequences to be faced by Mr X?

Where possible, use relevant case law examples or statutory provisions to illustrate the points you are making.

Assessment practice 3.1 A01

Lookout is a magazine focusing on current and controversial issues. This month's edition features the following case. The defendant has been given a fictitious name to preserve her anonymity.

Gemma's Story

Gemma had a difficult childhood and ran away from home at the age of 16. She was extremely vulnerable when she met and began a relationship with a man in his mid-thirties. He drank excessively and would become violent towards Gemma when he was drunk. This continued for two years. Gemma suffered from such physical and mental health issues that she decided to commit suicide. One evening, she took two knives from the kitchen drawer and took them to the bedroom. However, she heard her drunken partner entering the house and, in a panic, hid the knives under her legs. Her partner came to the bedroom. Fearing another beating, she took out the knives and stabbed him.

Explain and apply the law relating to fatal offences to this case. You should evaluate the possibility of a murder charge and the possibility of a voluntary manslaughter charge. Analyse the partial defences and the likely consequences for Gemma.

Plan

- I need to spend time planning my approach to the task, including research.
- I need to consider how the key facts of the case relate back to the law.
- I understand the legal complexities and concepts related to this case.
- I know how to access the resources I shall need to complete this task.

Do

- I need to relate the facts of the case to the law.
- I need to keep detailed notes and discuss any difficulties with my tutor.
- I need to think back to any discussions in class and use my notes to help with this task.

Review

- I can apply my knowledge of the law to a new case.
- I can discuss the law relating to voluntary manslaughter.

The laws relating to involuntary manslaughter

Involuntary manslaughter

Involuntary manslaughter occurs when the defendant lacks *mens rea* for murder. They had no intention to kill and may not have had any intention to harm the victim. There are two types of involuntary manslaughter:

- gross negligence manslaughter – this is where the defendant is so careless that their conduct that causes death is classed as criminal. An example could be a qualified electrician who repairs a cooker leaving live wires that electrocute the owner.
- unlawful act manslaughter – this is where someone is killed when the defendant was in the course of committing another crime, also known as constructive manslaughter. An example could be a burglar knocking an old man over in his home, who then suffers a fatal head injury.

Key term

Involuntary manslaughter – a death that occurs when the defendant had no intention to kill, or perhaps even harm, the victim.

Unlawful act manslaughter

For this offence to be defined as unlawful act manslaughter, liability is built up from a lesser crime – for example, if the defendant intended to commit an armed robbery and killed someone while carrying out the offence. The requirements of this offence are:

- the act committed was deliberate and criminally unlawful
- the act committed was dangerous
- the act committed caused the death of the victim.

Unlawful act

The unlawful act committed must be a crime and not a civil wrong. Some examples of constructive manslaughter are shown in Figure 3.3.

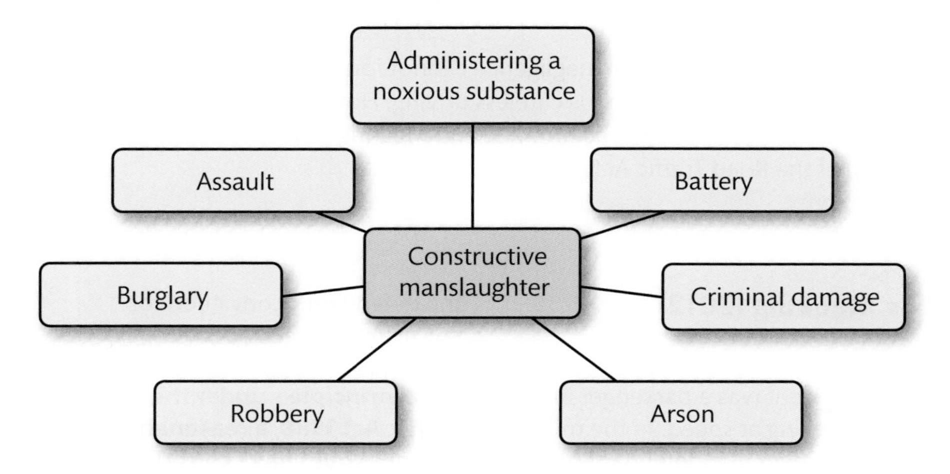

Figure 3.3 Examples of unlawful act manslaughter

The defendant must have the *mens rea* for the criminal act, but the prosecution does not need to prove that the defendant intended the result. In other words, the defendant need not have foreseen or intended death or harm, as illustrated in the following case.

Key case

R v Ball (1989)

Facts

The defendant took two cartridges from his pocket containing both live and blank cartridges. He loaded a shotgun and fired at the victim stating that his aim was only to frighten her. The cartridge in the gun was a live one and the victim died. The defendant was convicted of unlawful act manslaughter.

Legal principle – the defendant's act was deliberate and criminally unlawful. The test for whether the act was dangerous is not based on the defendant's viewpoint but on an objective test.

In DPP v Newbury 1977, the defendant pushed a paving stone from a bridge into the path of an approaching train. The train was struck and a guard was killed. The defendant committed a deliberate and positive act by pushing the stone over the bridge; the act would have constituted criminal damage, which is a crime; the act was dangerous and caused death. All of the requirements of constructive manslaughter were present.

For unlawful act manslaughter, the *actus reus* has to be a positive act and not an omission, which would be likely to fall under gross negligence manslaughter. The unlawful act committed must be a crime and not a civil wrong.

Key case

R v Lamb (1967)

Facts

The defendant pointed a gun at his friend in fun. He was aware that the gun was loaded with two bullets in a five-chamber cylinder but thought the gun would not fire unless a bullet was opposite the barrel. He knew that there was no bullet opposite the barrel but was unaware of the fact that the cylinder revolved when the trigger was pulled. The defendant pulled the trigger and a shot was fired, which killed his friend. The Court of Appeal held that there was no assault and therefore no unlawful act.

Legal principle – for unlawful act manslaughter, there must be a criminal act.

Crimes requiring the *mens rea* of negligence cannot form the basis of constructive manslaughter. An example of this is careless driving. However, in R v Meeking (2012) the unlawful act was a road traffic offence: 'endangering road users contrary to section 22(A)(1)(b) of the Road Traffic Act 1988 as amended'.

Key case

R v Meeking (2012)

Facts

The defendant was a passenger in a car travelling at speed. In the middle of an argument, the defendant pulled the handbrake to stop the car. The car spun and collided with another vehicle. Her husband, the driver, was killed. The Court of Appeal upheld the defendant's conviction for constructive manslaughter.

Legal principle – under the Road Traffic Act 1988, a reasonable person would have considered the defendant's actions of intentionally and unlawfully interfering with a motor vehicle as dangerous.

Dangerous act

The test to determine whether the act of the defendant is dangerous is objective. The reasonable person must recognise that the act of the defendant would cause the other person 'some harm', but the defendant does not need to foresee the exact type of harm.

There must be a risk of physical harm - a risk of emotional upset is not enough. However, in the case of R v Dhaliwal (2006), the Court of Appeal took into account physical or psychiatric harm when deciding whether the act of the defendant was dangerous. The type of harm and whether it had to be reasonably forseeable was further discussed in R v M (2012) summarised below.

Key case

R v JM and SM (2012)

Facts

The defendants were removed from a nightclub by the doormen. They later returned and assaulted the doormen. The victim, Mr Jopling, intervened and, due to a pre-existing condition, collapsed and died. Evidence was produced that the collapse was brought about by the shock and a sudden surge of blood pressure. The trial judge stated that this type of injury was different to what would normally be related to a fight, suggesting that the defendants should not be convicted of unlawful act manslaughter. The Court of Appeal overturned the trial judge's decision and stated that the reasonable person observing the affray 'would readily have recognised that all the doormen involved in the effort to control the defendants were at the risk of some harm, and that the fatal injury occurred while it was in progress or in its immediate aftermath while Mr Jopling was still subject to its effects'. The defendants were convicted of an unlawful act of manslaughter.

Legal principle - neither the defendant nor the reasonable person need to foresee any specific harm or the type of harm that was the result.

Causing the death of the victim

If the act committed by the defendant causes death, the courts would apply factual and legal causation. An intervening act might break the chain of causation, and this point has been argued in cases involving the supply of drugs such as R v Cato (1976).

Key case

R v Cato (1976)

Facts

The defendant injected the victim with heroin supplied by the victim. The victim died as a result of the injection. The defendant was convicted of manslaughter based on the unlawful act of administering a noxious substance.

The Court of Appeal held that injecting the victim was an unlawful act and upheld the conviction.

Legal principle - the defendant had unlawfully taken the heroin into his possession and had done an unlawful act.

The decision in R v Cato (1976) has been criticised because it linked the defendant's conduct to the end result (causation). Further problems have occurred when the defendant has prepared the injection, passed the syringe over and the victim has self-injected, as seen in R v Kennedy (2007).

Key case

R v Kennedy (2007)

Facts

The defendant prepared a mixture of heroin and water for the victim. He handed the syringe to the victim who injected himself, handed the syringe back and died. The defendant was convicted of unlawful act manslaughter. After two appeals to the Court of Appeal, the House of Lords quashed the conviction stating that the defendant had not committed an unlawful act and that the victim exercised free will in injecting himself, breaking the chain of causation.

Legal principle - self-injection by the victim breaks the chain of causation.

Scenario

You are on your placement at a law firm and have been given a summary of the facts of a current case, which the firm have passed on to a barrister to represent the client at a Crown Court trial.

The defendant is Mr G. It has been alleged that he had set fire to his council flat because he wanted the council to rehouse him in a larger property. The fire became out of control and his wife, his two-year-old son and another woman were killed in the fire.

You have to make notes on whether this case will lead to a conviction for murder, voluntary manslaughter or involuntary manslaughter and justify your decision.

Determine the *actus reus* and likely *mens rea*.

Explain the relevant area of law and refer to any tests used to determine liability. Apply any tests to the scenario relating to Mr G.

Check your responses by researching R v Goodfellow (1986).

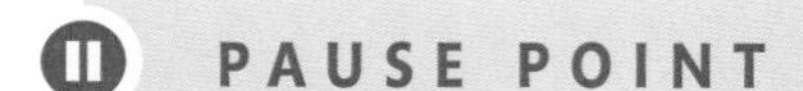

PAUSE POINT Produce a table to compare and contrast the offences of murder, voluntary manslaughter and involuntary manslaughter

Hint You could find examples of current or recent cases reported by the media to illustrate each type of offence.

Extend Research the human rights related to such offences.

Gross negligence manslaughter

Negligence means acting carelessly, but this definition is not enough for criminal liability. The negligence has to be gross. In other words, the negligence has to be so bad that the actions of the defendant are considered to be criminal.

The current tests applied in a gross negligence case were established in a case called R v Adomako (1995). The four relevant questions are as follows.

- Did the defendant owe the victim a duty of care?
- Did the defendant breach that duty of care?
- Did the breach of duty cause the death of the victim?
- Were the actions of the defendant so grossly negligent that they could be classed as criminal?

Foresight of the consequences is not required of the defendant, just of the reasonable person, but the jury may take into account whether the defendant's acts were influenced by factors such as stress, inexperience, mistake or confusion.

Key case

R v Adomako (1995)

Facts

The defendant was an anaesthetist and his role was to ensure that a patient undergoing an operation was safe and able to breathe while under anaesthetic. A tube supplying the patient with oxygen became disconnected. The defendant failed to notice the problem for four and a half minutes and he then misdiagnosed the situation. Evidence showed that a competent anaesthetist would have been aware of the problem within 15 seconds.

Legal principle – all of the elements for gross negligence were present in this case and confirmed by the House of Lords.

Duty of care

Sometimes the existence of a duty of care is obvious. For example, a duty of care exists between:

- a parent for their children
- a teacher for their students
- a doctor for their patients
- an employer for an employee
- a motorist for other road users.

Where it is difficult to decide whether there is a duty of care relationship, the courts have to decide whether it was reasonably foreseeable that the actions of the defendant would cause the death of the victim.

Reflect

For each duty of care relationship listed, give an example of the type of behaviour that could breach their duty of care and cause death. Can you think of any other obvious duty of care relationships?

Key case

R v Winter (2010)

Facts

The director and an employee of a fireworks company were held to owe a duty of care for a cameraman who worked for the fire services. The cameraman attended a fire to make a film for training purposes and was killed when a box of hazardous fireworks exploded. The director and employee were convicted of gross negligence manslaughter but appealed stating that they didn't owe a duty of care to the cameraman. The Court of Appeal upheld their conviction as it was reasonably foreseeable that a cameraman working for the fire service might film or photograph the site of the fire.

Legal principle – the test used to determine a duty of care relationship is reasonable foreseeability.

Breach of duty

The *mens rea* of a defendant on a charge of gross negligence manslaughter is negligence and carelessness, but the focus in these cases is whether the actions or conduct of the defendant were grossly negligent. An objective test is used to determine whether the act is grossly negligent, which is decided by the jury. The degree of negligence for the objective test was addressed in R v Misra and Srivastava (2004). The test was confirmed as whether the reasonable person would have foreseen a serious and obvious risk of death.

A recent and particularly disturbing case was when a child of four, Hamza Khan, had been found in his cot. He had starved to death and his body was found in September 2011, but he had died in 2009. The house was in squalor and five other siblings of school age lived in the house. The mother, who was addicted to alcohol, admitted child cruelty. She also admitted the charge of preventing the burial of a corpse. The jury, after five hours of deliberation found her guilty of gross negligence manslaughter. The law applied to the case as shown in Table 3.6.

Table 3.6: The law applied to the case of Hamza Khan

Duty of care	Breach of duty	Causing death	Grossly negligent to be classed as criminal
Established – parent and child	Failing to feed the child or care for the child sufficiently	The child died from malnutrition	A CPS spokesman referred to the death of the child as a 'horrific crime'

The breach of duty causing death

Legal and factual causation would be applied to any case of gross negligence manslaughter, as in the case of R v Wacker (2003).

Key case

R v Wacker (2003)

Facts

A lorry driver had hidden 60 Chinese illegal immigrants in his lorry so that they could be transported to England via the port of Dover. He had negligently closed the ventilation to the airtight container and when the lorry was searched in Dover, 58 of the immigrants had suffocated. The defendant was convicted of gross negligence manslaughter.

Legal principle – the factual causation was that if the ventilator to the container had not been closed, the immigrants would have survived.

Scenario

You are really enjoying your placement at the law firm, so much so that in your spare time you have been researching and reading up on fatal offences. It is the weekend and you have met up with a group of friends. They show you the following article from the local newspaper and have asked you to explain what happened in simple, easy to understand language.

Cellar death at Rave Bar

Mr B, manager of Rave Bar in Market Street, Bedlam, has been found guilty of manslaughter at Bedlam Crown Court. He will be sentenced at a hearing next month. Johnny had visited the bar with a group of friends. They thought he had left the bar, but Johnny had mistaken the cellar door for the toilets. The door was neither locked nor had any signs and Johnny fell to the foot of the stairs. Johnny's body was found four days later after his family had reported him missing. Rave Bar had been closed as Mr B was attending a training course. The jury were informed that Johnny had remained conscious but concussed for approximately four hours, crawling around the cellar.

1. Explain what type of manslaughter has taken place and what has to be proved.
2. Apply the law to Mr B's case.
3. Identify how Mr B could have avoided this situation.
4. Research and explain two other similar recent cases.

A car destroyed by dangerous driving was put on public display in July 2016 as part of a campaign for tougher sentences. The driver of this vehicle was using social media at the time of the fatal accident, he ran a red light and ploughed into a pedestrian killing him instantly.

 PAUSE POINT

Produce a list of actions that you think would fall into the category of dangerous driving.

Hint You could then compare your list to those listed on the CPS Dangerous Driving fact sheet.

Extend How could the risk of fatal accidents caused by dangerous driving be reduced?

Corporate manslaughter

In law, a company is classed as having its own **legal personality**, which means that it can operate just like an individual. For example, it can make contracts, buy property and sue or be sued by other individuals or companies. It is the owners and employees who act on behalf of the company because the company itself has no mind or body. In certain circumstances, a company can also be criminally liable, but there are certain offences it cannot be charged with, for example, rape, **bigamy** and **perjury**. A company cannot be criminally liable if the only punishment available is prison or community service.

When a crime requires proof of *mens rea*, such as manslaughter, it is difficult to apply liability to a company. In cases regarding corporate manslaughter, the courts have used the **principle of identification** to do this. The principle of identification meant that a person had to be found within the company who was 'the directing mind and will of the company'. This can be found in the case of R v Kite and OLL Ltd (1994)

Key term

Legal personality – a company can operate legally, like an individual. For example, it can make contracts, buy property, sue or be sued by other individuals or companies in its' own right.

Bigamy – marrying a person while still legally married to another person.

Perjury – telling lies while under oath in court.

The principle of identification – a person has to be found within the company who was 'the directing mind and will of the company'.

Key case

R v Kite and OLL Ltd (1994)

Facts

The defendant was the managing director of a small company that provided outdoor activity holidays for students. A group of sixth-form students were staying at the centre for five days and were canoeing in Lyme Bay when the weather worsened. Four of the group died when their canoes capsized. The court heard how the manager had been warned about his methods and inadequate safety. At the time of the incident, the students were given inadequate instructions from inexperienced instructors. Both the managing director and the company were convicted.

Legal principle – Mr Kite was the directing mind and will of the company under the principle of identification.

However, the problems with the method of finding the principle of identification are:

- The bigger the company, the more difficult it is to find this 'directing mind and will'.
- Where several people have contributed to a dangerous situation, the principle will not work.

In the 1980s and 1990s, several disasters occurred where it was clear that the companies involved were seriously at fault and were grossly negligent. However, a conviction could not be secured because of the principle of identification.

Research

Research one of the following disasters and extract evidence of serious failures or gross negligence by the companies involved.

- The Herald of Free Enterprise Disaster 1987
- Kings Cross Fire 1987
- Piper Alpha Fire 1988
- Marchioness Disaster 1989
- Southall Rail Crash 1997

What was the main problem with corporate manslaughter before the law changed in 2007?

The lack of successful convictions, and the fact that directors were more likely to be punished for financial irregularities rather than for causing death, led to campaigns and calls for change.

One such campaign group was Families Against Corporate Killings (FACK). They called for justice for the families of those killed at work as a result of negligence, and they wanted better law and stricter enforcement. They also wanted charges, convictions and penalties in the courts to act as a real deterrent in order to prevent needless deaths in the workplace.

In 1996, the Law Commission recommended a separate offence of corporate killing based on management failure in a company to provide a safe system of conducting the company's activities. The Corporate Manslaughter and Corporate Homicide Act 2007 came into force in April 2008.

The Corporate Manslaughter and Corporate Homicide Act 2007

An organisation is only guilty of an offence if the way in which its activities are managed or organised by its senior management is a major element of the breach. The Corporate Manslaughter and Corporate Homicide Act 2007 replaced the common law in relation to corporate manslaughter. For the purposes of the Act, an organisation includes companies, various public bodies, the police and partnerships.

Section 1 of the Act states that an organisation is guilty of an offence if the way in which its activities are managed or organised:

- causes a person's death
- amounts to a gross breach of a relevant duty of care owed by the organisation to the deceased.

Causation

The act does not define causation, but the established tests for factual and legal causation apply.

Duty

The Act lists some examples of relevant duty of care relationships such as employer and employee, occupier of premises and visitors/suppliers of goods or services/ consumers. The Act also notes the duties connected to construction and maintenance and the keeping or using of plant, vehicles or other things.

Proof of gross breach of duty

The breach of duty must fall below the standard of what would reasonably be expected of the organisation. Section 8 of the Act states factors that the jury must consider:

- how serious the breach was
- how much of a risk of death it posed.

The jury may also take the following into account:

- breach of health and safety laws
- guidance issued by enforcement agencies and company policies
- attitudes, systems or accepted practices that could have contributed to the breach.

The breach must be directly linked to serious management failure.

Proof of serious management failure

Senior management is defined to mean 'persons who play a significant role in the management of the whole or a substantial part, of the organisations' activities', as stated in s1 of the Homicide Act 2007.

What serious management failure is will become clearer as more corporate manslaughter cases are dealt with by the courts. Some examples of serious management failure can be identified in the cases that follow.

Key case

R v Cotswold Geotechnical Holdings (2011)

Facts

The victim was an employee of Cotswold Geotechnical Holdings. He was working alone in a deep trench when it collapsed and killed him. This was the first conviction under the Corporate Manslaughter and Corporate Homicide Act 2007 and the company was fined £385,000.

Legal principle – the serious management failure was that the company's system of work for digging trial pits was 'wholly and unnecessarily dangerous' and that industry guidelines had been ignored.

Key case

R v Lion Steel Ltd (2012)

Facts

The victim was an employee of Lion Steel Ltd. He was sent on to a roof to make repairs. He fell through a fibreglass section and died. The company pleaded guilty and was fined £480,000.

Legal principle – the serious management failure was that the company failed to provide suitable supervision, training and safety equipment.

Key case

R v Pyranha Mouldings Ltd (2015)

Facts

The victim was an employee of Pyranha Mouldings Ltd. He was working inside an industrial oven used in the manufacture of kayaks. While inside, the oven was switched on and the employee was trapped with no means of escape and no alarm. The unique design of the oven meant that the moment the oven was switched on the doors automatically closed and locked to save energy. The company was responsible for its safety. The company was fined £200,000 and a director was given a nine-month prison sentence, suspended for two years and fined £25,000.

Legal principle – the serious management failure was the 'fundamentally unsafe' maintenance work and the choice of this particular design of oven.

Key case

R v Baldwins Crane Hire Ltd (2015)

Facts

The victim was an employee of Baldwins Crane Hire Ltd. He died when the 16-wheel and 130-tonne crane he was driving crashed. The auxiliary brakes had been disconnected. The company was fined £700,000.

Legal principle - the serious management failure was that the crane had serious braking problems due to lack of maintenance.

Key case

R v Sherwood Rise Ltd (2016)

Facts

An elderly resident developed pneumonia and died weighing just 3 stone 12 pounds. Yousaf Khan, a director of the care home, pleaded guilty to a charge of corporate manslaughter. The defendant was sentenced to three years and two months in prison and disqualified from being a director for eight years.

Legal principle - the serious management failure was that despite warnings from outside agencies, he failed to ensure adequate care, nutrition, accommodation and support for this person.

Key term

Coroner's inquest - an investigation in a Coroners court to determine the cause of death.

Investigation, prosecution and penalties under the Act

When it is thought that an offence of manslaughter (either corporate or individual) has been committed, the police will take the lead in a joint investigation carried out by the police and the Health and Safety Executive (HSE). The police will help the **coroner's inquest** by establishing the circumstances surrounding a work-related death. The police have powers of arrest and refer cases to the Crown Prosecution Service (CPS) for review.

The HSE or another relevant authority, such as a local authority, will also investigate to identify potential breaches of health and safety law. Arrangements have to be made for a family liaison officer and a health and safety inspector to visit the bereaved family and to keep them informed of updates to the case.

Prosecution

The CPS is responsible for decisions about prosecution. The HSE may assist by providing information on relevant health and safety legislation, codes and guidance and suitably qualified HSE employees may provide expert opinion. The CPS makes the final decision.

Penalties

Following a conviction for corporate manslaughter, penalties may include a fine, a remedial order or a publicity order:

- There is no upper limit for fines. Guidance states that they should be high but also capable of being paid.
- A remedial order requires the company to address the serious management failure and fix the cause of the fatality.

- A publicity order requires the company to publicise:
  - the fact that it has been convicted of the offence of corporate manslaughter
  - the details of the offence
  - the fine imposed
  - the terms of any remedial order.

PAUSE POINT How important is health and safety at work? Why do some organisations cut corners when it comes to health and safety?

Hint You could research the latest statistics relating to fatalities at work on the HSE website.

Extend If you were the director of a large company, what would you do to make sure that all of your employees were safe?

Assessment practice 3.2

A02

You have noticed another interesting news report:

£600,000 Fine for Corporate Manslaughter

CAV Aerospace Ltd have been convicted of corporate manslaughter. Mr B died when a stack of metal sheets collapsed on top of him in a warehouse. He was trapped and crushed. The metal sheets had been delivered at the company's request but collapsed due to high levels of stock being stored in the warehouse. Senior management had received warnings over a period of years, which had also been made just prior to this incident. They had rejected any potential solutions to the storage problems based on the costs involved. Mr B had only recently been employed by the company and his death is a tragic loss.

The fine imposed was £600,000 and a further fine of £400,000 for breaking health and safety laws, plus costs of £125,000.

Explain and apply the law of Corporate Manslaughter to this case, using case law and statutory provisions where appropriate. Take into account the principles of duty of care, gross breach and serious management failure.

Plan

- I need to be clear what the law of corporate manslaughter is.
- I need to be clear what the principles of duty of care, gross breach and serious management failure are.
- I need to research what a publicity order contains so that I can be confident when writing my own for this case.

Do

- I need to organise my answer to include some discussion of each principle.
- I need to pick out the relevant parts of the case and apply them to the law of corporate manslaughter.

Review

- I can apply the law of corporate manslaughter to this case.
- I can pick relevant case law and statutory provisions to back up the points I am making.

C An introduction to offences against property: theft, robbery, burglary, fraud and criminal damage

Property crime includes situations where the aim is to steal or damage property. These types of offence made up 70 per cent of all police recorded crime in England and Wales in 2014–15. Many of the recorded property offences involved the theft of money, wallets and purses, although valuable electronic devices have become a popular target.

In general, the statistics show a decrease in relation to vehicle theft, criminal damage and domestic burglaries. One explanation for this is that people have become more security conscious and new technology can be used to make thefts more difficult and therefore less desirable to the **perpetrator**.

Statistics show that an area of increasing crime is **fraud** and **cybercrime**. In 2014–15, the National Fraud Intelligence Bureau recorded 600,000 victims of these crimes in the UK, compared with 79,000 victims of theft from the person recorded by the police.

Key terms

Perpetrator – a person who commits a crime.

Fraud – criminal deception intended to result in either financial or personal gain.

Cybercrime – criminal offences committed via the Internet or aided by computer technology.

Research

Research the latest property crime statistics and find out who is most likely to be a victim.

Shoplifting also showed a slight increase, accounting for 11 per cent of all recorded property crime in 2014–15 (a total of 326,440 offences).

Offences against property do not simply mean 'someone being robbed'. These offences cover theft, robbery, burglary or fraud. Each of these is different and requires different elements to be proved.

Theft: Sections 1–6 of the Theft Act 1968

Discussion

What are your most treasured possessions?

How would you feel if they were taken from you?

Criminal law seeks to protect not only people but also property. The main Acts dealing with property offences are the Theft Acts 1968 and 1978, which were amended in 1996.

Theft is defined in Section 1 of the Theft Act 1968 as follows: 'A person is guilty of theft if he dishonestly appropriates property belonging to another with the intention of permanently depriving the other of it.'

Sections 2–6 of the Act aim to clarify parts of this definition, with each section relating to either *actus reus* or *mens rea*, as shown in Table 3.7.

Table 3.7: The sections of the Theft Act 1968 and the areas they are related to

Section	Related to
2 - Dishonesty	*Mens rea*
3 - Appropriation	*Actus reus*
4 - Property	*Actus reus*
5 - Belonging to another	*Actus reus*
6 - Intention to permanently deprive	*Mens rea*

Actus reus of theft

Section 3 - Appropriation

Discussion

Collect news reports of recent, local theft offences and discuss how Sections 1 and 3 of the Theft Act apply to each case.

Appropriation means taking, using or assuming any of the owners' rights of something that does not belong to you. For example, if you borrow a very expensive law textbook from your tutor, you might assume the owner's rights by selling it, keeping it, lending it to somebody else or destroying it. It is more than just simply taking the book. Appropriation also covers situations where the defendant has come across the property innocently and later assumes any of the rights of the owner.

Appropriation can be more than just taking the property and this is illustrated in the following case.

Key case

R v Morris (1983)

Facts

The defendant had switched the price labels on goods in a supermarket in order to pay a lower price. He had taken the goods to the checkout and was arrested. He was convicted of theft and appealed but his conviction was upheld.

Legal principle - the court held that there does not have to be an assumption of all of the rights of the owner. The assumption of any of the rights of the owner will suffice.

The issue as to whether the appropriation could be authorised was addressed in a case called R v Gomez (1993).

Key case

R v Gomez (1993)

Facts

The defendant was an assistant manager in an electrical shop. He was asked to supply goods to the value of £17,000 to an acquaintance in exchange for two cheques, which he knew were stolen. The defendant persuaded the shop manager that the cheques were authentic even though they had no value. The defendant was convicted of theft and, on appeal the House of Lords, it was held that an appropriation had taken place even though the manager consented to supplying the goods.

Legal principle - an appropriation does not need absence of consent.

Borrowed property can become stolen property if the borrower later assumes the rights of the owner. For example, Jack borrows a book from his law tutor. She gave him permission to take the book home and use it until the end of the course. Jack made good use of the book and passed his law exam with flying colours. At this point, he had finished his college course, and knew he should return the book, but could not be bothered. Instead, he sold it on an Internet shopping site. Jack was behaving within the law until he interfered with the owners' rights by offering to sell the book.

Section 4 - Property

The Theft Act 1968 defines property as 'money and all other property, real or personal, including things in action and other intangible property'. Each point of this definition can be broken down further.

- Money - coins and bank notes in any currency.
- Personal property - moveable items, such as mobile phones, tablets, jewellery, cars, and also larger items like container ships. Very small items such as a packet of chewing gum or a pencil sharpener also fall into this category.
- Real property - land and buildings.
- Things in action - things such as debts, a credit balance in a bank account or an overdraft facility.
- Other intangible property -includes other rights that have no physical presence, such as gas or a patent.

Things that can't be stolen include flowers, fruit, foliage and fungi that grow in the wild. Foraging is allowed provided it is not for reward, sale or a commercial purpose. Wild creatures cannot be stolen.

When property is received by mistake, there is a legal obligation to give back the property. This can be seen in the case of Attorney General's reference (No 1 of 1983) (1985).

Key case

Attorney General's reference (No 1 of 1983) (1985)

Facts

The defendant had her salary paid into a bank account. Her employer by mistake had overpaid her to the value of £74.74. She was charged with theft but acquitted by the jury. The prosecution asked the Court of Appeal to clarify the law.

Legal principle - in this type of case there is an obligation to make restoration. If there is a dishonest intention not to make restoration, the case would be theft.

Section 5 - Belonging to another

This part of the definition of theft is given a wide meaning in Section 5 – 'property shall be regarded as belonging to any person having possession or control of it, or having in it any proprietary right or interest.'

Although the owner of property will normally be in possession and control of it, there are exceptions, for example if you borrow an item, or hire something. This issue was dealt with in R v Turner (no 2) (1971).

Key case

R v Turner (no 2) (1971)

Facts

The defendant left his car at a garage to be repaired and agreed to pay for the repairs on completion. The garage owner parked the car on the road outside the garage overnight when the repairs were complete and the defendant took his car using a spare set of keys. He had not paid for the repairs and had not gained the consent of the garage owner to remove it. The defendant was convicted of theft.

Legal principle – it is possible for someone to be convicted of stealing property that they own, if someone else has possession or control of it.

Mens reas of theft

Part of the *mens rea* of theft is that the defendant has to be acting dishonestly. The motive behind the theft is irrelevant. This can be shown in the following example:

- Simon took someone else's coat from the cloakroom that was similar to his own by mistake. This is not a dishonest act.
- Simon had a very old and shabby coat. If he decided to take the coat that was of the best quality and the most expensive instead of his own, this is a dishonest act.
- Simon decided to take a coat that was of the best quality and the most expensive instead of his own to give it to a homeless person. This is a dishonest act. The motive may be kind, but would still amount to theft.

Section 2 - Dishonesty

The Act provides three examples that would not be dishonest.

- The defendant believed they had a right to deprive the other of the property.
- The defendant believed the other would have consented if they knew of the appropriation and the circumstances.
- The person to whom the property belongs cannot be traced by taking reasonable steps.

In each of these examples, a subjective test is used and the defendant has to have a genuine belief to be considered not dishonest, even if the belief is unreasonable. Deciding whether a defendant is dishonest may not be straightforward. Over the years, the courts have provided guidelines established from decided cases such as R v Ghosh (1982).

The Ghosh Test attempts to answer the following questions.

- Were the actions of the defendant dishonest by the standards of reasonable and honest people, and if so
- Did the defendant know it was dishonest by those standards?

This test has been criticised as being too complicated and that there is no universal standard of dishonesty.

Key case

R v Ghosh (1982)

Facts

The defendant was a temporary doctor at a hospital and had to claim his own fees. He claimed for an operation that had not taken place. He claimed he was not dishonest because he was owed equivalent to those fees for consultations with patients. He was found to be dishonest and appealed. The Court of Appeal upheld his conviction and established a test for dishonesty.

Legal principle – the Ghosh test for dishonesty starts with an objective element, followed by a subjective element.

Section 6 – intention to permanently deprive

The intention to permanently deprive forms part of the *mens rea* of theft, along with dishonesty.

Section 6 of the Theft Act gives two examples of when a defendant will be considered to have intention to permanently deprive the owner of the property:

- where the defendant intends to treat the property as their own to dispose of without regard to the rights of the owner
- where borrowing or lending is equivalent to an outright taking or disposal.

Theft is a triable either way offence and the maximum sentence is seven years' imprisonment.

The following case shows that a defendant who treats property as their own can be classed as having intention to permanently deprive the owner.

Key case

R v Lavender (1994)

Facts

The defendant took off some doors from a council property, which was due to be demolished. He then fitted the doors in a property occupied by his girlfriend. This was also a council property. The defendant was convicted of theft.

Legal principle – treating the property as his own regardless of ownership amounted to an intention to permanently deprive the owner.

In the following case, the property was tickets sold by London underground – known as a chose in action (refers to property that can only be claimed or enforced by action), the tickets created a right that was appropriated.

Key case

R v Marshall (1999)

Facts

The defendant had obtained underground tickets from people leaving the underground and sold them on to others. London underground insisted that they had a right to expect that only the original purchaser would use the ticket. This right was disregarded by the defendant who was convicted of theft.

Legal principle – disregarding the rights of the owners amounted to intention to permanently deprive.

Scenario

Kamil, aged 16, and his brother Aleksy, aged 19, were home alone as their parents had gone on holiday. The two brothers wanted to raise money for a weekend of partying. They decided to sell the television and computer to get some extra cash.

1. Have they committed an offence?
2. Explain and apply Sections 2 to 6 of the Theft Act 1968 to their case.
3. Advise the brothers as to the potential consequences of their behaviour.

PAUSE POINT Create a visual memo depicting the contents of ss2 to 6 above, which could be a diagram or poster.

Hint Make your poster or diagram colourful and attractive so that when you visualise your creation, it will jog your memory about the law of theft.

Extend For each section, think about possible prosecution and defence arguments that could be used in court.

Robbery: Section 8 of the Theft Act 1968

In the Theft Act 1968, robbery is defined as follows:

> A person is guilty of robbery if he steals, and immediately before or at the time of doing so, and in order to do so, he uses force on any person or puts or seeks to put any person in fear of being then and there subjected to force.

In simple terms, robbery is the use of force, or the threatening of force, to commit a theft.

Actus reus of robbery

To be convicted of robbery, all the elements of theft must be present.

- A completed theft is an essential component of robbery. A completed theft means that all elements of theft are present. The wasn't proved in the case of R v Robinson (1977).

Key case

R v Robinson (1977)

Facts

The defendant was owed £7 from the victim's wife. He approached the victim to demand the money and threatened the victim. During a struggle, the victim dropped a five-pound note. The defendant took the note, claiming that he was still owed two pounds. The defendant was convicted of robbery but the Court of Appeal reversed the conviction as all of the elements of theft were not present. The defendant was not dishonest because he believed he had a right to the money.

Legal principle – all of the elements of theft have to be present for a conviction of robbery.

- The second requirement is that force must be used. The threat of force can be explicit or implied by gestures. Force was used in the case of R v Clouden (1987).

Key case

R v Clouden (1987)

Facts

The victim was carrying a shopping bag, which was wrenched from her hand by the defendant. The defendant was convicted of robbery.

Legal principle – the jury decides on what amounts to force, but the amount of force used can be small.

- The force can be directed at any person and not necessarily at the owner of the property.

Key case

Smith v Desmond (1965)

Facts

The defendants were carrying out a robbery from a bakery. The two men at the bakery were an engineer and a security guard; they were tied up and blindfolded. The defendants then took £10,447 from the safe.

Legal principle – the House of Lords ruled that the defendant had rightly been convicted of robbery.

- There must be a threat or use of force immediately before or at the time of stealing. This requirement has been challenged when there has been a delay between the threats and the theft, or where the theft has occurred before the threats or use of force. The case of R v Lockley (1995) shows this.

Key case

R v Lockley (1995)

Facts

The defendant had stolen some cans of beer from an off-licence. He used force on the shop assistant who was trying to prevent him from leaving.

The defendant was convicted of robbery. His appeal based on the fact that the force was after the stealing was dismissed.

Legal principle – theft can be classed as a continuing act.

- The force must be used in order to steal. This is similar to the previous point, but the timing of when the defendant formed an intention to permanently deprive the owner and the timing of the use or threat of force is important. For example, during an argument, one person threatens and then kicks the other. The victim is stunned and drops his mobile, and, seeing an opportunity, the attacker takes the phone. Here the force used was not in order to steal.

Mens rea of robbery

The *mens rea* of robbery is dishonesty and intention for theft and an intention or recklessness as to the use of force.

Scenario

One of the partners at the law firm has asked you to take notes in a meeting with a potential client. She is asking for advice about a particular situation that occurred the previous week. She is really upset as her 15-year-old son is being bullied at school. Five or six boys from his year group approached him. They asked him for money and he refused. Another five or six boys joined in and her son was surrounded. Two boys held on to his arms while another searched her son and took his wallet, travel pass and mobile phone from his pocket. The group of boys then pushed her son and ran off. She wants to know whether a crime has been committed.

1. Has an offence taken place?
2. Is the offence theft or robbery? Explain why.
3. What is the *actus reus* and *mens rea*?
4. What are the elements of the offence and are they all present?
5. What advice would you give to this lady?
6. Compare your answer to the case of B and R v DPP (2007).

Burglary: Section 9 of the Theft Act 1968

Section 9(1)(a) and (b) provides two offences of burglary.

- Section 9(1)(a) – A person is guilty of burglary if they enter any building or part of a building as a trespasser with intent to steal or to inflict or attempt to inflict grievous bodily harm or to do unlawful damage.
- Section 9(1)(b) – A person is guilty of burglary if, having entered any building or part of a building, they steal or attempt to steal or inflict or attempt to inflict grievous bodily harm.

Discussion

What are the differences and similarities of the two offences of burglary?

▶ Why is the sentence possibly greater if a home is burgled as opposed to business premises?

The common elements of the *actus reus* are that the defendant must enter a building or part of a building as a trespasser. Each element can be broken down further.

Entry

In most cases, the *actus reus* will be obvious, for example, where someone has broken into a house or factory to steal property, or where someone has gone behind a counter in a shop to take money from the till.

Entry can also include entering into a building by just part of the body, for example, smashing a window and reaching inside to steal items, as seen in R v Ryan (1996).

Key case

R v Ryan (1996)

Facts

The defendant had tried to enter a building at 2.30 a.m. but had got stuck. His head and one arm were through the window and the window was resting on his neck. When he was discovered, the fire service had to be called to release him. He was convicted of burglary and appealed on grounds that most of his body was outside. His conviction was upheld.

Legal principle – entry could involve part of the body and does not depend on whether enough of the body was inside.

A building or part of a building

A building should be reasonably permanent and includes outbuildings such as sheds, garages or greenhouses. A building may also include inhabited vehicles and vessels, which expands the meaning to include caravans, canal barges and campervans if they are being used as a dwelling.

A lawful visitor who has permission to be in one part of a building may become an unlawful visitor (a trespasser) if they enter an area of the building that they are not permitted to enter. For example, anyone can go into a shop or supermarket, but only the staff will have permission to enter the warehouse or stockroom.

Key case

R v Walkington (1979)

Facts

The defendant had noticed that a partly open till had been left unattended in a Debenhams store. He went behind the counter and found that the till was empty. He tried to leave the store but was stopped and arrested. He was convicted but appealed maintaining that because there was nothing to separate the counter from the rest of the store, he was not entering a prohibited part of a building. His conviction was upheld.

Legal principle – a lawful customer becomes a trespasser when entering an unauthorised area such as behind a till.

As a trespasser

A person entering a building is not a trespasser if the owner of the building has given them permission to be there. The permission may be express or implied, covering a customer's rights to enter the public areas of a shop. For criminal law, a trespasser must have the *mens rea* for trespass. The defendant must know or be reckless as to whether they are entering a building without consent. The case of R v Collins (1972) is an example of this.

Key case

R v Collins (1972)

Facts

The defendant had been drinking alcohol. On his way home, he saw an open window. He climbed a ladder to look inside and saw a naked girl asleep. He climbed down the ladder and removed all of his clothes except for his socks and climbed back up the ladder. He was on the windowsill when she awoke and, thinking that it was her boyfriend, she helped him inside and they had sex. The defendant was convicted of burglary as prior to 2003, rape or intending to rape was included in the definition of burglary. The defendant appealed and his conviction was rejected.

Legal principle – if a defendant honestly believed he had consent to enter the building, they cannot be a trespasser.

For both of the offences of burglary in s9 of the Act, the defendant must know or be reckless as to whether they are a trespasser. This is the *mens rea* of burglary.

- For the offence under s9(1)(a), the defendant must have had an intention to commit one of the offences listed at the time of entering the building.
- For the offence in s9(1)(b), the defendant must have the *mens rea* for theft or grievous bodily harm.

The maximum sentence for burglary of a dwelling is 14 years' imprisonment or 10 years if not a dwelling.

Fraud by false representation: Section 2 of the Fraud Act 2006

Under the Theft Acts 1968 and 1978, offences involving deception were very technical and became complicated and confusing. The law relating to fraud has been simplified and is now governed by one statutory offence, which can be committed in three ways as defined in s2 of the Fraud Act 2006.

A person is in breach of this section if they:

- dishonestly make a **false representation**
- intend, by making the representation, to make a gain for themselves or another or to cause a loss to another or to expose another to a risk of loss.

A representation is false if:

- it is untrue or misleading
- the person making it knows that it is, or might be, untrue or misleading.

Something is a representation if it is submitted in any form to any system or device designed to receive, convey or respond to communications (with or without human intervention).

Key term

False representation – making an untrue or incorrect statement or acting in a way to imply one thing while meaning another in order to make a gain or cause a loss.

Actus reus of fraud by false representation

The *actus reus* of fraud is making the false representation. A representation may be made through words or conduct. A representation may be explicit or implied.

Making a false statement through spoken or written communication was illustrated in the following case. The CPS Legal Guidance on the Fraud Act states: 'In most cases this will be the same as the deception under the old Theft Act offences.'

Key case

R v Adams (1993)

Facts

The defendant had filled in a form to hire a car. The form asked two questions: whether he had any previous convictions for motoring offences and whether he had ever been disqualified from driving. The defendant ticked the No box in each case. The defendant was found guilty as he had been disqualified four years before.

Legal principle – the representation made must be false or misleading.

The following case shows that conduct can contribute to making a false representation.

Key case

R v Lambie (1981)

Facts

The defendant went shopping and paid for goods using her credit card knowing that she was over her credit limit. The defendant argued that it was nothing to do with the shop that she was over her limit. The defendant was found guilty.

Legal principle – the act of using the credit card implied that she was authorised to do so.

Express representation

An express representation may be made through words or conduct.

Implied representation

Examples of implied representations are:

- getting into a taxi
- booking a holiday or a hotel room
- ordering food at a restaurant or putting petrol in a car.

In each of these cases, it is implied that someone will pay for goods or services. Using a cheque or debit card implies that the person has a bank account and that funds are available to pay for the goods.

Representations as to fact and law

A representation must be about fact, law or state of mind. It does not include statements of opinion.

Representations as to state of mind

A representation about present intention relates to state of mind. If a person borrows money and says that it is to pay for a wedding, but really they intend to spend the money in a casino, this is falsely representing their state of mind.

Representations as to a machine

Fraudulent transactions made through computers, websites and other forms of new technology are incorporated into the definition in the Fraud Act 2006.

Research

Research the most common Internet scams and ways of avoiding becoming a victim.

Figure 3.4 shows a 5 per cent increase in cases of fraud. The Crime Survey for England and Wales (CSEW) have estimated that there were 5.6 million cases of fraud and computer misuse from October 2015 to September 2016. The most common type of fraud was bank and credit account fraud, totalling 68 per cent of fraud. Non-investment fraud (which includes online shopping scams) accounted for 26 per cent. Other examples include advanced fee fraud and insurance fraud.

Fraud is difficult to measure as it is a deceptive crime that can target both individuals and organisations. Some may be unaware that they are victims and others fail to report such a crime as they are embarrassed that they have been conned.

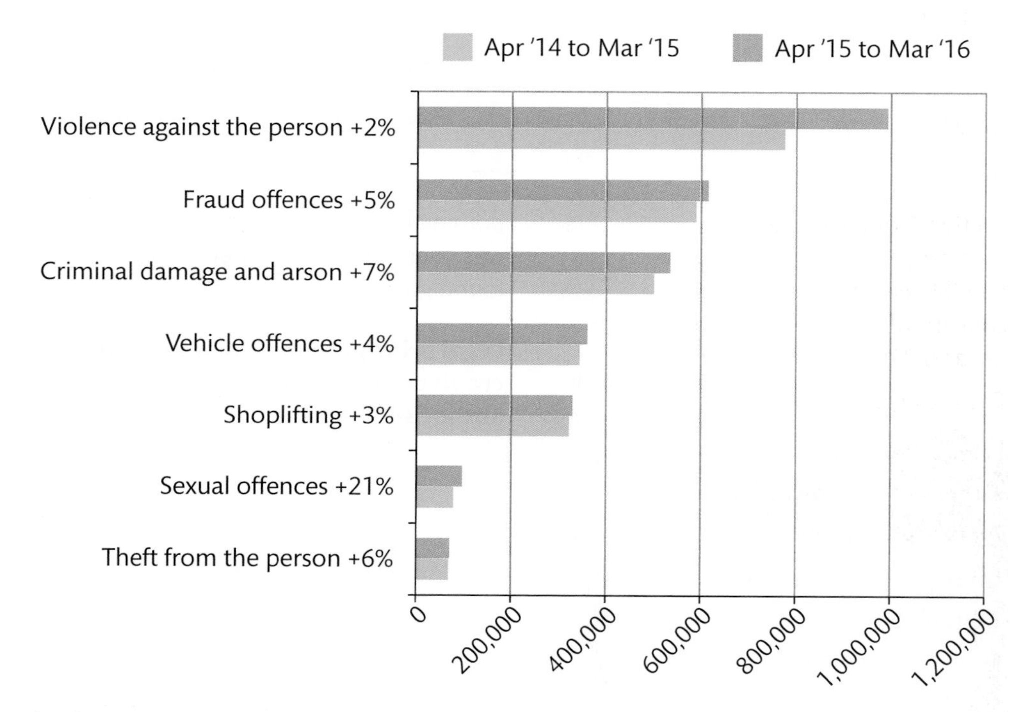

Figure 3.4: The increase in different types of recorded offences (police recorded crime figures)

Mens rea of fraud by false representation

The *mens rea* is dishonesty and the intention to make a gain or cause a loss to somebody else. As fraud is a conduct crime, it does not matter whether a gain or loss resulted.

Three criteria are used to establish the *mens rea* of fraud by false representation. They are:

- dishonesty
- intent to make a gain or cause a loss
- knowledge that the misrepresentation is or might be untrue or misleading.

On a recent visit to the local Magistrates Court, an offence being tried was fraud by false representation. The defendant had claimed to be a single parent and was claiming benefits. Evidence had emerged from her Facebook page that this was untrue as she was living with her partner – she was dishonest, had intent to make a gain and had full knowledge that she was living with her partner.

The two-stage Ghosh test as discussed in relation to theft is used to establish dishonesty and is illustrated in the following case.

Key case

R v Jeff and Bassett (1966)

Facts

The defendants told a householder that they had carried out the necessary work to repair his roof and that they had done the work well. The defendants had not carried out any repairs at all. They were convicted as they had dishonestly misled the householder.

Legal principle – all three elements of the *mens rea* of fraud by false representation were established in this case.

Criminal damage: Section 1 of the Criminal Damage Act 1971

Section 1 of the Criminal Damage Act creates a number of offences where property is destroyed or damaged. Property is defined in s10 of the Act as 'property of a tangible nature, whether real or personal'. There are similar sections to the Theft Act concerning animals being damaged or destroyed and excluding things growing wild on land. The property must belong to another.

The maximum sentence for criminal damage is ten years' imprisonment.

▶ What is the criminal charge where property has been destroyed by fire?

Section 1 (1) Criminal Damage Act 1971 (basic offence)

The basic offence of criminal damage is defined in s1(1) as:

> A person who without lawful excuse destroys or damages any property belonging to another intending to destroy or damage any such property or being reckless as to whether any such property would be destroyed or damaged shall be guilty of an offence.

Actus reus of criminal damage

The *actus reus* of criminal damage consists of damaging or destroying property belonging to another.

The jury decides whether or not the property has been damaged and the extent of the damage. If the damage caused is temporary and can be fixed, this will not prevent a conviction, but the cost and effort required to restore the property will be taken into account. Damage can result from permanent or temporary impairment, which affects the value and usefulness of the property. For example, in R v Fiak (2005), a prisoner blocked the toilet in his police station cell and the cell and two other adjoining cells were flooded. The prisoner had caused damage to the blanket and the cells, which could not be used until they were cleaned and dried.

Mens rea of criminal damage

The *mens rea* of criminal damage is the intention to cause damage or destroy property, rather than committing an act that caused damage. For example, Jake threw a stone at Luke. It missed Luke and smashed a window - there is no intention in relation to criminal damage.

If the defendant acted recklessly, the courts apply a subjective test by asking: did the actual defendant realise the risk and decide to take the risk? This test was applied in the case of R v G and another (2003).

Key case

R v G and another (2003)

Facts

The defendants were two boys aged 11 and 12. They were camping out and during the night went into the back yard of a shop and set fire to some newspapers under a large wheelie bin. They left the yard but thought that because the fire was on a concrete floor, it would go out by itself. The fire spread to the bin and then to the shop and other buildings. The boys were convicted under ss1 and 3 of the Criminal Damage Act. The boys' appeal was dismissed by the Court of Appeal but the House of Lords quashed the conviction stating that the appropriate test should have been subjective.

Legal principle - this case overruled the objective test from R v Caldwell (1982) in favour of the subjective test from R v Cunningham (1957).

Section 1(2) - aggravated criminal damage

The aggravated offence of criminal damage is defined in s1(2) of the Act. For this offence, damage can be to any property and the aggravating factor is that the offence involves endangering life by damage to the property. This section defines the offence of aggravated criminal damage as:

> A person who without lawful excuse destroys or damages any property, whether belonging to themselves or another: intending to destroy or damage any property or being reckless as to whether any property would be destroyed or damaged; and intending by the destruction or damage to endanger the life of another or being reckless as to whether the life of another would be thereby endangered; shall be guilty of an offence.

The *actus reus* is that the defendant damaged or destroyed any property. The *mens rea* is the intention or recklessness related to damaging or destroying property and intention or recklessness related to endangering life. These can be seen in the case of R v Dudley (1989).

Key case

R v Dudley (1989)

Facts

The defendant threw a petrol bomb at a house. The defendant was convicted for the aggravated offence.

Legal principle – the *actus reus* and *mens rea* were established as he threw the petrol bomb at the house and that he intended to endanger life by fire damage.

Lawful excuse

Each offence must be committed without lawful excuse but the Act states two lawful excuses could form a complete defence to a charge under s1(1) and to a simple offence of arson, but would not apply to the aggravated offence under s1(2) or aggravated arson.

The lawful excuses are contained in s5 –

- **a** he believed that the person or persons whom he believed to be entitled to consent to the destruction of or damage to the property in question had so consented or would have consented to it if he or they had known of the destruction or damage and the circumstances
- **b** he destroyed, damaged or threatened to destroy or damage the property in question in order to protect property belonging to himself or another.

Section 1(3) – arson

Section 1(3) of the Criminal Damage Act 1971 creates the offence of arson, which is defined as destroying or damaging property by fire. A charge of arson may be brought alongside the basic or aggravated offences in ss1(1) or 1(2). The maximum sentence for this offence is life imprisonment.

The *actus reus* of arson is the damage or destruction of property by fire.

The *mens rea* is intention or recklessness as to damaging property belonging to another by fire. The offence of aggravated arson in s1(4) also requires a *mens rea* element relating to endangering life.

Produce a table and summarise the requirement for each offence under the Criminal Damage Act 1971.

Hint For each offence, try to include a case example.

Extend What would happen if a person had accidentally damaged property belonging to another? Justify your answer.

Assessment practice 3.3 — AO3

You are in the middle of your law placement. The details of the following case are placed on your desk.

Irfan and Imran, two brothers aged 17 and 19, decided to play a trick at the local corner shop owned by one of their friends, Shamas. They arrived at the shop shortly after 10 p.m. in a black mini car driven by Imran. Irfan gained access to the shop by breaking a window in the back yard. Once inside, he unlocked the door and removed all of the fizzy drink stock. He loaded it into the car and the pair drove away after leaving a note stating that 'Fizzy drinks are bad for Shamas as they contain too much sugar.' After driving some distance into the countryside, the two brothers smashed all the bottles of fizzy drinks.

1 Identify the relevant areas of law.
2 Explain and analyse the law.
3 Apply the law to this case.
4 Advise Irfan and Imran on the likely consequences of their actions.

Plan

- I need to identify the laws that have been broken.
- I need to look at the facts of this case and decide how they relate back to the law.
- I need to be clear about the consequences of breaking these laws and what might happen to Irfan and Imran.
- I need to plan which resources I might need to complete this task.

Do

- I need to refer back to my notes and discuss any difficulties with my tutor.
- I need to explain the law clearly to Irfan and Imran.
- I need to look carefully at Irfan and Imran's individual actions.

Review

- I can apply the law to a new case.
- I can identify the key facts of this case and how they relate back to the law.
- I can advise on the likely consequences that Irfan and Imran's actions will have.

D Introduction to general defences in criminal law

Key term

Automatism – a defence where the *actus reus* is not established due to the fact that the defendant's acts were involuntary and caused by an external factor.

In criminal law cases, there are two sides – prosecution and defence. The prosecution makes the case to prove that the defendant is guilty, the defence solicitor or barrister seeks a 'not guilty' verdict. The defendant may raise a defence or a set of circumstances and facts that suggest a defence, giving an excuse or legal reason for the defendant's actions.

Criminal liability is based on proof of *actus reus* and *mens rea*, but there are various defences that can have an effect on the outcome of a case. Some general defences apply to any offence, and other defences apply to only some offences. The effect of a successful defence is that it will negate some aspect of the *actus reus* or *mens rea* and the defendant will be acquitted. The defences covered in this section are presented in Table 3.8.

Table 3.8: Different types of defence

Defence	Applicable to	Not applicable to
Duress	Most offences	Not available for murder or attempted murder
Intoxication	Offences of specific intent	Not available for basic intent offences
Self-defence	All offences for statutory definition, violent assault for common law definition	Not available if force is not necessary or unreasonable (excluding householder cases)
Insanity	All offences requiring *mens rea*	Not available for strict liability offences
Automatism	All offences	Not available for basic intent offences if self-induced

Duress

Duress is when the defendant is put in a situation where they are forced to commit a crime due to fear. The fear may have been caused by threats or circumstances.

Duress by threats

This is a defence used when there is a threat of death or serious injury. The defence is not allowed if the threat is less than this, such as a threat to punch the defendant in the face, or where the threat was of psychological harm. The defence has been allowed where there was a threat to rape the defendant. The defendant must have committed the crime to avoid death or serious injury. The threat need not be the only factor that forces the defendant to commit the crime, as seen in the case of R v Valderrama Vega (1985).

Key case

R v Valderrama Vega (1985)

Facts

The defendant was charged with illegally importing drugs. His defence was that he, his wife and his family had been threatened with death or serious injury made by a 'mafia type' organisation who were involved in drug smuggling. The defendant had also committed the crime while under financial pressures and because there was a threat to disclose his homosexuality. He was convicted as the trial judge thought the threat of death or serious injury had to be the sole cause for him committing the offence. The Court of Appeal decided that the conviction was safe but the judge's direction was incorrect.

Legal principle – the fear of death or serious injury need not be the only factor causing the defendant to commit the crime. Where there are several factors and the defendant acts because of the cumulative effect of them, the defence will be available.

Establishing duress by threats

A two-stage test was developed in the case of R v Graham (1982) to determine the impact of the threat.

- The defendant must reasonably believe and have good cause to fear the threat.
- A sober person of reasonable firmness sharing the defendant's characteristics would have acted in the same way.

The first stage is a subjective test but the requirement of a 'reasonable belief' suggests that an ordinary person would have believed and feared the threat.

The second stage is objective but the reasonable person can be attributed some of the defendant's characteristics such as age, sex, pregnancy, serious physical disability, recognised mental illness or psychiatric disorder.

Self-induced duress

Self-induced duress is where the defendant acts in a way that could place them under duress. If they know of the risk of this, they cannot use the defence. For example, if the defendant voluntarily joined a criminal gang, knowing its members were likely to use violence, and the defendant commits some offences. Later the defendant decides that its members do not want to carry on committing offences but they are compelled to do so as they are being threatened.

The following case illustrates the immediacy of threat.

Key case

R v Abdul-Hussain (1999)

Facts

The defendants had fled from Iraq to Sudan as they were at risk of being punished or executed because of their religious beliefs. Fearing being sent back to Iraq, they hijacked a plane, which landed at Stansted airport. The defendants released the hostages and surrendered. They pleaded duress of circumstances but the trial judge decided that the danger they were in was not sufficiently 'close and immediate'. They were convicted and appealed. The Court of Appeal quashed their conviction.

Legal principle – the threat need not be immediate but there must be an imminent peril of death or serious injury.

Duress of circumstances

Duress of circumstances was first recognised in R v Willer (1986). For a defence of duress by circumstance to be pleaded successfully, the defendant must have been in a situation where they feared death or serious injury, and in which the circumstances (as the defendant perceived them) were such that the defendant had no option but to commit a crime.

Key case

R v Willer (1986)

Facts

The defendant was driving down a narrow lane when his car was surrounded by a gang of youths who threatened the defendant and his passenger. He drove over a pavement to escape from the gang. The defendant was convicted of reckless driving but his conviction was quashed and the Court of Appeal created duress of circumstances.

Legal principle – the defendant must show that they acted in the way they did because they reasonably perceived a threat of death or serious injury.

The defence of duress has been problematic as there are so many factors. In the case of R v Hasan (2015), the House of Lords stated that the defence of duress needed six elements as follows:

1. The threat (or the circumstances) must cause the defendant to fear death or serious injury. This is a subjective element.
2. The threat must be directed against (or the circumstances must cause the defendant to fear for) themselves, a member of their immediate family, someone close to them or a person who relied on the defendant as responsible for their safety.
3. The jury must consider the reasonableness of the defendant's perceptions and conduct. This is objective and based on the reasonable person test.
4. The defence is only available where the criminal conduct that it seeks to excuse has been directly caused by the threats that are relied upon.
5. There was no evasive action that the defendant could reasonably be expected to take.
6. The defendant may not rely on duress if they have voluntarily laid themselves open.

The defence of duress is not available for the offences of murder or attempted murder, as decided in the case of R v Gotts (1992).

Key case

R v Gotts (1992)

Facts

The defendant was 16 and his parents had separated. The father of the boy threatened him with violence unless he stabbed his mother. The boy agreed and attacked the mother but he didn't kill her. He was convicted of attempted murder.

Legal principle – the defence of duress is not available for murder or attempted murder.

Scenario

Ali committed a robbery at a building society in order to pay money that he owed to Shabaz. Ali was a heroin addict and was intoxicated by drugs at the time of the robbery. Ali knew that Shabaz was a very violent person and he had threatened to shoot Ali unless he repaid the debt. Shabaz had given Ali a gun and had told him to get the money from a bank or building society.

1. Does Ali have a defence?
2. Apply the six elements from the Hassan case above and explain why they apply or do not apply.
3. Compare your answers to R v Ali (1995).

Intoxication

Criminal statistics now monitor the links between **intoxication** and violent crime where the defendant or victim (or both) are intoxicated at the time when the crime was committed. This causal link has been recognised by the courts for many years.

Key term

Intoxication – under the influence of alcohol, drugs (prescribed or otherwise) or other substances, for example glue sniffing.

Policy argument – an argument that assesses a decision in terms of how that decision affects society as a whole.

Public policy surrounding the availability of the defence

Policy arguments relating to intoxication are aimed at protecting the public from those who, by reason of intoxication, pose a threat of danger. Policy arguments reject intoxication being a factor to be considered in criminal cases because an intoxicated defendant should not be treated more favourably than a sober defendant.

On the other hand, criminal liability requires proof of *actus reus* and *mens rea*, and intoxication can have an effect on the defendant's state of mind. The aim is to balance public policy considerations against the legitimate defence argument that criminal liability cannot be established if the defendant did not form the required *mens rea* at the time the crime was committed. A compromise is achieved by setting restrictions on when intoxication can be taken into account. This can be seen in the case of R v Lipman (1970).

Key case

R v Lipman (1970)

Facts

The defendant and his girlfriend had been taking LSD, a drug that can cause hallucinations. The defendant believed that he was at the centre of the earth and was being attacked by snakes. When he awoke, his girlfriend was dead. He had strangled and suffocated her by pushing the bed sheet down her throat. The defendant was convicted of manslaughter because he did not have the intention required for murder. He appealed and his conviction was upheld.

Legal principle – voluntary intoxication is classed as reckless behaviour, therefore he had the appropriate *mens rea* for manslaughter.

There are two key questions for the courts:

- whether the defendant became intoxicated voluntarily or involuntarily
- whether the offence charged is classed as a crime of basic intent or specific intent.

Discussion

Should intoxication excuse the defendant? If so, in what circumstances? If not, why not?

Difference between voluntary and involuntary intoxication

Voluntary intoxication is where the defendant chooses to take intoxicating substances.

Involuntary intoxication is where the defendant does not know they are taking an intoxicating substance, such as where soft drinks have been 'spiked', or if a person takes illegal drugs thinking it is aspirin.

In a case of involuntary intoxication, the courts will assess whether the defendant had the necessary *mens rea* when the crime was committed. If they did, intoxication would make no difference. However, if the defendant was incapable of forming *mens rea*, they cannot be guilty of a basic intent or specific intent crime.

Key case

R v Kingston (1994)

Facts

The defendant was a homosexual paedophile. He had been lured to the flat of another man who wanted to blackmail the defendant. The man gave the defendant coffee that had been drugged. The man had also lured a 15-year-old boy to the flat and had drugged the boy. The man then invited the defendant to sexually abuse the boy. The man photographed and taped the sexual abuse taking place. The defendant was convicted of indecent assault. The House of Lords upheld the conviction.

Legal principle – if a defendant had formed the *mens rea* for an offence, involuntary intoxication cannot be a defence. In order for involuntary intoxication to be a defence, it must prevent the defendant from forming *mens rea*.

The rule in the case of DPP v Majewski (1977) applies to voluntary intoxication. As Figure 3.5 shows, a defendant can only be acquitted on the grounds of intoxication where the case is one of:

- voluntary intoxication only
- by alcohol or dangerous drugs
- the defendant lacks *mens rea*, and
- the crime is one of specific intent.

Figure 3.5: The impact of volunary intoxication

Key case

DPP v Majewski (1977)

Facts

The defendant was charged with an offence of Section 47 assault occasioning actual bodily harm (a basic intent crime) against a policeman after becoming voluntarily intoxicated by a large quantity of drugs and alcohol. The trial judge refused to allow evidence of intoxication and the defendant was convicted. The House of Lords dismissed his appeal.

Legal principle – voluntary intoxication may be used as a 'defence' in crimes of specific intent but not in crimes of basic intent.

Distinction between specific and basic intent crimes

Specific intent

Some examples of crimes of specific intent are shown in Figure 3.6. All of these offences require a level of *mens rea* higher than recklessness.

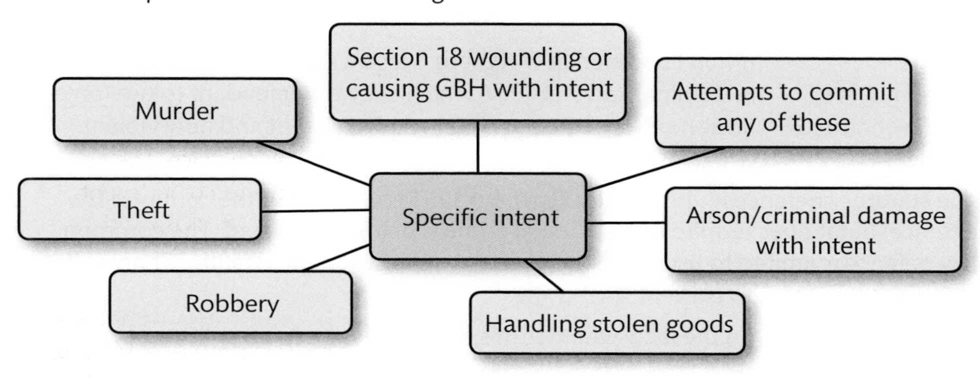

▶ **Figure 3.6:** Examples of crimes of specific intent

If a defendant is charged with a specific intent offence and there is no lesser charge, the defendant will be acquitted for lack of *mens rea*. If a defendant is charged with a specific intent crime and there is a lesser charge, the charge will be reduced as a result of the lack of *mens rea*. An example would be murder reduced to manslaughter.

There are different levels of *mens rea*; intention is the highest level that is attached to blame. Lower levels of *mens rea* are recklessness and negligence. Specific intent offences are those that require a *mens rea* of intent and nothing less.

Basic intent

Some examples of crimes of basic intent are shown in Figure 3.7.

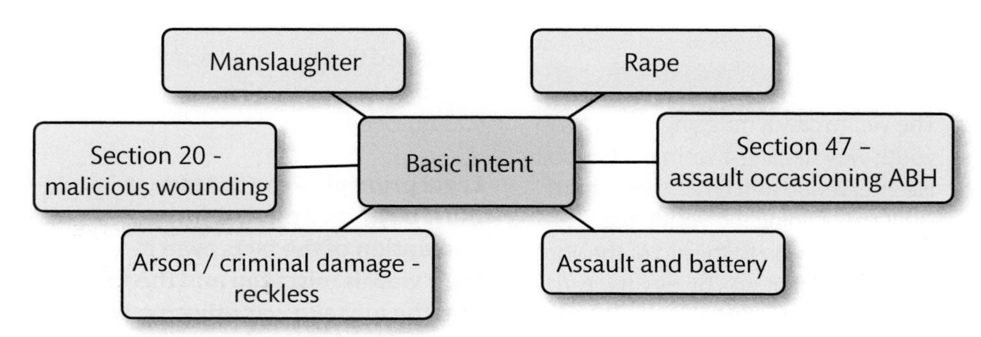

▶ **Figure 3.7:** Examples of crimes of basic intent

Basic intent crimes require a *mens rea* of recklessness. If a defendant has become voluntarily intoxicated, their conduct is reckless and therefore they have the required *mens rea*. Figure 3.8 shows the effect of voluntary intoxication by a non-dangerous drug.

Voluntary intoxication – non-dangerous drug → No *mens rea* → Defendant not liable if he is not reckless

Figure 3.8: The impact of voluntary intoxication by a non-dangerous drug

Self-defence

A person is allowed to use force that will negate the *actus reus* of a crime. This means that the defendant's conduct is lawful, if done to protect:

- themselves
- another
- property.

The difference between self-defence at common law and statutory defence

Self-defence is a common law defence, but there is also a separate statutory defence contained in s3 of the Criminal Law Act 1967, which allows a defendant to use force to prevent the commission of 'any' offence. This includes violent and non-violent offences and offences against property.

The statutory defence in the Criminal Law Act 1967 is wider than the common law defence, but it does require that an actual crime is being committed. The common law defence is limited to using reasonable force against violent assaults, whereas the statutory defence is to prevent 'any' crime.

The jury will decide on the facts whether this defence has been established, but there are two key questions.

- Given the circumstances, was force necessary?
- Was the amount of force used reasonable?

Discussion

If you saw a person being attacked in a public place, would you intervene? What factors would influence your decision?

Was the force necessary?

The defendant is judged subjectively based on whether they had an honest belief, in view of the facts, that force was necessary. If this view of the facts is mistaken, the defence is still available if the force used is objectively reasonable in the light of the defendant's belief. This was addressed in the case of R v Williams (Gladstone) (1987).

Key case

R v Williams (Gladstone) (1987)

Facts

The victim saw a mugging when a youth was stealing a woman's handbag. He intervened and chased the youth. While restraining the youth, the defendant came to the aid of the youth who he thought was being attacked. The defendant struck the victim and was charged with assault occasioning actual bodily harm. The defendant was convicted and appealed as the judge had stated that his mistake of the facts had to be reasonable. His conviction was quashed.

Legal principle – the defendant must be judged on their own perception of the facts even if their view is mistaken and the fact that the mistake was objectively unreasonable is irrelevant.

If an attack has not occurred but the defendant fears an imminent attack, then reasonable force can be used. Lord Griffith stated in the case of R v Beckford (1988) that 'a man about to be attacked does not have to wait for his assailant to strike the first blow or fire the first shot, circumstances may justify a pre-emptive strike'.

Where the defendant started the argument but the tables turned and the victim used a disproportionate amount of force to that used by the defendant, self-defence will be available as the positions of the two are reversed and the defendant becomes the victim.

Was the amount of force used reasonable?

Excluding **householder cases**, the degree of force will not be reasonable if it was disproportionate in the circumstances. Here the jury will take into account the size, strength and skill of the parties.

The aim of this provision in the Criminal Justice and Immigration Act 2008, was to give more legal protection to the householder (the person who owns the house or is in possession or control of it). In householder cases, the force used does not have to be proportionate to the circumstances in which the householder believed themselves to be. The householder has to be protecting themselves or another and not simply defending property. The Act states that the force used should not be 'grossly disproportionate', as argued in the case of R v Martin (2002).

Key term

Householder cases – this term has been defined in s76 of the Criminal Justice and Immigration Act 2008 as where:

- the defence concerned is the common law defence
- the force concerned is force used by the defendant while in or partly in a building, or part of a building, that is a dwelling
- the defendant is not a trespasser at the time the force is used
- at the time, the defendant believed the victim to be in, or entering, the building or part as a trespasser.

Key case

R v Martin (2002)

Facts

Martin lived in a remote farm called Bleak House. The farm buildings were in a poor state and the farm looked as if it was derelict. It had been a target for numerous break-ins. On one occasion, two males aged 16 and 30 broke into the farmhouse. Martin took a shotgun and went downstairs where he fired the gun indiscriminately towards the disturbance. The two intruders were shot and the 16-year-old died. Martin was charged with murder and pleaded self-defence. He was convicted and appealed on the grounds that his personality disorder had affected his perception of the circumstances and that this should have been put to the jury. The Court of Appeal ruled that the jury could not take into account a psychiatric condition for self-defence (to determine Martin's perception of the degree of danger) but quashed his conviction based on diminished responsibility.

Legal principle – if the defendant perceived the degree of danger as being far greater than would be perceived by a reasonable person, the defendant's mistake should be ignored.

PAUSE POINT Produce a PowerPoint presentation that summarises the law of self-defence.

Hint Consider reasonable force in different circumstances, for example, the person using force is a martial arts expert or is a frail pensioner.

Extend Provide a list of practical advice to keep yourself or your property safe.

Insanity and automatism

Insanity was a popular defence before the abolition of the death penalty. A defendant could plead legal insanity as being locked up in a secure mental institution indefinitely was preferable to being hanged. Today, it is rarely used as a defence but may be suggested by the prosecution. If the suggestion is that the defendant was insane at the time of committing the crime, the jury may find them to be not guilty by reason of insanity. Where it is asserted that the defendant is insane at the time of the trial, the issue is one of 'unfitness to plead' and the judge decides this issue.

Definition of insanity

The legal definition is different to the everyday definition and the medical definition of insanity.

The legal definition of insanity is provided by the M'Naghten Rules (1843) following the case of Daniel M'Naghten who had tried to kill Sir Robert Peel (the Prime Minister) but, by mistake, had killed his secretary. In this case, the plea of insanity was successful.

The rules state that if a defendant wishes to rely on the defence, it must be proved that they laboured under a defect of reason caused by a disease of the mind; so that either they did not know the nature and quality of their act or, alternatively, they did not know what they were doing was wrong. This rule can be explained in more detail.

A defect of reason

The disease of the mind must impair the defendant's power of reasoning and absent-mindedness or confusion is insufficient to show a defect of reason.

A disease of the mind

The question as to whether the defendant has a disease of the mind is a question of law to be determined by the judge. The condition must cause a malfunctioning of the mind and it is not relevant whether the condition is physical or mental in origin, or whether it is curable or temporary.

The case of R v Kemp (1956) illustrates this point.

Key case

R v Kemp (1956)

Facts

The defendant, who was a devoted husband, was suffering from a condition known as hardening of the arteries, which caused him to suffer from temporary loss of consciousness when his supply of blood to the brain was affected by the condition. He violently attacked his wife with a hammer in one of these moments, causing serious injury. He was charged with inflicting grievous bodily harm. At his trial, the defendant said he was suffering from 'a defect of reason' but not as a result of a disease of the mind as he was suffering from a physical condition. He was found not guilty by reason of insanity. He appealed and the Court of Appeal upheld the decision.

Legal principle – disease of mind is a question of law for the trial judge to decide.

Insanity has been considered in cases related to conditions such as epilepsy, diabetes, brain tumour, manic depression, schizophrenia and sleepwalking, as seen in R v Burgess (1991).

Key case

R v Burgess (1991)

Facts

The defendant had been watching television and asserted that he had attacked his girlfriend while asleep. He had smashed a bottle over her head and struck her with a video recorder. The jury accepted medical evidence of a sleep disorder and they returned a verdict of not guilty by reason of insanity. The Court of Appeal upheld the decision.

Legal principle - a condition caused by an internal factor will constitute a disease of the mind bringing the defendant within the scope of the defence of insanity.

In cases such as these, the prosecution argued that the defendants were not in control of their actions and were not capable of rational thought due to a malfunctioning of the mind, so the jury should decide that the defendant is insane. This does not seem to match with common sense even though it may match the legal definition. The growth of the defence of non-insane automatism has clarified the situation up to a point.

Not knowing the nature and quality of the act

This point is difficult to establish. It means that the defendant must not have known what they were physically doing and what the physical consequences of their actions would be. A defendant may be in this state as a result of:

- a state of unconsciousness or impaired consciousness
- a mental condition which causes them not to know or understand what they are doing even though they are conscious.

Not knowing what they were doing was wrong

This requires the defendant to fail to understand that what they were doing was legally wrong. The case of R v Windle (1952) illustrates this point.

Key case

R v Windle (1952)

Facts

The defendant's wife was suicidal and he gave her a fatal dose of aspirin. Although he was suffering from a mental illness, the defence of insanity was not available because when he was arrested, he had commented 'I suppose I'll hang for this.' These words showed that he knew that his actions were legally wrong. He was convicted of murder.

Legal principle - to rely on insanity the defendant must not have known that what they did was legally wrong.

Unfitness to plead

In order to plead, the defendant must be capable of understanding criminal proceedings, instructing a legal representative, challenging a juror and understanding the evidence. The judge decides whether the defendant is fit to plead. The prosecution, the defence or the judge may raise the issue of fitness to plead.

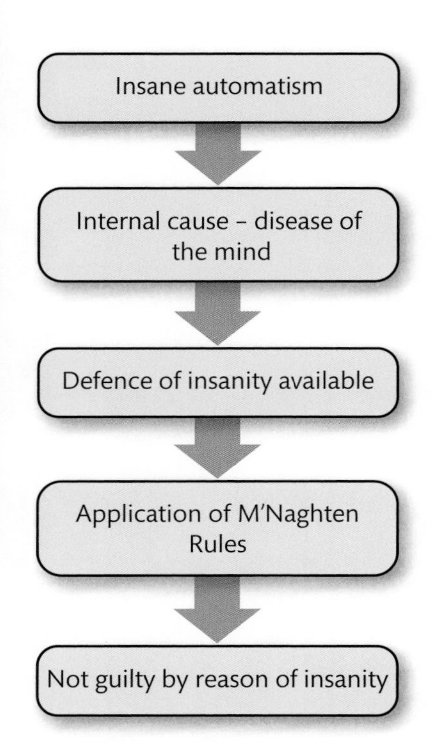

Figure 3.9: The availability of insanity

If the judge decides that the defendant is fit to plead, the trial proceeds. If the judge decides that the defendant is unfit to plead, the court will carry out a 'trial of the facts' to decide whether the defendant carried out the *actus reus* of the offence. The jury do not consider the *mens rea* element. Where the jury are sure beyond reasonable doubt that the defendant committed the *actus reus*, the options open to the judge are the same as for a verdict of not guilty by reason of insanity. If the jury decides that the defendant was not responsible for the *actus reus*, they will be acquitted.

The special verdict

In cases where the jury return a verdict of not guilty by reason of insanity, the judge has three options set out in the Criminal Procedure (Insanity and Unfitness to Plead) Act 1991, which are:

1. The judge can impose a hospital order (with or without restrictions as to when the defendant may be released).
2. The judge can impose a supervision order.
3. The judge can release the defendant with an absolute discharge.

If the defendant is charged with murder, the judge must impose an indefinite hospital order and the defendant will only be released when the Home Secretary agrees.

The difference between insanity and automatism

In the case of Bratty v Attorney General of Northern Ireland (1963), Lord Denning defined automatism as:

> An act which is done by the muscles without any control by the mind, such as a spasm, a reflex action or a convulsion, or an act done by a person who is not conscious of what they are doing, such as an act done while suffering from concussion or while sleepwalking.

A distinction is drawn between sane and insane automatism. A defendant who successfully pleads **sane automatism** will be acquitted but in a case of **insane automatism**, the special verdict of not guilty by reason of insanity will apply (see Figure 3.9). The courts distinguish insane and sane automatism by a test that considers the operation of internal and external factors.

- A condition caused by an external factor may give rise to the defence of sane automatism. If the condition is not self-induced, it will lead to a complete acquittal.
- A condition caused by an internal factor (disease of the mind) may give rise to the defence of insanity or insane automatism, which will lead to a special verdict.

The distinction between internal and external factors means that the defence of sane automatism has been taken away for those people such as diabetics and epileptics, meaning that on a finding of insanity, they would be subject to some sort of court order rather than being acquitted.

Two things need to be proved for the defence of sane automatism to succeed. These are:

- There was a total loss of voluntary control.
- This had been caused by an external factor.

Total loss of voluntary control

Loss of voluntary control means that even though the defendant committed the *actus reus*, their actions were involuntary and as a result they could not have the required *mens rea*. If the defendant retained partial or impaired control over their actions, the defence will fail - as shown in the case of Attorney General's Reference (No 2 of 1992) (1993).

Key terms

Sane automatism - when a defendant succesfully pleads sane automatism for an involuntary or unconscious action, they will be acquitted.

Insane automatism - when a defendant pleads insane automatism for an involuntary or unconscious action, the verdict of not guilty by reason of insanity will apply.

Key case

Attorney General's Reference (No 2 of 1992) (1993)

Facts

The defendant was a lorry driver travelling on the motorway. He had driven on the hard shoulder for about half a mile before crashing into a broken-down car that had stopped on the hard shoulder. Two people were killed and the lorry driver was charged. He raised the defence of sane automatism due to driving for too long on a flat and straight road and argued that the repetitive visual stimulus had caused him to 'drive without awareness'. The jury acquitted the defendant. The Attorney General referred a point of law to the Court of Appeal who stated that the defence of sane automatism should not have been put to the jury as the driver retained some control over his actions.

Legal principle - partial or impaired loss of control is insufficient for the defence of sane automatism.

Caused by an external factor

In a case of R v Quick (1973), the court explained what would not constitute a disease of the mind:

> A malfunctioning of the mind of transitory effect caused by the application to the body of some external factor such as violence, drugs, including anaesthetics, alcohol and hypnotic influences cannot fairly be said to be due to disease.

Key case

R v Quick (1973)

Facts

The defendant was a nurse caring for a disabled patient. While on duty, the nurse attacked the patient who suffered a broken nose, bruising and black eyes. The nurse was charged with assault occasioning actual bodily harm but raised the defence of sane automatism, stating that he had no control over his actions as he was in a hypoglycaemic state as a result of eating too little and taking too much insulin. The trial judge claimed this was insanity rather than automatism so the defendant withdrew the defence and changed his plea to guilty. The Court of Appeal quashed his conviction as his loss of control was caused by the insulin and not by the diabetes.

Legal principle - the loss of control must be caused by an external factor.

Some external factors include a blow to the head, injecting insulin, sneezing and being attacked by a swarm of bees.

Self-induced automatism

Self-induced automatism is when the defendant does something or fails to do something that they know will lead to an automatic state, such as drinking alcohol when taking prescribed medication against medical advice. In a case involving self-induced automatism, the courts use the same distinction as for intoxication-specific and basic intent crimes.

Key term

Self-induced automatism - when a defendant does something, or fails to do something, that they know will lead to an automatic state.

Discussion

How would you draw the line between insanity and sane automatism?

Self-induced automatism can be a defence to a crime of specific intent as the defendant lacks *mens rea*. The successful defence will lead to an acquittal or a charge of a lesser basic intent crime.

Self-induced automatism cannot be used as a defence for a crime of basic intent if the defendant has brought about that automatic state by being reckless.

Assessment practice 3.4

A04

As part of your placement at your local legal practice, you have been asked to talk to a group of GCSE students who are thinking about studying the law after they leave school. You decide to talk to them about the area of defence. You will talk to them about key points and cases relating to duress, intoxication, self-defence, insanity and automatism. You think this is an interesting area of law but understand that this is complex information for students just starting out. You need to make sure that your talk and hand-out resources are accessible and easy to understand.

You decide to talk for two minutes on each defence, and make a short hand-out on each defence, with a case that illustrates that defence. You also include some information about how fit for purpose each defence is, and whether there is any need for reform in the law.

Plan

- I need to pick cases that relate to each of the defences of duress, intoxication, self-defence, insanity and automatism.
- I need to know what criticisms of these defences exist and why reform might be necessary.
- I need to pick out the relevant points for each defence and explain them clearly in my talk and summarise them in my hand-out.
- I need to be clear which resources I might need to complete this task.

Do

- I need to practise and time my talk on each defence to make sure that I do not go over or under two minutes,
- I need to make use of my notes and discussions that have been held in class and discuss any difficulties with my tutor.

Review

- I can talk confidently about each defence.
- I can summarise the key points for each defence.
- I can identify areas of reform and any criticisms that there may be for each of these defences.

E An overview of police powers

Key term

Frontline duties – in relation to policing, frontline staff are directly involved in the public crime-fighting face of the force. This includes neighbourhood policing, response policing and criminal investigation.

There are 43 police forces in England and Wales and statistics for 2015 showed that the police employed 207,140 workers in a variety of roles. The numbers employed by the police have fallen but the proportion of staff on **frontline duties** has increased – 91.6 per cent of police officers are operational frontline staff, as shown by Figure 3.10.

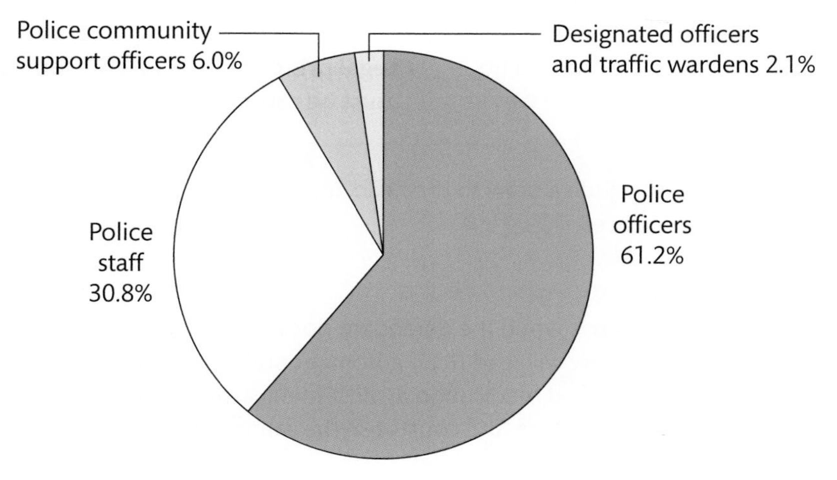

Figure 3.10: The roles of the police workforce

The core operational duties of the police include:

- protecting life and property
- preserving order
- preventing the commission of offences
- bringing offenders to justice.

The police have a difficult job and it is essential that there is a balance between individual rights and the powers of the police. The police deal with a wide variety of issues including crime, missing persons, family disputes, child abuse, sudden deaths and community tensions. Conflicting interests are inevitable; the police need to investigate but the individual has a right to go about their daily routine without interference. The powers of the police are limited by legislation and codes of practice.

The police have powers to:

- stop and search
- arrest
- detain, interview and investigate.

Stop and search

A police officer may stop and search you if they have reason to believe you are carrying illegal drugs, a weapon, have stolen property on you or have something in your possession that might be used to commit a crime. This power is defined in s1 of the Police and Criminal Evidence Act 1984 (PACE).

Stop and search is a powerful tool but it has been a controversial issue as in the past it has been used discriminately against specific sections of the community. A report on the Brixton riots in 1981 highlighted the improper use of police powers and consequently the Police and Criminal Evidence Act came into force in 1984.

People and vehicles in a public place

A police officer can stop and search any person or vehicle in a public place for stolen or prohibited articles. The Criminal Justice Act 2003 extended this power to include searching for articles intended to cause criminal damage. A public place is anywhere where the public have access either with or without payment, for example in the street, in a shopping centre or cinema, but not in a private house, garden or yard.

Prohibited articles

Prohibited articles are stated in s1 of PACE. They include stolen goods, offensive weapons and articles made or adapted for use in a criminal offence, such as theft, burglary, fraud or criminal damage. Police can also search for adult fireworks; this includes all fireworks with the exception of party poppers and sparklers.

Reasonable grounds for stop and search

The grounds for the stop and search or arrest cannot be based on factors such as age, sex, race or religion. The fact that the police knows the individual will not be reasonable grounds for suspicion alone.

Reasonable grounds are a suspicion that:

- the person is unlawfully in possession of, or has unlawfully obtained, a prohibited article
- the person is a terrorist or to prevent an act of terrorism.

Key terms

Warrant card – this is a form of identification that a police officer has. It has the authority related to being a police officer.

Home Secretary – a senior government minister in charge of the Home Office who has responsibility for crime policy, counter terrorism, immigration and passports.

Procedures that must be followed

Police officers using the stop and search power are trained to go through a process which has been given the name 'GOWISELY'.

- **G** – the police officer needs to have reasonable **grounds** for carrying out a stop and search.
- **O** – the person being stopped must be informed of the **object** or reason for the stop and search.
- **W** – if in plain clothes, the officer should produce a **warrant card**.
- **I** – **identity**, the officer should introduce themselves by name.
- **S** – the officer should name the police **station** they are attached to.
- **E** – explain that the person stopped is **entitled** to a record of the stop and search.
- **L** – explain from which Act the **legal** right to stop and search comes.
- **Y** – inform the person that '**you** are being detained for a search'.

The person who is being stopped and searched can only be required to remove outer clothing such as jackets, hats and gloves.

The legal powers to stop, search and arrest a suspect come mainly from PACE and also from other acts such as the Misuse of Drugs Acts 1971, the Terrorism Act 2000 and the Criminal Justice and Public Order Act 1994. For the Terrorism Act, the police do not need to establish reasonable suspicion but a senior officer must authorise the search procedure at particular places and at particular times, and the authorisation must be confirmed by the **Home Secretary**. Equally, reasonable suspicion is not required for Section 60 of the Criminal Justice and Public Order Act 1994; police officers may use the power of stop and search where there is a threat of serious violence or public disorder such as riots, gang fights or football hooliganism. Again, authorisation must be in place and the duration of the use of this power must not exceed 24 hours.

Reasonable force can be used during a stop and search but only if a person fails to co-operate and only as a last resort.

Research

Examine statistics available on the use of stop and search. Why are critics arguing that the power is still being abused and used disproportionately?

A recent report suggested that police forces using body cameras had reduced the amount of complaints against the police. Produce a short report on this issue.

Hint Think about the advantages and disadvantages of using body cameras.

Extend What other technological advances are used by police forces?

Arrest

An arrest occurs at the time a person loses their liberty (freedom). If a person is at a police station helping police with inquiries and they are free to leave at any time, an arrest has not taken place.

A lawful arrest must meet two main criteria:

- The person being arrested must be involved or suspected of involvement or attempted involvement in committing a crime.
- The police officer must have reasonable grounds for believing that it is necessary to arrest that person.

In a case called Castorina v Chief Constable of Surrey (1988), reasonable cause for an arrest was given consideration. The House of Lords looked at three questions:

1. Did the arresting officer suspect that the person arrested was guilty of an offence? This question depends on the facts and the officer's state of mind.

2 Assuming the officer had reasonable suspicion, was there reasonable cause for the suspicion? This is an objective requirement to be determined by the judge.
3 If the answer to the previous questions are affirmative, the officer has a discretion to make an arrest.

Legal powers to arrest are also derived from the common law in relation to arrest for **breach of the peace** or to prevent such a breach.

Key term

Breach of the peace – when harm is done or likely to be done to a person in their presence, to their property, or a person is in fear of being so harmed through an assault, an affray, a riot or other disturbance (R v Howell 1982).

Purpose of an arrest

An arrest is necessary:

- where the name and address of the person cannot be ascertained
- to prevent the person:
  - causing injury to themselves or another
  - suffering physical injury
  - causing loss of or damage to property
- to prevent an offence of public indecency or obstruction of a highway
- to protect a child or vulnerable person
- to allow the effective and prompt investigation of the offence
- to prevent the prosecution of the offence from being hindered.

On making an arrest, the police have to follow proper procedure, which involves:

- identifying themselves as police officers
- informing the person that they have been arrested and the circumstances
- explaining why the arrest is necessary
- explaining that the person is not free to leave
- cautioning the person with the following statement:

> You do not have to say anything. But it may harm your defence if you do not mention when questioned something which you later rely on in court. Anything you do say may be given in evidence.

The arrested person should then be taken to a police station as soon as is reasonably practicable. If the arrested person is under 18 or is a vulnerable adult, the police must contact parents, a carer, guardian or an appropriate adult as soon as possible after arrival at the police station.

In the case of R v Iqbal, the proper procedure for arrest was not followed.

Key case

R v Iqbal (2011)

Facts

The defendant had been arrested at a hearing of another person. A police officer had recognised the defendant as someone who was wanted by police for involvement with conspiracy to supply class A drugs. The police officer apprehended the defendant and handcuffed him. The defendant ran away and was later captured, charged and convicted of the common law offence of escaping from lawful custody. On appeal, the defendant's conviction was quashed stating that he was not under arrest because he had not been told he was under arrest.

Legal principle – a police officer must inform a person that they are under arrest and the reason why they are under arrest or the arrest will be unlawful.

Key term

Warrant – an official document signed by a judge or magistrate giving a police officer the right to arrest a person or people named in the warrant.

Powers of arrest with a warrant

Section 1 of the Magistrates' Court Act 1980 states that the issue of a summons requiring the defendant to go to court on a specified date can be the start of criminal proceedings. The magistrates' court can also issue a **warrant** for the defendant's arrest, but this is mostly used for serious cases.

To obtain a warrant, the police must gain permission to make an application and inform the magistrates of the person to be arrested and the reason for the arrest warrant.

The court will issue a warrant if:

- the suspect has committed or is suspected of committing a criminal offence
- the suspect is over 18
- the offence stated is indictable and if punishable would result in imprisonment
- the suspect's address is not so established as to make a summons appropriate, and
- the necessary information is provided in writing.

Powers of an arrest without a warrant

Most arrests are without a warrant because the police have to act quickly at the scene of a crime. A distinction used to be drawn between 'arrestable' and 'non-arrestable' offences, but this classification was confusing and police can now make an arrest relating to any offence as outlined in the Serious Organised Crime and Police Act 2005.

Make a list of dos and don'ts for a police officer to ensure that they act lawfully when carrying out a stop and search or an arrest.

Read back through this section on police powers and research the codes of practice.

Extend What are the potential consequences for the officer and the case against the defendant if the officer fails to follow proper procedure?

Right to search on arrest

The requirements of a lawful stop, search and arrest

- Is the person or vehicle in a public place?
- Are there reasonable grounds for a stop and search?
- Has the person been informed of the reason for the search?
- Has the officer identified themselves, name, police station, warrant card?
- Has the police officer explained the right to a written record of the search?
- Has the police officer explained the legal authority to carry out the search and the reason for it?
- Has the police officer informed the person that they are being searched?
- Is the person suspected of attempted or actual involvement in crime?
- Are there reasonable grounds for suspicion and is the arrest necessary?
- Has the person been informed that they have been arrested, and of the circumstances, why it is necessary and the fact that they are not free to leave?
- Has the person been cautioned?
- Has the person been taken to a police station as soon as reasonably practicable?

Detention, interviews, searches and samples

In this section you will look at interviews at the police station, the searches the police may do, and the samples they may take.

Detention

After arriving at the police station and being seen by the custody officer, the investigating officer will take over to gather evidence and to determine whether the suspect should be charged or released. The investigation may include:

- carrying out audio-recorded interviews with the suspect
- taking fingerprints or impressions of footwear
- carrying out an identification procedure
- taking photographs
- taking intimate or non-intimate samples.

Time limits

The Police and Criminal Evidence Act 1984 sets out time limits for the period of detention. The basic rule is that the suspect should be charged or released within 24 hours of being arrested.

Most cases are dealt with in the basic time period. However, in some cases the police need more time for questioning and investigation. The time limit can be extended to 36 hours if an officer of the rank of at least superintendent authorises the extension.

If the police wish to detain the suspect for a longer period, they need to request a warrant of further detention from the magistrates' court before the 36 hours expires. This warrant can extend the detention by 36 hours at any one time and up to a maximum of 96 hours in total.

The role of the custody officer

When a suspect has been arrested and taken to a police station, they will be put before a custody officer. A custody officer is responsible for the welfare of the suspect while they are held in detention. The custody officer must hold a position above a sergeant and must not be involved in the investigation involving the suspect. The role of the custody officer is to record all of the details of the detention including:

- arrival time
- property taken from the suspect
- interview times
- access to lawyers
- rest periods and refreshments.

The custody officer is also responsible for advising the suspects of their rights while in detention. The custody record will also include personal details of the suspect, the reason for and time of arrest and the reason for authorising ongoing detention.

The custody officer must review whether detention is still necessary after the first six hours and then after each period of nine hours. If reviews are not carried out, the detention becomes unlawful.

The rights of the detained person

The suspect has a right to free, independent legal advice from a solicitor or an accredited police station representative, either face to face or over the telephone. The consultation will be held in private and at any time it is requested. The police have a limited right to delay access to legal advice where it will lead to:

- interference with evidence connected to an indictable offence
- interference or injury to other persons
- alerting other persons suspected of having committed such an offence but who have not been arrested
- hindering the recovery of any property obtained as a result of such an offence.

The suspect has a right to request that one relative or other person is informed of their arrest and whereabouts. In certain circumstances, this right can also be delayed to preserve evidence.

The suspect has a right to rest, food and exercise. They must be kept in a clean, ventilated, adequately lit and heated cell. If the suspect is injured or suffering from a medical condition, they must be seen by a doctor as soon as possible. If the suspect is detained for more than one day, for each 24-hour period they must be given eight hours of continuous rest.

Interviews

An interview is the questioning of a suspect about their involvement, or suspected involvement, in committing an offence. The suspect must be cautioned at the beginning of the interview.

Interviews are recorded on three audiotapes.

- The first tape is the master and is sealed at the end of the interview. The seal is only broken when the trial takes place.
- The second tape is a working copy and will be used to produce a transcript of the interview.
- The third copy is given to the suspect or their legal representative.

Interviews can be recorded visually with sound but this is usually used in very serious cases or where the suspect has a disability and, for example, needs a signer as a result of a hearing defect.

Discussion

What safeguards are provided by having audio-recorded interviews?

Before an interview the investigating officer must consider whether the arrested person is capable of listening to and understanding questions as they may, for example, be under the influence of drink or drugs. For some people, special arrangements may have to be made. These include people who are:

- juveniles – if the arrested person is between the age of 10 and 16, an interview must be carried out with a parent, guardian or responsible adult present
- suspects with a mental disability – an appropriate adult must be present
- suspects who are deaf, dumb or blind – an appropriate adult and/or interpreter will be required
- suspects who cannot speak or understand English – an appropriate interpreter must be present.

If these arrangements are not made, the evidence gained will be inadmissible in court.

The investigating officer must not use inappropriate behaviour during the interview to get answers to their questions and there should be no **oppression**. Examples of inappropriate behaviour could be shouting at the suspect or using threatening words or gestures. The interview ends when sufficient information has been gathered and the suspect is given an opportunity to give an innocent explanation of the circumstances.

Key terms

Oppression – exercising power or authority in an unjust or cruel way.

Adverse inference – a legal inference that goes against the concerned party, for example, assuming that a suspect made no comment so that they could fabricate a story.

The right to silence

The right to silence is protected by the European Convention of Human Rights.

The Criminal Justice Act 1994 allows a court to draw an **adverse inference** when a suspect remains silent prior to charge, on charge or on trial. Section 34 of the Act states that the purpose of this is to:

- discourage an accused from fabricating a defence at the last minute
- encourage the accused to make a speedy disclosure of any genuine defence or any fact which may go towards a genuine defence.

In a case called R v Argent (1997), Lord Bingham set out six criteria to be met before a court could draw an adverse inference.

- There must be proceedings against a person for an offence.
- The alleged failure to mention a fact at trial must have occurred before the charge, or on charge.
- The alleged failure must have occurred during questioning under caution.
- The questioning must have been directed at trying to discover whether or by whom the alleged offence was committed.
- The alleged failure of the accused must have been to mention any fact relied on in their defence in those proceedings.
- The alleged failure must have been to mention a fact that in the circumstances existing at the time the accused could reasonably have been expected to mention when so questioned.

Searches and samples

One fascinating area of criminal investigation is **forensic science**, which has been developing for hundreds of years.

- The first **autopsy** to discover cause of death took place in Italy in 1302.
- The microscope was invented in the 1590s, leading to the ability to investigate blood cells, sperm cells and hair samples.
- The science of **toxicology** was developed in the 19th century, when stomach linings were examined for traces of poison. Bullet matching and **ballistics** soon followed.
- In the 1880s and 1890s, mug shots were introduced and the first fingerprint bureau was established. Blood analysis was first used to identify individuals (blood carries markers that are unique and allow for the identification of an individual).

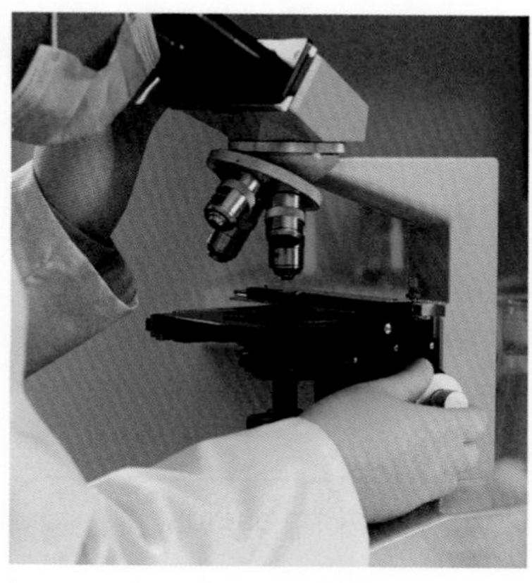

▶ How can science be used to help with criminal investigations?

- In 1910, the first crime laboratory was set up to carry out scientific tests to link the criminal to the crime scene.
- DNA analysis was discovered in 1984 and in 1995 the UK DNA Database was set up, which has had a major impact on criminal investigation.

Since then, computer reconstructions have been used to clarify the events of a crime. Facebook and mobile phone technology have provided evidence of communications and locations in court cases.

Key terms

Forensic science – the application of scientific knowledge and methods to legal problems and criminal investigations to provide objective and logical evidence for a court of law.

Autopsy – (also called a post-mortem) an examination of a body after death to determine the cause of death.

Toxicology – a scientific study of the nature, effects and detection of chemicals in living organisms.

Ballistics – the study of objects that are thrown or shot through the air such as bullets from a gun.

Fingerprints

Fingerprints may be taken where the suspect consents, or without consent and by using reasonable force if:

- the suspect is over the age of 10
- it is authorised by an officer of at least the rank of inspector
- the suspect has been charged with a recordable offence
- the suspect has been convicted of a recordable offence
- there is doubt about the identity of a person who has previously been fingerprinted and bailed.

When a suspect has been arrested, charged or told that they will be reported for a recordable offence, police officers may also take an impression of a suspect's footwear.

Samples

Police officers may take body samples in order to link the suspect to the crime. There are two types of samples – intimate and non-intimate.

- Non-intimate samples are defined in s63 of PACE and include saliva, footprints, hair (not pubic hair), sample of nail or under the nail, and mouth swabs. The suspect will be asked first if they consent but samples can be taken without consent if there are reasonable grounds to suspect the person has been involved in a recordable offence or if the suspect has been charged.
- Intimate samples are defined in s65 of PACE and include blood, semen, urine, pubic hair and swabs from body orifices other than the mouth. A medical practitioner must take the intimate sample if an inspector authorises it to prove or disprove a suspect's involvement in a recordable crime. If a suspect refuses to give consent to providing an intimate sample, this can lead to the court being informed and adverse inferences being drawn.

Breaches of PACE code of conduct

The aim of the provisions is to provide safeguards for the suspect and for the police and to make sure that if a suspect is charged, their right to a fair trial is upheld.

The consequences of a breach of the provisions will depend on the nature and extent of the breach. If a suspect is deprived of their right to legal advice or to have someone informed that they are being held at the police station, the likely outcome would be a complaint against the police. If a confession is obtained under oppression or if it is deemed unreliable because of things said or done, the confession will be inadmissible. Prosecution evidence can also be excluded if the admission of the evidence would affect the fairness of proceedings.

Key case

R v Khan (1996)

Facts

Police were investigating Khan for drug smuggling and, without authority, attached a listening device to his home. The police obtained a tape that showed Khan's involvement in importing heroin. The evidence was used in court and Khan was convicted.

On appeal, it was claimed that Khan's human rights had been breached. However, the House of Lords held that the evidence was rightly admitted and did not affect the fairness of the proceedings.

Legal principle – evidence can only be excluded if admitting it would affect the fairness of proceedings.

Assessment practice 3.5

A04

You are finishing a summer placement at your local legal practice. As part of your final week, all students on the placement are asked to create a presentation about different aspects of the law they have encountered and found interesting while they have been at the practice. You have decided to make a presentation on bail and bail without charge. You also decide to discuss the reasons why bail would be refused and the defendant would be held in custody pending trial in some cases.

You decide to also talk about government proposals to limit to 28 days the period of time a person can be on bail without charge, and the reasons why this might be a controversial decision.

Prepare a short, five-minute presentation that discusses these points.

Plan

- I need to be clear what the definition of bail is.
- I need to know the offences that may lead to a defendant being denied bail and why that may be so.
- I need to research what resources I need to complete this task.

Do

- I need to spend time to plan my approach to the presentation and identify the relevant information.
- I need to prepare and practise the presentation, making sure that it lasts five minutes.

Review

- I can draw links between this learning and prior learning.
- I can explain what I have learned and why it is important.
- I can identify how this experience relates to future experiences in the workplace.

Further reading and resources

Textbooks

Allen, M. J. – *Textbook on Criminal Law* (Oxford, 2015)

Martin, J. and Storey, T. – *Unlocking Criminal Law* (Routledge, 2015)

Ormerod, D. and Laird, K. – *Smith and Hogan's Criminal Law*, 14th Edition (Oxford, 2015)

Legal Journals

Criminal Law Review

Hazards Magazine

THINK FUTURE

Sardar Asghar

Criminal Defence Practitioner

I am proud to be a defender of rights, protecting the key legal principle – a person is innocent until proven guilty. I first developed an interest in law while studying at college and became fascinated with case law, statute, and legal procedure and its consequences. I then successfully completed an LLB qualification and a Legal Practice Course. Working in the legal profession is very competitive and initially, I worked at a local law firm on a voluntary basis. This gave me the opportunity to display my knowledge, skills and ability. I was soon offered a training contract at a firm of solicitors, which and I have now completed.

Although I am newly qualified, I already have experience working on a wide range of cases, from shoplifting to murder. My biggest challenge was working on a money laundering case where it was alleged that in excess of £200 million had been laundered. The case involved over 30,000 pages of evidence, 20 defendants and three separate trials.

There is no such thing as a typical day as no two days are alike! Some days I spend time in the office examining case files, preparing documents and liaising with counsel and clients in order to prepare for trial. Other days, I attend police stations and visit prisons, arranging and attending conferences with clients and counsel. I also regularly attend the Magistrates' and Crown Courts. It is very important to have a good working relationship with colleagues, the police, magistrates, the judge and the CPS.

My ultimate goal in a case is to achieve an acquittal. This provides enormous job satisfaction.

I look forward to further developing my career by achieving Higher Rights of Audience, so that I can represent clients in the Crown Court. Perhaps I will become a district judge and a partner in the firm.

Focus on skills

As Sardar highlights, communication, preparation and interpersonal skills are all important for a lawyer.

Planning is crucial when preparing for assignments or exams, as well as for your future learning and career. If you were planning for a case soon to start at the Crown Court, what would you consider? Think about the implications of:

- the nature of the case
- the legal arguments
- how long the trial will last
- whether there are any young or vulnerable witnesses
- whether or not the defendant wants legal representation.

Getting ready for assessment

This section has been written to help you to do your best when you take the external examination. Read through it carefully and ask your tutor if there is anything you are not sure about.

About the external assessment

It is crucial that you prepare for the external assessment throughout your study of this unit. Make sure that you have a comprehensive set of notes, case studies, hand-outs and news articles in an organised portfolio. You need to revise as you go through activities, applying the law to scenarios and making use of revision aids like flashcards and flowcharts. Match your portfolio to the unit specification and the contents pages to ensure there are no gaps. If there are any areas that you do not fully understand, ask your tutor to clarify these points.

Preparation

Ahead of your supervised assessment you will be issued with Part A of your assessment, which contains material for the completion of the preparatory work for the set task.

- Read all of Part A carefully.
- Highlight or underline key words.
- Remember the plan for applying the law – identify the relevant areas of law, explain and analyse the law, apply to the scenario and advise the clients. Consider any potential areas for discussion and the legal terminology which may be required or which may have to be explained.
- You will have time before the assessment to complete independent research around this. Make sure that you put time aside in your diary for this well in advance. Your teacher will give you more information.
- You can take a summary of your research into the supervised assessment, so make sure that your notes are clear and concise.
- Decide on where you will carry out this preparatory work so you are not disturbed.
- Get together everything you might need as directed by your teacher.

As the guidelines for assessment can change, you should refer to the official assessment guidance on the Pearson Qualifications website for the latest definitive guidance.

Sitting the external assessment

This unit is assessed under supervised conditions. Pearson sets and marks the task. As mentioned, you will be provided with a case study prior to a supervised assessment period in order to carry out research.

You will need to carry out a number of tasks, which will vary in each assessment.

- Always make a plan for your answer before you start writing. Sketch this out so you can refer to it throughout – remember to include an introduction and a conclusion where appropriate, and think about the key points you want to mention in your answer. On this plan, think about setting yourself some timeframes so that you make sure that you have time to cover everything you want to – and, importantly, have time to write the conclusion!
- Try to keep your answer as focused on your key points as possible. If you find your answer drifting away from that main point, refer back to your plan.
- Make sure that you understand everything being asked of you in the activity instructions. It might help you to underline or highlight the key terms in the instructions so that you can be sure your answer is clear and focused on exactly what you have been asked to do.

Make sure that you arrive in good time for your external assessment and that you leave yourself enough time at the end to check through your work. Listen to, and read carefully, any instructions you are given. Students often lose marks through not reading instructions properly and misunderstanding what you are being asked to do. There are some key terms that may appear in your assessment. Understanding what these words mean will help you understand what you are being asked to do.

Command word	Definition
Primary research	Research compiled directly from the original source, which may not have been compiled before. Learners could make use of their own observations of cases being dealt with in the Magistrates' or Crown Courts.
Secondary sources/ research	Published research reports and statistics, likely to be text books, case law, statute, etc.
File notes	A set of notes using relevant legal terminology and professional language to apply, analyse and evaluate the relevant law, defences and procedure

Sample answers

Look at the sample questions that follow and the tips on how to answer them well.

Worked example

Set task brief

- You must research information relevant to the scenario in Part A.
- You will carry out research on criminal law and legal procedure relevant to this type of case.
- In Part B, you will be asked to apply your research to tasks related to the case scenario.
- You will be allowed your own individually prepared notes to support you during the supervised assessment.

Part A: Set task information

The following are two recent and current news reports.

Case 1

'Catalogue of Errors'

Fineline Interiors Ltd has been charged with an offence following an investigation. Simon Smith, an employee of the company died at work when his forklift truck collided with stacks of flat-pack furniture causing the storage shelfing to collapse. Simon was pronounced dead at the scene of the accident.

Case 2

'Double Shock for Victim'

Jenny Atkinson was the victim of a violent attack in Bedlam town centre when she was pushed to the ground and a young white male snatched her handbag. After making statements as to what happened and visiting the local A and E, Jenny carried on with her routine and met several friends for drinks in the evening. Jenny had consumed too much alcohol to drive and decided to stay at a friend's house near to the bar. Her friend was away on holiday and Jenny had forgotten her key so she broke in through a small kitchen window and went

Underline the key words in the text to identify areas of law to research further and think of associated legal terminology.

Make a list of areas of law that you have studied in Unit 3 which are relevant to the scenario.

to sleep in the spare room. At 5 a.m. she was awoken by police officers at the door - a neighbour had reported a suspected break-in. Jenny was taken to the police station for questioning.

Part B of your assessment will be held under supervised conditions. You will be provided with further information relating to the subject of your preparatory work for Part A.

Search for key cases which are similar to the scenario and look for relevant statutory provisions. Circle or highlight the key information from your notes on which you might need to advise the parties involved.

Relevant areas, cases and statute

Case 1

Fatal offence, difference between voluntary and involuntary manslaughter, types of involuntary manslaughter, gross negligence, 3-stage test from Adomako, actus reus, mens rea and causation, old law and new law, Kite and OLL Ltd. case, Corporate Manslaughter and Corporate Homicide Act 2007, serious management failure, investigation, penalties, individual and corporate defendants.

Courts – Magistrates, Crown, indictable offence.

Reasons for new legislation, effect of scenario on parties involved.

Cotswold Geotechnical holdings case and Lion Steel case.

Case 2

Theft, sections 1 – 6, robbery and force, threat of or actual force in order to steal, Clouden case, burglary (section 9(1)(a) and (b)) - but what about intention, criminal damage, lawful excuse, Jaggard case, intoxication (specific and basic intent), actus reus, mens rea and causation, police powers – stop and search and arrest or helping police with enquiries.

Courts – Magistrates', Crown, indictable offence, triable either way, potential defences.

Evaluation of PACE safeguards.

Worked example

Part B: Set task information

Case 1

You have been given a placement at a large firm of solicitors called SummerScales for Justice prior to starting a degree course in law at university and you will work in the department dealing with criminal case work. You have been involved in preparatory work for the following cases and have been asked to prepare a report on case 1 for your line manager.

Fineline Interiors Ltd and Steve Clarke, the managing director, have been charged following a fatality at the company. Their case will take place in February.

Simon Smith aged 16, an employee and trainee at the firm, was pronounced dead at the scene of a forklift truck accident. He was driving the forklift, which collided with shelves stacking flat-pack furniture.

Following an investigation by police and the HSE, the prosecution has alleged that Simon had no induction training, no health and safety training and had not been trained to drive a forklift truck. Furthermore, they have found CCTV footage showing a lack of supervision for the young worker at the firm.

Refer to your notes for preparatory work completed in Part A.

Provide a report on the scenario to include:

- an explanation of the relevant fatal offences using professional language and legal terminology
- application of relevant case law and statutes
- analysis of any potential defences
- evaluation of the law relating to this offence.

Activity 1

Identify the area of law and explain the law relating to corporate manslaughter pre and post 2008. This offence is recent so the Corporate Manslaughter and Corporate Homicide Act 2007 will apply. Apply the law to the case:

Actus reus, *mens rea* and causation

Duty of care

Breach of duty

Carelessness so bad as to be classed as criminal

Gross breach

Serious management failure

Consider likely consequences to all involved and penalties for the individual director and the company.

Evaluate of the changes to the law, that is, simplification by removing the need for the principle of identification but some groups are still critical that companies may not take health and safety seriously.

Throughout your report, make sure that you make reference to case law and statute.

This task gives you the opportunity to identify the relevant area of law, explain and analyse the law, apply the law to the scenario and to evaluate the impact of the 2007 Act.

Part B: Set task information

You have been given a placement at a large firm of solicitors called SummerScales for Justice prior to starting a degree course in law at university and you will work in the department dealing with criminal casework. You have been involved in preparatory work for the following cases and have been asked to prepare case file notes on case 2 for your line manager.

Case 2

Jenny Atkinson was the victim of a violent attack in Bedlam town centre when she was pushed to the ground and a young white male snatched her handbag. Witnesses identified the suspect as Peter Parfitt, a heroin addict with previous convictions who is well known by the police.

After making statements as to what happened and visiting the local A and E, Jenny carried on with her routine and met several friends for drinks in the evening. Jenny had consumed too much alcohol to drive and decided to stay at a friend's house near to the bar. Her friend was away on holiday and Jenny had forgotten her key so she broke in through a small kitchen window and went to sleep in the spare room. At 5 a.m. she was awoken by police officers at the door – a neighbour had reported a suspected break in. Jenny was taken to the police station for questioning.

Meanwhile, in the early hours of that same morning police officers had spotted Peter Parfitt. They stopped and searched him and on finding him in possession of Jenny's purse and cash cards, he had been arrested. His right to legal advice and to have someone told about his whereabouts was delayed.

Refer to your notes for preparatory work completed in Part A.

Provide case file notes on the scenario to include:

- an explanation of the relevant property offences using professional language and legal terminology
- application of relevant case law and statutes
- analysis of any potential defences
- evaluation and legality of the police during stop, search, arrest and detention.

Do not just rely on the Internet for your research sources. Explore law books, journals and news reports.

Activity 2

Identify the relevant areas of law.

Explain and analyse the law:

Robbery – theft, force, immediacy – *actus reus*. *mens rea* and causation

Identification of the suspect

Would intoxication have an impact on Jenny or Peter?

Was the stop, search and arrest of Peter Prafitt lawful?

Have any rules been breached under the codes of practice in relation to his detention?

Did Jenny commit burglary?

Did Jenny commit criminal damage?

What are the implications of accompanying the police officers to the station?

Justify all your answers and refer to case law and statute where appropriate.

Evaluate police powers and the safeguards aimed at both police and suspects.

Incorporate relevant principles such as innocent until proven guilty.

You may be able to use contemporary cases in the news to illustrate your answers.

This task gives you the opportunity to identify the relevant area of law, explain and analyse the law, apply the law to the scenario and to evaluate the impact of PACE and the codes of practice.

Sample answer and commentary – Activity 1

Fineline Interiors Ltd and Steve Clarke, the managing director, have been charged following a fatality at the company. Their case will take place in February.

Report on the case for SummerScales for Justice.

Always make a plan first, think about the structure and format of your answer and the key points to include. Set yourself a timescale for each part of your answer so that you do not run out of time. Remember that you are being asked to explain and apply the relevant law, to analyse and evaluate the law – so you need to leave time for a conclusion.

Case 1

Introduction

1. The area of law relating to this case are homicide offences as there has been a fatality, homicide offences consist of murder, voluntary manslaughter and involuntary manslaughter. Murder is an intentional killing of another person with malice aforethought which means intention, this can be direct where the defendant's aim is to kill the victim or oblique intent where the defendant's aim is not to kill but to cause another outcome, never the less the defendant knows the death of the victim will be a virtual certainty. Voluntary manslaughter is the same as murder except there is a partial defence which reduces the charge from murder to manslaughter – the partial defences are loss of control and diminished responsibility which are explained in the coroners and justice act 2009.

This learner has made a good start by thinking about a professional format using legal terminology. Consider spelling and grammar, for example always use capital letters for the name of an act. Concentrate on 'relevant law', this learner didn't need so much explanation about murder and voluntary manslaughter as the case is about involuntary manslaughter. Going off onto other areas of law wastes time for discussion of relevant areas further on.

2. The case concerning the death of Simon Smith is about involuntary manslaughter and there are two types – constructive and gross negligence. In this case, it is alleged that the victim was given no training or supervision so I think this would be gross negligence and the company and a director are being blamed so it could be individual and corporate liability under the corporate manslaughter and corporate homicide act 2007.

3. For gross negligence you have to prove duty of care, breach of duty, damage and causation and the carelessness has to be so bad that it amounts to a criminal offence, these tests come from R v Adomako where a doctor was responsible for the death of a patient.

Paragraph 2 and 3 make a good effort at linking the relevant law to the scenario and use case law and statute – when quoting case law make sure that you give the date of the case and include enough explanation to show how the previous case links to the scenario.

In case 1, the employer has a duty of care for the employee – Simon, the employer was in breach of this duty of care as they did not provide any training or supervision and that breach of duty caused death. The company should train all employees and especially young ones who aren't used to the workplace. The actus reus which means the prohibited act is causing death and this happened, the mens rea which means the guilty mind is gross negligence and the director was very careless. The actus reus must cause the death and if the company had trained Simon properly he would not have died. This case is similar to Kite which happened before 2008 when the corporate manslaughter and corporate homicide act came into force, where the owner of a company and the company itself were responsible for the deaths of some students who were on holiday, they were canoeing and were not properly supervised, to find the company responsible two things were proved – gross negligence and the principle of identification which was about the 'directing mind and will of the company'. The law was updated in 2007 and now this principle is not used.

In the paragraph above, the learner has applied the law and has used and explained legal terminology well. The point about protecting young and inexperienced workers is a good one. Some other areas which could have been included are the objective test and reasonable foreseeability for the test for breach of duty, more case law could have then been incorporated such as R v Winter 2010 and R v Misra and Srivastava 2005. For the law pre-2008, the learner could have explained legal personality and why there were so few convictions for corporate manslaughter

Here, it would have been a good idea to include a paragraph about why the law was changed – the lack of convictions and the campaigns by groups like Families Against Corporate Killings. The learner could have used quotes and statistics on fatalities at work as well as conviction rates.

4. The courts look for a gross breach of duty resulting from a serious management failure.

In the Lion Steel case which happened in 2012, a man died at work and his employers were guilty. A company can't be sent to prison so the punishments were unlimited fines and remedial and publicity orders.

This section is very brief, the learner could have given a further explanation of what has to be proved and could have included Section 8 of the act, which states that a jury will consider the seriousness of the breach and the risk factor. More case law could have been used, for example - R v Cotswold Geotechnical Holdings 2010 and R v Sherwood Rise Ltd 2016.

5. The consequences of this case are that a coroners inquest would be carried out to determine the cause of death, the whole incident would be investigated by the police working with the HSE (Health and safety executive) and evidence would be passed on to the Crown prosecution service. The company and the director would be liable for Simon's death which means the company would be fined and the employer could be sent to prison.

6. Changing to the new act is a good thing because the law has been simplified and now it is easier for companies to be convicted which gives some justice to the victim's family who have lost their loved one and companies should not be allowed to treat people so badly.

This section is very brief, the learner has not left enough time for evaluation of the scenario and the changes in the law, but has made some valid points about the consequences. The learner could have included the new sentencing guidelines introduced in February 2016.

Sample answer and commentary - Activity 2

Jenny Atkinson was the victim of a violent attack in Bedlam town centre.

File notes

Case 2

This case is about offences against property and includes – theft, robbery, burglary, criminal damage. There are also possible defences and a commentary on police powers.

This is a good introduction – succinct and very informative with all of the relevant areas identified. This learner has made a good decision to deal with each part of the scenario chronologically which should ensure that nothing is missed out.

Jenny Atkinson was the victim of a violent attack in Bedlam town centre when she was pushed to the ground and a young white male snatched her handbag.

'A person is guilty of robbery if he steals, and immediately before or at the time of doing so, and in order to do so, he uses force on any person or puts or seeks to put any person in fear of being then and there subjected to force.' – This is the legal definition of robbery taken from section 8 of the Theft Act 1968 and shows that basically robbery is theft with forced used in order to steal. Robberies cover cases such as muggings to really violent cases such as armed bank robberies. Property crime includes situations where the aim is to steal or damage property, these type of offences accounted for 70% of all police recorded crime in 2014 – 2015.

The learner has accurately quoted statute law and has shown some evidence of researching recent statistics. The learner has explained the quote and shown an understanding of the range covered by robbery.

The elements which have to be proved are –

Actus reus – Theft and force or putting or seeking to put any person in fear, the relevant areas of theft are appropriation (which means taking, using, destroying or assuming the rights of the owner as in R v Morris 1983), of property belonging to another (this includes money and all other property real or personal which includes any of your belongings and it belongs to the person who is in possession or control of it.).

Mens rea - Dishonesty and intention as for theft and Intention to use force to steal. Dishonesty for theft is determined by using the two stage test from a case called R v Ghosh 1982 –

Were the actions of the defendant dishonest by the standards of reasonable and honest people, and if so

Did the defendant know it was dishonest by those standards?

Intention to permanently deprive means that the defendant does intend to keep the property even if initially it was borrowed and then not returned. The defendant must intend or be reckless as to the use of force. The force used must be in order to steal and must be more than trivial as in R v Clouden 1987 and must be used immediately before or at the time of the theft as in R v Lockley 1995.

This section has broken down the law into the essential elements, which have been explained making good use of case law. Maybe the learner could have made more reference to the scenario.

Jenny was the victim of a violent attack and her bag was stolen – the essential elements of robbery are present.

The arrest of the suspect –

Stop and search is defined in section 1 of the Police and Criminal Evidence Act (PACE). A police officer can stop and search any person or vehicle in a public place for stolen or prohibited articles. The Criminal Justice Act 2003 extended this power to include searching for articles intended to cause criminal damage. The police can only stop and search a person if they have reasonable grounds for suspicion, they cannot stop a person just because of the way they look or because they are a known drug addict. The person searched can only be required to move outer clothing.

This section is thorough and clear, making reference to statute law.

An arrest must be based on a two stage test -

The person being arrested must be involved or suspected of involvement or attempted involvement in committing a crime, and

The police officer must have reasonable grounds for believing that it is necessary to arrest that person.

The arrest of the suspect is based on reasonable grounds and he must be cautioned, taken to a police station as soon as reasonably practicable, seen by a custody officer and questioned. The police will not be in breach of the codes if they follow all of the rules and procedures relating to codes A to H. They must ensure that they follow the detention time clocks, that a suspect is given certain rights such as legal advice, that special procedures are used for juveniles and vulnerable adults. The aim of the provisions is to provide safeguards for the suspect and for the police and to make sure that if a suspect is charged, his right to a fair trial is upheld.

The consequences of a breach of the provisions will depend on the nature and extent of the breach, if a suspect is deprived of his right to legal advice or to have someone informed that he is being held at the police station, the likely outcome would be a complaint against the police. If a confession is obtained under oppression or if it is deemed unreliable because of things said or done, the confession will be inadmissible.

Peter is responsible for the actus reus and mens rea of robbery – he will be charged and his case will be taken to the Crown court as it is indictable.

This section is thorough and clear. The learner has used examples and has included some evaluation of the safeguards put in place by PACE as well as the consequences of non-compliance,

Was Peter intoxicated?

Peter is a heroin addict. Intoxication can be voluntary or involuntary such as when drinks are spiked, here Peter has chosen to take drugs. Intoxication can be used in relation to crimes of specific intent but not for basic intent crimes and this was established in DPP v Majewski (1977). Peter can claim intoxication if he lacks mens rea as robbery is a crime of specific intent. This occurred in a case called R v Lipman (1970) where the defendant had voluntarily taken drugs and murdered his girlfriend, murder is a specific intent crime and his charge was dropped to manslaughter

Intoxication can be caused by alcohol, drugs, solvents or prescribed medication. The arguments are that intoxication can have an effect on the guilty mind or mens rea. Public policy arguments however require that an intoxicated defendant should not have an advantage over one who is sober.

The learner has clearly understood this area, has distinguished voluntary and involuntary and specific and basic intent. There is a recognition with the need for *mens rea* and the consequences of agreeing to negate this with the policy arguments referred to.

Jenny broke into a house.

Section 9(1)(a) and (b) provides two offences of burglary –

> *A person is guilty of burglary if he enters any building or part of a building as a trespasser with intent to steal or to inflict or attempt to inflict grievous bodily harm or to do unlawful damage.*
>
> *A person is guilty of burglary if, having entered any building or part of a building, he steals or attempts to steal or inflicts or attempts to inflict grievous bodily harm.*

Jenny did enter the house but had not intention and lacks mens rea for either offence under section 9 of the Theft Act 1968.

Jenny did not enter the house as a trespasser as her friend would have consented to her being there.

This section is thorough and clear, making reference to statute law. The learner has provided justified reasons why liability would not apply.

Jenny broke the window.

The Criminal Damage Act 1971 defines the offence as -

'A person who without lawful excuse destroys or damages any property belonging to another intending to destroy or damage any such property or being reckless as to whether any such property would be destroyed or damaged shall be guilty of an offence.'

Jenny damaged the window but had a defence as she believed her friend would consent to her entering and staying in the house, this would be a lawful excuse as defined in section 5 of the Act. Jenny had the actus rea but no intention which is required for the mens rea – both elements are required for criminal liability so Jenny has not committed an offence and will not need to rely on intoxication as an excuse.

This section is thorough and clear, making reference to statute law. The learner has provided justified reasons why liability would not apply.

Jenny was taken to the police station. If Jenny has voluntarily accompanied the police to the station, she is free to leave at any time. She will only lose her liberty at the time she is arrested and then the Police and Criminal Evidence Act 1984 codes of practise come into play to strike a balance between the rights of the suspect and the powers the police need to investigate crime. Jenny will comply with the investigation and should not face any charges.

Though an overall conclusion would have been a good idea, this learner has included explanation, analysis and evaluation throughout and, given the time constraints, has produced an excellent answer.

Case 1

Selection and understanding of legal principles relevant to context - Band 2 to 3
Application of legal principles and research to information provided - Band 2
Analysis of legal authorities, principles and concepts - Band 2 to 3
Evaluation and justification of decisions - Band 2 to 3
Presentation and structure - Band 3

Case 2

Selection and understanding of legal principles relevant to context - Band 4
Application of legal principles and research to information provided - Band 3
Analysis of legal authorities, principles and concepts - Band 4
Evaluation and justification of decisions - Band 4
Presentation and structure - Band 4

Aspects of Family Law

4

Getting to know your unit

Assessment
This unit is internally assessed using a series of assignments set by your tutor.

Family law is an area of law that affects both children and adults. Many of us will have experienced for ourselves or known people who have family lives that are not straightforward. When relationships in family life break down there is a set of regulations to help resolve disputes. These regulations are part of family law. Family law also sets out the types of adult relationship that are legally recognised, such as marriage, civil partnerships and cohabitation (living together), and how these are formed, ended or dissolved. Often people need to make arrangements for their children following the break-up of a relationship and to settle financial matters. Family law can help to resolve these issues, as well as ensure that the children's own rights are protected.

In this unit you will examine the legal rules that apply to marriage, civil partnerships and cohabitation, and how courts may apply these rules. You will learn how the law affects adult relationships, both when they are formed and if they break down. You will examine the different ways in which a relationship between two adults can be legally ended, including looking at the reasons for this and how current law is applied. You will look at the rules concerning money and property on the termination of a relationship, and you will learn about financial and children orders in particular cases. You will examine how courts resolve disputes over children and you will learn how the law is applied with regard to parental responsibility and the rights of children.

How you will be assessed

This unit will be assessed by assignments set and marked by your tutor. You will need to work independently on these assignments. Keep all your notes and activities that you have completed together in one folder so that you are well prepared. You also need to to check the unit specification and assignment brief. This will help you to be clear about what is required when questions ask for explanation, analysis and evaluation. It may be helpful to practise the higher-level skills needed in order to achieve the Merit and Distinction grades, such as developing a point, analysing a situation or case study, and evaluating the law and its impact. Throughout this unit you will find activities that will develop your understanding of family law, which will help you prepare for your assignments. The recommended assessment approach for this unit is two assignments, to include the suggested criteria.

The assignments set by your tutor will consist of a number of tasks designed to meet the criteria in the table opposite. They are likely to include a written assignment but may also include activities such as:

- case studies where you make decisions about a case and provide legal advice
- presentations or scenarios where you can demonstrate your knowledge about legal practice and procedures.

Assessment criteria

This table shows what you must do in order to achieve a **Pass**, **Merit** or **Distinction**, and where you can find activities to help you.

Pass	Merit	Distinction
Learning aim A Explore the legal rules governing the formation of marriages, civil partnerships and cohabitation		
A.P1 Apply the legal requirements for a marriage and civil partnership in given case studies. **Assessment practice 4.1**	**A.M1** Apply and analyse the law on marriage, civil partnerships and cohabitation in given case studies. **Assessment practice 4.1**	**AB.D1** Evaluate the impact of the current law on the formation and dissolution of adult relationships. **Assessment practice 4.1 and 4.2**
A.P2 Explain the difference between the rights and obligations of marriage/civil partnership and cohabitation and apply the law in given case studies. **Assessment practice 4.1**		
Learning aim B Examine the various methods for dissolving a relationship		
B.P3 Apply the law on annulment, divorce and dissolution of a marriage and civil partnership in given case studies, explaining the applicable grounds. **Assessment practice 4.2**	**B.M2** Apply the law on divorce, dissolution and nullity in given case studies, analysing the current law. **Assessment practice 4.2**	
Learning aim C Investigate the legal rules governing the distribution of money and property on the breakdown of a relationship		
C.P4 Explain and apply the financial and children orders and relevant factors taken into account on divorce/dissolution in given case studies. **Assessment practice 4.3**	**C.M3** Analyse the financial orders and orders available for children in given case studies. **Assessment practice 4.3**	**C.D2** Evaluate the law on financial and other orders that the court can make on the breakdown of relationships. **Assessment practice 4.3**
Learning aim D Examine how the courts resolve disputes over children		
D.P5 Explain and apply the law on parenthood, parental responsibility and children's rights in given case studies. **Assessment activity 4.4**	**D.M4** Analyse how the court resolves disputes over children in given case studies. **Assessment activity 4.4**	**D.D3** Evaluate the impact of methods used by the courts to resolve disputes over children. **Assessment activity 4.4**

Getting started

In small groups, list the names of relationships that can exist between two adults. Discuss what happens when someone starts a new relationship. For example, will their money and possessions be affected? Think about ways in which the law can protect someone if a relationship comes to an end.

A Explore the legal rules governing the formation of marriages, civil partnerships and cohabitation

The legal regulations governing marriages, civil partnerships and cohabitation vary in different countries. Here you will explore the definitions of these relationships and how the law of England and Wales applies to them.

Marriage and civil partnership

The types of legally recognised adult relationships in which individuals have the strongest legal rights are marriage and civil partnership.

Definition of marriage

Marriage is the legally recognised union of two people as partners in a personal relationship. Until 2013, marriage was specifically a union between a man and a woman. However, the Marriage (Same Sex Couples) Act 2013 made marriage legal for same-sex couples in England and Wales.

The right to marry

The right to marry is a human right, as stated in the European Convention on Human Rights (ECHR), Article 12: 'Men and women of marriageable age have the right to marry and to found a family, according to the national laws governing the exercise of this right.' This is also part of English law under the Human Rights Act 1998.

Formation of a valid marriage

Marriage can only take place if:

- both parties have the legal capacity to get married
- the correct procedure is followed.

Getting married is a voluntary activity. There are safeguards in the law to help prevent marriage taking place through **coercion** or **fraud**.

Who you can marry

There are various rules governing marriage. These relate to, for example, age, gender, relationship to the other person and a person's marital status at the time of marriage.

- Age restrictions – both of the people who wish to marry must be over the age of 16 and have the mental capacity to consent to marry. If either of the two people is under the age of 18, then consent must be obtained from that person's parents or **guardians**. If permission is refused, in England and Wales you can apply to the Family Court for permission to marry. The law in Scotland has always been different, and couples wishing to marry used to flee to Gretna Green on the Scottish border.
- Prohibited degrees of relationship – you cannot marry a close relative or someone within the 'prohibited degrees of relationship'. These are sometimes referred to as rules of **consanguinity** and **affinity**. Consanguinity means a relationship between

Key terms

Marriage – the legally recognised union of two people as partners in a personal relationship.

Coercion – when you are being forced into doing something.

Fraud – unlawful or criminal behaviour by which you intend to deceive others, often for personal benefit.

Guardian – someone who has been named in a will as the person responsible for the will-maker's children if they are orphaned before reaching the age of 18.

Consanguinity – relationship between the intended marriage partners as a result of family ties through a blood relative.

Affinity – relationships developed as a result of marriage of one parent to a parent of the other party of the proposed marriage.

the intended marriage partners as a result of family ties through a blood relative. Affinity refers to ties developed as a result of marriage of one parent to a parent of the other party of the proposed marriage. These rules have been created on moral, social and genetic grounds, and are set out in the Matrimonial Causes Act 1973.

This means a person cannot marry any of the following relatives:

- a child, including an adopted child
- a parent, including an adoptive parent
- a brother or sister, including a half-brother or half-sister
- a parent's brother or sister, including a half-brother or half-sister
- a grandparent or a grandchild
- a brother's or sister's child, or a half-brother's or half-sister's child.

Cousins are permitted to marry under these rules despite the possible genetic difficulties that might arise.

Sometimes information may come to light at a later point, which can create difficulties, for example, if the true identity of a person's relative is only discovered after the marriage has taken place.

PAUSE POINT Explain the rules governing who a person is allowed to marry with regard to age and family relationships.

Hint Discuss the possible problems that could result if these rules were not in place.

Extend Research a case where consanguinity was discovered after marriage took place. What happened?

- Bigamy – **bigamy** occurs when a person goes through a ceremony of marriage while already married to someone else. This is most likely to occur when a person has not been divorced from an existing marriage and declares they have never been married. Bigamy is a criminal offence.
- Polygamy – in order for marriage to be recognised as valid in the UK, it must be monogamous. **Monogamy** means that a person can only have one partner at any one time. This contrasts with **polygamy** where more than one wife or husband is permitted. In some parts of the world, having more than one spouse is legal.

  For some purposes, a polygamous marriage, or a **potentially polygamous marriage**, may be considered valid in the UK. This often results in complications with respect to immigration, benefits, pension rights, and divorce and subsequent property rights.
- Transsexuals – since 2004, transsexuals have been allowed to marry using their new established gender. An unmarried transsexual can apply to a Gender Recognition Panel to obtain a Gender Recognition Certificate (see Appendix page 338) under the Gender Recognition Act 2004. This allows the established gender to be used in a marriage and a new birth certificate to be issued.
- Same-sex marriage – the Marriage (Same Sex Couples) Act 2013 makes the marriage of same-sex couples lawful. This means that same-sex couples can now marry and have the same legal protections as a married man and woman.

Marriage procedures

There are set legal procedures regarding marriage, including how the ceremony is conducted, the venue and notices. These must be followed for the marriage to be lawful.

- The conduct of the ceremony – the two people getting married must exchange some formal wording, sometimes called wedding vows. They should discuss other wording they want in the ceremony with the person conducting it. In a civil

Key terms

Bigamy – this occurs when a person goes through a ceremony of marriage while already married to someone else.

Monogamy – having only one wife or husband.

Polygamy – having more than one wife or husband.

Potentially polygamous marriage – a marriage that is in fact monogamous, but when the marriage took place, further spouses were permitted.

ceremony, readings, songs or music are allowed. However, this must not include anything that is religious, such as hymns or readings from a religious text. There must be at least two witnesses at the ceremony. The two people getting married and their two witnesses must sign the marriage register (see Appendix page 339).

- Wedding venues – the people getting married must give details of the venue in a special notice at their local register office. A ceremony can take place at:
  - a register office
  - any approved venue, for example, a stately home or hotel
  - religious premises where permission has been given by the organisation and the premises are approved by the local authority.
- Notice requirements – for most marriages both parties must give at least 28 full days' notice at their local register office although in certain circumstances this can be reduced to 15 days by the issue of a special license. The two people must have lived in the registration district for at least the past seven days. They need to include details of where they intend to get married. Their notice will be publicly displayed in the register office for 28 days (see Appendix page 341).

Research

Find out where your local register office is located. Check how it sets out its requirements. This information is usually found on your local council's website, such as: **http://www.northyorks.gov.uk/article/29862/Legal-requirement---the-notice-of-marriage-or-civil-partnership**

Make a list of everything you would need to take with you to register your intention to get married. Would this list apply equally to your proposed marriage partner?

PAUSE POINT Research a case where a marriage did not comply with legal requirements. Identify why the marriage was unlawful.

Hint Highlight evidence to support why the marriage should not have taken place. Use the information given above.

Extend Analyse the ways in which the law has been broken and mind map all the people directly and indirectly affected.

Distinction between marriage and civil partnership

There are many similarities between a marriage and a civil partnership. A civil partnership can be easily converted to a marriage. This is done by signing a 'conversion into marriage' declaration at the local register office and paying a fee. Some of the differences between marriage and civil partnership are outlined in Table 4.1.

Table 4.1: Some of the differences between marriage and civil partnership

	Marriage	**Civil partnership**
Relevant legislation	• Marriage Act 1949. • Matrimonial Causes Act 1973. • Marriage (Same Sex Couples) Act 2013.	• Civil Partnership Act 2004.
Formation	• Marriages are solemnised by saying a prescribed form of words. • Marriage can be between two people of the same sex or two people of different sexes. • Marriages can be conducted through either a civil or religious ceremony.	• Civil partnerships are registered by signing the civil partnership document, with no requirement for words to be spoken. • Civil partnerships can only be between two people of the same sex and cannot be between people of the opposite sex. • The formation of a civil partnership is an entirely civil event. Civil partners can choose to add a ceremony if they wish.

▶ **Table 4.1:** *Continued*

	Marriage	Civil partnership
Other points	• Married couples cannot call themselves civil partners. • Marriages are registered on paper, in a hard copy register. • Marriage certificates include the names of only the fathers of the parties. • Marriage is ended by divorce, by obtaining a decree absolute of divorce.	• Civil partners cannot call themselves married. • The details of civil partnerships are recorded in an electronic register. • Civil partnership certificates include the names of both parents of the parties. • Civil partnerships are ended by a dissolution order.

Formation of a valid civil partnership

As with marriage, there are regulations governing who is allowed to form a civil partnership and procedures that must be followed.

Who you can enter into a civil partnership with

A civil partnership is a legal relationship that can be registered by two people of the same sex. It cannot be registered between two people of different sexes. The advantage of registering a civil partnership is that the relationship is given legal recognition, resulting in certain rights and responsibilities.

Two partners can register a civil partnership providing:

- they are both 18 years old or over or, if 16 or 17, with written consent from both parents or guardians
- they have lived in the area of registration for at least seven days
- both are free to marry (no existing husband or wife or civil partner) and are not close blood relatives.

Civil partnership ceremonies

The Civil Partnership Act 2004 states that no religious activity may occur during the process of registering a union. The Act does not make provision for a ceremony; therefore a couple wishing to have a ceremony need to contact the registration authority where the union will be entered to see whether a ceremony is possible. Permission for a ceremony is usually granted.

Notice requirements

Notice must be given to the register office at least 28 days before the registration of the civil partnership (see Appendix page 340), following the same procedures as for marriage.

Discussion

In groups, think about the similarities and differences between marriage and the formation of civil partnerships. Then in pairs, discuss why you think some of these differences exist. Feed back your ideas to the group.

Cohabitation

In this section you will explore the legal rules governing cohabitation, as opposed to marriage or civil partnerships.

Definition of cohabitation and its legal recognition

Cohabitation is defined as living together with someone. People who are cohabiting have fewer rights than if they were married or in a civil partnership.

Some people make cohabitation agreements to try to allow for disputes or a split so that one party is not left without any assets. This is considered in more detail below.

Key term

Cohabitation – living with someone.

Distinction between married couples/civil partners and cohabitants

Married couples have far more individual rights and obligations than cohabitants. The rights of married couples are much the same as those of people who are in a civil partnership. There are important distinctions between these rights and those of people living together, particularly when a relationship ends, outlined in Table 4.2

(see page 187). Many aspects of a person's life are affected, including their property, possessions, housing and financial arrangements, and whether inheritance tax is due on **bequests** to the other party. Parental rights with respect to children are considered later in this unit.

Formalising status as a cohabitant - cohabitation agreements

The rights of unmarried couples are often more difficult to enforce than those of people who are married or in a civil partnership. If a relationship breaks down between two people who have many assets, it can be expensive and time-consuming to resolve matters.

A cohabitation agreement is an option for a couple who do not want to marry or enter into a civil partnership. Like a **prenuptial agreement**, it comes into effect when a relationship breaks down. It can protect one person's assets when that person has brought far more assets to the relationship than the other. The agreement protects each person's rights and makes it clear how assets should be divided, and what should happen with regard to any children. Usually both parties are encouraged to seek independent advice before signing an agreement. This is so that there is less risk of coercion, which would make the agreement invalid.

Key terms

Bequest - property given in a will.

Prenuptial agreement - a document drawn up before the parties marry that is designed to set out property rights in the event of subsequent divorce. This is sometimes called an antenuptial agreement.

Steps in making a cohabitation agreement

1. Agreement is reached on the following matters:
   - who owns and who owes what at the time of the agreement and how assets will be divided in the event of a split
   - where there are joint assets, what rights each person has to buy the other partner's share of that asset
   - what happens to assets and debts acquired after the agreement has been made
   - what should happen with regard to existing and future children.
2. The cohabitation agreement is drawn up. Each party signs the document and the signatures are witnessed, usually by a solicitor.

Other informal relationships - homesharers

Homesharing involves older or disabled householders with a spare room sharing their house with someone. That person is known as a homesharer, and is typically a young adult looking for affordable accommodation. This arrangement has conditions attached:

- Householders must have a home that is suitable for sharing, and be in need of some support or companionship.
- Homesharers must be able to spare the time to give support or companionship to the householder.

Most organisations helping to arrange homesharing make it clear that there needs to be a written homesharing agreement that sets out each party's legal rights. A homesharer may be expected to help with daily domestic tasks, for example, but should not have responsibility for the householder's personal care.

PAUSE POINT In small groups, list the benefits of being a householder and a homesharer.

Hint Think about any problems that could occur when a householder lives with a homesharer.

Extend Research and find a homesharing agreement. Do you agree with the legal rights it sets out for each party?

Legal rights and obligations of marriage/civil partnership and cohabitation

The legal rights and obligations of married people and those in a civil partnership as distinct from the rights of cohabitants are outlined in Table 4.2 below.

▸ **Table 4.2:** The legal rights and obligations of married couples/civil partners and cohabitants

	Married couples/civil partners	Cohabitants
Death and inheritance	If no will has been made, the surviving spouse/partner will inherit all or some of the estate. Married couples/civil partners are exempt from inheritance tax for bequests made under a will to each other.	Where one partner dies without leaving a will, the surviving partner will not automatically inherit anything. Jointly owned property is transferred to the survivor. Inheritance tax is payable on anything received under a will.
Ending a relationship	A married couple/civil partners can separate informally but if they want to end the marriage/partnership formally, they will need to go to court and obtain a divorce/dissolution. Both partners have a right to stay in the home until either there has been a divorce/dissolution or the court has ordered one partner to leave.	An unmarried couple can separate informally without the need to go to court. The court does, however, have power to make orders relating to the care of the children.
Financial support	Each partner has a legal duty to support the other. A court can enforce this right and can make arrangements for payments after divorce/dissolution.	There is no legal duty to provide financial support for the partner, but there usually is an obligation for support to be paid for children. There may also be complications with respect to state benefits that may have been received while cohabiting.
Housing	Both partners have the right to live in the matrimonial/partnership home. It does not matter in whose name the tenancy agreement was made or who owns the property. This applies unless a court has ordered otherwise, for example, in the course of separation or divorce/dissolution proceedings. If both partners come to an agreement as to who should live in the home, this can be confirmed as a court order as part of the financial arrangements.	The unmarried partner of a tenant will usually have no right to stay in the property if the partner who has the tenancy agreement asks the other to leave. To get any protection they would have to go to court. Many tenancy agreements are in joint names so each partner has the right to remain and an agreement will have to be reached to decide who will continue to live there. If their partner is the homeowner, they would need to seek legal help to achieve any rights with respect to the property and any contribution they made towards it. See Burns v Burns (1984).
Money and possessions	Both partners are entitled to own anything in their sole name or in joint names. On divorce/dissolution, any property a partner owned before marriage/civil partnership is usually theirs. On divorce, all property is taken into account in a financial settlement (see later in the unit). Wedding presents usually belong to the person whose family or friends gave the present. An engagement ring or wedding ring is usually taken to belong to the person who has been given it.	Property a partner owned before they started cohabiting remains theirs. If they have a joint account with their partner, then any money in it or overdraft is usually shared equally, but the contract with a bank usually makes both partners liable for the full debt. This means that if one partner does not pay the debt, the other can be made to do so through the courts.

Identify two areas where the rights of married couples or civil partners are different from the rights of cohabitants.

Hint Discuss whether you think these differences are valid.

Extend Evaluate whether the law should be changed with regard to these rights. What proposals would you make?

Key case

Burns v Burns (1984)

Facts

The parties lived together for 17 years but were not married. She took his name. She carried out normal household tasks but she made no direct financial contribution to the house. She brought up their two children over 17 years. As the children grew up, she went to work, but her earnings went on normal household expenses. The court decided that she had acquired no interest in the family home. There was no express agreement to indicate anything other than the fact that the house was bought in the man's sole name.

Legal principle - some substantial contribution is required from a cohabitant in order that they may take a share of assets in the event of a breakdown of a relationship. If the cohabitant makes no direct contribution to the purchase price, they would have to prove that there was a common intention that they should have a share in the property.

Assessment practice 4.1

A.P1 A.P2 A.M1 AB.D1

Beth and Ajay have been in a relationship for several years. After four months of seeing one another they began sharing a flat. Then two years later they got married. They have been married for seven years, and still live in the same flat. The tenancy agreement is just in Ajay's name, but Beth pays the rent. They have no children. Over the last six months their relationship has been deteriorating. Beth is sure that Ajay is spending a lot of money and getting into debt. Last Tuesday Beth received a voicemail message from Ajay telling her he wanted a divorce. He told her she must leave the flat in a week's time. Beth is upset but not surprised. She is worried about finding a new place to live. She is also concerned that Ajay will take things that belong to her, such as the jewellery she inherited from her mother. Beth wishes she had never married Ajay, as now she will have to go through expensive and stressful divorce proceedings.

1 Beth has come to you for legal advice. You need to provide her with information about her rights and obligations as a married person and those of Ajay as her spouse. Explain how these would have been different if she had been cohabiting with Ajay. How effective is the law in protecting Beth and Ajay?

To complete this task, you will need to show that you understand the legal requirements for a marriage and the difference in rights and obligations of marriage compared with those of cohabitation.

2 While considering your detailed advice for Beth, reflect on the requirements for a marriage or civil partnership. You remember your friend Alex who is in a same-sex relationship and is considering formalising this as either a marriage or a civil partnership.

It might be useful for Alex to have a simple guide as to the legal requirements for a marriage and for a civil partnership. You decide to produce a leaflet that includes an indication of how well the current law works in these situations to protect those entering the relationship and the distinctions between the two possible formal relationships.

Plan

- What is the task? What advice am I being asked to give?
- Do I have enough legal information to complete the task?

Do

- I need to list the rights and obligations of a married person and a civil partner, and the rights and obligations of a cohabitant.
- I need to compare these and identify the differences.
- I need to identify any information I am missing.
- I need to apply the information I have to a specific case and provide personal advice.

Review

- I can explain what the task was and how I compiled the legal advice for my client and the guidance for Alex.
- I can identify what I have learned.
- I can explain why it is important to have comprehensive information in order to provide legal advice.

Examine the various methods for dissolving a relationship

Nullity

The word **nullity** is used to describe something that is legally invalid or void, as though it never existed in the first place. It is often used with reference to a marriage. Annulling a marriage is a way of legally ending a marriage. It is different from divorce with different conditions and procedures. People who do not believe in divorce are usually prepared to have their marriage annulled if that is possible.

In both nullity and divorce court proceedings, the parties are known as **petitioner** and **respondent**. However, annulment is different from divorce in various ways.

- A **decree of nullity** can be applied for at any time, whereas an application for a divorce decree can only be started if the marriage is at least one year old.
- Instead of a decree of divorce from the court, the parties to the marriage are given a decree of nullity.
- A decree of nullity means that you have not been married, whereas a decree of divorce means that you have previously been married, but no longer are (until remarriage).

The distinction between void and voidable marriages/civil partnerships

A marriage can be annulled either because it is void or because it is voidable.

- A **void marriage** is not a valid marriage, and has never been valid. It is as though the ceremony had never taken place. This is sometimes called void *ab initio*, a Latin expression meaning 'from the start'.
- A **voidable marriage** is a valid marriage until the final decree of nullity is made. Some people who are in a voidable marriage never seek to have the marriage avoided (made void).

As with a marriage, a civil partnership may be void or voidable. The equivalent to a divorce in marriage is the **dissolution of a civil partnership**.

Consequences of a void marriage/civil partnership

A marriage or civil partnership is void if the requirements for a valid marriage or civil partnership have not been fulfilled (see learning aim A). The reasons may be to do with the age of either of the partners, their family ties, that one of them is already married or that they are in a polygamous relationship. If the formal procedures have not been followed, then that too will make the marriage or civil partnership void. The consequence of this is that a decree of nullity can be issued, and financial and property arrangements can be made.

Occasionally the court may decide the marriage is so flawed that it is considered a non-marriage. The difference between a non-marriage and nullity is that the courts are not able to intervene and make an order with respect to property for a non-marriage. This could be where the 'marriage' is part of a play or dramatic reconstruction of an event and occasionally relates to a marriage that is missing important elements.

Key terms

Nullity – as though something never existed.

Petitioner – the person starting a court case with respect to nullity of their marriage (or their divorce).

Respondent – the person responding to or defending a court case with respect to nullity of their marriage (or their divorce).

Decree of nullity – the final court order that annuls a marriage.

Void marriage – a marriage that is not valid and does not exist.

Voidable marriage – a marriage that is valid, but which may be made void at a later date.

Dissolution of a civil partnership – the equivalent to divorce for those in a civil partnership.

An example of a non-marriage can be seen in the case of Hudson v Leigh (2009).

Key case

Hudson v Leigh (2009)

Facts

Miss Hudson was a devout Christian, while Mr Leigh described himself as 'an atheist Jew'. They had had a relationship for over ten years, during which time they had a daughter. They decided to get married. Miss Hudson believed that the only way she would feel properly married was if she had a religious ceremony, whereas Mr Leigh wanted a ceremony in a register office. They agreed to have a religious ceremony on the roof terrace of Mr Leigh's home in Cape Town, South Africa. This would be followed by a civil ceremony at a register office in England.

However, shortly after the religious ceremony the couple split up, so the civil ceremony in England never took place. The religious ceremony did not in itself constitute a valid marriage in South Africa for many reasons. The English courts would therefore not recognise what had happened in South Africa as a marriage. If they had been married, she could have claimed financial support for herself. The court in England decided that this was an example of a new category, that of a non-marriage, so she was not able to claim financial support for herself.

Legal principle – a marriage can be considered a non-marriage when a ceremony that takes place is invalid and due legal procedures for a marriage are not followed.

Grounds for a voidable marriage

The grounds (the reason someone can apply) for a voidable marriage are listed in the Matrimonial Causes Act 1973, s12. These can be summarised as follows:

- non-consummation due to incapacity or wilful refusal
- lack of consent
- mental incapacity
- venereal disease
- pregnancy
- acquired gender.

Non-consummation due to incapacity or wilful refusal

Consummation means normal sexual intercourse after the parties have got married. In order to use this ground for nullity, the petitioner must prove that the marriage was not consummated for one of the following reasons:

- either party was incapable of consummating the marriage
- the respondent wilfully refused to consummate the marriage.

Neither of these grounds apply to marriages of same-sex couples.

Lack of consent

Consent to a marriage from both partners is essential, and it is a criminal offence to force someone to marry. This includes taking someone overseas to make them marry (whether or not the forced marriage takes place).

A forced marriage is when either or both participants have been pressured into it, without giving their free consent. This is not the same as an arranged marriage, which, for example, may have been set up by other family members, but the couple have willingly agreed to it. If there is any **duress** on a person to enter into a marriage, this can be grounds for nullity.

Key term

Duress – similar to coercion. It involves threats, violence or other action that is used to force someone into doing something against their will. This invalidates consent to a marriage.

Sometimes there is a problem with providing sufficient evidence of duress. In the case of Hirani v Hirani (1983), the court decided that duress was evident, and the marriage was considered to be void.

Key case

Hirani v Hirani (1983)

Facts

The petitioner was a 19-year-old woman, who lived at home with her parents. She formed a relationship with a Muslim man. Her Hindu parents were horrified and immediately arranged for her to marry a Hindu man, while telling her that if she did not go through with it she would be thrown out of the house. She went to the ceremony reluctantly and cried throughout. The court decided that there was enough evidence of lack of consent.

Legal principle – the test for lack of consent to a marriage is whether the pressure and threats were sufficient to destroy any consent.

Mental incapacity

The petitioner must show that at the time of their marriage they did not have sufficient mental capacity to consent to the marriage due to suffering from a mental disorder within the meaning of the Mental Health Act 1983.

Venereal disease

If the respondent had a communicable venereal disease (sexually transmitted infection) at the time of the marriage and they were aware of this at the time, but did not tell the petitioner, then the marriage is voidable.

Pregnancy

There are grounds for nullity if the respondent was pregnant with another person's child at the time of the marriage, and they were aware of this at the time but did not tell the petitioner.

Acquired gender

If the petitioner was unaware that the respondent's gender was an acquired gender under the Gender Recognition Act 2004 at the time of the marriage, the marriage is voidable. This usually occurs when the petitioner did not know that the respondent was a transsexual. This is best established by production of a Gender Recognition Certificate (see Appendix page 338).

Grounds for a voidable civil partnership

A civil partnership is voidable for these same four reasons as a marriage:

- lack of consent
- mental disorder
- pregnancy
- acquired gender.

The other two grounds do not apply to civil partnerships.

PAUSE POINT In pairs, list the legal grounds for the nullity of a marriage.

Hint For each of the grounds, explain what the petitioner must prove to the court.

Extend For one of the grounds, discuss a possible scenario where the petitioner has not provided sufficient evidence. One scenario is the case of Steve and Ann. Steve and Ann have only been married for 6 months. They have started to have arguments about starting a family and the fact that Steve believes if they did so, Ann's earning capacity as a freelance personal trainer would be compromised. Steve is now refusing to be with Ann until she agrees to ensure she does not become pregnant. Discuss whether Ann could petition for divorce now, and if so, on what fact. How might the scenario need to change to allow a divorce petition to be presented?

Procedure for obtaining a decree of nullity

There is a procedure for obtaining a decree of nullity supported by guidance notes issued by the Department for Justice. The procedure is very similar to that for divorce or dissolution of a civil partnership.

The process involves the following steps:

- filing the petition
- giving a statement in support of annulment
- the **decree nisi** (see Appendix page 337)
- the **decree absolute**.

Key terms

Decree nisi – the first stage in getting a decree of nullity.

Decree absolute – the decree of nullity.

Designated Family Centre – a principal Family Court location in a Designated Family Judge (DFJ) area. A DFJ has the role of managing the workload of the Family Court across each of the distinct areas of England and Wales, known as DFJ areas.

Filing the petition

A petitioner needs to give the court:

- three copies of their completed form D8N – the nullity petition (the petition contains a number of sections and the grounds for petition are set out in a series of tickboxes)
- an official copy of their marriage or civil partnership certificate
- the court fees (the petitioner may be able to apply for exemption).

The **Designated Family Centre** (DFC) will then send the petitioner form DH9 – 'Notice of issue of petition'. This is a receipt for the fees they have paid (if relevant). The form will also tell them when the petition was sent to the petitioner's spouse or civil partner, what to do if they do not reply to it and what the petitioner's case number is.

Discussion

There are four levels of judge working for the Family Court with each level reflecting the complexity of the cases. Lay magistrates, district judges, circuit judges, and High Court judges will be housed in the same court building. This new structure is designed to create a more effective and efficient use of all judges' time. Each DFC will have at least one Design DFJ who will be responsible for the administrative running of the family court.

What benefits do you think there will be of the judges all being in one court building for:

- the judges themselves
- those the judges are working with?

Giving a statement in support of annulment

The petitioner then has to give a statement in support of the petition, which outlines the facts. The petitioner may have to go to court to give further details, particularly if the respondent disputes any of the allegations the petitioner makes. The respondent may or may not agree with the facts stated.

The decree nisi

If the respondent agrees the details in the petition, then the petitioner can apply for a decree nisi (see Appendix page 337). A decree nisi literally means a 'decree unless'. The 'unless' here means 'unless there are objections to the petition'. So a decree nisi can be seen as a conditional order. Once there is a decree nisi, the court can consider financial arrangements, discussed later in this unit.

If it can be proved that the respondent spouse has been served with a copy of the petition, then the court can proceed without that party.

The decree absolute

Once a petitioner has obtained the decree nisi, they must wait six weeks and can then apply for the decree absolute, which is the final order. If the petitioner does not apply within three months of being able to do so, the respondent may apply for the decree absolute. The marriage or civil partnership is then formally ended.

Bars to annulment

A bar to annulment is a reason why a petition for annulment can be refused. There are two main bars to annulment. These are set out in the Matrimonial Causes Act 1973, 13: s13 and can be summarised as follows:

- The petition was not issued within three years of the marriage, unless the petitioner is relying on the grounds of incapacity or wilful refusal to consummate.
- The respondent can prove that the petitioner knew an application for nullity could be made but led the respondent to believe that no application would be made. This amounts to forgiveness of the other party and an indication of the desire for the relationship to continue.

Divorce and dissolution

The law governing the ending of marriage by divorce has many similarities with the law governing the ending of a civil partnership, referred to as dissolution.

- The law relating to divorce is set out in the Matrimonial Causes Act 1973 (for male/female marriages) or the Marriage (Same Sex Couples) Act 2013 (for same-sex marriages).
- The law relating to dissolution of a civil partnership is set out in the Civil Partnership Act 2004.
- Both divorce and dissolution are dealt with by the Family Court.

Most of the case law relating to dissolution comes from divorce cases as there have been far more divorces over the years than dissolutions of civil partnerships.

The law tries to prevent divorce or dissolution by encouraging reconciliation. There is only one ground for either divorce or dissolution – that the marriage or civil partnership has broken down irretrievably. A petition for divorce or a petition for dissolution of a civil partnership may be presented to the court by either party for that reason. No petition for divorce or dissolution can be issued until the parties have been married for at least one year.

Facts of irretrievable breakdown

The irretrievable breakdown of a marriage or civil partnership has to be evidenced by one or more relevant facts. The majority of these facts require a considerable period of time to have passed before the petitioner can apply for a divorce or dissolution.

While much of the detail of the law regarding these facts relates to both divorce and dissolution, there is one clear difference:

- For divorce there are five relevant facts that can serve as evidence that a marriage has broken down:
  - adultery and intolerability – the respondent has committed adultery and the petitioner finds it intolerable to live with the respondent
  - behaviour – the respondent has behaved in such a way that the petitioner cannot reasonably be expected to live with the respondent
  - desertion – the respondent has deserted the petitioner for a continuous period of at least two years immediately preceding the presentation of the petition
  - two years' separation with consent – the parties to the marriage have lived apart for a continuous period of at least two years immediately preceding the presentation of the petition and the respondent consents to a decree being granted
  - five years' separation – the parties to the marriage have lived apart for a continuous period of at least five years immediately preceding the presentation of the petition.
- For dissolution only four of these relevant facts can serve as evidence that a marriage has broken down:
  - behaviour
  - desertion
  - two years' separation with consent
  - five years' separation.

Adultery is not a fact on which a partner can rely, as the definition of adultery does not apply to a civil partnership.

Adultery and intolerability

Adultery requires proof of all of the following:

- the respondent spouse has voluntarily had sex with someone else of the opposite sex

- the petitioner finds it intolerable to live with the respondent any longer
- the petitioner and respondent have not lived together for more than six months after discovery of the adultery.

Sex that someone has been forced into, whether a man or a woman, is not adultery. Rape is therefore not adultery. Similarly if the spouse has consented to the sex, then this cannot be evidence for adultery.

Adultery requires the sex to be with someone of the opposite sex, so homosexual activity is not adultery. This is why this fact does not apply to dissolution of a civil partnership. Adultery can be grounds for divorce in same-sex marriage but the infidelity must involve a member of the opposite sex. If the infidelity is with someone of the same sex, then the petition would be based on unreasonable behaviour.

Proof of adultery often takes the form of an admission from the person who has committed the adultery. If that is not forthcoming, adultery can be inferred from other evidence. Where there is no admission of adultery by the petitioner's spouse, the petitioner may instead decide to use unreasonable behaviour as grounds for their petition.

Behaviour

This requires evidence that the respondent's behaviour is such that it is unreasonable for the petitioner to continue living with the respondent. This is not whether the behaviour is generally considered unreasonable but whether the petitioner finds it unreasonable.

What amounts to unreasonable behaviour, therefore, covers many different types of action. What is critical is how the behaviour affects the petitioner.

Examples of unreasonable behaviour include:

- one very serious incident such as a conviction for a serious criminal offence
- an incident of drug taking that has serious consequences for the petitioner.

Examples that on their own probably cannot be classed as unreasonable behaviour include:

- a catalogue of relatively minor incidents
- financial difficulties
- one incident of drunkenness
- a low sex drive.

As with adultery, it must be shown that the petitioner and respondent have not lived together for more than six months following the incident relied upon in the divorce petition. Living together for more than six months after discovery of adultery, or during the period of living apart, resets the clock or means the fact cannot be relied upon.

Research

Research two decided cases that have considered the question of unreasonable behaviour. One example is that of O'Neill v O'Neill (1975): **http://www.bailii.org/ew/cases/EWCA/Civ/1975/1.html**

In small groups list any evidence of unreasonable behaviour by the respondents, or reasons why you think the behaviour was not considered unreasonable. Do you agree with the decisions of the court?

Desertion

Desertion requires evidence that the respondent has abandoned the petitioner for a continuous period of two years or more and has left the household with the intention of not returning. Merely working abroad does not constitute desertion; there must also be evidence of an intention not to return.

The parties can have lived together for up to a total of six months in addition to this two-year period and still claim desertion. This could mean a period of two years and six months from the initial desertion. This means that, for example, a partner might desert the other partner for one year, but return and stay for a few weeks to attempt a reconciliation and then leave again. The few weeks that they returned are not counted in the two-year period required. This is to allow a chance at reconciliation and is consistent with the six-month time bar on behaviour as evidence of irretrievable breakdown of marriage.

Living apart for two years with consent of the other spouse

If the parties have lived apart for more than two years and both agree to divorce, this means that this fact is satisfied, and there is evidence of irretrievable breakdown of marriage. The parties can have lived together for a period or periods of up to a total of six months, as with desertion, and still claim this fact. This could mean a period of two years and six months of living apart. The petitioner must get the respondent's agreement in writing for this fact.

Living apart means living separate lives; this may not necessarily involve living in separate locations as the finances of the couple may not allow this to happen. Living apart is evidenced by the emotional behaviour of one party towards another. It may be seen through each party having separate bedrooms and living independent lives. If one party is undergoing military service or in prison, this does not automatically count as living apart.

Living apart for five years

This is much the same as living apart for two years except that the other party's consent is not required. A possible objection to this by the respondent is that divorce would result in extreme financial or other hardship.

PAUSE POINT Make a list of the five facts evidencing irretrievable breakdown of marriage, and consider which is most likely to cause a hostile divorce. You might consider whether hostility might make the process more expensive and might try to create misleading evidence.

Hint Think about the evidence involved in each fact.

Extend Discuss this question: 'How might a hostile relationship between two partners affect their divorce proceedings?'

Bars on petitions for divorce and dissolution

A bar to divorce or dissolution is a reason why a petition for divorce or dissolution can be refused. There are various bars on petitions for divorce and dissolution including the following:

- A petition for divorce or dissolution cannot be made during the first year after marriage or the creation of the civil partnership.
- Some of the facts of irretrievable breakdown have minimum requirements of time that must have lapsed in order for these to be used as evidence for a petition of divorce or dissolution. These include desertion, two years' separation with consent and five years' separation.
- The failure to agree financial arrangements or matters with respect to children can constitute a bar to divorce. (These are considered later in this unit.)

Encouraging reconciliation

The law on divorce has always encouraged reconciliation and counselling. Court proceedings can be adjourned at any time if there is a chance of reconciliation. If a solicitor is acting in a divorce case, a reconciliation certificate must be given to the court stating whether this has been discussed. While a solicitor is not required to discuss reconciliation and the help that is available, it is usually mentioned early on.

Apart from preserving the relationship, attempts at reconciliation can make it easier for the parties to come to an agreement about financial arrangements and the arrangements with respect to the children of the family. In most cases, it is a legal requirement to attend a **MIAM (Mediation Information and Assessment Meeting)** if you are going to take your case to court. The other person involved is also expected to attend a MIAM, but they do not have to go to the same meeting as you.

There are some cases where attending a MIAM would not be appropriate and the requirement is waived. These include the following situations:

- There is clear evidence of domestic violence.
- You do not know where the other party is or it would not be wise to let the other party know where you are. An example of this can be seen in the murder of seven-year-old Mary Shipstone by her estranged father in September 2016. He had been accidentally given the girl's safe house secret address by a solicitor in the case.
- The dispute is about money and one of the parties is bankrupt.
- Both parties are in agreement and there is no dispute.

Key term

MIAM (Mediation Information and Assessment Meeting) – a meeting between a couple and a mediator to find out whether there are alternative ways to find solutions to their problems.

Procedure for obtaining a divorce or dissolution

The procedure for obtaining a divorce or dissolution of a civil partnership is similar to that for a decree of nullity.

Procedure for obtaining a divorce

There are three stages to obtaining a divorce:

- filing a petition for divorce
- obtaining a decree nisi of divorce (see Appendix page 337)
- obtaining a decree absolute of divorce.

As with nullity, if the respondent agrees with the details of the petition, the petitioner can apply for a decree nisi. If the respondent spouse does not reply, but it can be proved that they have been served with a copy of the petition, the court can proceed without that party.

Procedure for obtaining a dissolution

There are three stages to obtaining the dissolution of a civil partnership:

- issuing a petition for dissolution of a civil partnership
- obtaining a conditional order of dissolution of a civil partnership
- obtaining an absolute order of dissolution of a civil partnership.

Defended and undefended divorce/dissolution

- If both parties agree to the divorce, this is an undefended divorce. If one of the parties does not agree to the divorce, it is a defended divorce. The vast majority of divorces are undefended.
- If both parties agree to the dissolution of a civil partnership, this is an undefended dissolution of a civil partnership. If one of the parties does not agree to the dissolution of a civil partnership, it is a defended dissolution of a civil partnership.

PAUSE POINT Make a list of the stages in obtaining a divorce.

Hint Alongside each point on the list, add the equivalent for obtaining a dissolution of a civil partnership.

Extend Consider whether the processes are really equivalent or whether they favour those who have been married.

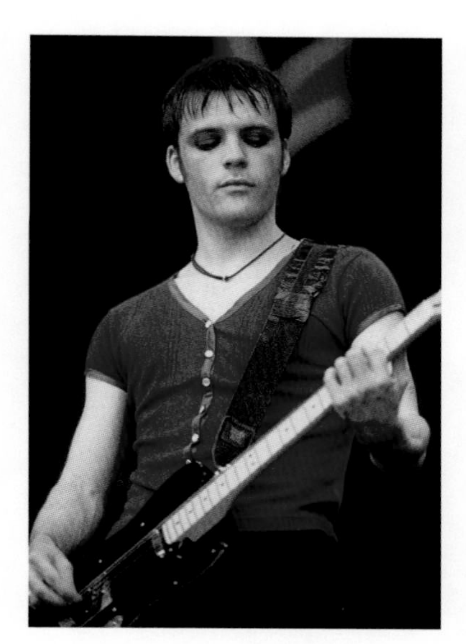

Richey Edwards, lyricist and guitarist of the group Manic Street Preachers was missing, presumed dead

Decree of presumption of death and dissolution of the marriage

Any missing person is generally assumed to be alive. Each year in the UK around 130,000 people are reported missing. Most of them are found but a significant minority each year remain missing. As well as being very distressing to friends and relatives, this can cause a number of problems, such as dealing with financial matters of the missing person. It also affects their spouse or partner in terms of any new relationships: the missing person is still their legal spouse or partner so they cannot remarry or enter into a new civil partnership.

The process for obtaining a death certificate of a missing person can be very lengthy. For example, Richey Edwards, lyricist and guitarist of the group Manic Street Preachers went missing and was presumed dead. It took his sister, Rachel Elias, 13 years to register her brother's death.

The Presumption of Death Act 2013 allows the High Court to issue a decree of presumption of death. This states that the missing person is presumed to be dead. The decree will confirm the ending of a marriage or civil partnership and can also deal with property matters. The date of the presumed death is the latest date in the seven years since the missing person was last known to be alive, or the end of any window of time in which death is known to have taken place.

Should the missing person return, any marriage or civil partnership is not automatically revived. The process would have to be gone through once more, assuming both were still free to marry or enter a civil partnership.

Reflect

Is it possible for courts to apply the law regarding nullity, divorce and dissolution consistently? Identify areas that might be open to interpretation.

Judicial separation

Judicial separation is an alternative to divorce. It is rarely used except in cases where the couple have moral objections, cultural reasons or religious beliefs for not wanting to obtain a divorce. For a civil partnership, this is known as a separation order.

Difference between judicial separation and divorce

The effect of a decree of judicial separation is that the parties remain married or in a civil partnership. However, the parties no longer have a duty to live together. The court can make financial orders as it can with divorce, with a few minor exceptions. Orders can be made with respect to children. The main differences between judicial separation and divorce or dissolution are outlined in Table 4.3.

Link

See Learning aim C of this unit for more information on financial orders.

Table 4.3: Differences between divorce or dissolution of a civil partnership and judicial separation

	Divorce or dissolution	**Judicial separation**
Must prove irretrievable breakdown	Yes	No
Time for application for decree	At least one year after marriage	At any time
Stages of making the order	Two stages: decree nisi and decree absolute	One stage only
Initial court fee (2016)	£550	£365

Requirements for a judicial separation

There is no requirement for a judicial separation to show that the marriage or civil partnership has irretrievably broken down. Otherwise, the requirements to obtain a decree of judicial separation are the same as the facts for divorce or dissolution of a civil partnership with insignificant differences in procedure. So for a judicial separation one of the five facts needs to be evidenced; for a separation order one of the four facts needs to be evidenced.

Legal effects of judicial separations

The legal effect of a decree of judicial separation is that the couple remains legally married. However, their normal marital obligations cease and they no longer have to go on living together. If they decide to resume their marriage, they can apply to the court to have the decree of judicial separation rescinded (ended).

Reasons for seeking a judicial separation

Judicial separation is rarely used except in cases where the couple:

- have moral objections, cultural reasons or religious beliefs for not wanting to obtain a divorce
- have been married for less than one year
- would have difficulty in proving that the marriage has irretrievably broken down.

Identify the main difference between the requirement for judicial separation compared with the requirement for divorce or dissolution of a civil partnership.

Hint Write down the legal effects of judicial separation for both parties.

Extend List and discuss the reasons why a couple may choose judicial separation over divorce or dissolution.

Assessment practice 4.2

B.P3 B.M2 AB.D1

You are doing a work placement in a law firm. The partner who manages the family law work wants to update the literature that is produced for clients so that it both reflects current law and is easily understandable. She would like you to prepare an informative and practical leaflet to give to clients on the formation of marriage and civil partnership and the ways in which these relationships may end. This should include promoting opportunities for reconciliation. The partner has suggested that you research decided cases, and provide simple analyses of these, so that clients can see how the law works in practice. Where relevant, this leaflet should refer to areas of the law that you feel are problematic, to show that it is not always easy to have laws that effectively and fairly cover any given scenario. You can also mention any legislation that is currently under consideration and evaluate how this might affect existing law if it is passed.

When undertaking this task, you need to think carefully about what information you include and how it is presented. The leaflet needs to be user-friendly but comprehensive and accurate. You need to show that you understand the law on the formation and dissolution of relationships, and how this applies to given situations. You should be able to explain the grounds for divorce, dissolution, nullity and judicial separation, including any bars to obtaining these, and the legal procedures involved. Use legal terminology where appropriate, and refer accurately to the cases you use as examples.

Having produced your leaflet, consider how the law might be applied in the following situations:

1. Guido and Lella are Italian students who were living together in London. When Lella's parents learned about their cohabitation, they immediately arranged to go through a valid ceremony of marriage in London. Her parents drove over to the wedding but immediately after the ceremony, Lella left in a car with her parents and was driven back to her hometown in Italy. She and her parents will not allow Guido to see her or communicate with her in any way. Guido wants to annul the marriage.
2. Anja and Virat have been married for ten years. Virat has become increasingly violent towards Anja. Police have been called on several occasions and she has now left the matrimonial home for a women's refuge. He wants to divorce her because he claims she would not cook his food as he liked it and objected to him drinking alcohol.
3. John and Ben are in a civil partnership. They have split up and have now lived apart with new partners for three years. Ben now wants to marry his new partner, Charles.
4. Graham went through a ceremony of marriage with Belinda. Belinda is now horrified to find that Graham is married to Svetlana. He says he is not really married to Svetlana as he only married her so she could fulfil the requirements to stay the UK. He did know the authorities suspected it was a sham marriage, so they lived together for three weeks. Belinda has just discovered that Svetlana had Graham's child which was conceived in that three weeks they were living together.

Plan

- What is the task? What is the purpose of the leaflet?
- Do I have sufficient understanding of the law? Do I need any clarification?
- What research do I need to do? Can I access the relevant information?
- How will I structure the leaflet? Will I use different features for presenting the information?

Do

- I need to present the information in a user-friendly way.
- I need to research decided cases, explain how the law was applied and evaluate the law, identifying any problem areas.

Review

- I can explain what the task was and how I approached the structure of the leaflet.
- I can explain what I found difficult and what I would do next time.

C Investigate the legal rules governing the distribution of money and property on the breakdown of a relationship

Financial orders available to the court on divorce / dissolution

In the case of a divorce or a dissolution of a civil partnership, the court can deal with financial matters and make a **financial order** with respect to:

- **money orders**
- **property orders**
- **pension orders**.

Another financial order the court can make is **maintenance pending suit**, which requires a spouse or partner to make payments in order to provide for the other party until a settlement has been reached.

For most couples, living apart requires more income than living together. The most hostile battles are usually about money and assets, often linked to the support of their children. For this reason, in nearly all cases, **family mediation** or **arbitration** takes place. Usually, a person who applies for a financial order will need to prove that they have considered mediation; exceptions are where domestic abuse has been present or the whereabouts of one partner is unknown. Financial matters are only settled in court when agreement has not been reached through mediation.

Family mediation and family arbitration

Family mediation

To use mediation, both partners must go along voluntarily. One of the parties may go by themselves, but will probably be referred to family mediation by a solicitor or other advisor. If there are children involved, the parties are likely to be referred to a CAFCASS (Children and Family Court Advisory and Support Service) officer.

A mediator can help to understand and resolve issues that face a family

An independent, trained mediator will meet the couple (either separately or together) to understand the issues they have and help them reach an agreement. The mediator will write up any proposed agreement.

Key terms

Financial order – a court order that deals with the assets of a separating couple.

Money order – a court order for the payment of money from one party to the other, either as regular payments or a lump sum.

Property order – a court order for the transfer of specific assets from one party to the other.

Pension order – a court order for the transfer of specific pension rights from one party to the other.

Maintenance pending suit – an order for periodic money payments to a spouse or partner until the financial aspects of divorce or dissolution proceedings are finalised.

Family mediation – an independent, trained professional helps a couple to work out an agreement about issues such as arrangements for children or their finances.

Family arbitration – enables couples going through family breakdown to resolve disputes more quickly, confidentially and in a more flexible and less formal setting than a courtroom.

The benefits of mediation are as follows.

- It gives couples a greater say in what happens.
- It is less stressful and involves less conflict than going to court.
- It improves communication between couples.
- It is quicker and cheaper than court action.
- Agreements can be changed when circumstances change.
- It considers the needs of children above the feelings of the parties.
- It is less upsetting for children involved and helps them continue important family relationships.

Family arbitration

Family arbitration also allows couples to reach an agreement about family disputes without going to court. However, it is a more formal process and is similar to court proceedings. An arbitrator's award is final and binding, whereas any agreement reached through mediation must be incorporated into a court order or other legal agreement to be binding.

PAUSE POINT In pairs, list the benefits of family mediation for a couple with two children.

Hint Which of these benefits will impact on the children most?

Extend List any disadvantages to resolving disputes through mediation rather than through the courts.

Maintenance pending suit

Maintenance pending suit is set out in Matrimonial Causes Act 1973, s22. It can be applied to help spouses and children in cases of nullity, divorce and judicial separation. Similar legislation exists with respect to civil partners under the Civil Partnership Act 2004.

Maintenance pending suit is defined as an order requiring either party to the marriage/civil partnership to make periodical payments to the other party or with respect to children. Payments continue until final arrangements are made. Typically an order is made when the parties to the relationship have separated prior to the start of proceedings. It can be helpful in dealing with short-term cash flow problems.

Money orders

Most cases do not require maintenance pending suit. The real need is to sort out long-term financial arrangements between the parties. Money orders are made in most cases: either as a periodical payments order or a secured periodical payments order.

Other orders are called property orders and include lump-sum payments and transfer of other property such as a house, car or specific item or investment. The primary objective is that, where possible, there is a clean break between the couple. This avoids the need for continuous contact even if only by bank transfer.

In this section you will only look at financial arrangements with respect to a spouse or civil partner. Orders for the support of children are considered later.

Periodical payments order

A periodical payments order is a payment made out of income by one spouse or civil partner to provide for the other. It is usually known as **maintenance**.

A periodical payments order is a weekly, monthly or annual payment (this is why it is called 'periodical'). It can be for any amount and is sometimes for a nominal amount of, say, £1 per year. This is to acknowledge the right to a money order. Any money order can be varied later by the court if there have been significant changes in one party's circumstances.

Where periodical payment orders have been made with respect to children, most will last until a child is 18.

Key term

Maintenance – the regular payment usually made out of income by one spouse or civil partner to provide for the other.

Secured periodical payments order

With a secured periodical payments order, the order is secured on the assets of the payer. This means that the order is backed up by any possessions or assets of the person who is paying. These orders are rare as the court will need to be satisfied of two conditions:

- There are reasons to believe the spouse getting the periodic payment needs protection against the paying party going bankrupt, disappearing or dying.
- There is an asset against which the payments can be secured.

This order requires the paying party to secure the annual amount of the periodical payments against a capital asset such as a lump sum deposit in a bank. As with a periodical payments order, a secured order will end on the death, remarriage or formation of a civil partnership by the receiving party. It will not end, however, on the death of the paying party.

PAUSE POINT Research several cases in which money orders were made by the court.

Hint Identify how the decision of the court varied depending on the circumstances of the case.

Extend Did you agree with the decision of the court in each case? Justify your reasons.

Property orders

Lump sum order

A lump sum order is an order requiring one party to pay a lump sum of money to the other. This could be:

- savings that were held in the name of one spouse only
- investments that are in one name only
- money from the sale of property whose ownership is not clear – for example, a work of art
- a sum payable by one party to the other to buy out the rights of the other in the former matrimonial home.

A lump sum can be made instead of periodic payments, when the spouse who is paying has sufficient money to make one substantial payment.

Property adjustment orders

A property adjustment order is an order requiring one party to transfer an interest in property to the other, such as a house, land, stocks and shares, car or other physical or non-physical asset. This kind of order, once made, cannot be varied. Typically, an order of this type will be made when there is a need to allow each spouse a share in the capital value of the family assets, especially the matrimonial home. It is very significant when dealing with high-value divorce cases, for example, when the transfer of shares in a business could affect control of a company. Similarly, it may well settle a dispute about the ownership of investment assets such as gold or a painting.

There are many forms and matters to consider with respect to property adjustment orders:

- Postponing the sale of the home

The court can order that the sale of the family home will not take place until a certain time, for example, when the youngest of the children reaches 18 years old.

- Orders for sale

The court usually only makes an order for sale of the matrimonial home if the marriage or civil partnership has been short and there are no children to consider. The court will not make such an order if that would leave either party homeless. This could also be

Key term

Negative equity – the amount owed on the mortgage of a house is more than the value of the house.

ordered if the sale of the matrimonial home will produce enough money to allow both parties to buy another home or if neither party can afford to buy out the other party. Where there is **negative equity** in the house, the court will not make an order for sale. The mortgage lender will usually require the house to be sold anyway if the parties cannot agree to continue to pay the mortgage.

Property adjustment orders may also cover:

- Transfer of property – the court can order that the ownership of the family home is transferred from one party to the other. The court can also order that the property is transferred and sold when a particular event takes place, and the proceeds of sale divided in particular proportions. This is often the case when it is agreed that one party shall remain in the former matrimonial home along with their children. The sale might take place when the children have finished education or reached a certain age.
- Settlement of property – this is an order requiring one party to transfer specified property for it to be held on trust. The trustees will hold the property for the benefit of the beneficiary (usually either the other party or the child of the marriage), in accordance with the terms of a trust deed. This type of order is not common and factors such as the child's welfare, the income, earning capacity, property and other financial resources that each parent has or is likely to have in the foreseeable future will be taken into account. It might be used, for example, to provide for a disabled child, with the assets under the trust being transferred to someone else on the death of the child.
- Variation of settlement – where a trust (which is sometimes called a settlement) is already in existence, the court can vary the terms of that trust or settlement. This is usually only relevant when the couple have had the benefit of a family trust and they are now getting divorced.

Pensions

Pensions are increasingly complex and important in cases of relationship breakdown. Often one party will have a large potential pension and the other may have little or nothing. Current law allows a person who has a pension pot to take some of it in cash rather than as a regular pension payment. This gives an opportunity for one party to withdraw a lump sum and reduce the income that they will get in later life.

If a person gets divorced, or has their civil partnership dissolved, the court will take their pension assets into account when making any financial order. Both parties will have to list the value of their individual pension pots. These will be calculated according to how much the pension benefits are worth at the date of divorce or dissolution of the civil partnership.

The court can make several types of order relating to pensions:

- Pension attachment order – this is an order requiring a proportion of a pension lump sum and/or pension income or a death in service payment to be paid. The order is set out as a percentage or fraction of the lump sum or income and is different to a pension sharing order as it applies to the value of the pension at the date of actual retirement. It therefore provides the recipient with a guaranteed pension or lump sum or payment when the pension holder reaches retirement age.
- Pension sharing order – the pension is split at the time of divorce or dissolution so that each party receives a separate pension pot to build for the future.
- Pension offsetting order – each party keeps their own pension benefits but the proportion of other assets is adjusted to balance things up.
- Pension earmarking order – this order ensures that when one person's pension benefits start to be taken, it will be paid directly to the other person.

Make a list of the individual orders available to a court on divorce or dissolution of a civil partnership.

Hint Think about the effects of each order on the couple, particularly if one party has far more assets than the other.

Extend Are court orders necessary to resolve financial matters?

Factors the court will take into account when deciding what order to make

Statutory factors and relevant case law

The court will take into account all relevant statutory factors when deciding which financial order to make. These factors should have been considered when coming to any agreement about financial matters before seeking a court order and before mediation. The factors referred to in the Matrimonial Causes Act 1973 and subsequent cases include:

- financial means
- financial needs
- lifestyle of the parties
- age of the parties
- duration of the marriage or civil partnership
- choices made in the relationship
- disability
- contributions
- conduct.

Financial means

This takes into account both parties' income, earning capacity, property and other financial resources. These are considered with respect to their current position as well as their situations in the foreseeable future. So if one party is currently unemployed but is looking for employment that will be taken into account. Otherwise, one party might choose to be unemployed and after the divorce revert to a highly paid job. A good example of this is a Premier League football manager.

In 2016 the Family Justice Council published guidance on this, called 'Sorting out Finance on Divorce', which:

- focuses on those cases where the available assets do not exceed the parties' needs
- provides a summary of the law as explained and developed in leading cases
- includes a number of helpful case studies of common scenarios.

The courts have dealt with many cases on this, most famously with the contrasting cases of Miller v Miller (2006) and McFarlane v McFarlane (2006). An appeal on these cases was taken to what is now the Supreme Court. The idea of fairness was discussed, and the following three important points were highlighted:

- the financial needs of the parties
- whether financial disadvantage had been caused by the way the parties arranged things in the marriage, including giving up work to look after children
- the principle of 'equal sharing', seen in the case of White v White (2000), which entitles each partner to an equal share of the assets of the partnership, unless there is a good reason to the contrary.

Financial needs

There is a difference between financial needs and financial wants. The parties and the court have to consider the needs, obligations and responsibilities that each party has now and in the foreseeable future. The first consideration is the need for somewhere to live.

These needs focus on providing a home for the children and the person who is going to be the primary carer for the children. Consideration for the other partner to the relationship comes after that, together with consideration of others for whom the couple have assumed responsibility during the marriage or civil partnership. This might include an elderly parent who has been living with the family.

Lifestyle of the parties

This factor involves a consideration of the standard of living before the split. In most cases, it is inevitable that the same standard of living cannot be maintained for both parties after the split. Even with wealthy couples, it is likely that some reduction of standards will follow a separation.

In the divorce cases of certain extremely wealthy people, there have been demands for very high settlements to enable petitioners to maintain their previous lifestyles. In the case of Preston v Preston (1982) it was said that a wife of 23 years of a millionaire could expect a very high standard of living. In the case of Christina Estrada (2006), her demands totalled £238 million; the estimate for the final settlement was £75 million. To avoid publicity, most divorces of very wealthy people never come to court and financial matters are settled in private.

Age of the parties

Age affects a person's earning capacity, particularly where the person has been caring for children rather than pursuing a career for many years. This is taken into account when deciding on a financial settlement.

Duration of the marriage or civil partnership

The duration of the marriage or civil partnership is an important factor. Normally any period of cohabitation prior to the marriage or civil partnership is ignored. Under exceptional circumstances, an earlier period of cohabitation can be taken into account. This might be the case when considering cohabitation before legislation allowed a civil partnership or same-sex marriage. In the case of Kokosinski v Kokosinski (1980), the husband had a wife in Poland from whom he could not get a divorce. That marriage was finally ended 25 years later during which time he had been cohabiting with the petitioner. Some months after they married, the relationship broke up and the court took their 25 years of cohabiting into account when considering financial arrangements.

Choices made in the relationship

This factor includes choices such as the decision for one spouse to stop working and bring up the children. The court considers financial and non-financial contributions to be of equal weighting.

Disability

Physical or mental disability is an important factor. This can have an effect on foreseeable financial needs and earning capacity as well as reduced life expectancy.

Contributions

Whether or not the couple have children is an important factor, and can affect one party's contribution to the finances as well as the overall financial state of the parties. Other contributions could include a party self-building a house or helping their partner develop their business while sacrificing their own career.

Conduct

Until the principle of no-fault divorce was brought in in the 1970s, fault had a significant bearing on financial arrangements. Now fault can only be taken into account if it would be unfair - or in legal terms not **equitable** - not to.

This includes circumstances where there has been 'gross and obvious misconduct'. This often refers to financial deception, such as:

- hiding funds prior to a divorce
- other financial deception on a large scale.

It does not take into account adultery or unreasonable behaviour; these are seen only as evidence that the marriage has irretrievably broken down.

The following cases show how the law was applied:

- In H v H (1999), the court decided that it was inequitable to disregard the husband's financial dishonesty during the last three years of cohabitation and thereafter.
- In Kyte v Kyte (1987), the court took into account the wife's conduct in actively assisting, or at least taking no steps to prevent, the husband's attempts at suicide together with her wholly deceitful conduct in relation to her association with another man.
- In Evans v Evans (1989), the wife was sentenced to four years' imprisonment for inciting others to murder the husband. This was taken into account.
- In H v H (1994), the husband's conduct in brutally assaulting the wife, resulting in his arrest and loss of employment, was taken into account.

Key term

Equitable - fair.

Scenario

Miller v Miller (2006) and McFarlane v McFarlane (2006)

Mr and Mrs Miller were engaged in July 1999 and they married a year later, on 14 July 2000. They did not live together before their marriage. They separated in April 2003 and the marriage was childless. When they separated, the husband was aged 39 and the wife was 33. At the time of the hearing, Mrs Miller had assets worth £100,000, of which half were in pension funds. She had legal costs outstanding in excess of £250,000. Mr Miller had assets of £17.5 million at the date of the first hearing, compared with £16.7 million when the parties married in July 2000 and £17 million when they separated in April 2003. The husband's basic salary was £181,000. He received a bonus of £3 million for 2003 and one of £1.2 million for 2004.

In the case of McFarlane v McFarlane, the couple were married for sixteen years and had three children. They were both aged 46 at the time of separation. They had both had successful careers but before the birth of their second child they agreed that the wife should abandon her career and bring up the children. This would also allow them to concentrate on the husband's career. The husband's career flourished and by the time of the separation his gross annual income was nearly £1 million. However, there was insufficient capital available for a clean break between the parties.

Identify the differences between these cases, considering the following:

- the financial needs of all parties
- the contributions each party has made over the course of the relationship
- any capital or other assets at the time of separation
- the needs of any children.

In each case, examine whether it was possible for the court to make a judgment that was fair to both parties. Give reasons for your answers.

Now consider other cases such as Paul McCartney v Heather Mills-McCartney (2008).

Clean break

Most divorce settlements have three main parts:

- periodical payments
- capital orders
- pension orders.

These can be replaced by a one-off settlement, called a clean break settlement. On divorce the court can make a clean break order. The result of this order is that each person's financial affairs are completely cut off from each other. The court is keen to ensure that, where possible, there is a clean break between the couple.

Advantages of a clean break

- The parties will have no financial ties once the order is agreed or ruled upon by a court.
- There are no periodical payments as they are covered by a lump sum.
- There is no danger of a payment being missed or arguments about timing or method of payment.

Disadvantages of a clean break

- There are some court costs involved.
- The parties cannot go back to court if there is a change of circumstances such as hard times or remarriage. Remarriage would normally end periodical payments.

Factors that will make a clean break appropriate or inappropriate

A clean break settlement is appropriate where there is a short, childless marriage or where the couple's resources are greater than their needs. Where there are children, one party is in poor health or where the parties are older, it may be less appropriate. This is largely a case of dependency of one party on another.

An example of not having a clean break order can be seen in the case of Kathleen Wyatt, ex-wife of Dale Vince. Wyatt won her case to get a 'modest lump sum payment' reputed to be £300,000 from her ex-husband's £100-million fortune. The case was brought more than 30 years after their divorce. At the time of divorce, no clean break order had been made as Mr Vince was a traveller and unable to provide any financial support for his ex-wife and child.

Prenuptial agreements

A prenuptial agreement, sometimes called an antenuptial agreement, is a document drawn up before the parties marry and is designed to set out property rights in the event of subsequent divorce.

- A prenuptial agreement can help to keep a divorce and a couple's financial affairs secret.
- A prenuptial agreement is not legally binding. However, in the event of divorce, the courts usually uphold the arrangement that has been outlined, provided the agreement was made freely and after independent advice offered to both parties.
- The law concerning prenuptial settlements is unclear at present. Such agreements have some value where there is little change in the overall situation between the parties at the time of divorce. The birth of a child may well change things, particularly where not envisaged in the prenuptial agreement.
- A prenuptial agreement should be drawn up by a solicitor and is likely to cost upwards of £900.

Variation of orders and appeals

The law on these orders and appeals can be found in the Matrimonial Causes Act 1973, s31. This section of the Act allows for some orders to be varied by the court at a later date.

Variation of orders

The usual reason for an application to vary a periodical payment order is because of changed circumstances. These orders automatically end in the following situations:

- if the recipient dies
- if the recipient remarries

- if the recipient enters into a registered civil partnership
- if the recipient cohabits with another partner for more than six months.

Property adjustment orders and lump sum orders cannot be varied.

When there is an application to vary a periodical payments order, the court must consider whether a clean break order is possible. This means, for example, being given a lump sum that is expected to generate £3,000 per annum (every year).

Appeals

Appeals are only allowed if the appeal is started soon after an order was made (usually a few days). Otherwise, court proceedings could be dragged out over a long period of time. This could have serious consequences for the parties, such as for a mother looking after children who is without a source of income or a place to live.

For an appeal to be successful, the party making the appeal must be able to point to a dramatic unforeseen change of their circumstances, which fundamentally changes the basis on which the order was made. This has become known as the Barder test, following the case of Barder v Barder (2007).

Key case

Barder v Barder (1988)

Facts

In divorce proceedings, an order was made, by consent, that the husband should transfer his interest in the family home to the wife within 28 days. Before the order had been executed, the wife killed the two children and committed suicide.

Legal principle – appeals and rehearings in divorce cases can only be allowed in exceptional circumstances.

Orders are generally unchangeable and the Barder test is very difficult to pass, so appeals and rehearings are very rare. Recent cases show that an unforeseen financial windfall, such as an unexpected inheritance, are not generally sufficient for a rehearing.

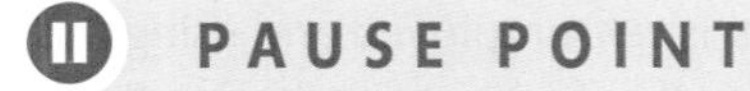

List the advantages of a clean break for a couple who are in divorce proceedings.

Hint: Under what circumstances might a clean break be a disadvantage for either party?

Extend: Do you think the courts are right to try to ensure a clean break for divorcing couples?

Orders for children

When a child's parents are no longer together, the welfare of the child is of paramount importance, and the law strives to reflect this. In this section, you will learn about financial orders with respect to children in the event of a breakdown of a relationship.

The best solution is to come to an agreement without the necessity for the court to intervene. Usually the parents propose the most satisfactory arrangement possible under the circumstances. Mediation can often help the couple come to such an arrangement.

Duty to maintain a child

If a person has parental responsibility for a child, they have a duty to:

- provide a home for the child
- protect and **maintain** the child.

Key terms

Maintain – provide basic necessities for someone.

Child support – periodical payment for a child, which is paid to the parent or legal guardian who lives with that child, by the other parent who does not live in the same home.

Parents have to ensure that their child is supported financially, whether they have parental responsibility or not.

Who child maintenance applies to

A mother automatically has parental responsibility for her child from birth. A father usually has parental responsibility if he is either married to the child's mother or named on the birth certificate. They both keep parental responsibility if they later divorce.

In the event of a divorce, a periodical payment for a child is paid to the parent who lives with that child, by the parent who does not live in the same home. This is known as **child support**. This periodical payment is made to assist the parent with the costs of raising a child. This payment can also be made to another family member or legal guardian if the child lives with them.

The payment is made to provide financial support and to confirm responsibility for the welfare of the child. These payments also help to minimise the need for other forms of periodic payments.

Powers of the courts

The Child Support Act 1991 contains the relevant law. The courts only have limited powers with respect to payment for a child, such as making a lump sum order for a specific purpose.

The best way to settle child support is if the parties agree on payments. This is called a family-based agreement. If this cannot be done, then the parties need to use the Child Maintenance Service. This service can work out payments and help ensure that the recipient receives the payments.

Research

Look at the child maintenance calculator at **https://www.gov.uk/calculate-your-child-maintenance.** Based on a father's weekly income of £400, calculate how much maintenance he would need to pay for two children who rarely stay with him. Now calculate the maintenance if they stay an average of two nights per week. Identify how this changes if his income goes up or down.

Where payments for a child are not made, the court has power to collect the money by various means. This will include:

- taking money from a paying parent's earnings or benefits
- taking money from a bank or building society account – either regular payments or a one-off payment
- taking court action over unpaid child maintenance, such as:
  - sending bailiffs to the non-paying parent's home to take and sell their belongings to get the child maintenance owed
  - sending the non-paying parent to prison
  - collecting money that is owed to the non-paying parent by someone else, such as money owed for work done where the non-payer is self-employed and using this to pay the child maintenance owed or forcing the sale of a house and using the money to pay the child maintenance owed.

There are also methods that can be used to undo attempts to hide assets that could be used to cover the payments.

Orders for a child of the family

Apart from financial orders, the court can make the following orders under the Children Act 1989:

- a child arrangements order, which can include:
  - a residence order
  - a contact order
- a specific issue order
- a prohibited steps order.

Each of these orders can be applied for separately or can be combined, depending on what the couple can or cannot agree on. These will be looked at again later in learning aim D of this unit.

Assessment practice 4.3

C.P4 C.M3 C.D2

Kamala is divorcing David because of his frequent affairs and his regular use of Class A drugs. David works for a film company. He earns £100,000 (plus bonus) with a generous pension scheme. Kamala earns £30,000 as a teacher. They have been married for ten years. The house is in David's name and has been valued at £550,000. Kamala wants to remain in the house with their two children aged eight and six. They own two cars, each worth £25,000, and many works of art. Kamala has evidence that one year ago they had joint savings worth £80,000. She also thought the mortgage on the house was £100,000. However, David's solicitor has disclosed that David recently extended the mortgage by an extra £150,000 and that the savings have disappeared. The mortgage has not been paid for three months. David will not say where the money has gone or why the mortgage is not being paid.

You are helping Kamala's solicitor to compile information on this case. Create a file note that lists the statutory factors that the court can take into account and note which details in this case are relevant for each factor. Which financial orders do you think would be most advantageous for Kamala and why? Who is responsible for the children and who will pay for their maintenance? Finally, evaluate the law with regard to this case: do you think Kamala can get a fair deal?

To complete this task, you need to understand the legal rules governing the distribution of money and property on divorce.

Plan

- What is the task? What information am I being asked to compile?
- Do I have sufficient knowledge on statutory factors and court orders to complete the task? Do I need to undertake any further research?
- How can I structure the information clearly and logically?

Do

- I need to spend sufficient time looking at the details of the case.
- I need to identify the relevant statutory factors, and financial and children orders.
- I need to identify any areas that require more information or analysis.

Review

- I can explain the stages I went through to compile the information required.
- I can explain what a court needs to take into account when making decisions on how property and assets should be divided.

D Examine how the courts resolve disputes over children

Those looking after children, whether they are parents or have parental rights with respect to a child, do not always agree on what is in the best interests of a child. When a dispute is brought to court, the interests of the child are of paramount importance. The law is concerned with safeguarding and promoting the child's welfare.

▶ If a family dispute involves children, it is their interests which are of paramount importance.

Parenthood and parental responsibility

Difference between being a parent and having parental responsibility

Being a parent means that there are certain legal duties such as a duty to maintain the child. Most parents also have parental responsibility for their children. However, as detailed in the Children Act 1989, parental responsibility may belong to someone other than the biological parents, including:

- a local authority with children in its care
- a child's legal guardian
- a child's step-parent
- others who may be able to acquire parental responsibility.

Definition of parenthood

There are many different meanings of the word 'parent'. The most obvious one is a biological parent of the child, sometimes called a natural parent. In most cases the biological parents are those with parental responsibility, but there are also many children whose 'parents' are not their biological parents. Examples of this include:

- where the child has been legally adopted
- where the child was conceived through egg or sperm donation
- where the child lives with adults acting as 'parents' who have informally taken on responsibility for the child.

Laws on surrogacy and assisted reproduction

Surrogacy is when a woman carries a baby for a couple who are unable to conceive or carry a child themselves. There are two different types of surrogacy:

- Straight surrogacy – the surrogate mother uses an insemination kit using the intended father's sperm. In this case, the surrogate mother is genetically related to the conceived child.
- Host surrogacy – when IVF is used, either with the eggs of the intended mother, or with donor eggs. The surrogate mother therefore does not use her own eggs, and is genetically unrelated to the baby. This has potential legal consequences for parental rights because, in law, the woman who gives birth is always treated as the mother.

Surrogacy is permitted under the Surrogacy Arrangements Act 1985. Surrogacy arrangements are not legally enforceable. It is illegal to make a surrogacy arrangement on a commercial basis or to advertise that a surrogate is available. Only the expenses of the surrogate can be paid.

The Human Fertilisation and Embryology Acts 1990 and 2008 regulate other aspects of who is the parent and who can acquire parental rights. This extends to married couples, civil partners and others.

The legal mother in surrogacy

The legal mother of a child born through surrogacy is always, at birth, the surrogate mother. This means that the intended mother is not recognised as a parent, even if she is her child's biological mother.

The surrogate mother has the legal right to keep the child, even if it is not genetically related to her. The surrogate will be the legal mother of the child until parenthood is transferred to the intended mother through a parental order or adoption after the birth of the child.

The legal father in surrogacy

If the surrogate mother is married, the legal father at birth is usually the surrogate's husband. This is irrespective of the biological relationships. This means that the intended father has no automatic claim to legal parenthood. However, the surrogate's husband may be able to show that he did not consent to the surrogacy arrangement. This also applies to a surrogate's wife when they are married or in a civil partnership. Her same-sex partner will be the child's second parent. This excludes both intended parents.

If the surrogate mother is not married or in a civil partnership at the time she conceives, the intended father may be treated as the legal father at birth.

The birth certificate of a child born to a surrogate mother

Where the birth is registered in the UK, only those who qualify as legal parents can be named on the birth certificate. The surrogate mother is responsible for registering the birth, and she is recorded as the child's mother. If she is married, her husband is recorded on the birth certificate as the father. If the surrogate mother is in a civil partnership, her same-sex partner is recorded as the second parent.

If the surrogate mother is single, the intended father (or whoever else is the second parent) can be named on the birth certificate, although he must attend the birth registration in person together with the surrogate mother.

The laws on assisted reproduction

Assisted reproduction is where medical help is taken to enable a couple to have a baby but does not involve another woman carrying and giving birth to a baby for the couple who want to have a child.

The laws on assisted reproduction are quite complex, but can be summarised as follows:

- Heterosexual couples conceiving with donor eggs only – in this situation, the woman who carries and gives birth to the child is the legal mother and the mother's husband or partner whose sperm is used with the donor egg is the legal father.
- Heterosexual couples conceiving with both donor eggs and sperm – as before, the woman who carries and gives birth to the child is the legal mother. The mother's husband is the legal father. If the mother is unmarried, the mother's partner is the legal father only if:
  - the fertility treatment takes place at a licensed UK clinic
  - the man in question is alive at the time of the treatment
  - written signed notices are given to the clinic by the mother and father stating that they both wish for the man to be treated as the father.
- Heterosexual, lesbian or gay couples using a surrogate mother – the surrogate mother is the legal mother. If the surrogate is married, her husband is the legal father. If the

surrogate is not married, the male whose sperm is used (usually the intended father) is the legal father. The intended parents need to apply for a parental order within six months of the child's birth to be registered as the legal mother and father.

Definition of parental responsibility

According to the Children Act 1989 Section 3, parental responsibility means 'all the rights, duties, powers, responsibilities and authority which by law a parent of a child has in relation to the child and his property'.

Key elements of parental responsibility

Duty to maintain a child

As mentioned earlier in this unit, someone who has parental responsibility has a duty to maintain their child. They must:

- provide a home for the child
- protect and maintain the child.

Decisions relating to the child

In practical terms, parental responsibility also means making important decisions in relation to a child such as:

- the religion (if any) with which the child should be brought up
- matters with respect to the child's education, such as where the child goes to school
- choosing, registering or changing the child's name
- appointing a child's guardian in the event of the death of a parent (one of the most important reasons why parents should make wills)
- giving consent to a child's vaccination, dental treatment or surgical operation
- giving consent to taking the child abroad for holidays or extended stays
- representing the child in legal proceedings.

Rights that are not included

It is important to remember that parental responsibility does not mean that a parent has the automatic right to:

- have contact with their child - a parent can apply to the court for a contact order as part of a child arrangements order
- know the whereabouts of other people with parental responsibility or where the child is living. In practice, this means that if the child lives with one parent the other parent does not have an automatic right to know the address of that parent. The parent can apply to the court for this to be disclosed, and it may be disclosed if it is in the best interests of the child.

Explain what parental responsibility means and identify its key elements. What does it not include?

Hint List the typical decisions that a parent needs to make with regard to their child.

Extend Is the principle of parental responsibility useful?

Automatic parental responsibility

Automatic parental responsibility is held by:

- the mother (the person who gives birth to the child)
- the father, if he is married to the child's mother and/or listed on the birth certificate.
  - If the parents of a child are married when the child is born, or if they have jointly adopted a child, both have parental responsibility. They both keep parental responsibility if they later divorce.

- If the father is married to the child's mother but not listed on the birth certificate, the birth can be re-registered to include the father on the birth certificate.

Acquired parental responsibility

Parental responsibility can be acquired by:

- an unmarried father of a child
- a civil partner of the biological mother
- step-parents
- a special guardian.

An unmarried father of a child

An unmarried father of a child can acquire parental responsibility if he:

- enters into a parental responsibility agreement with the child's mother
- obtains a court order for parental responsibility
- obtains a child arrangements order relating to residence in his favour (this will also include an order giving him parental responsibility)
- marries his child's mother
- is appointed as the child's guardian
- adopts his child.

Civil partner of the biological mother

A civil partner of the biological mother of a child can acquire parental responsibility if:

- she was in a civil partnership with the child's mother at the time of the child's birth
- her name is registered on the birth certificate
- she enters into a parental responsibility agreement with the child's mother
- she obtains a court order for parental responsibility
- she obtains a residence order.

Step-parents

Where a child's parent who has parental responsibility for the child is married to, or is a civil partner of, a person who is not the child's parent, that step-parent may acquire parental responsibility for the child either by:

- making an agreement with the parent(s) with parental responsibility that the step-parent will have parental responsibility
- obtaining a court order for parental responsibility.

Special guardians

Under the Adoption and Children Act 2002, the court can make a special guardianship order. This order:

- places a child with someone, to live with them permanently
- gives legal status for non-parents to care for that child.

Unlike adoption, a special guardianship order will not remove parental responsibility from the child's birth parents.

Losing parental responsibility and its effects

Parental responsibility terminates:

- when a young person reaches the age of 18
- when a holder of a parental responsibility order dies
- when a child or young person is adopted (this applies to both parents but is the only way a mother can lose parental responsibility)
- when parental responsibility had been obtained by a residence order or a child arrangements order and that order has been discharged or has expired
- through a court order – when parental responsibility has been granted to a female (same-sex) partner or step-parent through a parental responsibility agreement or a parental responsibility order, it can only be ended through a court order. Unmarried fathers can apply to the court for a parental responsibility order or agreement to be ended.

The effects of losing parental responsibility

Without parental responsibility you cannot make the decisions about a child's life, such as choice of school, religion, surname or guardian on your death. In other words, all the rights and responsibilities set out above end.

Discussion

At what age should parental responsibility end? Is it right that it should end on the child turning 18 years old or should a range of factors determine when parental responsibility ends? In small groups, list what these factors could be. Then share your findings.

Children's rights

Definition of rights

A right is an entitlement and a duty is an obligation. Any right must have a corresponding duty. Some rights are recognised at the international level through agreements between governments. The UK has signed up to the European Convention on Human Rights (ECHR) and the United Nations Convention on the Rights of the Child (UNCRC), both of which set out a number of children's rights.

The UNCRC defines a child as anyone under 18 years old. There has been much legislation to ensure that the rights of children are protected, including the Children Act 1989 and the Children Act 2004.

Some may view the restrictions on what a child may do as being restrictive and against a basic right of freedom, but the law in these cases is there to protect the child. For example, a child is protected by the law with respect to their freedom to work. The youngest age a child can work part-time is 13 years old, except children involved in areas such as television, concerts or modelling, when they can work if they have a performance licence. The person in charge of running the event must apply to the child's local council for a child performance licence. However, the question remains as to whether working under 13 years old ever benefits a child, given the well-documented problems some child performers have had in later life.

PAUSE POINT Make a list of five things a child is not allowed to do. These may relate to ownership, employment or decisions about their lives.

Hint For each restriction consider the benefit to the child.

Extend Are these restrictions fair? Do you think they should apply to all children whatever their circumstances?

Development of children's rights in the law

The right to protection

The right to protection has been developed over many years. In Victorian times, much of this related to child labour and the workhouse. Over the years, a great deal of legislation has been passed with varying degrees of success in protecting children.

The Children Act 1989 sought to address the failings. Subsequent legislation such as the Children Act 2004 widened the scope of safeguarding and protection. Further guidelines on safeguarding were published by the government in 2015.

The Children Act 1989 made it the general duty of every local authority to safeguard and promote the welfare of children in need within their area. In addition, local authorities are now required to promote the upbringing of children in their families. In order to do this, they must provide a range of appropriate services. Problems can arise when deciding who is a child 'in need' and what services are available.

The right to autonomy

Autonomy is the right to make your own decisions. As a child gets older, they have more independence and autonomy but protection is still needed. Teenagers usually have a great deal of autonomy but still need protecting. People often have different opinions on how far protection should extend and whether this infringes a child's autonomy.

The case of Gillick v West Norfolk and Wisbech Area Health Authority (1986) illustrates how the court upheld the right of doctors to give contraceptives to teenagers under 16 years old, under certain conditions, thereby allowing them a degree of autonomy.

Key case

Gillick v West Norfolk and Wisbech Area Health Authority (1986)

Facts

Mrs Gillick had five daughters under the age of 16. She challenged advice given to doctors in her local health authority allowing them to give contraceptive advice to girls under 16, and the right of doctors to act upon that advice. She objected that the advice infringed her rights as a parent, and would lead to what would be an unlawful assault on her daughters. She claimed it would be unlawful for a doctor to prescribe contraceptives to girls under 16 without the knowledge or consent of the parent.

The court stated that the law recognises that there is a right and duty of parents to determine whether or not to seek medical advice in respect of their child and, having received advice, to give or withhold consent to medical treatment. Nevertheless, the health authority's policy was capable of being lawful. A doctor could give such advice to a girl under 16 where she would understand it, where she could not be persuaded to involve her parents, she was likely to have sex irrespective of advice, her health was at risk, and it was in her best interests. A parent's rights of control over a child diminished as that child's understanding grew approaching adulthood.

Legal principle – the 'Gillick competence test' can be used to determine a child's competence in making decisions contrary to their parent's wishes.

In the case of Axon v Secretary of State for Health (2006), a mother sought to challenge guidelines that would allow doctors to protect the confidentiality of girls under 16 who came to them for assistance, even if the sexual activities they might engage in would be unlawful. The challenge was unsuccessful and the guidelines remained in place.

The right to be heard

Every child's right to express their views and have them taken seriously is enshrined in Article 12 of the UN Convention on the Rights of the Child.

However, most children are not included in discussions about issues that affect them. In the case of D (a child) (2016), the court established that the decision of whether a child should be involved in a court case was one for the courts, not the parents. In some cases, welfare implications might necessitate the child being excluded from the proceedings.

There are many ways to involve a child affected by court proceedings, and to ensure that their opinion is heard:

- full-scale legal representation of the child
- a report of an independent CAFCASS officer or other professional
- a face-to-face interview with the judge
- an invitation to the child to write a letter to the judge, setting out their views.

This is equally applicable in other matters where a child's views might be relevant. As the child gets older, their wishes and autonomy are more relevant.

Disputes over children

As you have seen, the Children Act 1989 deals with most aspects of decision-making with respect to children. There are a number of relevant orders relating to non-financial matters. These need to be explored along with the factors the court will take into account in making an order. Finally, you need to consider who can apply for an order.

Orders that can be made to resolve disputes over children

There are four main orders to consider in resolving disputes over children:

- A residence order – this specifies which person the child normally lives with, as well as how much time the child spends with each parent and when.
- A contact order – this specifies whether any contact should take place, and if so, what type of contact and when.
- A specific issue order – this specifies questions relating to how the child should be brought up.
- A prohibited steps order – this prevents one parent from making decisions about a child's upbringing.

A child arrangements order decides the usual arrangements for a child of the family. A residence order and a contact order often form part of a child arrangements order.

Residence order

A residence order decides which parent a child should live with. Each parent may wish to provide a home for the children of the family, but may not be able to agree about the detailed arrangements. In some cases, other relatives or foster parents may also be involved in the arrangements.

The idea of a residence order is misleading as the order relates to the person or persons with whom the child will live rather than the place. A condition that a parent should live at a certain address has been seen by the courts to be an unjustified interference, as the parent has the right to choose where they live. This means that a named person can take the child abroad for a period of up to one month without seeking the agreement of the court or anyone else.

A residence order names the person or people with whom the child is to live. This could be:

- one person, for example, the child's mother
- two people who live in the same household together, such as the child's parent and step-parent
- two people who live in different households (usually both parents). In this case, the order will set out how long the child will live in each household. This will be clearly defined so as to make settled arrangements for the child that will not confuse the child. A court can order shared residence under a child arrangements order to say that the child shall spend a period of time with one parent and a period of time with the other.

Contact order

An order regulating contact arrangements can form part of a child arrangements order. This is important when the couple cannot agree on when and how often contact with a child of the family should take place. It is also essential when one party refuses unreasonably to allow the other party to have contact with the child. The order normally continues until the child is 16 years old.

The court may order different types of contact arrangements:

- Direct and indirect contact arrangements
  - Direct contact arrangements involve the child having contact with a named person by staying with or visiting them.
  - Indirect contact is where the contact takes place indirectly. This could include email, Skype or similar software, instant message or phone. Indirect contact arrangements are ordered by the court if it is impractical or not appropriate for the child to see the person directly. This might be because of a risk to the child's well-being that cannot be managed.
- Overnight and visiting contact arrangements
  - Direct contact arrangements can involve the child visiting the person named for a fixed number of hours or staying overnight. This is particularly relevant when the child is a baby or very young. Often this means shorter but more frequent periods of contact.

- For older children, as they become more able to care for themselves, overnight contact arrangements are often ordered. Sometimes contact arrangements are gradually extended to longer periods of time as the relationship rebuilds.

- Supervised and unsupervised contact arrangements
  - In the majority of cases, the contact is unsupervised. However, if the court considers that there is a risk to the child's welfare, it can order contact arrangements to be supervised by a third party. This is to ensure the safety and well-being of the child.

Specific issue order

A specific issue order is used to determine a specific question about how the child is being brought up, such as the school the child should go to or the church the child should attend. It can be used for medical issues such as immunisation or with respect to a specific operation.

Prohibited steps order

A prohibited steps order can be made to stop the other parent from making a decision about the child's upbringing. For example, the order can prevent the other parent from taking the child out of the country or changing the child's surname. It can also stop the child associating with certain people.

PAUSE POINT Is the range of orders to resolve disputes concerning children useful?

Hint Identify any area you think should not be regulated through the courts.

Extend How else could disputes be resolved effectively?

Factors the court takes into account in making an order

The Children Act 1989, s1 states that the child's welfare is of paramount consideration. This applies to all proceedings where the child's welfare is directly affected. Various different principles are set out in the Act.

Welfare principle

The principle of the child's welfare is central to all types of order with respect to a child. Welfare is not measured by money or physical comfort. It is a much wider concept encompassing all aspects of a person's well-being. It is 'a holistic balancing exercise undertaken with the assistance, by analogy, of the welfare checklist, even where it is not statutorily applicable', as the court stated in the case of Re C (Internal Relocation) (2015). This case decided that a ten-year-old child should be allowed to move to Cumbria with her mother from London for her well-being, despite objections from the father.

No delay principle

A second very important principle set out in the Children Act 1989, s1(2) is that delay is presumed to be harmful for a child. This is evident in the strict time limits there are for applications to the court and the ability of the court to make emergency orders. The law says that there must not be any unnecessary delay in a case that concerns a child. Therefore, the court will decide a timetable for a case at the directions hearing (a court hearing where the judge sets out the case management plan) and can make a temporary order.

Presumption of continued parental involvement

The courts presume that both parents wish to continue to be involved with the upbringing of their child. This presumption can be overturned and access to the child can be legally prevented by a court order, if it can be shown that the parent (or parents) will affect the welfare of the child because of:

- criminal activity
- domestic abuse
- drug/alcohol misuse
- any other inappropriate behaviour that puts the child at risk.

Welfare checklist

The welfare checklist under the Children Act 1989 has seven criteria for the courts to consider when making a decision concerning a child, as follows:

1. The wishes and feelings of the child concerned – consideration is given to the age and level of understanding of the child in this criterion.
2. The child's physical, emotional and educational needs – in most cases this means that the child should stay with its natural parents even if all parties involved could provide equal care.
3. The likely effect on the child if circumstances would be changed as a result of the court's decision – in other words, the court will usually make an order that has the least impact or effect on a child's life.
4. The child's age, sex, background and any other characteristics that will be relevant to the court's decision – this may include religion, cultural background and lifestyle.
5. Any harm the child has suffered or may be at risk of suffering.
6. The capability of the child's parents (or of any other person the courts find relevant) at meeting the child's needs – this again may include lifestyle.
7. The powers available to the court in the given proceedings.

No order principle

The no order principle set out in the Children Act 1989, s1(5) states that the court should not make any order with respect to a child if it would be better for the child if there was no order at all. It could be more accurately described as the no 'unnecessary' order principle.

Scenario

Mistrust and the use of court orders

A husband and wife are in the process of getting divorced. Both are well-paid professionals but are functioning alcoholics. They cannot agree on anything. Each is suspicious of the other's conduct with respect to the children as each fears the other will remove the children from the country and make access to them impossible. During the summer holidays, the mother wants to take the children to Ireland so that they can attend a summer school and visit her family during their free time. The couple finally agrees to this happening on specific dates at a chosen residential summer school, which the husband will pay for. On the second day at the school, the children are collected by the mother to 'go and see their grandparents' with a promise that they will be returned at 7 p.m. that evening. The children are not brought back to the school.

1. Identify and explain the types of court orders that resolve disputes over children. Which apply particularly to this case, and why?
2. What decisions do you think a court would make with regard to the children's welfare?
3. Do you think the arrangements will be weighted in favour of the mother or father, or neither?
4. Where possible, illustrate your arguments using statutory provisions or examples of relevant case law.

Key term

Discharge – termination of an order.

Who can apply for an order to resolve a dispute over a child

Table 4.4 sets out who can usually apply to the court for an order with respect to a child, or for the variation or **discharge** of such an order.

Table 4.4: Types of orders for resolving a dispute over a child and who can apply for them

	Who can apply					
	Child (with permission from the court)	**Mother**	**Father**	**Step-parent**	**Guardian**	**A person with a residence order for the child**
Residence order	✓	✓	✓	✓	✓	✓
Contact order	✓	✓	✓	✓	✓	✓
Specific issue order	✓	✓	✓	✓	✓	✓

Table 4.4: *Continued*

	Who can apply					
	Child (with permission from the court)	**Mother**	**Father**	**Step-parent**	**Guardian**	**A person with a residence order for the child**
Prohibited steps order	✓	✓	✓	✓	✓	✓
Financial order	✓	✓	✓	✓	✓	✓
Parental responsibility order	✓	✓	✓	✓		✓
Special guardianship order	✓		✓	✓		✓

Assessment practice 4.4

D.P5 D.M4 D.D3

Rob and his wife Sally are in the middle of divorce proceedings. Rob is a police officer and Sally is a nurse. They have a son named Josh who is aged ten. Rob and Sally both wish to continue playing a part in Josh's life and to make joint decisions about his education and future. However, they are finding it difficult to come to a satisfactory arrangement about contact and residence, as they both have jobs that involve shift work, including at weekends. Rob's parents have offered to pay for Josh to go to boarding school, and Rob thinks this could be the perfect solution. However, Sally is opposed to this idea. Josh wants to stay in the family home with his mum and go to the local secondary school with his friends. Rob's parents are concerned that if this happens they will not be allowed to visit Josh and their relationship with him will deteriorate.

You are working for a law firm and have been asked to assess this case in a report. You need to outline the orders that a court might make with respect to Josh, and the reasons why. You should also evaluate the impact of any orders on Josh and other members of his family. In order to complete this task, you need to show that you understand the law regarding disputes over children, the factors that a court takes into account when reaching its decision and who can apply for what kind of court orders. How would your report vary if Rob and Sally were an unmarried couple who were splitting up?

Plan

- What is the task? Have I understood what information my report must contain?
- Do I need another look at any aspects of the law about disputes over children?

Do

- I need to decide how to structure a case report.
- I need to identify the orders that a court can make to resolve disputes about children and the factors that it takes into account.
- I need to apply the law to a given case and evaluate its impact on relevant parties involved.

Review

- I can explain what the task was and the skills I used.
- I can explain what I have learned and why it is important.

Further reading and resources

Information on polygamy.
www.parliament.uk/briefing-papers/sn05051.pdf

Information from Citizens Advice on the ending of relationships.
https://www.citizensadvice.org.uk/family/relationship-problems/

Guidance from the Family Justice Council on financial needs on divorce.
https://www.judiciary.gov.uk/related-offices-and-bodies/advisory-bodies/fjc/guidance/sorting-out-finances-on-divorce/

Guide on safeguarding published by the government.

https://www.gov.uk/government/uploads/system/uploads/attachment_data/file/419595/Working_Together_to_Safeguard_Children.pdf

THINK FUTURE

Ann Thomas

Specialist family law solicitor and civil and family mediator

I consider mediation to be beneficial in family law as it enables a couple to reach an agreement that a judge may not otherwise be able to make. It is a flexible process, quicker than going through the court, cheaper, and the parties are more inclined to be happier and abide by the outcome than they would if they had an order forced on them.

I am an advanced accredited specialist in international and private child law. Many of my cases have an international element. I have acted in several high-profile cases, and, as I am often contacted for comment, I have developed skills to deal with the media, sometimes at short notice. One particularly memorable case I dealt with involved the abduction of a two-year-old child who, as a result of orders against the father, was eventually delivered by a friend of the abductor to platform 12 at Waterloo station. The mother was standing with me to collect her child. As soon as the little boy saw his mother, he ran like the wind into her arms. The joy on their faces was immeasurable.

I am recognised as a leading international children's lawyer, particularly in relocation disputes. I have written a number of articles on the recent developments in family law for the legal profession. I am also a regular lecturer on international aspects of family law both in this country and internationally. I have trained family lawyers and the judiciary in Serbia in the mechanics of the Hague Convention and international aspects of family law.

As a litigator it is essential to have skills to analyse problems, and decide on a course of action, sometimes in an emergency. Quite often there is little time to engage in detailed research before attending court to issue an application and secure court orders, especially where there are issues of child abduction, domestic violence or removing assets overseas.

All lawyers need to maintain a professional distance from their clients to enable them to give advice without risk of bias or being influenced by their situation. I empathise with my clients but never allow myself to become close to them. All solicitors must be organised, confident, have a good memory for facts and keep up to date with the law. As Officers of the Court, integrity is paramount.

In addition to qualification, all solicitors in this country are now required to sign an annual declaration confirming they are committed to their own professional legal development. They are required to analyse their cases and establish what they have learned and whether a better outcome could have been achieved.

Finally, it is good to have a sense of humour as the job can, at times, be dry, so it is good to be able to smile.

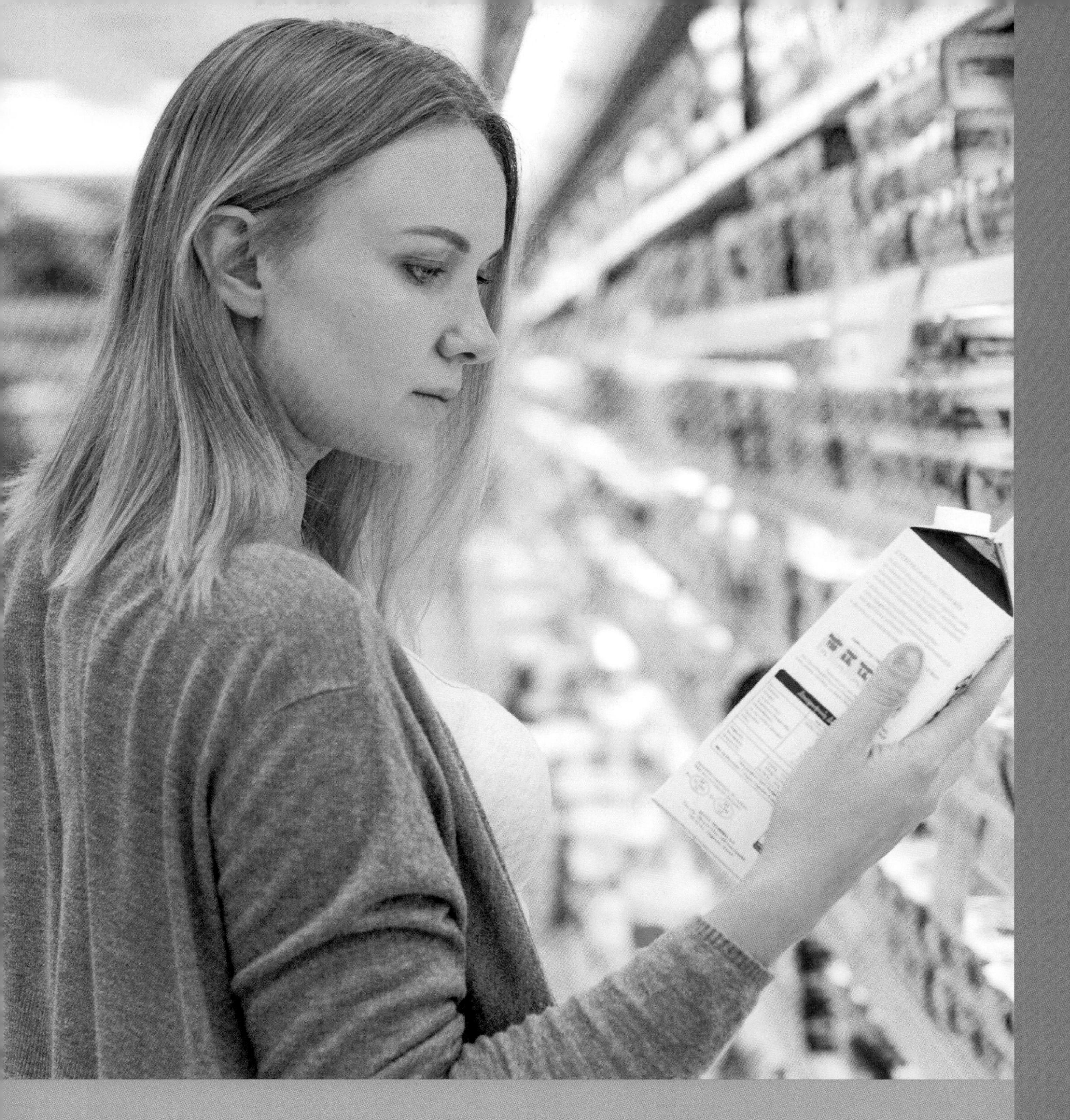

5 Consumer Law

Getting to know your unit

Assessment
This unit is internally assessed using a series of assignments set by your tutor.

A consumer is an individual who buys goods or services from a business. In order to avoid a business taking advantage of the consumer, there are several laws in place to protect the consumer. These laws deal with the sale of faulty goods, giving poor service or unfair small print in a contract. Most protection is contained in statutory laws.

How you will be assessed

This unit will be assessed by assignments set and marked by your tutor. You will need to work independently on these assignments. Keep all your notes and activities that you have completed together in one folder so that you are well prepared. You must also check the unit specification and assignment brief. This will help you to be clear about what is required when questions ask for explanation, analysis and evaluation. It may be helpful to practise the higher-level skills needed in order to achieve the Merit and Distinction grades, such as developing a point, analysing a situation or case study and evaluating the law and its impact. Throughout this unit
you will find activities that will develop your understanding of consumer law, which will help you to prepare for your assignments.

The assignments set by your tutor will consist of a number of tasks designed to meet the criteria in the table below. They are likely to include a written assignment but may also be activities such as:

- case studies where you make decisions about a case and provide legal advice
- presentations or scenarios where you can demonstrate your knowledge about legal practice and procedures.

Assessment criteria

This table shows what you must do in order to achieve a **Pass**, **Merit** or **Distinction**, and where you can find activities to help you.

Pass	Merit	Distinction
Learning aim A Examine the current law on the sale of goods and the availability of related advice and assistance for consumers, applying them in given case studies.		
A.P1 Explain, in given case studies, how consumers are protected in contracts for the sale of goods. **Assessment practice 5.1**	**A.M1** Apply the law on sale of goods in given situations, analysing the advice available to consumers. **Assessment practice 5.1**	**A.D1** Evaluate the impact of the Consumer Rights Act 2015 on consumers in given sale of goods case studies. **Assessment practice 5.1**
A.P2 Describe which organisations are available to give advice and assistance to consumers. **Assessment practice 5.1**		
Learning aim B Explore and apply the law on supply of goods and services and other areas of consumer protection law		
B.P3 Explain, in given case studies, how consumers are protected in contracts for the supply of goods and/or services. **Assessment practice 5.2**	**B.M2** Analyse the effect of consumer protection in contracts for the supply of goods and/ or services and other consumer protection legislation in given case studies. **Assessment practice 5.2**	**B.D2** Evaluate how beneficial the impact of the current law on supply of goods and services, unfair trading, aggressive practices and defective products is for consumers. **Assessment practice 5.2**
B.P4 Explain, in given case studies, how consumers are protected by other legislation. **Assessment practice 5.2**		
Learning aim C Investigate the law on exclusion clauses, applying this in given contractual case studies		
C.P5 Explain, in given case studies, how consumers are protected by common law and statutory provisions with respect to the validity of exclusion clauses. **Assessment practice 5.3**	**C.M3** Analyse the impact of exclusion clauses in given case studies. **Assessment practice 5.3**	**C.D3** Evaluate the protection provided by current common law and statutory provisions with respect to the validity of exclusion clauses. **Assessment practice 5.3**

Getting started

Have you bought goods from a shop or online that have not worked or later broke? Did you complain to anyone? Did you try to get a replacement or repair? Did the business you dealt with try to avoid helping you?
In groups, compare your experiences. After sharing your experiences, could you have done something differently?

A Examine the current law on the sale of goods and the availability of related advice and assistance for consumers

Sale of goods – Consumer Rights Act 2015

The Consumer Rights Act 2015 came into force on 1 October 2015. It applies to consumers buying goods from a business. The Act brought together much of the previous legislation from the Sale of Goods Act 1979, as well as introducing some new rules to make consumer rights more specific and relevant to the 21st century.

Section 2 – Definitions

Section 2 of the Consumer Rights Act 2015 covers the sale of goods and the rights of the **consumer**. The Act defines 'consumers' as individuals buying goods for personal use.

A **business** (in the Act called a 'trader') is defined in s2 as 'a person acting for purposes relating to that person's trade business, craft or profession'.

Section 3 – Goods

Section 3 the Act applies to the contracts a trader (business) uses to supply goods to a consumer.

Goods are defined in s3 as 'any **tangible** moveable items'. The rules apply to both new and second-hand goods bought from a business. The Act only applies to goods sold by a business to an individual. It does not apply to the sale of goods by one individual to another individual, for which the term ***caveat emptor*** applies.

Key terms

Consumer – somebody buying goods for their own personal use.

Business – a person or organisation selling goods or services. If a person describes themselves as a 'trader', they will be acting as a business.

Goods – Any solid, physical item that a person can touch or handle. The goods can be bought over the counter in a shop, by telephone order or online. Goods can be both new and used.

Tangible – something that you can touch and handle.

Caveat emptor – a Latin term meaning 'let the buyer beware'. In other words, an individual buying goods from another private person must check them thoroughly before completing the purchase as there will be no legal comeback once the purchase is completed.

Terms in contracts

In any contract for the purchase of goods, there will be both **express terms** and **implied terms**.

Implied terms are included within every contract for the sale of goods by the Consumer Rights Act 2015.

Key terms

Express terms – clauses set out in writing in any written contract. Express terms may also be agreed wholly or partly orally. They will cover matters agreed between the parties such as the make of the goods, the colour and the price of the item. If an express term has been broken (for example goods of the wrong make or colour have been supplied), there will have been a breach of contract. This means that the buyer must return the goods and recover all money previously paid.

Implied terms – matters that are not specifically agreed between the parties but are automatically included in the contract.

PAUSE POINT Explain the difference between express and implied terms in a contract.

Hint Where would you find each of them?

Extend What remedy has a consumer for breach of an express term?

Sections 9–11 – Rights

Section 9 – Satisfactory quality

Section 9 covers the quality of goods. Satisfactory quality is based on what a reasonable person would expect of the goods taking into account factors such as the price, appearance, safety and durability of the item. If there has been a breach of quality, the buyer has rights under the Consumer Rights Act 2015. The consumer can take action under this implied term if the goods do not work properly.

If the seller tells the buyer that there is a potential fault with the product, and the buyer continues to purchase the item, there can be no later complaint if it is more expensive to repair the item. This was seen in Bartlett v Sidney Marcus Ltd (1965).

Key case

Bartlett v Sidney Marcus Ltd (1965)

Facts

The claimant purchased a second-hand Jaguar car from a car dealer. The dealer told the claimant that the clutch was defective and that this was a minor repair costing a few pounds. He gave the claimant the choice of either taking the car as it was and knocking some money off the price, or he would repair it and charge the full price. The claimant chose to take the car with the fault and get the discount. The claimant later discovered that the fault would cost much more than he originally thought to repair.

The court decided that the dealer had brought the defect to the attention of the claimant and therefore the claimant had no right to say that the car was not of satisfactory quality.

Legal principle – if a defect has been brought to the buyer's attention before the sale was completed, the buyer has no comeback for that defect.

Section 10 – Fitness for purpose

The goods must be fit for the purpose for which they are made or intended. If the goods do not work properly, they will not be fit for their purpose and action can be taken by the buyer for breach of this term. An example is given in the case of Baldry v Marshall (1925).

Key case

Baldry v Marshall (1925)

Facts

The buyer asked the seller to supply him with a fast, flexible and easily managed car that would be comfortable and suitable for ordinary touring purposes. The seller supplied a Bugatti racing car, which was not at all suitable. The court decided that the buyer was entitled to reject the Bugatti.

Legal principle – there was a breach of the fitness for purpose term.

Usually, if the goods do not work properly there will be a breach of both the satisfactory quality term and the fitness for purpose term. As long as the buyer can prove at least one of the implied terms has been broken, they will have rights under the Consumer Rights Act 2015.

Section 11 – Description

The goods must match their description – this can include its colour or make. If the seller tells the buyer the goods will be the same as any sample shown, the goods when received should conform to the sample that has been seen. An example of this is shown in Re Moore & Landauer (1921).

Key case

Re Moore and Landauer (1921)

Facts

A contract for the sale of 3100 tins of peaches described the tins as being packed in cases of 30. When they arrived, the tins were packed in cases of 24. A total of 3100 tins were supplied. The court decided that the purchaser was entitled to reject the goods because they were not as described. This can be seen as a harsh decision as the purchaser received the correct number of tins, even though incorrectly packed.

Legal principle – if the goods do not correspond exactly with the agreed description, there will be a breach of an implied term.

There can be a sale by description even if the buyer inspects the item before purchasing it, as seen in Beale v Taylor (1967).

Key case

Beale v Taylor (1967)

Facts

Taylor advertised a car, describing it as 'white, 1961, Herald convertible'. Relying on that description, Beale inspected the car. As he did not have a driving licence, he did not take a test drive, but sat in the passenger seat. He saw a metallic disc on the rear of the car with the figure '1200' on it. He bought the car believing it to be the 1961 model. After he got his licence, he found the car unsatisfactory to drive. When he had it examined, he was told that the car was made up of two cars welded together; the front portion was a 948 model while the rear portion was the 1200 model. Further, the car was unroadworthy and unsafe. Beale filed a claim for damages. There was a sale by description even though the buyer saw the car before purchasing it. There had been a breach of this implied term and Beale was entitled to damages.

Legal principle – there can be a sale by description even if the buyer inspects the goods before the purchase.

Goods are sold by description as long as they meet a particular description. In Beale v Taylor (1967), the buyer relied on the particular description of the car. However, if the item is inspected and approved by an expert on behalf of the consumer, there will be no sale by description.

Key case

Harlington & Leinster v Christopher Hull Fine Art (1991)

Facts

The claimant bought a painting from the defendant for £6,000. An auction catalogue described the painting as being by German impressionist artist, Gabrielle Munter. Both the buyers and the sellers were London art dealers. The sellers were not experts on German paintings while the buyers specialised in German paintings. The buyers sent their experts to inspect the painting before agreeing to buy. After the sale, the buyers discovered that the painting was a fake and worth less than £100. They brought an action claiming that the painting was not as described. The court decided that, by sending their experts to inspect the painting, this meant that the sale was no longer by description and the buyers had no protection.

Legal principle – if goods have been inspected and approved by experts on behalf of the buyer before a sale is completed, there can be no sale by description.

Section 20 – Remedies

If one of the implied rights has been broken, the Consumer Rights Act 2015 gives the buyer rights to do something about the goods. These rights depend on when the consumer tells the business that one of these implied terms has been broken.

Rights within 30 days of receiving the goods

If the goods do not work and the consumer acts within 30 days of receiving them, the consumer can return the goods to the business and is entitled to a complete refund. However, the consumer could opt for a replacement or a repair instead.

The only exception to the 30-day rule is if the goods are perishable, such as food. In this case, there is a shorter period depending on the goods.

The same rights apply to digital goods as to physical items. In addition, s46 of the Consumer Rights Act 2015 allows the consumer to require the supplier to repair or pay for repairs to any device damaged by the digital content.

Case study 1

Greg buys a digital radio from a shop for £90. After two weeks, he finds that it will only receive the FM frequency and no digital stations. He immediately takes the radio back to the shop and demands a refund as he says the radio is not of satisfactory quality (it does not work properly); nor is it fit for its purpose as a digital radio.

He could insist on a refund or replacement. He could also accept a radio of a different brand at £100 (and pay the difference). If he was particularly attached to the radio (as he liked the individual colour), he could request it to be repaired.

The shop cannot insist that they do not give refunds. Also, they cannot insist that he returns the radio to the manufacturer, as Greg's contract is with the shop.

Case study 2

Sara buys an e-book online for her e-reader. When she starts reading, she finds that some of the wording does not make sense and some pages are missing. The content is not of satisfactory quality. She can reject the book and demand her money back. Alternatively, she can demand a new e-book that is compatible with her e-reader and where the content is complete.

Rights between 31 days and 6 months after purchase

If the item stops working between 31 days and 6 months after purchase the consumer must return the item and claim either.

- a repair (at the expense of the business)
- a replacement of the same type or value
- (if the consumer wants to keep the item) a discount to reflect the fact that it does not work/work as well as it should.

The consumer will not have to prove who caused the fault to the item.

Rights six months or longer after purchase

If the item stops working more than six months after purchase, the consumer may be able to claim a refund, replacement or a part refund. The business chooses which option it offers to the consumer. These options will be available if the item should last longer than six months. There will be a stronger case if the item is expensive, or sold as good quality or top of the range. The seller may require the consumer to prove that they did not cause the fault.

These consumer rights are summarised in Table 5.1.

Key case

J & H Ritchie Ltd v Lloyd Ltd (2007)

Facts

Mr Ritchie was a farmer and bought a seed drill and harrow from the defendant. It was advertised at a reduced price because it had been repossessed from a previous owner. It did not work. The defendant agreed to repair it. It was returned to Mr Ritchie but the defendant refused to say what the problem had been. Mr Ritchie found out informally that there had been a serious defect and rejected the machine. The question for the court was whether he could still reject the machine. The House of Lords agreed that Mr. Ritchie was entitled to reject the equipment, even though it had been repaired.

Legal principle - if the buyer is not informed that the goods have a defect and they do not work properly, they can be rejected.

Other consumer information

The following information is not directly in the Consumer Rights Act 2015 but is likely to affect a consumer:

- Receipt - evidence of payment and the date of purchase. The business is likely to require sight of this as proof of purchase. By itself, it gives the consumer no rights.
- Refund policy - some retailers or suppliers may have a separate refund policy, for example, a 14-day 'no-quibble' refund. This allows the consumer to obtain a refund if there is nothing wrong with the goods but they change their mind about their purchase.
- Guarantees or warranties - a manufacturer may give their own guarantee (also known as a warranty) to the consumer. This will operate in addition to the consumer's rights under the Consumer Rights Act 2015. If there is a defect in the product, the consumer could follow the terms of the guarantee and deal directly with the manufacturer. A guarantee will usually provide for a repair by the manufacturer or, if that is not possible, a replacement.
- Paying by credit card - if the consumer pays for the item using a credit card and the cost of the item is more than £100, s75 of the Consumer Credit Act 1974 applies. This gives the consumer additional protection. It means that if the retailer or supplier fails or refuses to refund the consumer, a claim can be made against the credit card company for the cost of the item. The card provider is jointly liable with the retailer so the consumer could just claim against the card provider. There is no time limit for such a claim.
- Paying by debit card - the consumer can ask for a chargeback or refund from their bank or card provider for the full cost of the item. A claim can only be made within 120 days of the purchase. This scheme will only operate if all other attempts to claim against the retailer or supplier have failed.
- Trader goes out of business - if a retailer or supplier closes or goes out of business before refunding a consumer, then a claim can be made under s75 of the Consumer Credit Act 1974 if the item cost more than £100 and the consumer paid by credit card. A chargeback claim could be made within 120 days of the purchase if payment was made by debit card. If the consumer paid by cash, they are unlikely to get any money back.

Table 5.1: A summary of the consumer rights for a faulty product

Time of claim	Consumer Rights
Within 30 days	Reject and claim refund
31 days - 6 months	Consumer claims repair, replacement or discount
After 6 months	Business decides whether to offer repair, replacement or refund

Scenario

Emma bought a new phone on a two-year contract over the counter at a shop. The phone was described as 'having a beautifully curved, full aluminium body that seamlessly blends into a full HD screen to give a premium feel and look. Stereo speakers pump out fantastic sound and the unique Duo Camera makes photos and videos really stand out.'

Emma transferred all her music and photos onto the new phone. A week later, Emma could not get either the camera or video to work and neither she, nor the technicians at the shop, can get it to work or to recover the photos she has taken. A few days later, she was unable to get her music to play and the technicians cannot recover any of the tunes.

1. What implied terms from the Consumer Rights Act 2015 apply to the contract between Emma and the shop?
2. Ignoring the sentimental value of the photos and music, what would you advise Emma to do?
3. Does the Consumer Rights Act 2015 give consumers greater rights when purchasing defective goods than previous legislation?

Table 5.2 provides a comparison of the pre-2015 legislation with rights introduced by the Consumer Rights Act 2015.

Table 5.2: A comparison of pre-2015 consumer legislation with the Consumer Rights Act 2015

Pre-2015 legislation (Sale of Goods Act 1979)	Consumer Rights Act 2015
Consumer purchases from a business.	Consumer purchases from a business.
Goods must be new.	Goods can be new or second-hand.
Digital goods or goods with digital content are not covered.	Same rules apply to digital goods and physical goods.
Goods must correspond with description - failure to do so allows the consumer to reject.	Goods must correspond with description - failure to do so allows the consumer to reject.
Goods must be fit for their purpose - failure to do so allows the consumer to reject.	Goods must be fit for their purpose - failure to do so allows the consumer to reject.
Goods must be of satisfactory quality - failure to do so allows the consumer to reject.	Goods must be of satisfactory quality - failure to do so allows the consumer to reject.
Consumers have right to reject goods provided they have not been 'accepted'. Time limits will depend on the goods.	Specific time limits set.
Consumer can claim the cost of goods from the trader, if any implied term has been broken.	Consumer has right to reject goods within 30 days of purchase. Consumer can claim repair, replacement or discount if goods returned after 30 days and within 6 months. Consumer may be able to claim a refund, replacement or a part refund if goods stop working 6 months or more after purchase.
Private purchases are not covered.	Private purchases are not covered.

Close your book and complete a table showing when a consumer can reject goods bought from a retailer. Try to use case law.

Hint Think about each of the implied terms.

Extend Add references to express terms into your table.

Obtaining help and advice

If you have a consumer-related problem, where can you go to get help or advice? You may immediately think of a lawyer. However, consider the following first:

- The lawyer will charge a fee based on the time spent on giving advice or taking action.
- The cost of the item may not justify spending lots of money on lawyer's fees.
- Lawyers traditionally will know the general rules that relate to buying and selling goods and services, but are unlikely to have been involved in cases involving the specific rules as covered in this unit.
- Involving a lawyer is likely to bring about confrontation with the retailer or supplier instead of resolving the issue.

Discussion

In pairs, think about where you might go for help and advice about a consumer-related problem other than a lawyer.

Trading Standards

One option is to contact your local Trading Standards department. They are part of your county or city council services and are funded by council taxpayers. They have duties laid down by statute.

What do Trading Standards do?

Trading Standards departments work with other agencies covering concerns of consumers, traders and the general public. Their aim is to regulate business and trade in order to create a fair trading environment.

They have the power to enforce national laws relating to the supply of goods and services. They can take action, in court if necessary, against traders who have broken the law. In more serious cases, they can carry out investigations with other agencies such as the police, HM Revenue & Customs, Citizens Advice and trade organisations. If necessary, and with the necessary information, they can take formal action by:

- prosecuting traders in criminal courts
- issuing a caution
- applying for injunctions
- issuing a statutory notice
- entering premises
- seizing goods and/or documents.

Link

Aggressive trading is discussed later in this unit.

In less serious cases, they can take informal action against a trader preventing court action. However, they can also advise and educate traders in order to prevent any future breach of law.

Trading Standards officers can carry out routine inspections of restaurant and hotel kitchens, and can check price displays in retailers to ensure that they are accurate. They can investigate complaints about the selling of age-restricted products to underage children.

They can offer advice and help to individual consumers, particularly on how to make a complaint to a trader. They can take action against traders on behalf of individuals, especially where this involves protecting vulnerable individuals from rogue traders and scams.

In a more general way, they can publicise changes in the law and ensure that consumers know and understand their rights.

Research

What action have Trading Standards officers taken about unsafe skin lightening products?

Why do you think it has been necessary to take action about such products?

What other actions can you find where Trading Standards have taken action to protect consumers in your county or city?

Research

Look on the Which? ® website **www.which.co.uk** for a list of their achievements on behalf of consumers. Which do you think is their best achievement in the last ten years?

Which?®

Which?® was formed in 1957 and is now the largest consumer body in the UK, with over a million members who subscribe to their magazine and online services.

They are well known for testing and unbiased reporting on household products, including everything from washing machines to digital cameras, and services such as banking and energy supply. It is an independent, not-for-profit organisation. By giving independent advice, it helps consumers to make informed decisions and choices. They carry out campaigns on behalf of consumers to bring about changes in the law for the benefit of consumers.

You can pay to become a member of the organisation and receive advice about your problem. If you are not a member, you can look at their website to find out general information about consumer rights, which may apply to your particular problem.

The media

The media can include:

- newspapers – both national and local
- magazines
- TV and radio
- the Internet
- social media.

There are lots of places where a consumer can find a review of a product or service

Before buying a product or service, a consumer might read reviews posted by journalists or other consumers. If there is a problem with a product after purchase, the consumer could use one or more of these sources to obtain help or advice on their particular problem.

Newspapers

Newspapers sometimes publish consumer help and advice sections, particularly appearing in weekend editions. Readers write in with a problem that is taken up by a journalist on behalf of the paper. Usually the reader will have tried to resolve the issue with the business, but for a variety of reasons the issue will be unresolved. The journalist will contact the business on behalf of the consumer. Often, in order to avoid further bad publicity, the business will offer a solution that the consumer was unable to achieve by themselves.

Magazines

Magazines will often review products or services and make recommendations to their readers to consider before a purchase is made. An example could be the magazine *Good Housekeeping*, which reviews a number of products each month and gives an award or recommendation to the product that achieves the best score in its category.

TV and radio

Some TV channels broadcast consumer-related programmes that test items or services, or feature consumers' problems with a retailer or provider that often have been experienced by many viewers. These programmes include *Watchdog* and *Rip Off Britain* on BBC channels. There are programmes on Channel 4 giving information on food and other products such as *Supershoppers*. Some radio stations, both local and national, have consumer-related programmes and articles. Radio 4 broadcasts the regular weekday programme *You and Yours*, and many stations have phone-in sessions, either dealing with specific issues or more general consumer problems. Time constraints often mean that the advice given is limited.

Internet

Internet searches will usually provide help or advice from other individuals who have or are suffering similar problems. However, it will have to be carefully noted whether the advice is given by other consumers in the UK or in other countries, where the rules may differ. Many retailers have review sections on their websites for consumers who have bought an item to post their thoughts on the quality and use of the item. These comments may help other consumers decide whether to purchase an item or what to do with it in the event of a problem occurring.

Social media

Social media allows for the sharing of information, advice and reviews from other users. These comments may help other consumers decide whether to purchase an item or what to do with it in the event of a problem occurring.

Citizen's Advice (CA)

Citizens Advice (previously known as the Citizens Advice Bureau) is a network of independent charities throughout the UK that give free, confidential information and advice to assist people with a variety of problems, including consumer matters.

It is the largest independent advice provider in the UK. Advice is given face to face in local offices, community venues, people's homes, by phone, by email and online.

At some CA offices, solicitors may offer short appointments on a *pro bono* basis as a way of gaining clients. Its Adviceguide website was visited by one third of the UK's online population in 2013.

Each CA office operates differently. Some will have specialist staff who deal with certain cases. Others operate a 'Gateway' system, which means clients are booked for advice at a later appointment while others offer 'drop in' general advice sessions.

CA also operates on a national level. It is the government-funded provider of consumer education in Great Britain. There are 11 Consumer Empowerment Partnerships that work closely with the Trading Standards Institute. CA produces resources to improve consumer education. It uses clients' problems as evidence to influence policy makers to review laws or administrative practices which cause undue difficulties to clients, in a process referred to as 'Social Policy'. It also engages in policy research in order to recommend policy changes.

Consumer ombudsman

If a consumer has a complaint about goods or services purchased after 1 January 2015, this service may be able to help. The trader has to be a member of a trade association that offers this service. Consumers will receive a free, fair and independent service for dealing with their dispute.

The service can deal with complaints about:

- faulty goods/service
- poor service or workmanship
- failed/incomplete or non-delivery of goods or services
- pricing issues.

However, they cannot deal with a complaint if it is already subject to court proceedings.

A consumer must tell the business involved in the dispute about their complaint within 12 months of the date of purchase of the goods or service. If a company is willing to work with the ombudsman to resolve the complaint, the ombudsman will aim to reach a resolution within 90 days. If both sides agree to the resolution, it will be binding. If the consumer chooses not to accept the resolution, the consumer can still take the matter to court.

If it is decided that a trader has made a mistake, treated the consumer unfairly or that the goods or services supplied were not fit for purpose, the ombudsman can require an award which returns the consumer to the position they would have been in had the mistake not occurred. The trader can be required to apologise for the time and the trouble it has caused as a result of the dispute. As part of this, the trader may be required to make a payment to the consumer in recognition of the problems it has caused.

Trading associations

Many businesses and service organisations have established a trade association to represent members. They are usually not-for-profit organisations which, as well as representing their members, will set and promote quality standards and represent their members within government. They are likely to license their members and may offer training schemes. They can also provide independent and impartial advice to their members and, if contacted by a consumer with a problem, may put pressure on members to resolve a dispute. Members may be required to offer ombudsman or arbitration schemes to deal with disputes within their contracts.

Arbitration

Arbitration may be available if there is a clause in the contract between the consumer and the trader that requires this method of dispute resolution. The clause may require the parties to enter into mediation or conciliation before arbitration is available. The process of arbitration will usually be an alternative to taking court action.

The arbitrator's decision is final and both sides will have to follow the terms of the decision and pay any money owed. The consumer must firstly complain directly to the trader and then wait a short time before going to arbitration, unless a **letter of deadlock** has been issued by the trader.

Some arbitration schemes are free while others charge a fee for making an application for arbitration. The cost depends on how complicated the case is and whether it can be dealt with without a hearing. Most cases are dealt with on paper, without either party attending.

The arbitrator will usually make a decision within three months of the consumer making the application. Arbitration is generally quicker, cheaper and less formal than taking court action and it should maintain the relationship between the consumer and the trader.

Key term

Letter of deadlock – letter that states a trader and consumer have been unable to agree on a solution to a given problem.

Link

See Unit 1 for more on alternative dispute resolution.

 **PAUSE POINT** Close your book and make a list of the most useful sources of advice for a consumer.

Hint List the services that each advice agency provides.

Extend Rank the different sources from most useful to least useful.

Assessment practice 5.1

A.P1 A.P2 A.M1 A.D1

Vin tells you that he bought some drinks from Tim, who owns a health food and drink shop. He promoted the sale of expensive 'recovery' drinks, which he claimed would significantly reduce recovery times after physical training sessions. In fact, the drinks were no more effective than just drinking water. Vin tells you he paid £60 for a pack of 'recovery' drinks but found, after strenuous gym sessions, that the drinks were not at all effective in helping his recovery.

1. Write a letter on behalf of Vin to Tim setting out his right under the Consumer Rights Act 2015.
2. Where can Vin go to get specialist help and advice about his rights?
3. Vin asks whether the rights given to consumers such as him are more or less effective as a result of recent changes in the law. Write a detailed evaluation for him about this.

Plan

- I need to find out what Vin's rights are in this case.
- I need to know which sections of the Consumer Rights Act 2015 apply to this case.

Do

- I need to explain Vin's consumer rights carefully and clearly to him.
- I need to advise Vin on where to go to for impartial advice.

Review

- I can identify the particular area of law that applies to this case.
- I can clearly communicate which sections of the Consumer Rights Act 2015 are applicable.

Explore and apply the law on the supply of goods and services and other areas of consumer protection law

Supply of goods and services – Consumer Rights Act 2015

Definitions

The Consumer Rights Act 2015 covers all contracts for services supplied by a business to a consumer.

As stated in s2, a consumer is defined as an individual acting wholly or partly outside that person's trade, business, craft or profession. In simple terms, this means that the Act applies to an individual buying a service for personal use.

A 'contract' has the definition as set out in s48: a 'contract for a trader [business] to supply a service to a consumer'.

Section 48 - Services

Services are not specifically defined in the Act. However, they are considered **intangible** (something that is not physical) and cover such things as:

- repairing a car
- giving a haircut
- taking photos of a special occasion such as a wedding
- making a cake or
- decorating a house or room.

Key term

Services – a task that is performed by a business or individual for money.

Intangible – something that you can't touch or handle.

Terms in contracts

The contract between the parties, either spoken or written, will contain both express and implied terms.

- Express terms include exactly what service has to be done, when it has to be done by and the price of the service. If there is a breach of one of the express terms – for example, if the work is not completed in time, there will be a breach of contract allowing the innocent party, usually the consumer, to get all or part of their money back. The consumer may also charge the business if they get another new business to complete the work.
- As with contracts for goods, there are implied terms included in contracts for services. These implied terms will not be written down but will automatically be included by the Consumer Rights Act 2015 to give consumers certain protections. Implied terms are included within every contract for the supply of services by the Consumer Rights Act 2015. These implied terms are discussed under Rights, overleaf.

Before this Act was introduced, the consumer had the right to have the service completed by a different supplier and charge the original supplier, which is not part of the Consumer Rights Act 2015. This could limit the consumer's rights as they will have to still deal with the original supplier and the best they can achieve will be a price reduction. However, consumers have been given an additional right, not included in the previous law, to claim if they have relied on statements given by the service provider. This should encourage businesses to be honest in pre-contract statements made to the consumer.

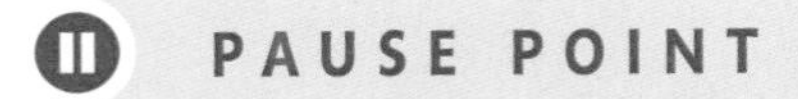

PAUSE POINT List the express terms found in a contract for a haircut for an important event.

Hint Think of what you would want to agree with the hairdresser before they started.

Extend What could you do if one of the express terms was broken and you did not like the end result?

Rights

Section 49 – Reasonable care and skill

According to s49 of the Consumer Rights Act 2015, the trader must perform the service with reasonable care and skill. This focuses on the way a service has been carried out, rather than the end result of the service. This means that, if a business has not provided a service with reasonable care and skill, they will be in breach of this implied term, whatever the end result.

There is no definition of what 'reasonable care and skill' means. This is deliberate to allow the standard to be flexible between different service sectors. Industry standards or codes of practice for particular services can be taken into account. The price paid for the service is also likely to be relevant. For example, a consumer might expect a lower standard of care and skill from a quick and cheap repair service for a laptop than from a more expensive and thorough service.

On the other hand, if a consumer contracts with a high-cost, specialised gardener to landscape their garden, that service must be provided with reasonable care and skill. If the gardener does not cut and treat the grass to the industry standard, it is likely that a court would find that the gardener did not exercise reasonable care and skill and this implied term would be broken.

If the claimant is injured abroad as in Wilson v Best Travel, the implied term of the contract of reasonable care and skill may have a different interpretation from that applying in England.

Key case

Wilson v Best Travel (1993)

Facts

The claimant, Wilson, was injured when he fell through some glass patio doors while on holiday in Greece. The glass conformed to Greek safety standards but did not conform to British safety standards. The claimant brought an action against the travel agent asking for a term to be implied, as a matter of law, that all accommodation offered by the travel agents should conform to British safety standards, and that their failure to do so was a breach of the implied term that the service will be carried out with reasonable care and skill.

It was decided that no term should be implied. The travel agents had inspected the premises, made sure it complied with local safety requirements and had made sure that reasonable holidaymakers would not be put in danger. They had not breached the implied term of carrying out a service with reasonable care and skill.

Legal principle – where an accident occurs abroad the defendant is to be judged by the relevant local standard of care, which may not be of the same level as the standard applying in England.

Section 51 – Price

Section 51 of the Consumer Rights Act 2015 states that if there is no price stated in the contract for the service, it must be carried out at a reasonable price. What is considered a reasonable price is different for each case. Normally, the price will be set in the contract as an express term. However, in an emergency this may not be the case.

For example, if a home owner engages a plumber to fix an urgent leak, they may not discuss the price before fixing the problem and the plumber would not know until they start work how much time might be involved. If the leak was fixed in a few minutes and with only a small replacement part, £1,000 is unlikely to be a reasonable price to pay and this implied term would have been broken.

Section 52 - Time

According to s52 of the Consumer Rights Act 2015, if there is no time set in the contract for the service to be completed, it must be completed within a reasonable time. Again, what is considered a reasonable time is different for each case. For example, a consumer hires a builder to rebuild a 1-metre-high, 25-metre-long garden wall. The consumer agrees the price with the builder, but not a deadline for completion of the work. If, six months later, the work has not been completed, the builder would most likely not have carried out the work within a reasonable time and this implied term would have been broken.

Proving that a service provider has breached any of the implied terms of care and skill, time and cost will require the consumer to obtain evidence from other service providers or a trade association. This may prove lengthy and potentially costly and may delay completion of the original service.

Section 50 - Information

Section 50 of the Consumer Rights Act 2015 is a rule that has not appeared in any previous laws. It states that if the consumer receives any information - either spoken or written - about the business or the service that influences the consumer to buy the service or make a decision about the service provider, then this amounts to an implied term.

In other words, if the consumer makes up their mind to use a business because it says they are experts in their field, this can be an implied term. For example, a consumer invites a window company to fit new windows. The consumer chooses that company to fit wooden windows because the salesman said that the company would install and paint the frames. If, after fitting the windows, the fitter would only prime the frame and told the consumer to paint them himself, the company would not have complied with the information it gave the consumer. Again this implied term would have been broken.

Remedies

Section 54 - Enforcement of terms

If the service has not been carried out with due care and skill and within a reasonable time, the consumer is entitled to either repeat performance by the business or a price reduction. The amount of the price reduction will be the difference in value between the service the consumer paid for and the value of the service provided.

Section 55 - Repeat performance

If the service a business provides is not done with reasonable care and skill (s49), the consumer can require the business to properly perform the service and require the business to fix the problem within a reasonable time, and at the cost of the business concerned.

For example, if you take your car to a garage to have a new battery installed but you later find that it has been installed incorrectly, you can take the car back and require the garage to install the battery correctly so that it does work properly. This should be done at their expense.

Section 56 - Price reduction

If the business cannot, or it is impossible to, fix the problem, s56 allows the consumer to claim a price reduction of up to 100 per cent.

For example, a consumer engages a decorator to redecorate the whole interior of their house. It is accepted that one room was not done with reasonable care and skill. In this case, the consumer can insist that the decorator re-does the relevant work without any extra cost to the consumer. If the decorator does not do that within a reasonable time, the consumer would be entitled to a price reduction. The amount would reflect that only some of the work was done with reasonable care and skill.

If there is a term in the contract which limits the liability of the business to less than the contract price or which excludes the business's liability for completing the service with reasonable care and skill, this clause is invalid but the rest of the contract will remain in force.

For example, the consumer makes a written contract with a bakery to make and decorate a cake for a special birthday party for £200. There is a clause in the small print of the contract that says the maximum discount for any problems with the cake is £100. When it arrives, the cake is stale and undecorated. There is a breach of the implied term that the service will be completed with reasonable care and skill (s49). The contract cannot be repeated as it is a one-off party, but there is a right to a price reduction under s56 that may be close to 100 per cent. The clause in the contract to limit liability to £100 is invalid and will not operate.

If there is a breach of the implied term of charging a reasonable price, the consumer is entitled to require the business to refund the amount in excess of a reasonable price.

Goods supplied with services

Under s4 of the Supply of Goods and Services Act 1982, if goods are supplied with the service there is an implied term that the goods will be of satisfactory quality.

For example, if you needed a new exhaust fitted to your car, it is implied that the garage will use an exhaust that fits your car and that it works properly.

Scenario

Garfield comes to you with a problem. He paid Lewis, a specialist repairer of books, £3,000 to rebind a set of rare books that he owns. In view of the nature of the work, no date was set for completing the rebinding, but Lewis suggested that it would take him a couple of months. After hearing nothing for six months, Garfield received a phone call from Lewis asking for a further £1,000 to complete the work as it was so complicated. Garfield reluctantly paid the extra £1,000. When Lewis finally finished the work a few months later, Garfield found that the work had been poorly completed as a number of pages had been damaged. He also found that he could have had the work done by another specialist company for £500 less.

1 What implied rights are contained in the contract between Garfield and Lewis?
2 What would you advise Garfield to do?

Unfair trading

Key term

Unfair trading – misleading or unethical ways of doing business.

Unfair trading covers aggressive practices by a business to a consumer. A practice is aggressive if it significantly damages or is likely to damage the consumer's freedom of choice. It covers harassment (pestering) of the consumer or coercion (pressure), which could be carried out by a salesperson overstaying their welcome or pressure selling.

Consumers are given some protection when dealing with aggressive selling in the home, but only after the event. There is no specific right given to eject an aggressive salesman from the consumer's home.

Protection from aggressive selling

Consumer Protection from Unfair Trading Regulations 2008

The law regarding aggressive selling is contained in the Consumer Protection from Unfair Trading Regulations 2008. Under these regulations, a criminal offence is committed by the business if they commit an aggressive practice and, as a result, the consumer enters into a contract. The consumer can report the business to their local Trading Standards department, who can take action in the criminal courts against the business. These regulations do not allow a consumer to take any action themselves against the business.

Link

A full list of aggressive practices is set out in Schedule 1 of the Consumer Protection from Unfair Trading Regulations 2008, which can be looked at here: **http://www.legislation.gov.uk/ukdsi/2008/9780110811574/contents**.

Consumer Protection (Amendment) Regulations 2014

There was a deficiency in the law that meant that businesses who undertook aggressive selling could only be prosecuted in the criminal courts, leaving the consumer with little action to benefit themselves. The law has been updated by the Consumer Protection (Amendment) Regulations 2014, which allow the trader to be prosecuted in the criminal courts and for a consumer to take a civil action to recover any money paid.

From 1 October 2014, consumers have new rights under the Consumer Protection (Amendment) Regulations 2014 if they have been the victim of misleading actions or aggressive selling by a business.

There is now a general ban on unfair commercial practices, which occur if the practice falls below the standards of skill and care that a trader in that industry would be expected to show towards customers, and they affect, or are likely to affect, a consumer's ability to make an informed decision about whether to buy a particular product.

There is a ban on misleading and aggressive practices that influence a consumer to enter into a contract with the business. These can include:

- advertising goods which do not exist
- offering a few items at the advertised price with no hope of meeting large demand
- making misleading comparisons with other products
- misleading consumers about their rights.

Any information must be displayed clearly and not hidden in small print.

There is a 'blacklist' (a list of actions that are unacceptable) of 31 commercial practices, including:

- claiming something is free when it is not
- constant cold-calling
- bait advertising (luring the customer in with the promise of a free or cheap item, but then saying it is unavailable and then directing them to more expensive items)
- limited or false free offers
- pressure selling
- aggressive doorstep selling.

For any of these practices, it is enough to show wrongdoing. There is no need to show that it influenced the consumer in any way. A trader taking part in any of the blacklisted practices is committing a criminal offence.

In addition, the regulations implement the European Unfair Commercial Practices Directive (2005/29/EC), which gives a consumer the same protection against unfair practices and rogue traders whether the consumer is buying locally or purchasing from a website based in another country.

Additionally to any criminal action, a consumer can:

- unwind any contract they have entered into, as long as notice is given to the business within 90 days of it being made. This will allow the consumer to recover the price paid.
- return the goods
- claim damages for any additional loss including distress and inconvenience.

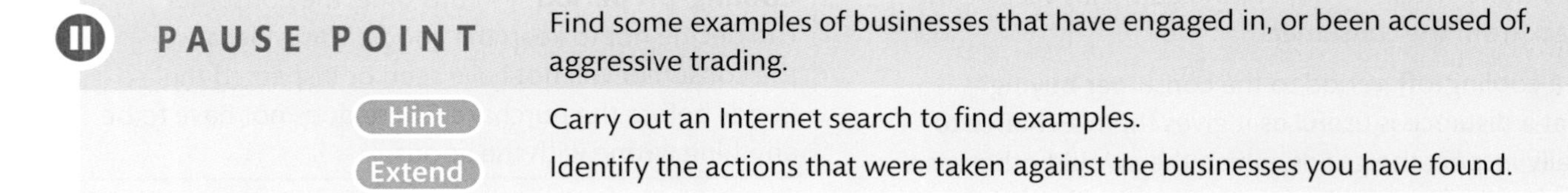
PAUSE POINT Find some examples of businesses that have engaged in, or been accused of, aggressive trading.

Hint Carry out an Internet search to find examples.

Extend Identify the actions that were taken against the businesses you have found.

The combined threat of criminal prosecutions and civil remedies may encourage businesses not to undertake aggressive selling. There are few publicised cases so there may be limited consumer or business awareness of the possible action that can be taken. However, the Department for Business, Energy and Industrial Strategy has issued a guidance booklet on these regulations. You can also refer to the CA for more guidance.

Distance selling

Distance selling covers buying goods online, by telephone or by mail order.

The Consumer Rights Act 2015 applies to goods bought from a distance in the same way as if they are bought face to face. A retailer has to ensure that the goods are of satisfactory quality, that they are fit for their purpose and meet any description. If the goods are faulty and any of these implied terms are broken, the consumer has the same rights as if the goods were bought face to face.

Key term

Distance selling – goods not bought in person, but online, by telephone or by mail.

PAUSE POINT

Remind yourself what rights a consumer has when buying face-to-face goods that do not work.

Hint: Just consider implied terms.

Extend: What remedies has a consumer with faulty goods?

Consumer Contracts (Information, Cancellation and Additional Charges) Regulations 2013

In addition to the rights given to consumers by the Consumer Rights Act 2015 if the product does not work, the consumer has additional rights given by the Consumer Contracts (Information, Cancellation and Additional Charges) Regulations 2013.

These regulations give consumers an automatic 14-day **cooling-off period**.

- This starts as soon as the ordered goods are received.
- There does not need to be anything wrong with the item.
- The consumer needs to tell the seller that they do not want the goods within the 14 days.
- Once the seller has been told, the consumer has another 14 days to return the goods.

If the goods are returned within this time, the consumer is entitled to repayment in full. If the consumer paid for standard delivery, the seller has to refund this in addition to the cost of the item. If a more expensive delivery option is chosen, the consumer will have to pay the difference between that and the standard delivery. The seller has to pay the refund within 14 days of the date they receive the item back from the consumer.

Giving a cooling-off period to the consumer buying goods at a distance is useful as it gives them a chance to physically inspect the goods, which they would otherwise do in a shop before purchasing. Distance selling is advantageous for consumers as they have the right to return goods they do not like. This right is not always available when buying goods face to face.

The additional rights given to consumers when purchasing at a distance may increase costs for a business and require them to have additional procedures to accept returned goods.

There is no cooling-off period for:

- a product that deteriorates quickly, such as flowers or food
- an item that was personalised or custom-made for the consumer
- a CD, DVD or computer software, if the wrapping is unsealed
- an item bought from a private individual rather than a business.

At the time the purchase is made, the sellers must give the consumer certain information. This includes:

- the seller's business address and phone number
- a full description of the goods
- the total price (including delivery charges)
- when the goods will be delivered
- how the goods are being paid for
- confirmation of the contract
- for digital material, details of its compatibility
- details of the consumer's right to cancel.

If this information is not given, the cooling-off period is extended. The notice can be sent to the consumer by email.

Key term

Cooling-off period – in this time, the consumer can decide not to keep the goods. This is because the consumer will not have seen or inspected the goods before the purchase. There does not have to be anything wrong with the goods.

Consumer Rights – Consumer Protection Act 1987

Consumers injured by defective products

If a consumer has suffered personal injury or damage to their property caused by a faulty product, a claim can be

What advice would you give a friend who had received faulty goods from an online retailer?

Hint: What do the terms of the contract say? What are your friend's statutory rights?

Extend: What advice would you give if your friend had changed her mind about the goods, rather than something being wrong with them?

made using the ordinary rules of negligence. This is also known as product liability.

To claim in common law negligence, the claimant has to prove that:

- a duty of care is owed by the manufacturer
- the duty of care has been broken
- injury, loss or damage has been caused.

The consumer will have to prove that there was some fault in the manufacturing process that caused the injury or damage. Specialist evidence will be needed for this, which is not easy or cheap. If a consumer in the UK wants to sue a manufacturer based abroad, they will have to take action in a foreign court, which again is not easy or cheap.

To deal with these problems and to make it easier for consumers to sue, the Consumer Protection Act 1987 was introduced. The Act gives a consumer the right to claim against a wider range of potential defendants than in negligence. So, if the manufacturer is based abroad or has gone out of business, it may be possible to claim against the supplier or the importer.

So what products are covered and what is meant by defect?

Definitions

Consumer

A claim can be brought under the Act where 'any damage is caused wholly or partly by a defect in a product'. Therefore, a 'consumer' is defined in the Consumer Protection Act 1987 as the user of the product. They do not have to have bought the product.

Producer

Where there is a defect, the consumer has a right to sue the producer. This term includes:

- the manufacturer
- the importer of the product into the UK
- a company involved in the manufacture of a part
- own-branders – any company which labels goods under its own name
- the retailer or supplier.

Product

A product is defined as 'any goods or electricity' and includes any product that is part of another. For example, the engine of a car is considered a product on its own even though it is part of the car.

Products that are not included under the Act are:

- fresh food which has not been processed in any way
- buildings
- nuclear power.

Safety

Section 3 of the Consumer Protection Act 1987 defines a **defect** as being present when 'the safety of the product is not such as persons generally are entitled to expect'. The standard of safety that 'persons generally are entitled to expect' is to be assessed in relation to all the circumstances, including:

- how the product has been marketed
- any instructions for, or warnings with, the product – for example, if a toy has a notice 'Not suitable for children aged under 3' written on it, the product should be safe for use by older children
- what might reasonably be expected to be done with or in relation to the product
- the time when the product was supplied by its producer to another
- the consumer's care for their own safety.

The fact that older products were less safe than newer ones does not, of itself, render the older products defective. The defect can be a fault in:

- design
- processing or manufacturing
- instructions
- a lack of warning that might affect the way the product may be used, installed or assembled.

The main benefit of taking action under the Act is that it forces strict liability on the producer. This means that the consumer does not have to prove how or why the product was defective or faulty – merely that it caused loss or injury to the consumer.

Key term

Defect – a fault in a product.

Damage

In order to claim, the consumer must show that the product caused damage. This includes:

- death
- any personal injury caused by the defective product
- loss or damage to property of at least £275. The property has to be of a type usually intended for private use and intended for private use by the consumer.

It does not include:

- damage to property worth less than £275
- damage to business property
- damage to the product itself.

There have been very few reported cases based on the Consumer Protection Act. However, the case of Abouzaid v Mothercare was reported and the claim was based on both negligence and Consumer Protection Act liability.

Key case

Abouzaid v Mothercare (2000)

Facts

The claimant was a boy whose mother bought a Cosytoes sleeping bag from Mothercare. It was designed to be attached to a child's pushchair with elastic straps. Shortly after the purchase, the boy, who was aged 12 at the time, helped his mother attach the product to his younger brother's pushchair. One of the elastic straps slipped and lashed back. The buckle attached to the elastic strap hit him in the eye causing serious, permanent damage. The boy sued Mothercare both in negligence and using the Consumer Protection Act 1987.

Legal principle – the court decided that Mothercare was not at fault in any way as it merely supplied the sleeping bag and so the claim in negligence failed. However, the court decided that the sleeping bag was defective and that it caused injury to the boy so they were liable under the Consumer Protection Act 1987.

When considering liability, the court may take into account the consumer's knowledge of, and care for, their own safety as in Bogle v McDonald's (2002)

Key case

Bogle v McDonald's (2002

Facts

Several young children were injured by spilled hot drinks served in McDonald's restaurants. A claim was brought under the Consumer Protection Act 1987. The main issue was whether the defendant was negligent in dispensing and serving hot drinks at a hot temperature, and whether, as a result, they were in breach of the Consumer Protection Act 1987 if injury was caused. The judge found that the public using McDonald's wanted to buy drinks that were served hot, even though there was a risk of scalding if the drink was spilled. Further, there was no evidence that suggested that a risk of injury would have been reduced if the drinks were served at lower temperatures.

Legal principle – while McDonald's owed a duty of care to those who visited its restaurants, that duty was not such that it ought to be stopped from serving hot drinks at all.

Defences

The Consumer Protection Act 1987 provides some defences to the producer. These include:

- The product complies with statutory or EU standards.
- The defect did not exist at the time it was supplied by the defendant.
- The product was not supplied in the course of business.
- The defendant did not supply the product to anyone.
- The state of scientific and technical knowledge at the time of production meant the defendant could not be expected to have discovered the defect. This is often known as the development risks defence.

Remedies

A claim has to be brought within three years of the accident. If the consumer succeeds in the claim, the court can award compensation for any personal injuries suffered and for any damage caused. The total damages have to be above £275. The cost of replacing the defective product cannot be claimed.

Table 5.3 compares the differences between claims for defective products in negligence and defective products under the Consumer Protection Act 1987.

Table 5.3: Differences between claims in negligence and under the Consumer Protection Act 1987

Defective products in negligence	Defective products in the Consumer Protection Act 1987
• There must be a duty of care owed. • The duty has been breached – this shows that fault has to be proved. • Injury or damage to property has resulted from the breach of duty.	• It is a strict liability tort. • Claim can be made if injury or damage caused by the use of the product. • There is no need to prove duty, breach or damage.
The claimant is any person who buys or uses the product or who is affected by it, including bystanders.	• The claimant is a person who suffers injury or damage caused wholly or partly by a defect in a product. • The claimant does not have to have bought the goods – merely to be injured while using them.
The claimant can sue if there is a breach of duty by the defendant.	• The claimant can sue if there is a defect in a product that causes them injury. There is a defect in a product if the safety of the product is not such as persons generally are entitled to expect in the circumstances. • No fault is needed.
The defendant is the person or company that breached the duty of care.	The producer can be sued. These include: • the manufacturer • the importer • the supplier • the own-brander • the person or company who made the defective component.
Defences available: • contributory negligence of claimant • consent to injury by claimant.	Defences available: • contributory negligence of claimant • development risks defence • product complies with the law • product not supplied • the use of the product was commercial • defect did not exist when product made.

• Claimant can claim damages for personal injuries and damage to other property caused by the defective good (whatever the amount).
• However, the claimant cannot recover the value of the item itself (unlike in contract law).
	• Claimant can claim for personal injuries, loss or earnings, damage to property provided it totals more than £275.
	• There is no claim for:
	  • damage to property worth less than £275
	  • damage to the defective item itself
	  • damage to anything being used for business use.

PAUSE POINT What action would you advise for a consumer who has been injured by a defective product?

Hint What can the consumer claim for and against whom?

Extend Use Table 5.3 to compare taking action using common law negligence and under the Consumer Protection Act 1987.

Scenario

Ezra tells your firm that when he was standing on some steps and putting up curtain poles in his son's house, he suffered an electric shock and burns while using his new electric drill. As a result of the shock, he fell off the steps breaking his ankle. He was off work for several weeks. The shirt he was wearing was damaged and the drill was completely burned out. The drill had been a present from his son.

Your firm's enquiries show that the drill had faulty wiring due to a defect in the manufacturing process.

1. What law would apply to this situation and what rules are contained in that law?
2. What advice would you give Ezra on what he should do?

Assessment practice 5.2

B.P3 B.P4 B.M2 B.D2

A family of three women come to see you for consumer advice.

The grandmother, Joan, had suffered a leaking roof to her house. After checking local websites and talking to some neighbours who had suffered similar problems, she contacted Martin. Martin looked at the roof and described himself as being in the roofing business for the past 25 years and was experienced in all kinds of roofing repairs. As a result of this statement, Joan asked him to repair her roof. Martin replaced some roof tiles and repaired the joints between brickwork and tiles. Joan paid him £5,000, due as, he said, it was 'a difficult job'. Two months later, Joan discovered that rain was penetrating the poorly repaired joints and had caused further damage to material stored in the loft. She found out that Martin had only worked in the building trade as a general labourer and that she had been considerably overcharged.

1 Joan has made an appointment with a senior partner about this and other matters. Write a file note for the senior partner to advise Joan.

Joan's granddaughter, Emma, has also had problems. She had several visits at home in the last month from a salesman representing Stylesafe trying to persuade her to buy some double glazing. She told him that she did not need their product as her house was fully double glazed. On one occasion, she told the salesman not to return but he came back the next day, trying to persuade her to buy and telling her that he was likely to lose his job if Emma did not place an order. Emma was persuaded by this to buy some new units costing £4,000. She signed a contract and paid £1,000 deposit.

2 Emma asks you to draft an email to the company saying that she does not want the double glazing and wants her money back.

Emma also ordered an e-book reader from Books-R-Us, an online retailer. When she ordered, the site said that there was a 'special offer' and the price of the reader was £50. When she received the e-book she found that her credit card had been charged £100. She queried the amount and found that Books-R-Us had not originally confirmed her order. She was told the 'special offer' had ended when her order was placed and she had been charged an additional delivery charge.

3 Emma asks you to draft a letter to Books-R-Us saying that she does not want the reader and wants her money back.

Finally, Emma's mother, Christine, tells you that she bought Emma a new washing machine as a present. It was manufactured in Korea, but imported into the UK and delivered to Emma by Whitegoods Ltd. The first time she used the machine, there was a small explosion and fire. Emma's expensive designer dress worth £750 was ruined, and she suffered burned hands.

Emma wants to know what action she can take, and against whom, for her damaged dress and injuries.

4 You promise to research the law and write a letter to advise her.

5 It is some time since your senior partner was asked about matters of consumer law. He asks you to write a file note for him evaluating how beneficial the impact of the current law on the supply of goods and services, unfair trading, aggressive practices and defective products is for consumers.

Plan

- I need to be sure about the facts of the three cases and which laws apply to them.
- I need to be clear about the law on the supply of goods and services, unfair trading, aggressive practices and defective products.
- I need to be sure how compensation applies to each case.

Do

- I need to be clear about how current consumer protection law is beneficial to the consumer, and areas where it might be lacking.
- I need to write each letter and file note clearly and reference the applicable laws.

Review

- I can evaluate different areas of consumer protection law.
- I am confident I can identify which areas of law are applicable to each case.

Investigate the law on exclusion clauses, applying this in given contractual case studies

Contractual clauses

In the small print of a contract you will often find a clause that tries to exclude the business's liability in the event of a breach of contract, for example, in the event of goods not being delivered or being broken. Such clauses can also commonly be found on signs in car parks. Many clauses are written in such a way that the meaning is not clear and so it is necessary for consumers to have some protection. This type of small print is also known as exemption clauses. They can be divided into **exclusion clauses** and **limitation clauses**.

Key terms

Exclusion clause – where the person who is selling goods or who is providing a service tries to avoid all liability in the event of a breach of contract.

Limitation clause – where the person who is selling goods or who is providing a service tries to limit their liability in the event of a breach of contract.

Exclusion clauses

The party with the stronger bargaining position, usually the business, puts exclusion clauses into a contract. They are not ordinarily negotiable and the effect of them is to put the consumer at a disadvantage. For example, in a package holiday contract a clause might read 'We are not responsible for any services that do not form part of our contract with you.' The approach of the law has been to try to protect the party in the weaker bargaining position (the consumer).

Protection can be given both by case law and statute, though in the case of consumers buying from a business the old case law has, from 1 October 2015, been overtaken by statutory protection in the Consumer Rights Act 2015.

Limitation clauses

Limitation clauses are also put into a contract by the party with the stronger bargaining position, usually the business. They are not ordinarily negotiable, and the effect of them is to put the consumer at a disadvantage. For example, in the same holiday contract another clause might read 'Where we are found liable for loss of, delay and/or damage to property, the maximum amount we will have to pay you is £1,000 per person.' The approach of the law has been to try to protect the party in the weaker bargaining position (the consumer).

Research

Find a contract that contains small print. Examples could be for upgrades on your phone, for iTunes or Amazon. Can you find an exclusion clause in the small print? Try to explain the effect of the clause to a friend.

Common law rules

It is fair that common law rules provide some protection for consumers when buying from a business, by ruling that consumers are only bound by clauses included in the contract at the time of entering into it.

A written contract will contain clauses to do with the type of product, its price, its colour and when it will be delivered. There may be other clauses in the small print, such as the clause seen in the case of L'Estrange v Graucob (1934).

Key case

L'Estrange v Graucob (1934)

Facts

The claimant purchased a cigarette vending machine for use in her café with accent. She signed an order form that had the following clause in the small print: 'Any express or implied, condition, statement of warranty, statutory or otherwise is expressly excluded.' The vending machine did not work. The claimant tried to reject it and get her money back. The court decided that by signing the order form she was bound by all the terms contained in it whether she had read the form or not. As a result, her claim was unsuccessful.

Legal principle – the consumer will be bound by the written terms in the contract, whether they have been read or not.

Incorporation

Not every contract containing small print is signed by the parties. If this is the case, the party seeking to rely on the exclusion clause (the business) must show that the other party (the consumer) knew of, or should have known of, the existence of the term. This can be done either by referring to it in a contractual document or by having a clear notice that is seen before the contract is made. This was addressed in the case of Olley v Marlborough Court (1949).

Reflect

What advice would you give anyone before they sign a contract containing small print?

Key case

Olley v Marlborough Court (1949)

Facts

The claimant booked into a hotel and a contract for her stay was made at the reception desk, where there was no mention of an exclusion clause. On the back of the door of the room, a notice tried to exclude the hotel's liability for any lost, stolen or damaged property. The claimant had her fur coat stolen. The court decided that the notice was not effective. The contract had already been made by the time the claimant saw the notice and so it was not part of the contract.

Legal principle – the consumer must know the terms, or have had the terms of the contract drawn to their attention, before the contract is made.

Interpretation

There is a difference between a ticket that is a receipt, such as a cloakroom ticket, and one that everyone knows is likely to contain or refer to terms such as a rail ticket or a plane ticket. An example of ticket interpretation can be seen in the case of Chapleton v Barry UDC (1940).

Key case

Chapleton v Barry UDC (1940)

Facts

The claimant hired a deck chair from Barry Council. There was a notice on the beach where the chairs were stored requesting the public to obtain tickets from an attendant. The claimant obtained a ticket and put it in his pocket without reading it. On the ticket was an exclusion clause excluding the council's liability for personal injury caused when using their chairs. The claimant was injured when he sat on a chair. He claimed against the council for his injuries. They relied on the exclusion clause. but the court decided in favour of the claimant.

Legal principle - the exclusion clause was not incorporated into the contract. A reasonable person would regard the ticket as a receipt and would not expect it to contain contractual terms.

Protection given by statute

Before the introduction of the Consumer Rights Act 2015, the law on unfair terms was contained in two separate pieces of legislation:

- Unfair Contract Terms Act 1977
- Unfair Terms in Consumer Contracts Regulations 1999.

These pieces of legislation had inconsistent and overlapping rules, creating uncertainty for consumers, businesses and lawyers.

With effect from 1 October 2015, both pieces of legislation were replaced by the Consumer Rights Act 2015 in respect of business-to-consumer contracts.

Consumer Rights Act 2015 - Section 63 and Schedule 2

Section 63

In s63 of the Act, there is a requirement for consumer contract terms and notices to be fair. Terms will only be binding upon the consumer if they are fair.

There is no definition for 'fair', but a contract can be 'unfair' if it:

- puts the consumer at a disadvantage
- limits the consumer's rights or
- unreasonably increases their obligations compared to the obligations and rights of the business.

Section 63 sets out factors that a court should take into account when deciding whether a term is fair (the 'fairness test'). The court should consider:

- the specific circumstances existing when the term was agreed.
- other terms in the contract
- the nature of the subject matter of the contract.

For example, if a consumer subscribed to a magazine, the contract could contain a term allowing the publisher to cancel the subscription at short notice. In deciding whether this is fair or not, the court could consider issues such as whether the consumer can also cancel at short notice or obtain a refund if the publisher cancels the contract.

If a term is found to be unfair it is void (invalid) and of no effect, though the remainder of the contract could contain terms which are fair and continue in force.

Schedule 2

Schedule 2 of the Consumer Rights Act lists 20 terms that are automatically unfair in a consumer contract. This includes, in point 2, a clause that excludes or limits the liability of the business in the event of a breach of the contract.

Returning to the magazine subscription example again, a consumer enters a 12-issue subscription contract. If the contract includes a term that allows the publisher, but not the consumer, to cancel the subscription at short notice, that term may be regarded as unfair. Schedule 2 covers a term which allows 'the business to dissolve the contract on a discretionary basis where the same facility is not granted to the consumer'. The remainder of the contract remains valid so that subscriptions would start and continue throughout the 12 issues of the contract.

Link

Look at Schedule 2 Consumer Rights Act 2015 for the complete list of terms that are automatically unfair.

A term that sets the main subject matter of the contract (the magazine, for example), or a term that sets the price, are only exempt from the test of fairness if they are both **transparent** and **prominent**.

Key term

Transparent – the clause is written in plain and clear language.

Prominent – the term is brought to the consumer's attention in such a way that the average consumer would be aware of the term.

An example of this could be when buying an airline ticket. One of the terms says 'extra fees may apply', but does not say what they are or when they will be charged. The consumer buys the ticket and finds at the airport that an extra charge is payable for hand luggage. This could be considered unfair as the clause about the extra fees was not clear.

The Act also provides that some terms are not automatically unfair, but may be held to be unfair by the court even when the consumer has not complained of unfairness. For example, if you agree with a catering company for them to provide you with lunch, and the contract includes a term that you will pay £100 for a three-course meal, the court cannot look at whether it is fair to pay £100 for three courses. It may, however, look at other things, such as the rights of the company and the consumer to cancel the lunch, and when the price of the lunch is due to be paid.

Identify three examples of exclusion clauses.

Hint Find examples in the small print of contracts.

Extend Compare exclusion clauses and limitation clauses.

Scenario

Catherine has just moved into a new house that had no curtains or blinds fitted. She paid £1,500 to Lightbloc for the supply and fitting of curtains and blinds in the bedrooms. Catherine bought deep blue 'blackout' blinds. The invoice included a statement that 'in the event of any complaint about goods supplied or work undertaken, repair, replacement or refund (subject to payment of a maximum of 20 per cent of the contract price) will be entirely at Lightbloc's discretion'. She did not read this statement at the time and nor was it pointed out to her.

After the blinds had been fitted, Catherine found that they did not block out sufficient light.

Catherine complained to Lightbloc who referred her to the statement in the invoice.

What law applies to this situation?

Assessment practice 5.3

C.P5 C.M3 C.D3

Vicki has recently entered into a contract with Fitness4health, a business offering training sessions for personal fitness and health. Vicki tells you that she had not exercised for some years. She signed a contract in which she agreed to pay £20 per session for 20 training sessions over five weeks. One clause in the small print, which she did not read, said that Fitness4health would not be liable for any injuries suffered by Vicki as a result of the sessions. A notice in the changing room stated that precise start and finish times could not be guaranteed and that Fitness4health would not be liable for any additional costs incurred by learners. All the sessions in the first week started at least 30 minutes late, causing Vicki major inconvenience and extra childcare expense. The sessions had also been too strenuous, causing Vicki to suffer from a back injury, which prevented her from working for two weeks.

1. Vicki wants to know whether she is bound by the clauses in her contract with Fitness4health. You write her a letter informing her of her rights.
2. She also wants your views on the protection provided by common law and statutory rules on the validity of exclusion clauses. You promise to write her a short report about this.

Plan

- I need to be clear about the protections offered by common law and statutory rules.
- I need to be clear about when exclusion clauses are fair and when they are not.

Do

- I need to apply my knowledge of exclusion clauses to this case.
- I need to give Vicki clear advice and explain the law simply.

Review

- I can apply the law to this particular case.
- I can evaluate the validity of exclusion clauses.

Further reading and resources

http://www.bbc.co.uk/news/business-34403005

THINK FUTURE

Roger Cohen

Senior Trading Standards Officer

My work and that of my small team involves acting on behalf of consumers and businesses, advising them, and, if necessary, enforcing laws that govern the way goods and services are bought, sold and hired. I have 40 years' experience in the field and am employed by a county council in the south of England. My role is to protect the county's consumers and businesses by promoting a safe and fair trading environment.

To become a Trading Standards Officer, a degree is an initial requirement, followed by professional qualifications administered by the Chartered Trading Standards Institute. Although not a lawyer, I am responsible for understanding the effect of a range of legislation and case law together with its implementation and enforcement.

I am involved in preventing, detecting and prosecuting consumer-related offences. A particular problem in my county at present is the sale of illicit tobacco. As well as evading national taxes, the sale of these products may involve personal health and fire risks and, in certain cases, a range of wider offences such as people trafficking and slave labour. I will often liaise with other agencies including the police, HM Revenue & Customs, Citizens Advice, trade organisations and legal professionals to build up intelligence.

Other areas of my work can include animal welfare, especially that of cattle and sheep, and protecting vulnerable individuals from rogue traders and scams. I have to be aware of new methods of trading, which, in my area, have included selling puppies and illicit tobacco through social media. In addition, I have certain statutory duties including enforcing rules on underage selling and weights and measures.

I enjoy the wide variety of my work, which could include gathering information while investigating suspected offences. Sometimes this has to be done undercover, though it may also include obtaining court orders for the disclosure of material. I may have to visit business premises, perhaps supported by the police, and on certain visits it is neccesary to wear a protective stab vest as you can never anticipate the reaction of a suspect. My work also includes advising or taking evidence from members of the public and businesses, and sometimes presenting evidence at court. My office-based work includes writing reports, statements, letters, articles and consultation documents.

In my work I need good written and oral communication skills, including the ability to talk to people from different backgrounds. I must be able to analyse and evaluate often detailed legal rules, and apply them to evidence obtained. I must have keen investigative skills, and once I have decided to investigate an issue I must have the determination to see it through. I must also be tactful and diplomatic while I am building a case, and sometimes resilient in order to cope with occasional aggression. My experience of knowing how to approach and deal with people, especially vulnerable victims, is also important as I may be required to negotiate between a victim and suspected rogue trader.

Contract Law 6

Getting to know your unit

Assessment
You will be assessed by a series of assignments set by your tutor.

Contract law is the law that applies to anything you buy or sell, and to the conditions under which you work. Contract law governs formal written contracts as well as everyday transactions, such as buying a cup of coffee, a train ticket or an app. A contract is an agreement that the law will enforce. The law sets out how and when a contract comes into existence and the rights and duties that follow from the contract. These come from the terms of the contract that may be specifically stated or may be implied by an Act of Parliament or the law generally. When things go wrong, you need to know what remedies are available and how these are decided in law.

In this unit, you will learn about the legal requirements for setting up a valid contract and the effect of the law in negotiating a contract. You will be able to evaluate how parties can draw up enforceable contracts when using modern communication methods. In addition, you will explore the types of terms that are used in contracts and be able to evaluate their meaning in a standard form contract. Using given cases, you will investigate the validity of a contract to determine contractual rights. You will look at the different ways in which a contract may be ended, what effect this has in each case, and the remedies in the event of a contract being breached.

Most of the law in this area comes from decided cases. It is therefore important that you can demonstrate knowledge of these cases, as well as showing you can apply the relevant law in given scenarios.

How you will be assessed

This unit will be assessed by a series of assignments set and marked by your tutor. You will need to work independently on these assignments. You will find activities as you read this section of the book that will help you prepare for those set by your tutor. Keep all your notes and activities that you have completed together in one folder so that you are well prepared. It is also important for you to check the unit specification and assignment brief. This will help you to be clear about what is required when questions ask for explanation, analysis and evaluation. It may be helpful to practise the higher-level skills needed in order to achieve the Merit and Distinction grades, such as developing a point, analysing a situation or case study and evaluating the law and its impact. Throughout this unit you will find activities that will develop your understanding of contract law that will help you prepare for your assignments. The recommended assessment approach for this unit is three assignments, to include the suggested criteria.

The assignments set by your tutor will consist of a number of tasks designed to meet the criteria in the table opposite. They are likely to include a written assignment but may also include activities such as:

- case studies where you make decisions about a case and provide legal advice
- presentations or scenarios where you can demonstrate your knowledge about legal practice and procedures.

Assessment criteria

This table shows what you must do in order to achieve a **Pass**, **Merit** or **Distinction**, and where you can find activities to help you.

Pass	Merit	Distinction
Learning aim A Examine the necessary legal requirements to form a valid contract		
A.P1 Explain in given case studies, whether the legal requirements for the formation of a contract have been met. **Assessment practice 6.1**	**A.M1** Apply the law on formation of contracts in given case studies, analysing the impact of each stage of a series of negotiations up to formation of contract. **Assessment practice 6.1**	**A.D1** Evaluate, using current case law to justify a conclusion, how parties would ensure enforceable contracts when using modern communication methods. **Assessment practice 6.1**
A.P2 Explain using given case studies, the rules on offers, counter-offers and invitations to treat. **Assessment practice 6.1**		
Learning aim D Explore the types of terms that are found in a contract		
B.P3 Explain the types of express terms in a given standard form contract. **Assessment practice 6.2**	**B.M2** Apply the law on express and implied terms in given contracts, analysing their impact on the parties. **Assessment practice 6.2**	**B.D2** Evaluate the meaning and legality of terms in specific case study contracts. **Assessment practice 6.2**
B.P4 Outline the different ways that terms can be implied in a contract. **Assessment practice 6.2**		
Learning aim C Investigate the validity of a contract to determine contractual rights		
C.P5 Explain in given contract case studies rights under contract and the different ways contracts can be invalid. **Assessment practice 6.3**	**C.M3** Apply the law on validity and rights in given contracts, analysing any impact on the parties. **Assessment practice 6.3**	**CD.D3** Evaluate the legal position and appropriate remedies in given contract case studies. **Assessment practice 6.3**
Learning aim D Review the ways in which a contract may end and the remedies available		
D.P6 Discuss using given contract case studies, the ways in which a contract may be discharged and the remedies available. **Assessment practice 6.3**	**D.M4** Apply the law on discharge and remedies, analysing the impact in given case study materials. **Assessment practice 6.3**	

Getting started

Have you bought a cup of coffee recently? If so, was it hot? What was included in the price: sugar, milk, a lid, a stirrer? Was your coffee served in a cup or mug? Did you pay in cash or by card? These are all terms of a consumer contract. The same principles apply in commercial dealings.

A Examine the necessary legal requirements to form a valid contract

A **contract** is an agreement that the law will enforce. A contract requires agreement as a starting point. An agreement requires an **offer** to do or sell something that the other person agrees to. This is known as offer and **acceptance**. This agreement, together with an intention for the agreement to be legally binding and something of value passing from each party to the other, known as **consideration**, makes the agreement a contract. You will look at the legal rules of these requirements so that you will be able to explain whether a legal contract has been formed or not and when the contract came into existence.

Key terms

Contract – an agreement that the law will enforce.

Offer – a statement of the terms upon which the offeror is willing to be bound in a contract.

Acceptance – clear assent by the offeree to the terms set out by the offeror.

Consideration – something of value given by each party to a contract to the other.

Offeror – the person making an offer.

Offeree – the person to whom the offer is made. An offeree can accept the offer.

Offers and invitation to treat

Only an offer can be accepted to make a contract. It is therefore essential to be able to work out whether there is an offer open for acceptance at the time that a contract is made.

Offers

An offer is a statement of the terms on which a person is willing to be bound in a contract. It must be made to the person who wishes to accept it. This means that the offer is communicated from the **offeror** to the **offeree**. This is generally not a problem. Usually, if you wish to sell something, you are happy to sell it to anyone. This can be seen in the famous case of Carlill v Carbolic Smoke Ball Company (1892). One of the legal points decided in that case was whether an offer could be made to anyone in the world. The court decided that this was not a problem so long as the person accepting the offer knew about the offer. This case will be looked at in more detail when you consider the differences between an offer and an invitation to treat, later in this section.

An offer can be made in various ways:

- in a written document
- stated verbally, either face to face or on the telephone
- by a machine.

An example of an offer made by a machine can be seen in the case of Thornton v Shoe Lane Parking (1971), also discussed later on in this unit.

Key case

Thornton v Shoe Lane Parking (1971)

Facts

The contract was made by putting coins in the machine next to an automatic parking barrier for a car park. This meant that the terms of the contract were those that were made known at the time that the money was exchanged.

Legal principle – an offer can be made by a machine on behalf of a person or organisation.

Counter-offers and other ways an offer can come to an end

An offer can come to an end in the following ways:

- counter-offer
- rejection
- revocation
- lapse of time
- death.

Counter-offer and rejection

A **counter-offer** is a different offer made in response to the original offer. It happens during negotiations leading up to a contract and is made by the offeree. For example, if someone offers to sell you their car for £1,900, you might well say, 'How about £1,800?' Your statement is a counter-offer that ends the original offer.

If the person then replies to you, 'No', they would be making a **rejection** of your offer, which also ends your offer to them. At this point there would be no offer open for the sale of their car, so you could not say, 'Actually, I have changed my mind and I accept your offer to sell at £1,900.' You would have just made a new offer to buy the person's car for £1,900, which they could accept or reject.

The following diagram in Figure 6.1 illustrates this principle.

Key terms

Counter-offer – an offer by the offeree that is in response to and different from the offeror's offer.

Rejection – the offeree saying no to an offer made.

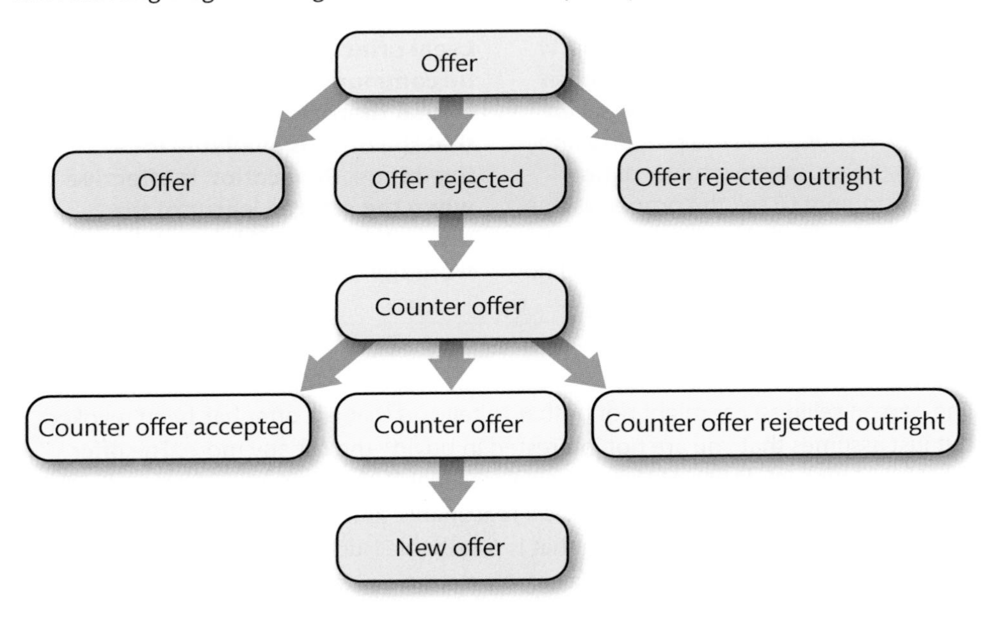

Figure 6.1: The relationship between offers at different stages of a simple negotiation

A case that illustrates these principles is Hyde v Wrench (1840).

Key case

Hyde v Wrench (1840)

Facts

There was an offer made to sell a farm for £1,000. The offeree responded with an offer of £950 (a counter-offer and therefore a rejection of the offer). The seller of the farm rejected the counter-offer. The original offeree then tried to accept the original offer to sell the farm for £1,000, but could not do so as his counter-offer had ended that offer.

Legal principle – a counter-offer ends the original offer.

 **PAUSE POINT** In pairs, identify what an offer is.

Hint — List the ways that an offer can be made and how it can come to an end.

Extend — In groups, identify everyday situations where offers are made and accepted.

Key terms

Revocation – the offeror withdrawing their offer.

Lapse of time – after a period of time has passed.

Revocation

You might not reply to the person's offer to sell the car for £1,900 at the time, but decide to go away to think about it. The person can change their mind at any time and end the offer. This is known as **revocation** of the offer. However, revocation does not end an offer until you, the offeree, know about the revocation – revocation must be communicated to the offeree before the offer is ended. This can be seen in the case of Routledge v Grant (1828).

Key case

Routledge v Grant (1828)

Facts

There was an offer to sell a property, with the offer to remain open for six weeks. Three weeks later, the seller decided not to sell the property and told the prospective buyer of his decision not to sell the property. One week after that, the prospective buyer tried to accept the offer, but could not do so as the offer had already been ended by the revocation.

Legal principle – revocation can be communicated at any time, even if there has been a statement that the offer is available for a fixed time. Revocation is effective when the offeree learns of the revocation, even if it is not directly from the offeror.

Lapse of time

The person selling a car might not bother to tell you that the offer has been revoked, but just assumes that you are not interested in buying the car any more. The offer would end through **lapse of time** when a reasonable time has passed or any fixed period for the offer has ended. What is a reasonable time depends on the nature of the offer. An offer to sell something that is perishable (such as a cake) will obviously lapse more quickly than an offer of a car. An example of lapse of time can be seen in the case of Ramsgate Victoria Hotel v Montefiore (1866).

Key case

Ramsgate Victoria Hotel v Montefiore (1866)

Facts

An offer was made to buy shares in a hotel. No reply was made to the offer for over five months. The court decided that this was too long a period to wait and that the offer had lapsed.

Legal principle – an offer ends after a reasonable period of time, if the time period during which it should remain open is not specified.

Death

The death of either party will end the offer when the other party learns of the death. The exception to this is an offer to perform a personal service. If someone offered to give you private tuition in law, their offer would end as soon as they died even if you had not learned of their death. This makes sense, as it would then be impossible for them to perform the contract. However, it would be unfair if you were unable to accept an offer for goods, as the ability for the goods to be transferred to you would not end on the person's death. For example, if the owner of a one-person business died, the owner's spouse would not have any income until renegotiations had started.

Invitation to treat

An **invitation to treat** is not an offer. It is something that encourages negotiations and offers. Therefore a request for information and the reply to this is not an offer, but an invitation to treat – it is just a common courtesy to reply to such a request. This can be seen in the case of Stevenson v McLean (1880).

Key terms

Invitation to treat – something that encourages negotiation but is not an offer.

Key case

Stevenson v McLean (1880)

Facts

A query about whether credit terms were available in a proposed contract was said to be a request for information and not a counter-offer.

Legal principle – a request for information and a reply to that request do not form an offer or a counter-offer.

In general, advertisements, goods in a shop window (even with a price ticket attached) and goods on a supermarket shelf are invitations to treat and not offers. This makes sense as a shop may only have a few items in stock or there may be legal restrictions on the sale of items such as knives, fireworks and aerosol paint cans.

You can see the difference between an invitation to treat and an offer in the following cases.

- In Partridge v Crittenden (1968), an advertisement was not an offer to sell.

Key case

Partridge v Crittenden (1968)

Facts

There was an advertisement to sell birds. It was illegal to offer these birds for sale. The defendant was not guilty of offering the birds for sale, however, because the advertisement was not an offer to sell but an invitation to treat.

Legal principle – an advertisement is not an offer to sell but an invitation to treat.

- In Fisher v Bell (1961), goods in a shop window with a price ticket on them were not an offer but an invitation to treat.

Key case

Fisher v Bell (1961)

Facts

A gravity knife in a shop window with a price ticket on it was not an offer but an invitation to treat, so the shopkeeper could not be guilty of offering restricted weapons for sale.

Legal principle – goods in a shop window even with a price ticket are not an offer but an invitation to treat.

- In Pharmaceutical Society of Great Britain v Boots Cash Chemists (Southern) Ltd (1952), goods on a self-service shop shelf were an invitation to treat and not an offer.

Key case

Pharmaceutical Society of Great Britain v Boots Cash Chemists (Southern) Ltd (1952)

Facts

Pharmaceutical products that could only be sold on the authority of a qualified pharmacist were on a shelf for sale in a self-service shop. Normally, offer would be made by the customer to buy the goods and the offer would then be accepted or rejected by the pharmacist, so complying with the law. A case was brought as pharmaceutical products that could not be legally sold without the authority of a qualified pharmacist were on a shelf for sale in a self-service pharmacy. However, the court ruled that this complied with the law, as the goods on the shelf are merely an invitation – the pharmacy was not offering the items for sale.

Legal principle – goods in a self-service shop are invitations to treat and not offers.

One exception to the rule that advertisements are invitations to treat and not offers is when the advertisement contains an offer that is intended to be taken seriously, such as a reward. This can be seen in the case of Carlill v Carbolic Smoke Ball Company (1892).

Key case

Carlill v Carbolic Smoke Ball Company (1892)

Facts

The Carbolic Smoke Ball Company placed an advertisement offering a cash reward of £100 to anyone who used the advertised product but still caught flu. To make it clear this was meant to be a serious offer, the advertisement claimed that £1,000 had been deposited with a bank. The court stated that this was an offer that could be accepted and become a contract, so Mrs Carlill could claim her reward.

Legal principle – an advertisement can be an offer in reward cases.

▶ The advertisement in the case Carlill v Carbolic Smoke Ball Company (1892)

PAUSE POINT Explain the differences between an offer and an invitation to treat.

Hint Define an offer and define an invitation to treat.

Extend Look at the case law that illustrates the difference between the two. Can you remember and explain the legal principles?

Acceptance

Acceptance of an offer is what changes an offer into an agreement. Acceptance must be unequivocal. This means that the communication by the offeree to the offeror is definite and certain.

Discussion

In small groups, think of situations where you have accepted an offer. How did you communicate your acceptance of the offer? Was it clear to all parties? Do you think the contract you made would be easily enforceable by law?

Communication of acceptance

Acceptance must be communicated to the offeror to take effect. There are many possible forms of communication, and the rules vary as to when communication takes place. The actual time for communication is critical as it can decide whether there is a contract or not.

Acceptance by post

Acceptance by post is governed by the posting rules. These were developed when the use of post was the only effective way of communicating other than face to face.

The posting rules require these three parts to be proved.

1 The post is the usual or expected means of communication.
2 The letter must be properly addressed and stamped.
3 The offeree must be able to prove the letter was posted.

If these three parts are proved, then acceptance takes place as soon as the letter is posted. A contract would be made at that moment even if the letter was lost or delayed. This can be seen in the case of Adams v Lindsell (1818).

Key case

Adams v Lindsell (1818)

Facts

The offeror sent a letter offering to sell wool and requested that the offeree accepted by post. A letter accepting an offer of the wool was posted the day before the offeror sold the wool to someone else. It was then a further day before the letter accepting the offer arrived with the seller of the wool. The court decided that a contract had been formed by the exchange of letters. Therefore the offeror had broken his contract and would have to compensate the disappointed buyer of the wool.

Legal principle - a letter of acceptance is effective from the moment of posting, providing that it can be proved that the three posting rules have been complied with by the offeree.

Verbal and telephonic acceptance

Verbal acceptance is completed once the offeror has heard the acceptance of the offer. If you are not communicating face to face, there can be an opportunity for confusion when a phone call drops out. For this reason, confirmation by letter, email or SMS (text message) is a good way to ensure that the agreement has been made.

Electronic

The Electronic Commerce (EC Directive) Regulations 2002 apply to online sales and advertising services, as well as services carried out via email and SMS. These regulations state that offer and acceptance are deemed to have taken place when the person to whom they are addressed is able to access them. For example, an offer to buy goods from a website is open when the web company can access the message. Their acceptance takes place when the buyer can receive the message, such as when you agree to subscribe to an online streaming service.

Silence

Acceptance cannot be silent. This means that a positive action must be taken to be considered an acceptance, as seen in the case of Felthouse v Brindley (1862).

Key case

Felthouse v Bindley (1862)

Negotiations took place about the sale of a horse. The seller stated, 'If I hear nothing more, consider it yours.' This could not be the basis of acceptance when there was no further communication.

Legal principle - acceptance must be communicated to the offeror.

Acceptance by conduct

We have seen acceptance by conduct in the case of Carlill v Carbolic Smoke Ball Company (1892) where Mrs Carlill's acceptance of the offer was made by using the smoke ball. This is seen in reward cases, such as a poster for a lost dog offering a reward. There is no need to telephone and say you are looking for the dog as acceptance takes place when you return the pet to its owner.

PAUSE POINT Explain the different ways acceptance can take place and when it actually happens.

Hint List the different ways and use examples to show your understanding.

Extend Consider whether the law is confusing as to when acceptance takes place. How could it be improved?

Scenario

Byrne v Van Tienhoven (1880)

After an enquiry, Van Tienhoven posted a letter from its office in Cardiff to Byrne in New York, offering 1000 boxes of tinplates for sale on 1 October. Byrne received the letter on 11 October. They sent a telegram with acceptance on the same day and also posted a letter confirming the details of the telegraphed acceptance. However, on 8 October Van Tienhoven had sent another letter withdrawing their offer because tinplate prices had just risen 25 per cent. They refused to go through with the sale.

1 If you set out the facts of the scenario in chronological order, you can identify each part as an invitation to treat, offer or acceptance, and show when each came into effect and the consequence, as in the table below.

2 Explain why Van Tienhoven's revocation was not effective before 20 October.

3 By this time (20 October) a contract had already been made - identify the two possible ways this had been made and the dates.

4 Discuss how the case might have been different if modern methods of communication had been used.

September	Enquiry made by Byrne.	Invitation to treat - no legal consequence.
1 October	Van Tienhoven posted a letter offering goods for sale.	Offer not open until communicated to Byrne & Co.
7 October	Letter of 1 October arrived with Byrne.	Offer open.
8 October	Van Tienhoven revoked the offer in a letter.	Revocation would be effective when communicated to Byrne - therefore offer still open.
11 October	Byrne accepted the offer by telegraph and also posted a letter confirming acceptance.	Posting rules applied as letters were the normal means of communication. So if Byrne could prove when they posted the letter and it was properly addressed and stamped, acceptance took place when it was posted (11 October). If they could not prove that, acceptance would have taken place on arrival of the telegram. Contract made.
20 October	Letter of revocation arrived.	Offer ended.

Consideration

Once there is an agreement between the parties, there must also be **consideration**. The law is concerned with deals and not gifts; a gift will not have consideration. Consideration is defined as the parties of a contract each giving the other something of value, which can be something now or something in the future. For example, if someone makes a contract for delivery of a computer next week, but pays now, consideration is the person's payment and the company's promise to deliver a computer next week.

Key terms

Consideration – the parties in a contract giving the other something of value.

Duress – when a person enters an agreement as a result of threats, traditionally of unlawful physical violence. In recent times, courts have recognised economic duress.

Executed consideration – consideration that has been performed after the formation of a contract.

Executory consideration – consideration that has to be performed in the future.

Promisor – the person making the promise.

Promisee – the person to whom the promise is made.

Past consideration – a promise to pay for something already done. It is not valid consideration as it has no value in law.

Types of consideration

Valid consideration must have some value. It does not have to be of equal value – otherwise, businesses would never make a profit! This can be quite extreme and high-value items may be bought for very little money. It should be noted that if the bargain is very extreme, it might be an indication of some form of **duress** that might affect the legality of the contract.

There are certain terms normally used to describe consideration in legal materials. For example, imagine a scenario in which you have agreed to buy someone's Ferrari for £1. If you drive the Ferrari away and the contract is to pay the seller the £1 next week, you having the Ferrari would be **executed consideration** and the promise to pay £1 would be **executory consideration**. In other words, because you have the Ferrari in your possession, this is consideration which has taken place or been executed. However, you have not yet paid your £1, so this is consideration that is waiting to happen. With respect to the £1, you would be the **promisor** and the seller would be the **promisee**.

The rules of consideration

The rules that set out whether there is valid consideration for a contract are:

- Consideration must have some value.
- Consideration must not be past.
- Consideration must move from the promisee.

Consideration must have some value

An example of consideration requiring some value can be seen in the case of Chappell v Nestlé (1960).

Key case

Chappell v Nestlé (1960)

Facts

Nestlé's customers were able to claim a record of a song in exchange for some chocolate bar wrappers. The question was whether the wrappers formed part of the consideration or were of no value. It was held that the chocolate bar wrappers provided the consideration on one part and the record the other.

Legal principle – consideration must have some value but each party's consideration does not have to be equal.

Consideration must not be past

Past consideration is a promise to pay for something that has already happened. This has no value in law and cannot form the consideration in a contract.

An example of this can be seen in the case of Re McArdle (1951).

Key case

Re McArdle (1951)

Work on a house was voluntarily undertaken by the tenant Mrs McArdle. After the work was finished, the owners of the house said they would pay £488 for the work done. This promise was unenforceable, as all the work had been done before the promise to pay was made and was therefore past consideration.

Legal principle – past consideration has no value and cannot be used to form a contract.

Similarly, a promise to perform an existing obligation cannot form consideration as there is already a legal obligation to perform the task or pay the money. Sometimes there can be shown to be an extra benefit to both parties, for example, by paying an additional sum to ensure that building work is finished on time, as in the case of Williams v Roffey Bros & Nicholls (Contractors) Ltd (1990).

Key terms

Privity of contract – the principle that only a party to a contract can sue on it.

Damages – an award of money to compensate the innocent party.

Consideration must move from the promisee

This rule means that the promisee, and not another party, must follow through on their side of the agreement. In conjunction with this, a person cannot sue or be sued under a contract unless that person has provided consideration under the contract. This is the basis of a principle called **privity of contract**.

The courts have tried to find ways to avoid injustice caused by this rule as in the case of Jackson v Horizon Holidays Ltd (1975).

Key case

Jackson v Horizon Holidays Ltd (1975)

Facts

Mr Jackson booked a holiday for himself and his family. The holiday was very disappointing. He sued the holiday company for **damages** for his and his family's disappointment. The court decided that it would be unfair to only pay damages to Mr Jackson and to ignore the claims of his family purely on the basis that he was the one that made the contract.

Legal principle – the court can look at ways to avoid the harshness of the privity of contract rule to avoid injustice.

This situation has been helped by the Contracts (Rights of Third Parties) Act 1999. Under the Act, someone who is not a party to a contract (a 'third party') may enforce the contract against either or both of the actual parties to the contract.

 **PAUSE POINT** Make a list of the rules on consideration.

Hint Use decided cases to illustrate each of the rules you have mentioned.

Extend Consider the rights of third parties. Do you think third parties should always be allowed to enforce contracts which affect them?

Intention to create legal relations

People tend to assume that some things are legally binding and some things are not, and in many situations are unaware of the relevant law. Often there is no need to find out whether something is legally binding until things go wrong. For example, people think that buying something is a legally binding contract and that they will have certain rights and obligations in making the contract. They also assume that an arrangement to meet someone for a coffee is not legally a contract, even though it is annoying if the other person does not turn up.

In terms of the law, agreements fall into two categories:

- social and domestic agreements
- business and commercial agreements.

Key terms

Presumption – a fact assumed to be true.

Rebutted – shown not to be valid, using evidence.

Social and domestic agreements

Social and domestic arrangements are presumed not to be legally binding. Like any **presumption**, this can be **rebutted** by showing that it does not apply to a particular case in question.

The two contrasting cases of Balfour v Balfour (1919) and Merritt v Merritt (1970) illustrate how the law is applied. Both cases involve a husband making an agreement with his wife to pay her an allowance.

Key case

Balfour v Balfour (1919)

Facts

Mr Balfour worked abroad and agreed to pay his wife an allowance while he was away. The marriage later failed and he stopped paying the allowance. The court decided that this was a domestic arrangement and that the court in divorce proceedings should make a decision on the amount to be paid.

Legal principle – a domestic agreement, such as to pay an allowance, is not legally binding.

Key case

Merritt v Merritt (1970)

Facts

A couple, who were already living apart, met to agree financial arrangements. This was seen to be legally binding as the fact that they were trying to sort out a financial agreement before matrimonial proceedings started was evidence of the intention to make the agreement legally binding, rather than only a domestic arrangement.

Legal principle – the presumption that a domestic agreement is not legally binding can be rebutted where there is evidence that there is an intention to create legal relations.

The legal principle in Merritt v Merritt (1970) is very relevant to lottery syndicates and similar arrangements. It is generally advisable to put such agreements in writing so there is no doubt about the arrangement. If there is no written agreement, other evidence of the arrangement must be evident, as in the case of Simpkins v Pays (1955).

Key case

Simpkins v Pays (1955)

Facts

Mr Simpkins was a lodger at Mrs Pays' house along with her granddaughter. They regularly entered competitions in the newspaper on the basis that any prize money would be shared equally. All three contributed to the entry fee and one form was sent off containing all three entries. The entry was in the sole name of Mrs Pays and they won £750. She did not share the winnings as agreed. The court decided that although the agreement was made in a social setting, there was clearly an agreement that this was a joint enterprise with the intention of sharing the winnings.

Legal principle – agreements in a social setting can be legally enforceable and, in some cases, it is possible to rebut the principle that social agreements are not legally binding.

Business and commercial agreements

With business and commercial agreements, the opposite presumption applies. Business agreements are presumed to be legally binding, but the presumption can be rebutted by evidence such as that in the case of Jones v Vernon's Pools (1938).

Key case

Jones v Vernon's Pools (1938)

Facts

This case involved a football pool competition entry form that stated: 'This contract is binding in honour only.' This meant that Mr Jones could not take legal action against the football pool company when he thought he had won but they declined to pay.

Legal principle – an honour clause in an agreement rebuts the presumption of an intention to create legal relations.

Explain the difference between social and commercial agreements.

Hint Look at the cases that show the difference.

Extend Do you think that all agreements should be legally binding?

Assessment practice 6.1

A.P1 A.P2 A.M1 A.D1

Jay is a musician and recently travelled from Manchester to London to have a meeting with Emily about whether his band could perform at a music festival. Jay told Emily that his band's fee would be £500. Emily said she would be in touch in the next three weeks.

Two weeks after they spoke, Jay's band's new video went viral. Emily saw the reaction online and realised that an appearance by Jay's band would sell out the festival. She immediately emailed Jay, stating that she agreed to pay £500 for a performance by his band. An hour later, Jay emailed back, saying that the band's fee was now £2,000. In the email, he also asked Emily to pay for his train fare for their previous meeting.

However, another band member named Steve thought Emily would look for a different band now. Without telling Jay, Steve phoned Emily the following day, saying that they could drop the price to £1,500.

Emily is now unsure of her legal position and has come to you for advice. You need to assess each stage of negotiations, using correct legal terminology. You must evaluate the offers made by all parties and determine whether any contracts have been made. In order to complete this task, you need to apply your knowledge of the law on formation of contracts and to think about the means of communication used. Referring to current case law, evaluate how enforceable any contract may be in the current circumstances.

Plan

- What is the task? What advice am I being asked to give?
- Do I need to research any aspect of current case law before I begin?

Do

- I need to identify the different stages in negotiations and apply the rules on these to given scenarios.
- I need to explain what constitutes acceptance and how this can be communicated.
- I need to discuss how enforceable different types of contracts are, referring to current case law.

Review

- I can explain how I approached this task.
- I can apply the law on the formation of contracts to a given scenario.
- I can explain what I have learned.

B Explore the types of terms that are found in a contract

Every contract has terms. The terms of a contract detail what the parties to the contract have agreed. These terms can either be those that have been specifically agreed between the parties, known as express terms, and those that the law will imply in the contract, known as implied terms. These implied terms can be implied by the courts or by an Act of Parliament.

Express terms in different types of contract

Express terms in a contract are agreed during the process of negotiation leading up to the acceptance of an offer. It can be very straightforward – for example, buying a cup of coffee in a café for the price in the menu.

Different types of contracts use different express terms. The following are types of express terms:

- conditions
- warranties
- innominate terms.

The same categorisation applies to those in standard form contracts and also to implied terms.

Conditions

A **condition** is a term that is central to the contract. If someone makes a contract to rent a car, it is central to the contract that the car actually runs and brakes reliably. If a condition is broken, the person affected is entitled to end the contract there and then. A condition can be seen in the case of Poussard v Spiers and Pond (1876).

Key case

Poussard v Spiers and Pond (1876)

Facts

An opera singer agreed to perform the lead role in a production for a season of performances and relevant rehearsals. After she failed to attend the first few performances, her role was given to an understudy and she was not allowed to take up the role. She sued for breach of contract but the court stated that she had broken her contract by not attending the important opening nights. This was a breach of **condition** and, therefore, the production company was entitled to end her contract.

Legal principle – a breach of condition entitles the affected party to repudiate (end) the contract.

Key terms

Condition – a term in a contract that is central to the contract; if it is broken the contract can be ended.

Warranty – a minor term in a contract, breach of which does not end the contract but allows a claim for damages only.

Innominate term – a term in a contract that is not set out as a condition or a warranty. The way it is treated depends on the consequences of the breach.

Warranties

A **warranty** is a minor term of the contract that allows a claim for damages to be made by the affected party to the contract. Even though damages may be payable, the contract continues, as the term is not central to the contract. For example, if a radio in a rented car only works intermittently, this would be classified as a warranty.

The case of Bettini v Gye (1876) is similar to Possard v Spiers and Pond (1876) but instead illustrates a warranty.

Key case

Bettini v Gye (1876)

Facts

A singer was contracted to perform at a series of concerts and six days of rehearsal. He failed to attend the first three days of rehearsals. He was replaced and so sued the concert organiser. The court decided that the rehearsals were not central to the contract to sing, so the concert organiser could not end his contract. His absence might have caused extra expense but rehearsals could have been arranged in another way. He therefore won his case and got an award of damages for loss of earnings.

Legal principle – a breach of warranty only allows a claim for damages. The contract continues and is not ended by the breach.

Innominate terms

The court will decide on the category of term based on all the evidence, particularly on any description of the term in a contract. Sometimes a term may not fall into the simple classification of either a condition or a warranty. The courts tend to call any term that is not clearly defined as a condition or a warranty in a contract as an **innominate term**.

The effect of an innominate term may be a condition or a warranty. It is often unclear whether a term in a contract is a condition or a warranty until the breach of that term and its consequences have been investigated by the courts. This was seen in the case of Hong Kong Fir Shipping Co Ltd v Kawasaki Kisen Kaisha Ltd (1962).

Key case

Hong Kong Fir Shipping v Kawasaki Kisen Kaisha (1962)

Facts

Kawasaki Kisen Kaisha chartered a ship for two years from Hong Kong Fir Shipping. One of the contract terms stated that the ship was 'in every way fitted for cargo service'. Within the first year, 20 weeks of the charter were lost due to problems with the ship. They could only end the charter if the term was a condition and not a warranty.

The court stated that the effect of the breach would determine whether it was a breach of condition or a breach of warranty. It decided that there was insufficient breach for the term to be treated as a condition.

Legal principle – some terms in a contract are innominate. In that case, the effect of the breach determines whether the breach is a breach of condition or a breach of warranty.

PAUSE POINT Explain how different types of term are classified.

Hint Look at the definitions and the cases related to warranties, conditions and innominate terms.

Extend Does this distinction make it easy to work out each party's rights and remedies?

Research

Research a standard form contract you would have to agree to in order to buy something direct from an online retailer of your choice. These are usually found under 'Terms & Conditions'.

Individually agreed contract terms and terms in standard form contracts

Individually agreed terms are those express terms that the parties to a contract specifically agree. We have seen the example of the cup of coffee for £1. If a business buys 100 tons of steel to make cars at an agreed price per ton on their standard terms of trading, these are the express terms. There are other implied terms such as those that we will investigate later under the Sale of Goods Act 1979.

There are more complex contracts that are made every day that have standard conditions of trading included by the seller of the goods or service. Individuals rarely have any power to negotiate changes to these. However, it is very important to understand what each of the terms means.

Scenario

Here is an example of a term in a contract:

'Confirmation of receipt of an order or other information, or any email, telephone or verbal correspondence from Hereton Ltd or from a representative of Hereton Ltd does not constitute an order confirmation or acceptance from Hereton Ltd. Acceptance of your order will take place upon despatch to you of the product or service ordered unless we have notified you that we do not accept your order or you have given Hereton Ltd adequate notice of your wish to cancel the order. 'Despatch' means making a product or service accessible to you, including but not limited to sending you a printed publication or CD-ROM, or providing you with passwords or other access codes so that you may access a product or service provided on the Internet. '

At first sight this can seem complicated. However, it can be explained easily if you understand the underlying law and break the term down:

a 'Confirmation of receipt of an order or other information, or any email, telephone or verbal correspondence from Hereton Ltd or from a representative of Hereton Ltd does not constitute an order confirmation or acceptance from Hereton Ltd.'

This makes it clear that none of the ways stated that might be viewed as an acceptance of an offer is, in fact, to be acceptance. It also stresses that the customer is making the offer.

b 'Acceptance of your order will take place upon despatch to you of the product or service ordered.'

This states that acceptance of the customer's offer takes place when Hereton Ltd sends out the goods or service.

c '... unless we have notified you that we do not accept your order'

This states that Hereton Ltd can reject the customer's offer.

d '... or you have given Hereton Ltd adequate notice of your wish to cancel the order.'

This states that the customer can revoke their offer, providing it is done with 'adequate notice'. What is considered to be adequate notice is not stated.

e 'Despatch' means making a product or service accessible to you, including but not limited to sending you a printed publication or CD-ROM, or providing you with passwords or other access codes so that you may access a product or service provided on the Internet.'

This just explains what dispatch means so that it can be differentiated from physical goods data.

1 For each of the individual points above, identify what advantages or protections the wording will give to either Hereton Ltd or the customer.

2 Now analyse the following term, dividing it into separate sentences or sections and writing the meaning below:

> 'Prices are reviewed periodically by Hereton Ltd. The price charged to you for a product or service that you have ordered will be the price that is current when the order is processed by Hereton Ltd or the price that was current when Hereton Ltd received your order, at Hereton Ltd's discretion. Products or services may be provided free of charge or at a discount at Hereton Ltd's discretion. Products or services provided in a digital format may be subject to VAT charges in addition to the quoted prices. Quoted prices will normally but not necessarily include postage and packing for UK destinations.'

Implied terms

All contracts have some express terms, but nearly all contracts have terms implied in them too. Implied terms can arise in two main ways:

- by the courts because they are obvious and needed in the contract
- by an Act of Parliament that gives rights to one party, such as the Consumer Rights Act 2015.

Terms implied by the courts

The courts imply terms where the parties to the contract would have included the term had they thought about it. It is usually very obvious. Two tests are traditionally used to decide whether a term is implied in a contract:

- The 'business **efficacy**' test – the suggested term will be implied if it is necessary to give business efficacy to the contract (or, in other words, so that the contract makes business sense).
- The 'officious bystander' test – the proposed term will be implied if it is so obvious that, if an **officious** bystander observing what was going on suggested to the parties that they include it in the contract, the response would be, 'Of course.'

An example of terms implied by the court using the 'officious bystander' test can be seen in the case of The Moorcock (1889).

Key terms

Efficacy – the ability to produce the desired or intended result.

Officious – An officious person is someone who is objectionably aggressive in offering unrequested and unwanted services, help, or advice.

Key case

The Moorcock (1889)

Facts

A ship owner agreed on paying a fee to moor his ship, *The Moorcock*, at a mooring so that it could be unloaded. Both the owner of the mooring and the owner of the ship knew the ship would rest on the seabed when the tide went out. When the tide did go out, the ship was badly damaged by a rocky shelf under the mooring. The court implied a term in the contract that the mooring would be safe to use, as that was necessary for the effectiveness of the contract and both parties would have agreed that it was obvious to have such a term in the contract.

Legal principle – a contract will include terms that would obviously have been agreed, had the parties thought about it.

Terms implied by statute or regulation, in outline only

There are many terms that are implied by statutes or regulations, rather than the courts. It would be too complex to discuss the details of how this relates to every area of law. However, there are some useful general points that can be made.

Different types of contract

The law makes a distinction between different types of contract. Contracts can be either for business-to-business, business-to-consumer or private sales, and terms can be implied in each of these types of contract by the relevant laws.

- Business-to-business – there are a number of implied terms that apply in business-to-business contracts. These terms are implied by the Sale of Goods Act 1979 and the Supply of Goods and Services Act 1982.
- Business-to-consumer – where a business makes a contract with a consumer, the Consumer Rights Act 2015 implies terms in the contract. These include terms that are similar to those implied in business-to-business contracts, but there are additional protections.
- Private – private sales of goods are transactions between individuals. The Sale of Goods Act 1979 (ss12 and 13 only) implies terms in these types of contract.

Link

See Unit 5 for more detail on business-to-consumer contacts from the point of view of a consumer.

Implied terms under the Sale of Goods Act 1979

In sale of goods contracts, there are various terms implied by the Sale of Goods Act 1979. These may apply to business-to-business contracts, business-to-consumer contracts or private sales, depending on the section(s) of the Act. Terms implied include the following:

- The person selling the goods will pass on good title to the goods to the buyer – this usually means that the buyer will become the owner of the goods. This is obviously not the case if the item you are buying is in fact stolen goods, as in the case of Rowland v Divall (1923).

Key case

Rowland v Divall (1923)

Facts

The claimant bought a car that turned out to be stolen. When the car was returned to its rightful owner, the claimant could recover the full price of the car from the seller.

Legal principle - under the Sale of Goods Act 1979, s12, in sale of goods contracts, a term is implied that the person selling the goods will pass on good title to the goods to the buyer.

- The goods must correspond to any description applied to them - this might be something stated, written down or a sticker or badge. This is applied quite strictly, as can be seen in Beale v Taylor (1967).

Key case

Beale v Taylor (1967)

Facts

A buyer of a car was influenced by the description of it as a '1961 Triumph Herald'. It turned out to be a mix of two cars badly welded together, one of which was an earlier model. The buyer successfully argued breach of the Sale of Goods Act 1893, s13 (now restated in the Sale of Goods Act 1979, s13).

Legal principle - the Sale of Goods Act 1979, s13 implies a term that the goods must correspond to any description applied to them.

- The goods are of satisfactory quality - this is an objective test. Quality of the goods refers to their state and condition on being supplied. The Act states that the term 'satisfactory quality' should take into account factors such as:
  - fitness for all purposes for which goods of the kind in question are commonly supplied
  - appearance and finish
  - freedom from minor defects
  - safety and durability.

However, this does not apply if defects were brought to the buyer's attention or if the goods were examined by the buyer and the defect should have been noticed.

The goods are fit for their purpose providing that the buyer 'either expressly or by implication makes known to the seller ... any particular purpose for which goods are being bought ... whether or not that is a purpose for which goods of that kind are commonly supplied'.

In other words, the term is implied if the buyer either directly or by implication lets the seller know why they are buying the item, even if that reason is not the most obvious or frequent reason for buying the goods. An example of this implied term can be seen in the case of Grant v Australian Knitting Mills Ltd (1936).

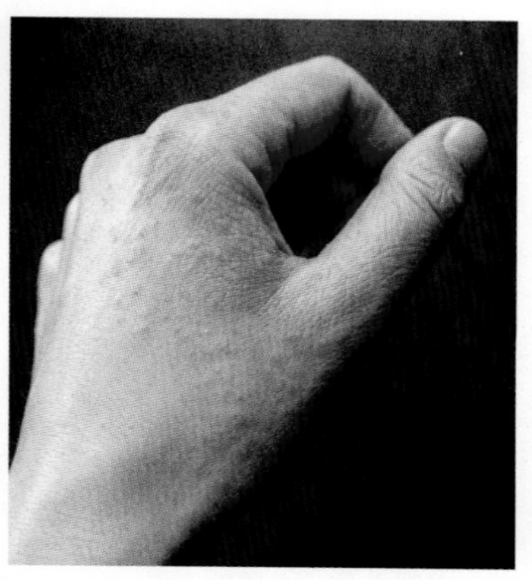
Dermatitis is a skin condition caused by an external agent or allergic reaction

Key case

Grant v Australian Knitting Mills Ltd (1936)

Facts

Dr Grant contracted dermatitis from chemicals in underpants that he had bought. The court accepted that the buyer would have impliedly made known the purpose for which he was buying the underpants even if he had not actually stated it to the seller.

Legal principle - Section 14(3) implies a condition that the goods are fit for their purpose providing the buyer makes known the purpose for which the goods are being bought and the buyer relies on the seller's skill and judgment about that.

PAUSE POINT In pairs, list some of the main terms implied by the Sale of Goods Act 1979.

Hint Add any detail you can to each one, including factors to be taken into consideration or conditions.

Extend Discuss whether these are of equal importance or not to the buyer.

Exclusion clauses

Exclusion clauses are sometimes called exemption clauses. The purpose of these terms in a contract is to protect the person selling the goods or providing the service by avoiding liability in the event of breach of contract. This can be done in many ways, but however they are set out, the idea is to limit or totally exclude liability.

Discussion

In a small group, choose two or three contracts that you have made recently and list the terms of the contract as you think they might be. Did you notice any exclusion clauses? Do you read notices on signs and tickets? Do you read the terms, for example, on iTunes?

A sign attempting to exclude liability

The effectiveness of exclusion clauses in different situations

The law has struggled with exclusion clauses as they are nearly always put in a contract by the party with the stronger bargaining position. They are usually not negotiable, particularly in consumer contracts and those made by businesses with limited bargaining power. This can be seen in the famous case of L'Estrange v Graucob (1934). Nowadays, protection is given by various **statutory provisions**. The protection means that exclusion clauses imposed on consumers and some businesses may have no legal effect so the business imposing the exclusion clause is still liable for their breach of contract.

Key term

Statutory provisions – sections of an Act of Parliament that cover the area of law in question.

Key case

L'Estrange v Graucob (1934)

Facts

The company's order form contained a clause providing them with complete exemption from liability. The cigarette vending machine Mrs L'Estrange bought never worked properly, but the exclusion clause meant she could not claim against the supplier of the machine.

Legal principle - if the exclusion clause is part of the contract then it will be effective if there is no statutory protection given to the party suffering the term.

When an exclusion clause is not part of a contract

The first way an exclusion clause can be found not to be effective is if it can be shown that it is not incorporated in the contract. This goes back to the idea of offer and acceptance. The exclusion clause must be part of the offer made and not introduced after the contract has been formed. Mrs L'Estrange's problem was that she had signed the contract with the term in it. It was irrelevant that she had not read the contract first.

When no document has been signed

However, when the term is in an unsigned document, then the party seeking to rely on it must show that the other party knew or should have known of the term's existence. This can be either by having reference to it in a contractual document or by a prominent notice that is seen or indicated before acceptance of the offer. You have already seen that in the case of Thornton v Shoe Lane Parking (1971). In that case, the terms were those displayed before Mr Thornton got his ticket and not those he saw later. The terms inside the car park had not been referred to on the ones outside the car park. The term outside the car park stated 'Cars parked at owner's risk' and other terms about payment - nothing was mentioned about personal injuries. Inside the car park, a notice excluded liability for personal injury to car park users. Mr Thornton's car was not damaged but he was injured in the car park. There is also a distinction between a ticket that can be considered to be merely a receipt, such as a cloakroom ticket, and one that everyone knows is likely to contain terms such as a rail ticket or a plane ticket.

Regular dealing

A term can also be implied by a course of regular dealing between the parties to a contract. If you take clothes to the cleaners on a regular basis, then the occasion when you do not pick up a ticket is governed by the terms on the ticket you normally collect. This can be seen in the case of Hollier v Rambler Motors (1972).

Research

Look up cases concerning tickets and see whether you can distinguish the different cases and legal principals involved. Examples include Chapelton v Barry UDC (1940), Olley v Marlborough Court Hotel (1949) and Thompson v London, Midland and Scotland Railway Co. (1930).

Key case

Hollier v Rambler Motors (1972)

Mr Hollier left his car with the garage for repair. He had brought his car to this garage several times before and had always been asked to sign a document excluding liability for any damage. However, this time he made the arrangement over the phone. While the car was at the garage it was damaged by fire. The garage was able to rely upon their terms excluding liability, as the terms had been incorporated by implication through the course of dealings between the parties over a number of occasions.

Legal principle - a term can be part of a contract through its regular use.

Exclusion clauses in standard form contracts

Terms in a standard form contract have to be standardised, in that they are terms which the company in question uses for all, or nearly all, of its contracts of a particular type without alteration (apart from blanks which have to be completed showing the price, name of the other contracting party and so on). You can see similar terms on a regular basis – when buying goods over the Internet, by mail order or when buying a ticket for travel. These terms are not varied from transaction to transaction.

Apart from the specific statutes and regulations that prohibit or limit exclusion clauses in consumer contracts, the main protection is found in the Unfair Contract Terms Act 1977.

Link

See Unit 5 for more detail on exclusion clauses in consumer contracts.

A clause excluding or limiting liability for breach of contract must pass a 'reasonableness' test set out in the Unfair Contract Terms Act 1977, s11. The assumption is that a standard form exclusion clause will not be enforced unless the term is a fair and reasonable one to include in the contract. This is judged by all the circumstances of the case that were known, or ought to have been known, by the parties at the time the contract was entered. It is up to the party seeking to enforce the term to show that it was fair and reasonable.

There are a number of factors that must be taken into account by the court in applying the reasonableness test. The five considerations in the guidelines to interpreting 'reasonableness' laid down in the Act are:

- the relative strengths of the parties' bargaining positions – the bigger the difference, the more likely the term is to be unfair
- whether the customer received any incentive to accept the term – if it was cheaper for the buyer to take the risk of the item not working
- whether the customer knew or should have known that the term was included – this can be linked to regular dealings as in Hollier v Rambler Motors (1972)
- in the case of a term excluding liability if a condition is not complied with, the likelihood of compliance with that condition at the time the contract was made – did it seem likely or unlikely that specific terms would be complied with such as one relating to time for delivery of goods?
- whether the goods were a special order rather than normal stock items – for example, a non-standard finish on a domestic appliance.

An exclusion clause may be invalid either as a result of case law and it therefore not being incorporated in the contract or, failing that, under the Unfair Contract Terms Act 1977. Prepare a flow chart showing how you would assess the validity of an exclusion clause.

Hint List the points to be made in order.

Extend Give examples of the factors that might make a term unreasonable.

Assessment practice 6.2

B.P3 B.P4 B.M2 B.D2

Geeta is thinking of buying a new mobile phone and getting a SIM-only contract from a mobile phone company. She has found a phone she likes but is unsure what some of the terms mean in the mobile company's terms and conditions. The terms are as follows:

'16. Liability on pay monthly and SIM-only contracts

Limits on our liability

16.1 All of our obligations to you relating to our service are set out in this agreement. If you wish to make any change to this agreement or rely on any other term, you must obtain our agreement to the change of term in writing.

16.2 Except as set out in 16.3:

1 All other terms, conditions and warranties relating to our service or products are hereby excluded;

2 Our liability to you is limited to £3,000 for all claims;

3 We do not accept liability for any loss of income, business or profits, or for any loss or corruption of data in connection with the use of our service. We do not accept liability for any loss or damage that was not reasonably foreseeable when you entered into the agreement; and

4 We do not accept liability for any service, goods and content you may take from third parties, including if they are defective or deficient, and any dispute with a third party will not affect your obligations to us.

16.3 Nothing in this agreement removes or limits our liability for fraud, death or personal injury caused by our negligence or for any liability which cannot be limited or excluded by law. If you are a consumer, the terms of this agreement does not affect any of your statutory rights which you have, which cannot be excluded by this agreement.'

Geeta would like you to advise her on what these terms mean and any implication on her as a consumer buying a SIM-only contract. You need to identify and explain the express terms and exclusion clauses that would apply to Geeta. You must also list and describe some of the implied terms of a SIM-only contract. Where appropriate, evaluate the meaning and legality of these terms and how difficult they might be to enforce. In order to complete this task, you need to show that you understand the types of terms found in a contract and how they impact on parties to that contract.

Plan

- What is the task? What should my advice contain?
- Do I need to research any information before I begin?
- How am I going to present my advice to Geeta?

Do

- I need to identify and explain the express terms used, and list the terms that could be implied in this contract.
- I need to analyse the impact of express and implied terms on a party to a contract.
- I need to give clear and accurate advice.

Review

- I can explain how I structured my advice.
- I can explain what I have learned.

Investigate the validity of a contract to determine contractual rights

Validity of a contract

An agreement may have been reached and all the requirements for a valid contract may have been fulfilled, yet the contract may still be void or voidable.

- A **void contract** is not a valid contract; it has never been valid and it is as though the agreement had never been made so it is unenforceable in a court of law. This is sometimes called 'void *ab initio*', a Latin expression meaning 'from the start'.
- A **voidable contract** is a valid contract until one party exercises their right to make the contract void.

Key terms

Void contract – a contract that does not exist.

Voidable contract – a contract that is valid, but may be made void at a later date.

> **Key term**
>
> **Misrepresentation** – a false statement of material fact made by a party to the contract that induces the other party to enter into the contract.

Misrepresentation and remedies for different types of misrepresentation

A **misrepresentation** may only occur during the formation of a contract. Misrepresentation can be defined as a false statement of material fact made by a party to the contract that induces the other party to enter the contract. This concept is broken down as follows:

- False statement – the statement made must be untrue. As there must be a statement to be a misrepresentation, silence cannot be a misrepresentation. However, silence in not correcting a statement that was true when made but later becomes false can be a misrepresentation as seen in the case of With v O'Flanagan (1936).

> **Key case**
>
> ### With v O'Flanagan (1936)
>
> **Facts**
>
> Mr With purchased a medical practice from Dr O'Flanagan. Mr With was induced to buy the practice by Dr O'Flanagan's statement that the practice took £2,000 per annum. This statement was true at the time it was made. However, Dr O'Flanagan became ill and many patients went elsewhere. He did not tell the prospective purchaser of changes to the situation. By the time the sale was completed, the practice was virtually worthless.
>
> **Legal principle – silence is not a misrepresentation except where a seller does not correct information that has changed between statement and contract.**

The statement does not have to be written or verbal; it can be anything that would influence the other's decision. This can be seen in the case of Spice Girls Ltd v Aprilia World Service BV (2000).

> **Key case**
>
> ### Spice Girls Ltd v Aprilia World Service BV (2000)
>
> **Facts**
>
> The Spice Girls had signed a sponsorship agreement with Aprilia, but while the agreement was being negotiated, unknown to Aprilia, Geri had given notice to leave the group. Filming of promotional material took place with all the girls together. As one member of the group was going to leave, these were now worthless for promotional purposes. The Court of Appeal ruled that misrepresentation had led to Aprilia signing the contract, as they had believed that all five girls would remain in the group.
>
> **Legal principle – generally, a person who is about to enter into an agreement is under no duty to disclose material facts that they know but which the other party does not know; the exception to this is when key information has been withheld which affects the terms of the contract.**

- Material fact – the misrepresentation must be material, in the sense that it would have led a reasonable person to make the contract. Most importantly, it must be a statement of fact rather than opinion; future intention is not a fact.

- Made by a party to the contract – a person is not liable for statements made by others unless they are an agent or other paid representative.
- Induces the other party to enter the contract – the false statement of material fact must lead the other into making the contract. In other words, the misrepresentation was a critical part of making the decision. For example, if you were going to a club that advertised that a particular DJ was playing and he was not appearing there, the question would be whether his proposed appearance affected your decision to go or not. If you were going largely because of the DJ, then it could be a misrepresentation. If you would have gone anyway – perhaps you had never heard of the DJ or you just wanted a night out with friends – then his name had no bearing on your decision and so could not be a misrepresentation.

Different types of misrepresentation

Misrepresentations are of three possible types – innocent, negligent and fraudulent:

- Innocent misrepresentation – a false statement made by a party who honestly believed it to be true. If a person can be shown to have genuinely held an opinion and did not intend to mislead the other party, there can be no misrepresentation.
- Negligent misrepresentation – a false statement made by a person who had no reasonable grounds for believing it to be true. If it can be shown that the person making the statement could not have held such an opinion or had no such future intention then there will be a misrepresentation. This can be seen in the cases of Bisset v Wilkinson (1927) and Edgington v Fitzmaurice (1885).

Key case

Bisset v Wilkinson (1927)

Facts

Mr Wilkinson, the seller of a farm that had never had sheep on it, gave his opinion that it would support about 2,000 of them. This turned out to be false. However, the statement had not been a representation of fact but merely an expression of the seller's honestly held opinion.

Legal principle – if the person expressing an opinion genuinely believes it, it is not a misrepresentation.

Key case

Edgington v Fitzmaurice (1885)

Facts

The claimant invested in a company that stated that the money raised would be used to buy new equipment and upgrade buildings. In fact, the money was used to clear existing debts. The statement was a statement of fact as they were proved not to have the intention of buying new equipment and doing the upgrades. It was therefore a misrepresentation.

Legal principle – if a person making the statement can be shown not to have the stated intention, their statement can be treated as a statement of fact and is therefore a misrepresentation.

- Fraudulent misrepresentation – defined in Derry v Peek (1889) as a false statement that is made:
  - knowingly
  - without belief in its truth
  - recklessly as to whether it be true or false.

  In other words, it involves telling a deliberate lie.

Different types of remedy

Each misrepresentation has different possible remedies, summarised in Table 6.1.

- The remedy of **rescission** – the ending of a contract. The aim of rescission is to put the parties back in their original position, as though the contract had not been made. In other words, it is making the contract void. However, rescission is an equitable remedy and is awarded at the discretion of the court. The right may be lost under the following circumstances:
  - if the injured party does not act quickly
  - if the injured party, knowing of the misrepresentation, carries on with the contract
  - if rescission is impossible (for example, the goods have been used to make something else)
  - if others have rights under the contract.

In all these cases, it would not be fair to rescind (end) the contract so the court would not allow the remedy.

- The remedy of damages – the financial compensation awarded by a court when a contract has been breached.

Key term

Rescission – the cancellation or repeal of an agreement, order or law.

Link

Damages in negligence have been dealt with in Unit 1. Damages in contract are dealt with later in this unit (see learning aim D).

Table 6.1: A summary of the types of misrepresentation, their remedies and the key cases

Type of misrepresentation	Requirement on maker of the statement	Remedy	Key case
Innocent	Honestly believed it to be true	Rescission or damages under Misrepresentation Act 1967	Leaf v International Galleries (1950)
Negligent	Has no reasonable grounds for believing it to be true	Rescission and damages in the tort of negligence	Esso Petroleum v Mardon (1976)
Fraudulent	Knew the statement to be false	Rescission and damages in the tort of deceit	Cherrilow Ltd v Butler-Creagh (2011)

PAUSE POINT Explain with examples different types of misrepresentation and the remedies available.

Hint Research decided cases of misrepresentation and identify the remedy in each case.

Extend Make up your own scenarios. In groups, discuss whether there is a misrepresentation and, if so, what type of remedy would be appropriate.

Illegal contracts and their enforceability

A contract that exists for an illegal purpose is void; it cannot and will not be enforced by a court. For example, a contract to supply illegal drugs or kill someone is void. Therefore, the money paid and the goods are not recoverable.

There are a number of categories of illegal contract, but the most common is a contract of employment that is designed, for example, to evade immigration rules. There are a number of complex issues with respect to these types of contract and it may be that some aspects of the 'illegal' contract will be enforced.

Frustration of contract and the remedies available when that occurs

Frustration of contract is one way in which a contract can end – other methods of discharge of contract are dealt with later in this unit.

What amounts to frustration of contract?

Frustration occurs where a contract that was capable of being performed when made becomes impossible to perform, through no fault of either of the parties to the contract. There are two key points here:

- It becomes impossible to perform – this does not just mean more expensive to perform, as in the case of Davis Contractors v Fareham (1956).

Key case

Davis Contractors v Fareham (1956)

Facts

Davis Contractors agreed to build houses for the council within eight months for an agreed price. However, there was a shortage of skilled labour and materials so the contract took longer and was much more expensive to complete. This was not frustration of contract.

Legal principle – frustration occurs where performance of a contract is prevented by outside events beyond the control of the parties.

- It occurs through no fault of either party – this means that there was no breach of contract, merely that circumstances prevented performance of the main purpose of the contract. This can be seen in the case of Fibrosa Spolka Akcyjna v Fairbairn Lawson Combe Barbour Ltd (1943), usually known as the Fibrosa case.

Key case

Fibrosa Spolka Akcyjna v Fairbairn Lawson Combe Barbour Ltd (1943)

Facts

A contract made in July 1939 for the supply of textile machinery by English company Fairbairn Lawson Combe Barbour Ltd to Polish company Fibrosa Spolka Akcyjna was valid at the start. However, the proposed delivery by November 1939 to Poland was frustrated by the invasion of Poland and the outbreak of war. All contracts to enemy or enemy-occupied countries were made illegal and therefore frustrated.

Legal principle – subsequent illegality of a contract frustrates the contract.

Research

Look at cases involving illness in the performance of a contract by a party to that contract. Examples include Condor v Barron Knights (1966) and Atwal v Rochester (2010). Discuss the judgments in these cases and whether you think these were fair.

What happens when a contract is frustrated?

The Fibrosa case happened just as the Second World War was starting. It was recognised that there would be many other similar disputes and the law, as it stood then, did not provide a just remedy. The result was the Law Reform (Frustrated Contracts) Act 1943, which sets out a very straightforward resolution to the problem:

- Money paid before the frustrating event is recoverable.
- Money payable before the frustrating event ceases to be payable.
- If, however, the party to whom such sums are paid/payable incurred expenses before frustration, the court may award them expenses up to the limit of the money paid or payable before the frustrating event.

Who has rights under a contract

The rules on privity of contract

As referenced earlier in the unit, the rule of privity is that only those who are parties to a contract are bound by the contract. Only they can enforce the contract and get a court order to enforce their rights.

The justification for this rule is that it would be unfair for two parties to make a contract that would make a third person do something. Similarly, it would be unfair for a third person to sue either or both of those making the contract if the third person was not a party to the contract. This can be seen in the case of Dunlop Pneumatic Tyre Company Ltd v Selfridge (1915).

Key case

Dunlop Pneumatic Tyre Company Ltd v Selfridge (1915)

Facts

Dunlop did not want their tyres sold cheaply, but wanted to maintain a standard resale price. It agreed that its dealers (in this case, Dew and Company) would not sell them below a certain price. It required its dealers to get the same undertaking from their retailers (in this case, Selfridge). Dunlop was thereby a third party to a contract between Selfridge and Dew. When Selfridge sold the tyres at below the agreed price, Dunlop sued to enforce their contract with Dew against Selfridge. They could not do so as there was no privity of contract.

Legal principle - only a party to a contract can sue on it.

The exceptions to the rules on privity of contract

There are some exceptions when the rule of privity does not apply. These include:

Agency

An agency arises when one person, the agent, is authorised to make a contract on behalf of another person, the principal. In a valid agency situation, the principal will be bound by the terms of the contract even though they did not make the contract themselves. Typically, this will be the situation when an employee makes a contract on behalf of a business.

Collateral contracts

The courts occasionally avoid the privity rule by finding a second contract alongside the main agreement, called a collateral contract. This can be seen in Shanklin Pier Ltd v Detel Products Ltd (1951).

Key case

Shanklin Pier Ltd v Detel Products Ltd (1951)

Facts

A contract was made for a pier to be painted. The contract required a particular type of paint that would last for seven to ten years. The manufacturer of the paint gave that assurance to the painter. However, the paint lasted only three months. There was no direct contract between the pier company and the manufacturer of the paint. However, the court decided that a second (collateral) contract between the pier and the paint manufacturer existed alongside the original contract between the pier and the painter.

Legal principle – the privity rule can be avoided by finding a collateral contract.

Restrictive covenants

Under land law, if a purchaser of land promises the seller in the purchase contract that they will not do something on the land (a restrictive covenant), that promise will 'run with the land'. This means that all subsequent purchasers of that land are legally bound by that promise even though they are not parties to that initial contract. Most houses have restrictive covenants on them that can be enforced against any owner of the house (land), often preventing a business being carried on from the house.

The rights of third parties to a contract

As you have seen, third parties do not usually have rights under someone else's contract. This is despite the best efforts of the courts in cases such as Jackson v Horizon Holidays (1975) that you explored earlier. The strict rule has been modified by the Contracts (Rights of Third Parties) Act 1999. Under the Act, someone who is not a party to a contract (a 'third party') may enforce the contract against either or both of the actual parties to the contract.

This Act now allows a third party to sue under a contract if:

- the third party is expressly identified by name, or as a member of a class of people, or as answering a particular description AND
- the contract expressly states that the third party may enforce the contract OR
- the contract term is an attempt to give the benefit of the term to the third party.

However, if it appears the parties did not intend the term to benefit a third party then the Act will not apply. Therefore, the parties to the contract have the right to exclude it from benefiting a third party. Most commercial contracts now include such a term.

Make a list of the cases you have studied regarding frustration of contract and contract rights, together with the relevant legal principles.

Hint: Make sure that the list concentrates on the law and not just the facts.

Extend: Explain how the facts of each case illustrate the legal principle so that you can apply the law to given situations.

D Review the ways in which a contract may end and the remedies available

Discharging a contract based on performance or breach

Reflect

Reflect on how fair you think the law is, and whether it is always clear whether performance is complete. For example, if a taxi driver dropped you 5 metres from your door, rather than directly outside, would that constitute complete performance? Now research the case of Cutter v Powell (1795) – was that decision harsh or fair?

You have already seen how a contract can be discharged through frustration and the special rules that apply in that situation. You will now consider what amounts to performance of a contract and, where there has not been performance, what amounts to breach and whether the breach is so serious that one party can treat the contract as ended.

Performance of contract

The general rule is that performance of the terms of a contract must be complete and exact. This can appear to be very harsh. This is seen in Re Moore and Landauer (1921).

Key case

Re Moore and Landauer (1921)

Facts

The contract provided for the sale of 3000 tins of peaches. The tins were to be packed in cases of 30 tins. It was discovered on delivery that half the cases contained only 24 tins although the total number of tins was still 3000. The court decided that the buyer was entitled to reject all the goods as they should have been delivered as specified, namely with 30 tins to a case.

Legal principle – performance must be complete and exact.

Discussion

Divisible contracts

Where a contract can be seen as being made up of separate parts, it can be seen as a number of separate contracts. This is typically the case in employment contracts where an annual salary is divisible into monthly payments; so an employee leaving after three months is entitled to three months' salary. Can you think of any other situations where this type of contract is applicable? What are the benefits of this type of contract to the person or organisation issuing one?

There are three ways this rule can be modified by the courts:

- where the contract is divisible
- where there is substantial performance
- where part performance is accepted by the other party.

Substantial performance

When a person fully performs the contract, they should get paid in full. Substantial performance occurs where there is almost full performance, but there are minor defects. The court can decide whether there has been substantial performance of the contract. Where substantial performance is allowed, the court may then require payment of the contractually agreed price and deduct sums to reflect the amount not performed. This is done on a ***quantum meruit*** basis.

Key term

Quantum meruit – a Latin term meaning 'as much as it is worth'.

The two contrasting cases of Hoenig v Isaacs (1952) and Bolton v Mahadeva (1972) illustrate when substantial performance is deemed to have occurred or not.

Key case

Hoenig v Isaacs (1952)

Facts

Mr Hoenig was contracted to decorate and furnish a room for Mr Isaacs for £750. Some of the furniture was defective but could be repaired for £55. The court decided that the contract was substantially completed on a financial basis. Mr Hoenig was entitled to be paid for what he had done on a *quantum meruit* basis minus the cost of repairing the defective furniture.

Legal principle - minor defects amount to substantial performance of a contract.

Key case

Bolton v Mahadeva (1972)

Facts

Mr Bolton agreed to install a central heating system in Mr Mahadeva's house for £560. However, the installation was defective and repairs cost £170. The court decided that Mr Bolton was not entitled to any payment as there had not been substantial performance of the contract.

Legal principle - significant defects prevent substantial performance of a contract.

Part performance

Where one party freely agrees to accept part performance of a contract, then a sum is payable for the work completed on a *quantum meruit* basis.

 **PAUSE POINT** Write down the difference between substantial and part performance.

 Hint: Give a definition for each.

Extend: Consider arguments for and against the use of substantial performance as opposed to the strict rule of performance. Are there any negative aspects to the rule on part performance that you can think of?

Breach of contract

Contracts can be broken either by a breach of conditions or by a breach of warranties. You have already looked at the distinction between a condition and a warranty (see learning aim B). This is particularly important with respect to time for performance of the contract.

Breach of warranty

Failure to complete a contract on time is usually seen as a breach of warranty. This means that the contract continues but damages can be awarded.

Research

Breach can be actual breach or anticipatory breach. Actual breach can be either a failure to perform at all or poor performance. Anticipatory breach is where one party makes it known that they will not perform their part of the contract. This can be seen in the case of Hochster v De la Tour (1853). Research online to look for a case that covers actual breach.

Mr Hochster agreed to be a courier for Mr De la Tour. Before the contract was due to start, Mr De la Tour informed Mr Hochster that he would not be employing him after all, but refused to pay any compensation. Where a party makes it clear that they will not perform their part of the contract, the other party may either sue immediately or wait until the breach occurs.

Breach of conditions

If a condition is broken, the injured party can rescind (end) the contract and is not bound to accept any goods that were part of the contract.

Sometimes a term regarding the time for performance can be a condition. This is often used in building contracts, for example, in completing renovations or even for buying a flat 'off-plan' (before it has been built). This can occur where the parties have expressly stated in the contract that time is 'of the essence', or if the circumstances show that time for completion is critical. This can be seen in the case of Charles Rickards Ltd v Oppenheim (1950).

Key case

Charles Rickards Ltd v Oppenheim (1950)

Facts

A buyer of a Rolls-Royce car chassis agreed for a body to be built on it by a fixed date. The body was not completed by the agreed date. Mr Oppenheim accepted the lateness, but as delays continued, he gave notice that unless delivery of the car with the completed body was delivered within four weeks he would cancel the contract. More than four weeks later, the car was delivered and the buyer rejected it.

The court ruled that, as time was of the essence in the initial contract, the right to reject the car had been waived. However, the buyer exercised his right to make time of the essence again with the final four-week deadline which, when not met, allowed him to reject the goods.

Legal principle – where the contract states expressly that time is of the essence, any delay in completion constitutes a breach of conditions.

Rejection of goods or damages

When someone has a choice as to rejecting the goods or claiming damages and continuing with the contract, there is a simple decision to be made. Do they want the item, possibly at a later date than agreed or at a reduced price (the effect of damages) or do they wish to start again? The conclusion that is reached will depend on the situation. The rejection of the goods is available as of right for breach of condition.

Discussion

In a small group, discuss the merits of either getting a price reduction or rejecting the following goods:

- a second-hand car that has done 120,000 miles rather than the stated mileage of 60,000 miles (consider at what mileage difference you would accept the car)
- a new £600 computer that failed after two days, which the supplier has offered to fix by installing a new hard drive
- a horse that when collected has become lame
- a pair of shoes described as red but, when the sealed box is opened, are blue.

Compare your answers with other groups.

Damages and injunctions as remedies for breach

A breach of contract may be remedied either by damages or by an injunction.

General and special damages

Damages are the financial compensation awarded by a court for the breach of contract that has occurred. In contract law, the purpose of an award of damages for breach is to compensate the injured party. Damages are meant to place the claimant in the same position as if the contract had been performed.

Where damages include a sum to cover future losses, they are called general damages, whereas those that are quantifiable before trial are sometimes called special damages. These terms are more commonly used in claims for negligence.

The first matter to be dealt with is the extent of the loss, namely, which losses follow from the breach of contract. This is a question of **remoteness of damage**. The second matter is the actual amount of money to be paid as compensation for the losses. Damages are awarded for **loss of bargain** and wasted expenditure.

Key terms

Remoteness of damage – the extent of the consequences of a breach of contract that can be claimed as damages.

Loss of bargain – what you have lost out on as a result of the breach.

Legal principles with respect to remoteness of damage

A breach of contract may have many consequences. The court has developed tests to set out the extent of the losses for which the party in breach is responsible. The court set out two tests in the case of Hadley v Baxendale (1854).

Key case

Hadley v Baxendale (1854)

Facts

A crankshaft in the claimant's mill broke. He agreed with the defendant carrier to take the shaft to someone who would use it as a model for the new shaft. The carrier took longer than agreed to deliver the shaft. The mill was out of action for longer than anticipated and so lost profit. The carrier had not been told the mill would be out of action until the new shaft arrived.

The court decided that the carrier was not liable for the loss of profit as he was entitled to assume the mill owner had a spare shaft or could borrow one.

Legal principle – damages for breach of contract may be awarded when: a) it is reasonable to argue that the loss was a foreseeable result of the breach, and b) it can be reasonably supposed that such damages were considered by the parties at the time of making the contract.

These two tests are objective and subjective:

- Objective test – would a reasonable person foresee the loss as a consequence of the breach of contract? If so, then the defendant is liable.
- Subjective test – were any potential losses in the minds of the parties when the contract was made? If so, then the defendant is liable.

The use of the tests can be seen in the case of Victoria Laundry (Windsor) Ltd v Newman Industries Ltd (1949).

Key case

Victoria Laundry (Windsor) Ltd v Newman Industries Ltd (1949)

Facts

Newman Industries Ltd was five months late in delivering a boiler to the laundry. The company knew it was needed by the claimant to run its business. The laundry sued for normal business loss of profits for this period (Claim 1). It also sued for the loss of profit on a special government contract it had just obtained, which gave greater profits (Claim 2).

The court decided that the defendant was liable for Claim 1 under the objective test. However, Claim 2 failed under both tests.

Legal principle – as for the case of Hadley v Baxendale.

Key terms

Reliance loss – this is otherwise called wasted expenditure. This refers to the expenses incurred by a claimant who relied on a contract being performed.

Loss of a chance – this is for a lost opportunity. In rare circumstances, the courts have allowed claimants to recover a loss that is entirely speculative, although generally in contract law a speculative loss is not recoverable.

Legal principles with respect to loss of bargain

The second matter to be considered is the basis for assessing how much a successful claim is worth. This is easily seen as the loss of bargain, although occasionally other matters are considered such as **reliance loss** or **loss of a chance**.

This places the claimant in the same financial position as if the contract had been properly performed. At its simplest, it is the difference in value between the goods or services stated in the contract and those actually occurring when the contract is performed. This sum can be assessed according to the decrease in value or the cost of bringing them up to the contract quality. This can be seen in the case of Bence Graphics International Ltd v Fasson UK Ltd (1996).

Key case

Bence Graphics International Ltd v Fasson UK Ltd (1996)

Facts

The defendant supplied vinyl film on which the claimant printed decals to put on bulk containers. There was a term that the decals would survive in a readable form for five years. In fact, they lasted only two. The claimant sued for damages to cover the losses resulting from the failure of the product to be as durable as agreed.

The court decided that the claimant was entitled to recover the actual loss resulting from the failure in durability of the product.

Legal principle – loss of bargain can be claimed when a product fails to meet the agreed specification.

Key term

Mitigation of loss – a party who has suffered loss has to take reasonable action to minimise the amount of the loss suffered.

Where there is a market for goods and there has been non-delivery, the buyer must go into the market and get the goods elsewhere, subject to the idea of **mitigating their loss**. Mitigation of loss is the duty to ensure that a claimant minimises the loss suffered by taking reasonable steps to ensure that, where possible, the loss does not increase, and to not take unreasonable steps that may increase the loss.

Damages will be the difference between the contract price and the price obtained or required to be paid in the market. If the claimant can still make their profit, there is no loss to be compensated. This can be seen in the case of Charter v Sullivan (1957).

Key case

Charter v Sullivan (1957)

Facts

The defendant agreed to buy a car, then refused to take delivery. At that time, demand for the particular model easily outstripped supply, so the dealer could easily sell the car to someone else. As a result, he recovered only nominal damages.

Legal principle – if the claimant can still make their profit, there is no loss.

The claimant can be awarded damages for the profit that they would have been able to make except in the case of a breach of contract.

Prohibitory and mandatory injunctions

An injunction is a court order instructing a party against performing an action. This is known as a **prohibitory injunction**. This is the most common form of injunction and is used to prevent someone from breaking their contract. This might be used to stop someone disclosing information under a confidentiality agreement.

Occasionally, an injunction will order a party to complete an action. This is known as a **mandatory injunction**. This might be used to order someone to hand over goods. However, the goods in question must be unique, such as a painting, rather than an item where many others are available, such as a Ford Focus car.

An injunction is an equitable remedy rather than a legal remedy such as damages. Legal remedies are available as of right to the injured party, whereas equitable remedies are only made at the discretion of the court where a legal remedy does not seem satisfactory. For example, an injunction will not be awarded for a party to complete a personal service as the court is unable to supervise such an order. An example of a court refusing to make an injunction can be seen in the case of Page One Records Ltd v Britton (1967).

Key terms

Prohibitory injunction – a court order instructing a party to a contract against performing an action.

Mandatory injunction – a court order instructing a party to a contract to complete an action.

Key case

Page One Records Ltd v Britton (1967)

Facts

A band had a five-year contract with their manager. They sacked their manager, therefore breaking the contract. The manager wanted an injunction to stop the band employing any other manager.

The court decided that an injunction would not be granted as this would mean that the band could only employ the manager they had lost confidence in and sacked. The court awarded the manager damages instead.

Legal principle – a court will not create an injunction if it forces a contract of personal service to be continued and damages are an adequate remedy.

PAUSE POINT Make a list of remedies available for breach of contract. Define each and give examples of when each might be used.

Hint Make sure that you know the difference between remedies that are available as of right and those that are only awarded at the discretion of the court.

Extend Add to your list the advantages and disadvantages of each remedy.

Assessment practice 6.3

C.P5 C.M3 D.P6 D.M4 CD.D3

Anji owns a courier business, which uses small vans. She won a contract with Beechers to carry out home deliveries for their products. The contract required three vans, in Beechers colours and logo to be ready for deliveries from 1 October. Anji agreed with Chris, a signwriter, to pay £1,000 per van for this work. Chris agreed to complete the work by 27 September in readiness for deliveries.

On 25 September, Chris had finished work on two vans, but had not started the third. He told Anji that he could not finish the work on time. Anji immediately cancelled the contract and took the remaining van to Desi who did the work in time, but at a cost of £2,500.

1 In file notes to Anji's solicitors, discuss the issues involved in the contracts between the different parties and their respective rights and remedies. Evaluate how effective you think the law is in a situation such as this.

Anji decided to supply shirts with the company logo on for her drivers. She contacted UNICO who told her that all their shirts were made from fair trade cotton in the UK. She thought that fitted her company image so she ordered shirts from them. She took delivery of the shirts and gave them to her drivers. A week later, one driver complained that his did not appear to be made of fair trade materials.

2 Explain how the law and remedies of misrepresentation might apply to this contract.

Anji also bought ten baseball caps to give away in a promotion. One cap was given to Lance who wore the cap once, but the strap broke as it had not been properly secured.

3 Has Lance any rights against the supplier of the cap?

Plan

- What is the task? What should my report contain?
- Do I need to research any information before I begin?
- How am I going to present the information to Anji's solicitors?

Do

- I need to apply my knowledge of contract law to this case study.
- I need to explain where breach of contract has occurred and what remedies are appropriate.

Review

- I can explain how I structured my file notes.
- I can explain what I have learned.
- I can identify any aspects of the task that I found difficult.

Further reading and resources

Government advice, such as: **https://www.gov.uk/unfair-terms-in-sales-contracts/overview**

Newspaper articles, such as: **https://www.theguardian.com/small-business-network/2016/aug/25/consumer-rights-small-firms-unfair-contract-petition**

Commercial solicitors' websites.

Most textbooks are very detailed, but revision guides may give good pointers, for example:

Duxbury, R. – *Nutshells Contract Law*, 10th Edition (Sweet & Maxwell, 2015)

Finch, E. and Fafinski, S. – *Law Express: Contract Law*, 5th Edition (Pearson, 2016)

Aspects of Tort 7

Getting to know your unit

Assessment
This unit is internally assessed using a series of assignments set by your tutor.

A tort is a civil wrong which causes personal injury or loss, such as loss of earnings or damage to property. The injured claimant usually claims damages for their loss. Many of the rules setting out what needs to be proved are based on judicial precedent. The court will ultimately decide on civil cases but settlements made between the parties are encouraged.

How you will be assessed

This unit will be assessed by assignments set and marked by your tutor. You will need to work independently on these assignments. Keep all your notes and activities that you have completed together in one folder so that you are well prepared. You also need to check the unit specification and assignment brief. This will help you to be clear about what is required when questions ask for explanation, analysis and evaluation. It may be helpful to practise the higher-level skills needed in order to achieve the Merit and Distinction grades, such as developing a point, analysing a situation or case study and evaluating the law and its impact. Throughout this unit you will find activities that will develop your understanding of tort law, which will help you prepare for your assignments.

The assignments set by your tutor will consist of a number of tasks designed to meet the criteria in the table below. They are likely to include a written assignment but may also be activities such as:

- case studies where you make decisions about a case and provide legal advice
- presentations or scenarios where you can demonstrate your knowledge about legal practice and procedures.

Assessment criteria

This table shows what you must do in order to achieve a **Pass**, **Merit** or **Distinction** and where you can find activities to help you.

Pass	Merit	Distinction
Learning aim A Examine the principles of tort and liability in negligence for psychiatric harm		
A.P1 Explain and apply the law on negligence and psychiatric harm. **Assessment practice 7.1**	**A.M1** Analyse liability in given scenarios for negligence and psychiatric harm, providing a reasoned opinion on outcome based on current law. **Assessment practice 7.1**	**AB.D1** Evaluate the development of the law relating to the imposition of duty of care and limitations imposed in situations of psychiatric harm, negligent misstatements and pure economic loss claims. **Assessment practice 7.1**
Learning aim B Explore liability for economic loss and negligent misstatement		
B.P2 Explain and illustrate, based on case studies, how the law deals with negligence claims based on economic loss. **Assessment practice 7.1**	**B.M2** Analyse liability in given case studies for economic loss and negligent misstatements, providing a reasoned opinion on outcome based on current law. **Assessment practice 7.1**	
B.P3 Explain based on case studies how the law demonstrates liability for negligent misstatements. **Assessment practice 7.1**		
Learning aim C Investigate the law on occupiers' liability and vicarious liability		
C.P4 Explain the law contained in the Occupiers' Liability Act 1957 and Occupiers' Liability Act 1984 and apply in given case studies. **Assessment practice 7.2**	**C.M3** Analyse liability for occupiers and vicarious liability in given case studies, providing a reasoned opinion on outcomes based on current law. **Assessment practice 7.2**	**C.D2** Evaluate the working and impact of the law of occupiers' and employers' liability. **Assessment practice 7.2**
C.P5 Explain and illustrate how an employer can be held vicariously liable for acts of an employee using given case studies. **Assessment practice 7.2**		
Learning aim D Explore liability for private nuisance and Rylands v Fletcher		
D.P6 Explain the law to demonstrate liability for private nuisance and Rylands v Fletcher using given case studies. **Assessment practice 7.3**	**D.M4** Assess liability for nuisance and Rylands v Fletcher in given case studies, providing a reasoned opinion on outcomes based on current law. **Assessment practice 7.3**	**D.D3** Evaluate the effectiveness of liability in private nuisance and Rylands v Fletcher. **Assessment practice 7.3**

Getting started

Civil wrongs are less well publicised than crimes but will often have substantial implications for an injured claimant. How many civil wrongs can you think of? What would you hope to achieve by taking action? Can you think of any problems you might face in taking a civil court action?

Examine the principles of tort and liability in negligence for psychiatric harm

Objectives of the law of tort

As you will have seen in Unit 1, a tort is a civil wrong that results in some form of injury, loss or damage. The claimant will be taking action to recover compensation for that injury, loss or damage.

The main objectives of tort law are:

- to show that the defendant was at fault
- to compensate victims of accidents, which may give some justice to the injured claimant and punish the defendant to send a message to others not to act carelessly (also known as deterrence).

Key term

Fault - the legal blame for causing an accident. The fault will have to be proved on the balance of probabilities and evidence will have to be produced to show the fault.

Fault

Fault means the legal blame for causing the injuries or damage to the victim. In many torts, the fault of the defendant has to be proved in order to successfully claim. However, proving fault may be difficult or costly for the victim. Evidence will be required to show how the injuries occurred, for example, from eyewitnesses and paid experts. Medical evidence may be required to show the extent of the injuries and the effect on the victim in the future. If property is lost or damaged, valuations will have to be obtained. All or any of these costs of proving fault can deter a potential claimant from bringing an action.

In many cases a person or company will be covered by insurance. Sometimes, insurance cover is compulsory, such as for driving motor vehicles. In the event of an accident where injury or damage is caused, a report will be passed to the insurance company who are likely to take over the case. The benefit of having insurance cover is that the victim can be reassured, if they can prove their case, that they will receive compensation.

However, this need to prove fault can cause problems and only a small number of victims of accidents actually receive full compensation for their injuries. This may be for a number of reasons, including:

- The person who caused the injuries or damage cannot be traced - in motor vehicle claims, the Motor Insurers Bureau funds claims against uninsured drivers or drivers who cannot be traced. They are funded by a charge on all insurance companies who provide motor insurance cover. There are no similar bodies for injuries caused in other areas.
- The fault cannot be proved, even though injury or damage is suffered - for example in Bolton v Stone (1951), Miss Stone suffered injury from being hit by a cricket ball but received no compensation as it was considered that the cricket club had done everything to cover the low risk of injury. Another example is Bolam v Friern Hospital Management Committee (1957), where the victim was unable to prove the fault of the doctors as the court considered that they reached the standard of other doctors in the profession. Again in Roe v Minister of Health (1954), the victim was unsuccessful as the risk of contamination of glass tubes was then unknown.

- There is no fault – the injuries or damage were completely accidental or not covered by any insurance policy risk.
- The victim is prevented from claiming for public policy reasons – for example, in the case of Hill v Chief Constable of West Yorkshire (1988), Mrs Hill was prevented by the courts from pursuing a claim against the police as they could not be expected to know that she, or her daughter, would be a victim of the Yorkshire Ripper.
- Expert evidence and specialist lawyers are required to deal with cases where severe injuries have been caused – these experts and lawyers will be expensive and will have to be paid in order to obtain the evidence to assess whether there is a valid claim and later to prove the claim in court.

Some torts are said to be torts of **strict liability** where the claimant does not need to prove fault. These include:

- private nuisance – this is where the defendant is causing an unreasonable interference to the claimant's enjoyment of their property. The judge will decide whether the defendant is acting unreasonably and will take various factors into account. The defendant will only be at fault if they are found to have acted maliciously (intending to do harm).
- Rylands v Fletcher liability – this is an alternative to a claim in negligence. If the claimant can show that there was a) storage of a non-naturally occurring material on property, b) that it escaped and c) that it caused reasonably foreseeable damage to the adjoining property, then **damages** will be awarded. The claimant does not have to show any fault on the part of the defendant for the storage or escape.
- vicarious liability – this is where the claimant has been injured by an employee. If it can be shown that the person causing the injury, loss or damage was employed (as opposed to being self-employed), and they were acting in the course of employment, the employer will be liable to pay compensation.

Link

For more on Rylands v Fletcher liability, see learning aim D.

Key terms

Strict liability – the claimant will not have to prove any fault on the part of the defendant in order to win their claim. These torts should be easier and cheaper to prove.

Damages – the payment of money by the defendant to the claimant for the loss, injury or damage suffered. Damages are the most common remedy in civil law.

Loss of amenity – the inability to do something after an accident that a person was able to do before.

Compensation

If the claimant can prove fault, the court will award compensation (damages). This is a financial sum paid for the injuries suffered ('pain and suffering'), any **loss of amenity** (for example, no longer being able to play sport), loss of earnings and any past or future medical expenses.

If the defendant is insured, the insurance company will pay this compensation. If the defendant is not insured, the claimant may not receive any or all the compensation awarded. This objective of tort law is therefore heavily dependent on there being suitable insurance cover, which may be either 'before the event' cover or a more expensive 'after the event' cover.

Deterrence

The idea of deterrence is to send a message to others that behaving in a certain way is wrong and that such behaviour may result in punishment or penalties. In the case of tort, this is usually the payment of damages.

It could be argued that motorists are deterred more by the threat of motoring penalties such as fines, penalty points and disqualification, than the threat of paying compensation. A business may be more deterred by the threat of prosecution for breach of health and safety laws than paying compensation to injured victims.

Justice

A successful claimant will achieve a certain amount of justice (fair treatment) by receiving compensation for their loss. However, a seriously injured claimant, who has perhaps lost a limb, would not think that any amount of money could fully compensate them for their loss or that they have received justice.

Punishment

If the defendant is liable, they will be punished by having to pay compensation to the claimant for their losses and injury. However, in most cases the defendant's insurers will pay the compensation. The defendant will only be punished by having to pay higher premiums in the future.

Alternatives to and comparison of the fault-based system

The UK uses a fault-based system of compensating victims of accidents. Table 7.1 lists the differences between fault and no fault compensation.

Table 7.1: The differences between fault and no fault liability

Fault	No fault
Proving fault is costly - proof of how the accident happened and medical evidence for the claimant's injuries is required.	Cheaper - there is no need to show how accident happened.
Claims can be lengthy - it can take a long time to prove fault and consider the effects of accident on the claimant.	Claims can be dealt with quicker as no need to prove fault.
Few claims succeed due to cost and lack of evidence.	More claims are possible.
Fault-based claims can be a deterrent, ensuring that people take greater care to avoid accidents.	No deterrent as claims are paid by insurance - apart from higher premiums, the cost to the defendant is small.

One alternative to the current system of compensation is a state-run benefit scheme that pays out compensation, either in lump sums or regular payments, to all victims of accidents without the need to prove how or why the accident happened. This could be funded through general taxation or by a levy on motorists or employers. Canada has had a state-run compensation scheme in place for many years. Employers are required to pay a contribution, based on the dangers in their workplace, to fund an employee's compensation scheme.

Another alternative is to enforce a requirement for every adult to have personal liability insurance, which would pay out in the event of an accident.

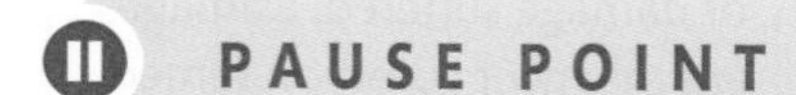

What is fault and when does it have to be proved in tort law?

Hint: Identify the difference between fault and no fault liability.

Extend: List some problems with fault-based liability.

Law relating to duty of care, breach and damage

Link

You have studied the law of negligence and the effect of public policy on duty of care in detail in Unit 1.

The law of negligence is concerned with a person's claim for compensation when they have been injured or someone has damaged their property.

Negligence can result from either an act or a failure to act (an omission). Baron Alderson's interpretation in the case of Blyth v Birmingham Waterworks Company (1856) was that negligence involved two alternatives - either failing to do something which the reasonable person would do or doing something which the reasonable person would not do.

There are three elements to negligence.

- The defendant must owe a duty of care to the claimant.
- That duty must have been broken through a failure to reach the required standard of care.
- The broken duty must have caused the damage or injury.

Duty of care

Whether a duty of care is owed to the claimant can be assessed by a three-part test.

- Could a reasonable person see that some damage or harm is reasonably foreseeable to someone in the claimant's position?
- Is there a sufficiently proximate (close) relationship between the claimant and the defendant?
- Is it fair, just and reasonable to impose a duty of care (the public policy consideration)?

This test comes from the case of Caparo Industries v Dickman (1990) and all three parts must be satisfied if there is to be a duty of care owed by the defendant to the claimant. In most cases, it will be clear when a duty is owed by defendants such as manufacturers, drivers and employers.

Breach of duty

If a duty of care is owed, the next stage is to prove that the duty of care has been breached (broken). This occurs when the defendant fails to reach the required standard of care. The standard of care required is an objective test. This means that the standard is that of the reasonable person performing the task competently.

There are special tests for professionals, learners and young persons to decide whether they have fallen below certain standards. Remember the cases of Bolam v Friern Hospital Management Committee (1957), Nettleship v Weston (1971) and Mullin v Richards (1988).

In addition, there are various risk factors to be taken into account such as:

- special characteristics of the claimant, such as in Paris v Stepney (1951)
- the risk of harm, for example in Bolton v Stone (1951)
- social utility, for example in Watt v Hertfordshire (1954)
- taking precautions, for example in Latimer v AEC (1953).

Loss or damage

The third element of negligence is that the breach must have caused the damage or injury. There are two parts to damage and both parts have to be proved for a negligence claim to succeed.

- Causation – which requires the breach of duty to have caused the injury or loss in the case. This is factual causation, such as in Barnett v Chelsea and Kensington Hospital Management Committee (1969).
- Remoteness – which decides if the actual loss was reasonably foreseeable (not too remote). This is legal causation such as in The Wagon Mound (No. 1) (1961).

If all three aspects of negligence can be proved, the claimant should be awarded damages.

Link

Damages and remedies are covered in more detail at the end of learning aim A and in Unit 1.

Discussion

The next time you are a passenger in a car, identify who is owed a duty of care on your journey. Examine whether the driver breached a duty of care on any occasion.

Most claims in negligence are for personal injury or damage to property. For some torts such as claiming for psychiatric harm or for negligent misstatement, the injury or loss is different. In psychiatric harm, the victim will have suffered mental injuries and in negligent misstatement the victim will have suffered financial loss. In both of these actions, it will be necessary for the claimant to prove that the defendant has been negligent before dealing with the special rules that apply to those actions.

 **PAUSE POINT** A claim for negligence requires proof of duty, breach and damage by the person causing the accident, all of which amount to fault. How easy is it to prove negligence?

Hint: What is negligence?

Extend: What are the benefits of a no fault claim for accident compensation?

Psychiatric harm

Psychiatric harm is a branch of the law of negligence. It deals with situations where the claimant has suffered mental injury instead of, or as well as, physical injury.

For cases of psychiatric harm, the courts have restricted claims in the interest of public policy for fear of opening a floodgate of other claims. This is similar to claims of negligent misstatement.

Link

See learning aim B for more on negligent misstatement.

See later in this section for more on the Alcock criteria.

To be successful in claiming psychiatric harm, a claimant first has to prove that:

- there was an accident or event where someone was negligent and caused the injury
- they have suffered a recognised mental injury
- they pass certain criteria (known as the Alcock criteria) to allow them to claim.

Then, the mental injury has to be proved. This must be:

- supported by medical evidence
- sufficiently serious that the claimant is badly affected by it
- more than mere shock or grief
- triggered by a sudden event
- a long-term injury that, for example, prevents the claimant working.

The claim can therefore include loss or earnings while suffering from the condition. Proving a long-term serious mental injury will need medical evidence and may be difficult and expensive. Examples of injuries covered include post-traumatic stress, depression and acute anxiety. However, if the claimant has, for example, nursed a loved one over a period and then suffered mental injuries following death, this cannot be claimed for.

Historical development of the law

The law regarding psychiatric harm has developed as a result of decisions of judges over time. A claim must be brought to court for the law to be extended. Initially, a claim could be made only if the claimant suffered mental injury as a result of fearing for their own safety. This was as a result of Dulieu v White and Sons (1901).

Key case

Dulieu v White and Sons (1901)

Facts

The claimant who was pregnant was working in a bar when a coach and horses crashed into the bar. She suffered such fear for her own safety that she gave birth prematurely. This was one of the first claims allowed for suffering mental injury.

Legal principle – a claim can be made if you suffer mental injury due to fear for your own safety.

The next development was in Hambrook v Stokes Brothers (1925).

Key case

Hambrook v Stokes Brothers (1925)

Facts

A claim was allowed when a mother feared for the safety of her children. Her children were walking ahead of her when a runaway lorry passed her and she heard it was involved in an accident involving a child. She suffered such severe shock that she died.

Legal principle – a claim can be made by those suffering shock due to fearing for the safety of a family member.

As a result of Hambrook v Stokes Brothers (1925), claims could be made as a result of fearing for your own safety or fearing for the safety of other family members. The next case that developed the law, Bourhill v Young (1943), considered whether a claim could be made by a stranger.

Key case

Bourhill v Young (1943)

Facts

A pregnant woman heard an accident involving a motorbike as she was getting off a tram. She went to look at the scene and suffered such shock when she saw blood on the road that she miscarried. Her claim against the estate of the dead motorcyclist, who had caused the accident, failed as she was not related to him and she was not in the range of those who might suffer shock.

Legal principle – claims are limited to those suffered by the claimant or a member of their family.

The decision in Bourhill v Young (1943) confirms the previous cases that shock has to be suffered due to injury to oneself or a member of family and unrelated bystanders could not claim. In McLoughlin v O'Brian (1982), the law was developed further as the victim suffered shock a short while after the accident.

Key case

McLoughlin v O'Brian (1982)

Facts

Mrs McLoughlin was at home when her husband and children were involved in an accident due to the negligence of a lorry driver. She was informed of the accident and went to the hospital where she suffered shock as a result of seeing her family being treated and learning of the death of one of her children. Her claim was allowed.

Legal principle – a claim can be made by someone who had close ties of love and affection with the victims of the accident, and if they suffered the shock at the scene of the accident or in its immediate aftermath. No time was set for this but Mrs McLoughlin arrived at the hospital and suffered shock within two hours of the accident.

Primary and secondary victims

Key case

Page v Smith (1996)

Facts

Mr Page was involved in a car accident due to the defendant's negligence. He suffered no physical injury but a recurrence of chronic fatigue syndrome. He was able to claim for this injury.

Legal principle – the House of Lords developed the categories of primary and secondary victims for claims of psychiatric injury.

The important point from this case is that the House of Lords developed two categories of victims:

- Primary victims – those involved in the accident and who suffer mental and/or physical injury. They have to prove the negligence of the person causing the accident.
- Secondary victims – those who are not directly involved in the accident but who suffer shock as a result of what they have witnessed or heard. They can claim if they can prove negligence and also the Alcock criteria.

There is also a threshold test that has to be satisfied. This means that a claimant can only succeed if a reasonable person in that position would have suffered the shock as well.

The Alcock criteria

Key case

Alcock v Chief Constable of South Yorkshire (1992)

Facts

This case came about following the Hillsborough disaster in which 96 fans died and hundreds were injured at the Hillsborough football ground. The deaths and injuries were caused by the negligence of the police in allowing too many people into an already crowded part of the ground. Those who were injured were able to claim compensation from the police and were called 'primary victims'. This particular case involved claims by families of the victims for mental injuries suffered as a result of discovering that a family member had died. Family members were called 'secondary victims' as they were not directly involved in the accident.

Legal principle - secondary victims can only claim if they have close ties of love and affection with the victim, they suffered psychiatric injury at the scene or in its immediate aftermath, and they witnessed the incident with their own senses.

The House of Lords developed the following three criteria for claims by the victims' relatives as well as for future claims by secondary victims:

- The claimant had to have close ties of love and affection with the victim - this means either that they were related to the victim or a close friend. Closeness has to be proved whether the claimant was a family member or not. Proving close ties of love and affection may be difficult as it can require gathering evidence of previous contacts, visits and phone calls at a time when they are struggling with their illness.
- The claimant suffered the mental injuries at the scene of the accident or in its immediate aftermath - the time limit for 'the immediate aftermath' is unclear - the two-hour period in McLoughlin v O'Brian (1982) was approved. However, some of the claimants in the Alcock case saw the bodies of their family members in the mortuary eight hours or more after the events and these claims were not allowed. It appears that if the claimant suffers the shock closer to the two-hour period than the eight-hour period they will be able to pass this criteria.
- The claimant suffered the shock when using their own unaided senses - in other words they saw or heard the accident or its aftermath and did not suffer the shock when watching TV, listening to the radio or hearing about the accident by a phone call, for example.

All three of these criteria have to be satisfied for a claim to succeed. If a claimant cannot prove all the Alcock criteria, they will be left without compensation. The rules are unfair on work colleagues who may have been present at an accident and suffered mental injuries. This unfairness is illustrated in Duncan v British Coal (1998) when a miner saw a work colleague crushed in a roof fall, which was due to the negligence of the employers, and he suffered mental injuries. As he was unable to prove the Alcock criteria, his claim failed.

Reflect

Why do you think the courts have developed these restrictions? Following the events at the Hillsborough ground, who could have claimed if these restrictions were not put in place? Are the restrictions fair?

Special categories of victims

Bystanders

A witness to an accident who is not related to the victim is a secondary victim and has to prove the Alcock criteria as well as negligence. In McFarlane v E.E. Caledonia (1994), a worker suffered shock from witnessing the rescue of victims following an explosion on the Pier Alpha oil rig. He was not related to any of the victims and was unable to satisfy the Alcock criteria and could not claim.

Rescuers

Rescuers are in a different category to bystanders. They will have been actively involved in helping victims of the accident. The courts do not wish to discourage rescuing and it is likely that their claim for mental injuries suffered in the act of rescuing will be allowed. They do not have to prove the Alcock criteria. In Chadwick v British Railways Board (1967), the claimant suffered mental injuries as a result of helping those involved in the Lewisham train crash. His widow's claim was allowed as he was a rescuer, not just a bystander.

Property owners

If a claimant has suffered mental injuries as a result of seeing their property damaged they may be able to claim. In Attia v British Gas (1987), a woman saw her house had been badly damaged by a gas explosion caused by the negligence of British Gas workmen. Her claim for the mental injuries she suffered was allowed.

'Near missers'

These are people who were close to the scene of the accident and could easily have suffered physical or mental injuries. They do not have to be related to the victim of the accident. They are regarded as primary victims and can claim for their injuries if they can prove negligence.

Relationship with victim, the aftermath and loss

In order to prevent too many claims against the person causing the accident, the courts have developed control mechanisms that have to be satisfied before a person can bring a claim for psychiatric injury. These are that the claimant has to have some form of relationship with the victim, the shock is suffered at the scene of the accident or within the immediate aftermath of the accident and that the claimant suffers the shock through their own unaided senses and not through third party means.

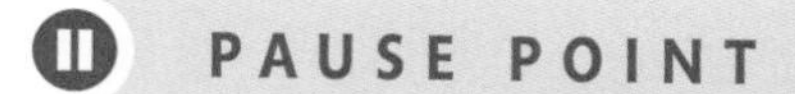

What are the reasons for restricting claims for psychiatric injury?

Hint Identify the reasons for the decision in Alcock v Chief Constable of South Yorkshire (1992).

Extend Examine each of the Alcock criteria to identify those who might be affected.

Aim and calculation of damages

In a successful tort claim, the court can award a successful claimant compensation for the injuries they have suffered or damage to their property. This award is known as damages.

The aim of the award of damages is to place the claimant in the same position as if the tort had not been committed – as far as money can do so. This is possible where the claim is for damage to property. However, if the claimant has suffered disabling personal injury, this is not possible as no amount of money can fully compensate for the loss of a limb, for example.

Special damages

Special damages are amounts that can be calculated specifically up to the date of the trial or settlement. In other words they are the **pecuniary loss**. This could include the cost of repairing a vehicle and the hire costs of a replacement, replacing damaged clothes or bags. Any loss of earnings while recovering from the accident could also be claimed.

Tip

To help you remember the difference between special and general damages: Specific amounts of money = special damages; Undefined amounts of money = general damages.

General damages

General damages are **non-pecuniary losses** and are looking forwards from the trial or settlement date. They can include:

- an amount for pain and suffering
- loss of amenity
- future loss of earnings
- future medical expenses, including adapting a house or car to be suitable for a severely injured person and paying for specialist care.

Claims for general damages require evidence to support the claim, for example, medical evidence of the effect of the accident on the victim and how long the suffering or injuries will take to heal, if at all. For future loss of earnings and future medical expenses, there will have to be an annual calculation of the loss multiplied by the number of years of the loss. For example, five years' loss of earnings at £25,000 each year will lead to a total loss of earnings of £125,000. The claimant will be expected to **mitigate the loss**, so if they can work part-time or at a lower rate of pay, this will be taken into account when deciding the award.

For example, the claimant cannot claim for private treatment for the injury if there is suitable treatment available under the NHS. However, if treatment is only available privately, damages can be claimed for the private treatment.

The same applies to property damage. If property, such as a car, has been damaged beyond repair, the cost of replacing that property with something of similar value can be claimed. Replacing the damaged item with a more expensive item would not be allowed.

Lump sums and structured settlements

When the courts make an award for pain and suffering and loss of amenity, they can only award a single **lump sum**. The claimant cannot come back to court to say that they have exhausted the damages.

This can be unfair to the claimant whose condition in the future might become worse. On the other hand, an award of a lump sum might be unfair to the defendant if the claimant's condition improves considerably and there is no longer a need to pay for care. This is why detailed medical reports are important evidence and are used to calculate damages more accurately.

The Damages Act 1996 allows for **structured settlements** to be set. It allows parties who settle a claim to agree that all or part of the damages can be paid as periodical payments, which can be an amount each month or year. This is arranged by the defendant (or, more likely, their insurer).

Key terms

Pecuniary loss – a loss that can be easily calculated in money terms, for example, the cost of hiring a car while your own car is being repaired.

Non-pecuniary loss – a loss that is not wholly money-based.

Mitigate the loss – a duty to keep the loss to a reasonable level.

Lump sum – a once only payment of damages awarded by the court, or agreed in a settlement.

Structured settlements – damages paid regularly over a period.

The effect of death on claims and damages

The Fatal Accidents Act 1976 covers the situation if either party dies as a result of, or after the accident:

- If the claimant dies as a result of the accident, their survivors, such as a spouse or children, can take action against the defendant. If the action has started before the claimant died, the survivors can continue the action.
- If the defendant dies before the claim has been finalised, the action can continue against their estate.

The amount of damages that can be claimed will be the amount of the annual loss multiplied by the number of years the loss would have been suffered. In addition, funeral expenses may be claimed and the spouse of a dead claimant can claim bereavement damages currently set at £12,980. Any benefits such as insurance or pension payments paid out as a result of death are ignored. If the claimant died partly as a result of their own fault, and partly of the fault of the defendant, contributory negligence will apply and the damages will be reduced proportionately.

PAUSE POINT Are financial damages an adequate remedy for someone injured in an accident?

Hint What is the purpose of the award of damages in tort?

Extend Is there another remedy that would be more appropriate for an injured victim?

B Explore liability for economic loss and negligent misstatements

This section is a development of the law of negligence that you studied in Unit 1. It deals with claims of pure financial loss, rather than physical loss or damage. It covers two areas:

- economic loss
- negligent misstatement.

A claimant can always recover financial loss caused by a negligent act – a positive action, which causes an accident. This is providing they can prove that the defendant's act caused the loss and it was not too remote. This financial loss could be any lost earnings as a result of being injured or any property damaged in the accident.

A negligent misstatement will take place where there is no contract between the parties, but where one party is trying to persuade the other party to enter into a contract. A statement will usually be given orally by someone who has some sort of expert knowledge. The person who hears the statement will act on it but suffers financial loss as the statement turns out to be incorrect. The person who loses money will want to take an action in tort to recover their loss.

Key term

Pure economic loss – money loss that is a loss of profit that cannot be claimed. Goods that are damaged by a negligent act or omission can be claimed.

Economic loss

The courts have been clear that financial loss arising from a breach of contract should be a matter of contract law, not tort law. Therefore, actions for **pure economic loss** or loss of profit are not generally recoverable in tort law. This approach is considered to be a matter of policy, not necessarily based on a legal principle. The approach was established in the case of Spartan Steel v Martin (1973).

Key case

Spartan Steel v Martin (1973)

Facts

The claimants made steel alloy melts in their factory. Due to the negligence of the defendant's workers, an electricity cable supplying the factory was cut, leading to a loss of power for several hours. There were three parts to the claim:

- the damage to the melts on the production line – this could be claimed as it was a foreseeable consequence
- the loss of profit on those melts – this could be claimed as again it was a foreseeable consequence
- the loss of profit while the factory was out of action – although this was a foreseeable consequence of the loss of power, it was decided by the Court of Appeal that, as a matter of policy, this part of the claim was not allowed.

Legal principle – loss of profit cannot be claimed in tort. Only damage to goods or loss that is reasonably foreseeable can be claimed.

In Spartan Steel v Martin (1973), the distinction between the three types of financial loss is very small and the contractors should have forseen that if they negligently cut the electricity cable the factory would be without power for a period, affecting production and profit. This could be seen as allowing the negligent defendant to get away with their behaviour.

On the other hand, it could be argued that the loss of profit is really a failure to make a gain. The aim of tort law is to compensate the victim of a tort for their loss, so allowing a claim for loss of profit (gain) goes against the principle of tort law.

Negligent misstatements

If a person receives negligent advice, acts on that advice and loses money as a result, then the person should be able to use the ordinary law of negligence to claim for their loss. This will apply to advice directly given by professionals such as a solicitor, accountant or architect.

Key case

Hedley Byrne v Heller and Partners (1964)

Facts

An advertising company, Hedley Byrne, were approached by Easipower to place adverts in newspapers and magazines. They had not previously dealt with Easipower so they requested a reference form Easipower's bank. The bank gave a favourable reference and Hedley Byrne went ahead with the campaign. However, Easipower went into liquidation without paying for the campaign. Hedley Byrne sued Easipower's bankers for the loss suffered as a result of their reliance on the reference.

Legal principle – the House of Lords decided that, in principle, a claim could be made for the negligent misstatement if a special relationship could be proved. In this case, the reference contained a disclaimer of liability, which meant that Hedley Byrne could not succeed.

Negligent advice given directly by a professional to a client that causes loss can be claimed for

Key term

Special relationship – a legal device approved by the courts that allows a person who receives advice or information to sue the person giving the advice for any loss suffered as a result of acting on that advice.

As a result of the case of Hedley Byrne v Heller and Partners (1964), claims may be made by those who have suffered financial loss as a result of relying on a statement. However, it has to be established that:

- the statement was made negligently
- that there is a **special relationship** between the parties.

The case of Caparo v Dickman (1990) set out the features of a special relationship, which in effect means that the person giving the advice owes a duty of care to the claimant.

Key case

Caparo Industries v Dickman (1990)

Facts

Caparo were shareholders in a company called Fidelity Ltd. Caparo considered the annual books of audit of Fidelity, prepared by Dickman. These books showed a profit and Caparo decided to launch a takeover to completely own Fidelity. When they had completed the deal, Caparo found that Fidelity was almost worthless and they sued Dickman for their loss. The preparation of the annual books of audit was a statutory requirement. The House of Lords decided that the books of audit were not designed as a guide for new investors, or existing investors to increase their shares, and Dickman did not owe a duty of care to Caparo.

Legal principle – a special relationship requires all of the following to be proved:

- **special skill or expertise on the part of the person giving the advice**
- **the claimant relied (acted upon) the advice**
- **the advice is communicated directly to the claimant**
- **the person giving the advice knows that it is needed for a purpose and is used for that purpose**
- **there is no disclaimer to act as a defence.**

If the claimant successfully proves the negligent misstatement, they can claim damages for the loss suffered. However, as the law on claiming losses for negligent misstatement has been developed by cases that have come before the courts, it is complicated and unsettled.

The case of Chaudhry v Prabhakar (1988) sets out that a special relationship can exist even if the advice was given in a social relationship, rather than a business relationship. The decision in Chaudhry v Prabhakar (1988) seems to conflict with the general approach of the courts that advice given in an informal setting, which turns out to be negligent, cannot be claimed for.

Research

- What were the facts of Chaudhry v Prabhakar (1988)?
- What did the court decide about Miss Chaudhry's claim against Mr Jandoo?
- What area of law was used for this part of the claim?
- What did the court decide for Miss Chaudhry's claim against Mr Prabhakar?
- What area of law was used for this part of the claim?
- Do you think that the result of the case was fair?

What is the difference between pure economic loss and negligent misstatements?

Hint Which loss is claimable in tort?

Extend What are the public policy reasons for restricting claims?

Assessment practice 7.1

A.P1 A.M1 B.P2 B.P3 B.M2 AB.D1

Malcolm and Jack consult your legal firm about a recent accident in which they were involved. A delivery driver, Andzej, was seen driving at speed and sending a text on his mobile. As he approached Malcolm's house, Andzej lost control of his van, which crashed into the front wall of the house. Malcolm was in his front garden and the wall collapsed on him. Malcolm tells you he was screaming in pain from a broken leg and was covered in blood.

Jack had been driving his car behind Andzej. He was on his way to deliver a book manuscript, which had to be received within the hour. When he saw the crash, he ran to help by lifting the brickwork off Malcolm. Since the incident, Jack has been suffering severe panic attacks. Also, as a result of him helping he did not meet the deadline and estimates that he will lose possible royalties of about £5,000.

1 Write to Malcolm to advise him about his rights and remedies against Andzej in the tort of Negligence. Write to Jack to advise him about his rights and remedies against Andzej in the torts of psychiatric harm and economic loss.

Malcolm also tells you that his friend, Imran, is an investment consultant. Malcolm asked Imran for advice on investing £100,000 that he had just inherited. Imran advised Malcolm, free of charge, to invest all the money in shares in the General and Legal Company. Malcolm took this advice and invested all of his inheritance. Without Imran's knowledge, Malcolm also told his neighbour, Mick, about Imran's advice. As a result of this, Mick invested £10,000 in the same company. Malcolm tells you that he has just heard that the company has collapsed and it is likely that he and Mick have lost all their money.

2 Write to Malcolm to advise him of any rights and remedies he and Mick may have against Imran for negligent misstatement.

3 You tell your senior partner about these two cases and she asks you to write a briefing note evaluating the development of the law relating to the imposition of a duty of care and the limitations in situations of psychiatric harm, negligent misstatements and pure economic loss claims.

Plan

- How many parts of the task are there? Who am I advising or writing to in each part?
- Am I clear on the law of each part? Are any parts of the law unclear?

Do

- I need to use relevant case law to support each point.
- I need to tailor the advice to each specific client.

Review

- Have I provided clear and balanced advice?
- Have I covered the remedies that may be available in each case?

C Investigate the law on occupier's liability and vicarious liability

Occupiers' liability is a branch of negligence. While negligence is a common law tort created by judges, occupiers' liability has been created by statute. The main remedy for a successful claim of occupiers' liability is compensation for any injuries sustained or damage suffered.

Occupiers' Liability Act 1957

The Occupiers' Liability Act 1957 provides that an **occupier** of a premises owes a duty of care to **lawful visitors** and if that duty is broken and the visitor is injured, they are entitled to receive compensation from the occupier.

Key terms

Occupier – person who is in control of the premises, usually owner or tenant.

Lawful visitor – someone who has permission to be on another's premises.

Adult visitors

Lawful adult visitors include:

- people who have been invited to enter and who have express permission to be there
- people who may have express or implied permission to be on the land for a certain length of time
- those with contractual permission, for example a person who has bought an entry ticket for an event
- those given a statutory right of entry such as meter readers and police constables exercising a warrant.

An adult visitor is owed the common duty of care. According to s2(2) of the Occupiers' Liability Act 1957 this means to 'take such care as in all the circumstances is reasonable to see that the visitor will be reasonably safe in using the premises for the purpose for which he is invited... to be there'.

The occupier does not have to make the premises completely safe for the visitor – only to do what is reasonable.

Key case

Laverton v Kiapasha (Takeaway Supreme) (2002)

Facts

The defendants owned a small takeaway shop. They had fitted slip-resistant tiles and they used a mop and bucket to mop the floor if it had been raining. When the claimant went into the shop, it was very busy and it had been raining. She slipped and broke her ankle. The Court of Appeal decided that the shop owners had taken reasonable care to ensure that its customers were safe. They were not liable as they did not have to make the shop completely safe.

Legal principle – an occupier does not have to make premises completely safe, only to do what is reasonable.

Key case

Dean and Chapter of Rochester Cathedral v Debell (2016)

Facts

The claimant was injured when he tripped and fell over a small lump of concrete protruding about two inches from the base of a traffic bollard in the precincts of Rochester Cathedral. The bollard had previously been slightly damaged by a car.

The Court of Appeal decided that:

- Tripping, slipping and falling are everyday occurrences. No occupier of premises such as the Cathedral could possibly ensure that the roads or the precincts around a building were maintained in a pristine state. Even if they were, accidents would still happen. The obligation on the occupier is to make the land reasonably safe for visitors, not to guarantee their safety. In order to impose liability, there must be something over and above the risk of injury from the minor blemishes and defects that are habitually found on any road or pathway.
- The risk is reasonably foreseeable only where there is a real source of danger that a reasonable person would recognise as obliging the occupier to take remedial action. A visitor is reasonably safe even if there may be visible minor defects on the road that carry a foreseeable risk of causing an accident and injury.

Legal principle - an occupier does not have to make premises completely safe, only to do what is reasonable.

The judgments in both cases emphasise that the common duty of care imposes a duty on the occupier to keep the visitor reasonably safe, not necessarily to maintain completely safe premises. The state of premises must pose a real source of danger before foreseeability of the risk of damage can be found. It is possible that if the cases had been decided in favour of the visitor, it could have opened the floodgates to a tide of claims against occupiers and created a very high level of responsibility for the safety of visitors.

A visitor may be a lawful visitor for the purposes of the Occupiers' Liability Act 1957 but if they exceed their permission, for example, by entering a room they have been told not to enter, they may become a **trespasser** and lose the protection of the Act.

Key terms

Trespasser - someone who has no permission to be on another's premises or who has exceeded their permission.

Allurement - an attraction to a child visitor.

Other visitors

Children

The occupier will owe children coming onto the premises the common duty of care, but there is an additional special duty owed to child visitors.

Under s2(3) of the Occupiers' Liability Act 1957, the occupier 'must be prepared for children to be less careful than adults' and as a result 'the premises must be reasonably safe for a child of that age'. So, for children, the standard of care is measured according to the age of the child. Also, the occupier should guard against any kind of **allurement** or attraction that places a child visitor at risk of harm.

Reflect

What sort of things could amount to an allurement for a child?

Key case

Taylor v Glasgow Corporation (1923)

Facts

A seven-year-old child ate poisonous berries from a shrub in a public park and died. The shrub on which the berries grew was not fenced off in any way. The council was liable to the child's parents. They were aware of the danger and the berries amounted to an allurement to young children.

Legal principle – an occupier owes a duty to protect children from allurements on the premises.

There is a defence for the occupier when very young unsupervised children are injured. The courts consider that the child should be under the supervision of a parent or other adult and they will not find the occupier liable.

Key case

Phipps v Rochester Corporation (1955)

Facts

A five-year-old child was playing on open ground owned by the council with his seven-year-old sister. He fell down a trench and was injured. The court decided that the council was not liable because he should have been with his parents.

Legal principle – the occupier is entitled to expect that parents should not allow their young children to go to places that are potentially unsafe.

The difficulty with this defence is that there is no set age limit. Even if there is an allurement on the premises, there will be no liability on the occupier if the damage or injury suffered is not foreseeable.

Key case

Jolley v London Borough of Sutton (2000)

Facts

The council had failed to move an abandoned boat situated on their land for two years. Children regularly played in the boat and it was a potential danger. When two boys aged 14 years jacked the boat up to repair it, the boat fell on one of them, seriously injuring him. The House of Lords decided that it was foreseeable to the council that children would play on the abandoned boat. It was not necessary for the council to foresee exactly what they would do on it. They considered that children often find ways of putting themselves in danger, which needed to be taken into account by an occupier when considering how to keep them safe.

Legal principle – an occupier owes the common duty of care to child visitors for injuries that are reasonably foreseeable.

Professionals

The occupier will owe the common duty of care to a professional coming onto the premises. However, by s2(3)(b) of the Occupiers' Liability Act 1957, an occupier can expect that a person in the exercise of their work will 'appreciate and guard against any special risks ordinarily incident to it so far as the occupier leave him free to do so'.

The effect of this rule is that an occupier will not be liable where a professional fails to guard against risks that they should know about or should be expected to know about. For example, a carpenter should know about the risks of working with wood, but they would not be expected to know about the possible dangers of working with water or electricity.

Key case

Roles v Nathan (1963)

Facts

Two chimney sweeps died after inhaling carbon monoxide fumes while cleaning the chimney of a coke-fired boiler. The sweeps had been warned of the danger. The occupiers were not liable as they could have expected chimney sweeps to be aware of the particular danger.

Legal principle - an occupier can expect that a professional will guard against risks associated with their work.

This rule, which acts as a defence to an occupier, only applies where the professional visitor is injured by something related to their trade. If the professional is injured by something different, the occupier will still owe the common duty of care.

Independent contractors

As discussed, a lawful visitor will be owed the common duty of care while on the occupier's land. However, if the visitor is injured by a professional's negligent work, the occupier may have a defence and be able to pass the claim to the professional. Section 2(4) of the Occupiers' Liability Act 1957 states:

- Where damage is caused to a visitor by a danger due to the faulty execution of any work of construction, maintenance or repair by an independent contractor employed by the occupier, the occupier is not to be treated without more as answerable for the danger if in all the circumstances he had acted reasonably in entrusting the work to the independent contractor and had taken such steps (if any) as he reasonably ought in order to satisfy himself that the contractor was competent and that the work had been properly done.

From this, three requirements will apply and all have to be satisfied:

- It must be reasonable for the occupier to have given the work to the independent contractor - the more complicated and specialist the work, the more likely it will be that the occupier gives the work to a specialist.
- The contractor hired must be competent to carry out the task - the occupier should be advised to take up references or recommendations or check with a trade association, and check that the contractor is properly insured. If the contractor fails to carry appropriate insurance cover, this could be a fair indication that the contractor is not competent.
- The occupier must check that the work has been properly done - the more complicated and technical the work, and the less expert the occupier, the more likely that this condition will require the occupier to employ an expert such as an architect or surveyor.

If all three conditions are satisfied, the occupier will have a defence to a claim and the injured claimant will have to claim directly against the contractor.

Key case

Bottomley v Todmorden Cricket Club (2003)

Facts

A cricket club hired a stunt team to carry out a 'firework display'. The team chose to use ordinary gunpowder, petrol and propane gas rather than more traditional fireworks. They also then used the claimant, who was an unpaid amateur with no experience of pyrotechnics, for the stunt. The claimant was burned and broke an arm when the stunt went wrong. The stunt team had no insurance. The Court of Appeal decided that the club was liable as it had failed to exercise reasonable care to choose safe and competent contractors.

Legal principle – an occupier is expected to check, or at least enquire about the qualifications and competence of contractors.

Figure 7.1 summarises the duty of care owed by an occupier to lawful visitors.

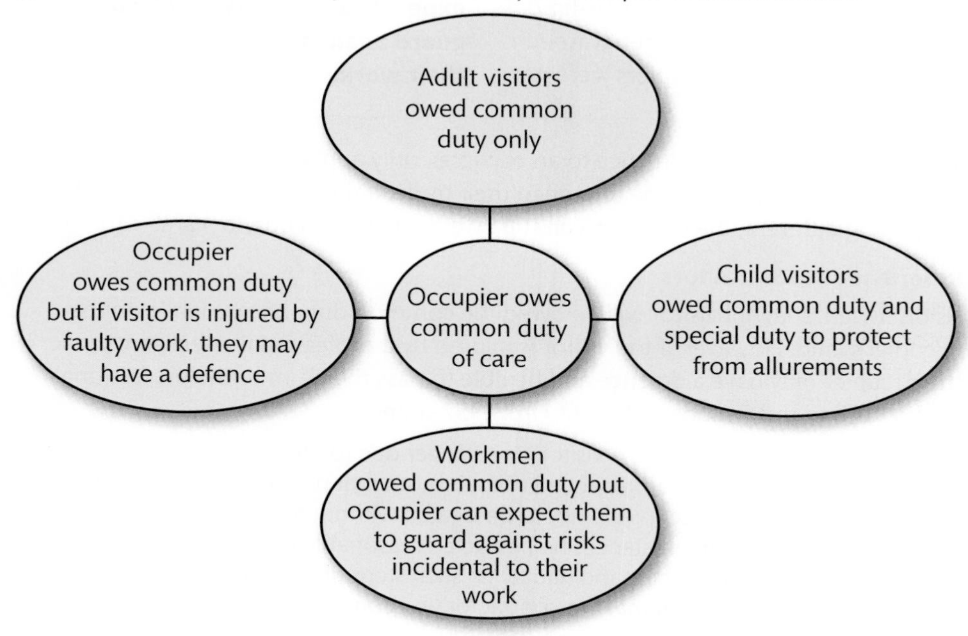

Figure 7.1: The common duty of care owed to lawful visitors

Defences

Warning signs and exclusion notices

A sign warning of danger can amount to a full defence for the occupier. The warning of the danger has to be clearly set out.

The existence of a warning sign can be a full defence against an adult visitor. Whether it will be a defence against a child visitor will depend on the age and understanding of the child. The older the child, the more likely it will be a valid defence.

On the notice, an occupier may attempt to exclude (completely remove) or limit (put a maximum figure on) their responsibility. If the occupier is a business, it cannot exclude liability for death or personal injury caused by negligence, but it can exclude liability for damage to property such as clothes, bags or tools. This is now contained in the Consumer Rights Act 2015.

▶ Examples of warning notices

Consent

If the visitor has consented or agreed to run the risk of injury on the occupier's premises, this acts as a complete defence for the occupier and they will not be liable to pay any damages to the injured visitor. For example, this could operate if the visitor has been advised not to go onto the premises but the advice is ignored.

Contributory negligence

If the visitor is partly to blame for the accident, the occupier can allege that the visitor has been **contributory negligent**. This could operate if, for example, the visitor has not worn protective clothing or shoes as recommended when going on to the occupier's land. If this is the case the court can, under the Law Reform (Contributory Negligence) Act 1945, fix a percentage of the visitor's responsibility and the damages will be reduced by that percentage.

The defences of warning notices, consent and contributory negligence apply to child visitors, but whether the occupier can rely on these as a defence will depend on the age and understanding of the child. For example, the older the child, the more likely they are to be able to read and understand the warning.

Key term

Contributory negligence – the claimant is partly responsible for the accident and their injuries. The amount of damages that can be claimed will be reduced by an appropriate percentage.

Remedies

If the occupier is liable for breach of their duty of care to the visitor, the remedy is damages. The court can award damages for personal injury suffered and for any property damaged.

PAUSE POINT Close your book and complete a table showing when an occupier is liable for injury caused to a lawful visitor.

Hint Have a column for each of adult visitors, child visitors, professionals and independent contractors.

Extend Add to the table which of the possible defences could apply.

Occupiers' Liability Act 1984

Lawful visitors are covered by the Occupiers' Liability Act 1957. Non-visitors, or trespassers, may be covered by the Occupiers' Liability Act 1984. According to s1(1)(a), a duty is owed by the occupier to people other than lawful visitors for 'injury on the premises by reason of any danger due to the state of the premises or things done or omitted to be done on them'.

A non-visitor or trespasser can be any of the following:

- someone who has entered the occupier's premises without any permission
- a lawful visitor who stays on premises after permission to be there has been removed
- a lawful visitor who has entered premises with permission, but then exceeds their permission and enters part of the premises where they are not supposed to go.

The Occupiers' Liability Act 1984 gives trespassers a right to claim compensation when they have been injured while trespassing. Damage to property is not covered. However, there have been a number of court decisions that have restricted whether a duty is owed to trespassers and, if a duty is owed, whether the occupier is liable.

The occupier will only owe a duty under s1(3) under the following circumstances:

- They are aware of the danger or have reasonable grounds to believe it exists – this could be, for example, where the owner or site manager of a construction site knows that there are hazards, such as holes in the floor of a building or dangerous tools or equipment lying around.
- They know, or have reasonable grounds to believe, that the other is in the vicinity of the danger – this could be, for example, where the owner or site manager of a construction site has been warned that children are entering to play on the site after the workers have gone home.
- The risk is one against which, in all the circumstances of the case, they may be expected to offer the other some protection. This could be, for example, where the owner or site manager of a construction site could have made the site more secure to prevent entry after the workmen have gone home and placed visible warning signs showing that the site is dangerous.

The duty owed under s1(4) is to:

- Take such care as is reasonable in the circumstances to see that the trespasser is not injured by reason of the danger – this could be, for example, where the owner or site manager of a construction site could have made the site more secure to prevent entry after the workers have gone home and placed visible warning signs showing that the site is dangerous.

The danger referred to in these sections is the object or part of land on which the trespasser is injured. The standard of care is an objective one – in other words, what the reasonable person would have done to secure their premises. What is required of the occupier depends on the circumstances of each case. The greater the risk of injury, the more precautions the occupier will have to take. The following will have to be taken into account:

- the type and condition of the premises
- the amount of danger
- whether it is possible to take precautions
- the age of the trespasser.

Adult trespassers

When considering claims under the Occupiers' Liability Act 1984, the courts have introduced the concept of obvious dangers, especially for adult trespassers. This concept is broken down in the following ways:

- The occupier will not be liable if the trespasser is injured by an obvious danger.

Key case

Ratcliff v McConnell (1999)

Facts

A 19-year-old student climbed the fence of his open-air college swimming pool at night and dived into the pool hitting his head on a ledge. He was seriously injured.

Legal principle – an occupier is not required to warn adult trespassers of the risk of injury against obvious dangers. In this case, there was no hidden danger as it is well known that swimming pools vary in depth and diving without checking the depth is dangerous.

- The time of day and the time of year when the accident happened will be relevant as to whether the occupier owes a duty of care.

Key case

Donoghue v Folkestone Properties (2003)

Facts

The claimant was injured when he was trespassing on a harbour and dived into the sea, hitting a submerged object. The object would have been visible at low tide. The injury happened in the middle of winter, at around midnight. The court decided that the occupier did not owe the claimant a duty of care under the Occupiers' Liability Act 1984 as they would not expect that a trespasser might jump into the harbour at that time of day or year.

Legal principle – an occupier does not owe a duty of care to a trespasser who is injured by an obvious danger at an unexpected time of day or year.

- An occupier does not have to spend lots of money in making premises safe from obvious dangers.

Key case

Tomlinson v Congleton Borough Council (2003)

Facts

The council owned a park including a lake. Warning signs were posted prohibiting swimming and diving because the water was dangerous, but the council knew that these were generally ignored. The council decided to make the lake inaccessible to the public but delayed start on this work because of lack of funds. The claimant, aged 18, went swimming in the lake, struck his head on the sandy bottom and suffered paralysis as a result of a severe spinal injury. The House of Lords decided the following:

- In order to be liable under the Occupiers' Liability Act 1984, there had to be a danger due to the state of the premises or things done or omitted to be done. In this case, the danger was not due to the state of the premises but was due to the claimant diving into the water.
- It was not the sort of risk that an occupier should have to guard against but one where the trespasser has to take some responsibility for their actions.
- The council would not have breached its duty even if the claimant was a lawful visitor as it was not reasonable for them to spend a lot of money preventing visitors being injured by an obvious danger.

Legal principle – the occupier does not have to make premises safe for trespassers against obvious risks.

It could be thought that the court decided the case of Tomlinson v Congleton Borough Council (2003) in favour of the occupier because they were providing a social benefit enjoyed by many visitors each year. If they, and other similar attractions, had to spend a lot of money making premises safe, they might be forced to close and prevent the majority of the public who use them properly from enjoying the attraction.

- The occupier will not be liable if they had no reason to suspect the presence of a trespasser.

Key case

Higgs v Foster (2004)

Facts

A police officer investigating a crime entered the occupier's premises to carry out surveillance. He fell into an uncovered inspection pit suffering severe injuries, causing him to retire from the police force. The police officer was judged to be a trespasser on the premises. Although the occupiers knew the pit was a potential danger, they could not have anticipated his presence on the premises or in the vicinity, so they were not liable.

Legal principle – an occupier will not be liable if they are unaware of the presence of a danger.

- The occupier will not be liable if they were not aware of the danger or had no reason to suspect the danger existed.

Key case

Rhind v Astbury Water Park (2004)

Facts

The occupier did not know of a submerged fibreglass container resting on the bottom of a lake on its premises. The claimant ignored a notice which said 'Private Property. Strictly no Swimming', and jumped into the lake and was injured by objects below the surface of the water. Section 1(3)(c) of the 1987 Act requires the occupier to owe a duty if 'the risk is one against which, in all the circumstances of the case, he may be expected to offer the other some protection'. As the occupier did not know of the dangerous objects, no duty was owed and the claimant was unsuccessful.

Legal principle – an occupier will not be liable if they are unaware of the presence of a danger.

Discussion

Discuss in pairs whether you think all these rules are fair for:

- an occupier
- a trespasser who has been injured.

Child trespassers

The law provides protection to child visitors if an occupier has dangerous premises where, or close to where, children might play. Children, depending on their age, are held to a different standard to adults because they do not have the same knowledge and experience. A danger that is obvious to an adult may not be obvious to a child.

Key case

Keown v Coventry Healthcare NHS Trust (2006)

Facts

An 11-year-old boy climbed a fire escape on the exterior of a hospital to show off to his friends, fell and was seriously injured. The Court of Appeal decided that, as the boy appreciated the danger, it was not the state of the premises (the existence of the fire escape, which was not faulty) that caused his injuries, but what the boy was doing on it. There was no danger due to the state of the premises and the hospital was not liable.

Legal principle - an occupier will not be liable to a child trespasser where the danger is not due to the state of the premises but because the child has acted in a dangerous manner themselves.

Key case

Baldacchino v West Wittering Estate plc (2008)

Facts

On a summer's day, a 14-year-old boy climbed a navigational beacon sited off a beach as the tide was ebbing. He dived off the beacon suffering neck injuries and tetraplegia. He was a lawful visitor to the beach but a trespasser to the beacon. It was decided that there was no duty on the part of the occupiers to warn against obvious dangers and the injuries did not result from the state of the premises. The beacon was not by itself dangerous - the beach company had no grounds for believing that the boy would come into the vicinity of any danger (based on the previous warnings given by the lifeguards) - and the precautions taken by the defendant (having lifeguards on the beach) was as much as could reasonably be expected for a busy beach that was visited by 11,000 or so visitors each day. His claim failed.

Legal principle - an occupier does not have to specifically tell a visitor (including children) to keep off their property.

The court will take into account the child trespasser's age and understanding in deciding what it is reasonable for the occupier to do to protect their property against injury by obvious risks. The reasoning may be similar to that used in the case of Tomlinson v Congleton Borough Council (2003) above, in that the occupier was providing a social benefit to many visitors. If they were found liable, it could mean that the benefit would be closed in the future and prevent the majority of the public who used the facility properly from enjoying it. Occupiers' liability to trespassers is summarised in Figure 7.2.

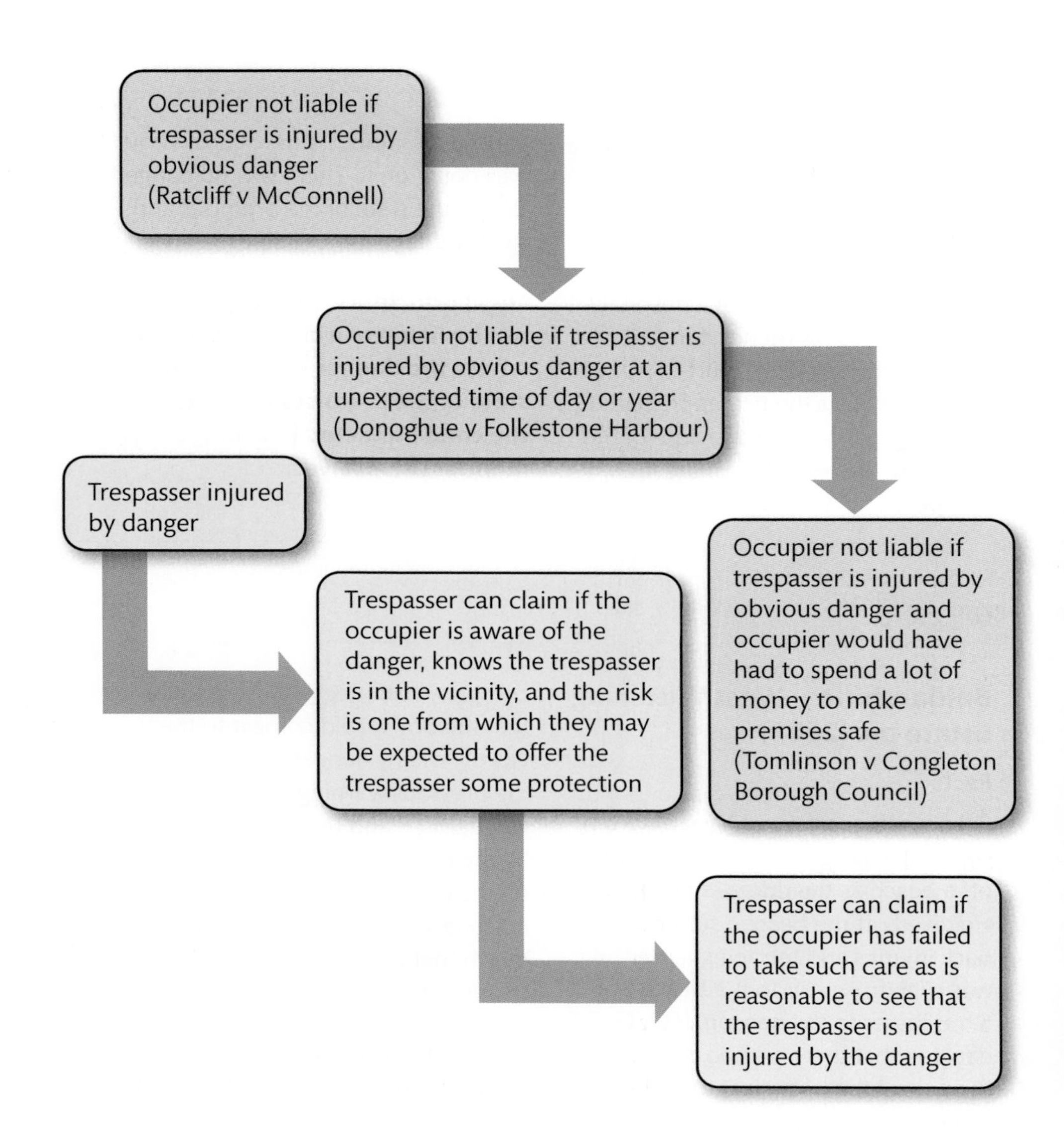
Occupier not liable if trespasser is injured by obvious danger (Ratcliff v McConnell)
Occupier not liable if trespasser is injured by obvious danger at an unexpected time of day or year (Donoghue v Folkestone Harbour)
Trespasser injured by danger
Trespasser can claim if the occupier is aware of the danger, knows the trespasser is in the vicinity, and the risk is one from which they may be expected to offer the trespasser some protection
Occupier not liable if trespasser is injured by obvious danger and occupier would have had to spend a lot of money to make premises safe (Tomlinson v Congleton Borough Council)
Trespasser can claim if the occupier has failed to take such care as is reasonable to see that the trespasser is not injured by the danger

Figure 7.2: Claims by trespassers

Defences

The defences of consent, contributory negligence and warning notices, as explained in the section on the Occupiers' Liability Act 1957, apply to trespassers as well as lawful visitors. In the case of child trespassers, whether these defences will be successful will depend on the age and understanding of the child.

Remedies

If the occupier is liable for breach of duty to a trespasser, the remedy that can be claimed is damages for personal injury only. Damage caused to personal property, such as clothes, cannot be claimed.

Comparison

Table 7.2 compares the 1957 and 1984 Occupiers' Liability Acts.

▸ **Table 7.2:** A comparison of the 1957 and 1984 Occupiers' Liability Acts

Occupiers' Liability Act 1957	Occupiers' Liability Act 1984
For the common duty of care to exist the occupier must take such care as is reasonable to see that the visitor will be reasonably safe.	For a duty to exist the occupier has to be aware of the danger and knows, or has reasonable grounds to believe, that the trespasser is in the vicinity of the danger. This is a subjective test, which is opposite to that in the Occupiers' Liability Act 1957 and to many other torts that are judged objectively.
It could be said to be unfair that an occupier is liable even if they have no knowledge of reason for the accident or the allurement.	It requires the occupier to have actual knowledge of the danger. So if the occupier has no knowledge of it then they will not owe a duty, as in Rhind v Astbury Water Park (2002). This could be unfair on trespasser.
The occupier will be judged objectively. In other words, doing what the reasonable occupier would have done.	There is a duty owed if the occupier may reasonably be expected to offer some protection against the danger. Whether the occupier may be judged to have acted reasonably may depend on the claimant - what is reasonable for that particular claimant taking into account their age and understanding.
In a claim based on injury while swimming, there is a duty to make sure that the premises are reasonably safe.	There is no obligation on the occupier to check for the existence of a danger.
Judges will often find in favour of lawful visitors. It is in the interests of the public that lawful visitors are safe and an occupier should be responsible for their safety if they are behaving in a normal way.	Statutory rules appear to give trespassers the right to claim. However, the approach of judges has been to often find against trespassers. The public would consider it unfair that a trespasser should gain from their own illegal or irresponsible actions.

Vicarious liability

Vicarious liability shifts the burden of compensating the victim of an accident onto someone other than the person who committed the tort. The clearest example is where an employer has to pay for a tort committed by an employee. It imposes strict liability on the employer as they will not be at fault themselves, or have directly caused the accident, but will still be liable to pay compensation. Vicarious liability can be justified because the employer is taking a benefit from the employee and should be in control of what they do. Therefore they should accept responsibility for the actions of their employees. An employer is also more likely to have the financial resources to pay compensation than the employee - either from funds or through liability insurance.

There are two conditions to be satisfied:

- The person who committed the tort is an employee as opposed to an independent contractor (or a **self-employed** person).
- They were acting in the course of their employment.

Key term

Self-employed - also known legally as independent contractor. Unlike an employee, they will have to accept legal liability for any acts and omissions that cause injury to another.

Tests used to determine employment status

Whether a worker is regarded as employed or self-employed for the purposes of vicarious liability is a legal test, as opposed to a person's employment status for tax purposes. There are several tests that can be used:

- The control test - this determines how much control the employer had over the employee in the way the employee did their work, which may be difficult as employers are often not in full control of their employees if they are working away from the place of employment. In Yewens v Noakes (1880), it was said that this test involved asking whether the master (employer) had the right to control what was done and the way in which it was done. Subsequently, the features that could be taken into account included the power to employ the worker, the right to control how the work was done, the right to suspend or dismiss the worker and the payment of wages. This test does not apply to many workers now but a case where it did was Hawley v Luminar Leisure Ltd (2006).

Key case

Hawley v Luminar Leisure Ltd (2006)

Facts

A bouncer who was supplied to nightclubs by a firm of specialist suppliers assaulted a customer outside the club. The suppliers went into liquidation so the injured claimant sued the club. The court decided that, as the club exercised so much control over the bouncer in how he should do his work, it employed him and was vicariously liable for his actions.

Legal principle – a person can still be considered an employee if the employer controls how they should work, even if there are other factors present which suggest they are self-employed.

- The integration test – if a person's work is fully integrated into the business, the business will be vicariously liable for the person's actions. For example, a captain of a ship is an employee but a pilot bringing the ship into port is not; a chauffeur is an employee but a taxi driver is not.
- The economic reality or multiple test – this looks at the whole situation between the worker and the employer including factors such as:
  - tools, equipment or uniform – who owns any tools, equipment or uniform used in the work?
  - payments – an employee will receive regular payments on weekly or monthly terms, but a self-employed person is likely to receive a single payment for the whole job.
  - tax, pension and National Insurance – an employee will usually have these deducted from the regular payments and these payments will be sent to HM Revenue and Customs (HMRC). A self-employed person will deal with their own tax arrangements and make tax payments directly to HMRC.
  - description – how the worker describes themselves (as employed or self-employed), though this should not be conclusive.
  - how much independence is present – whether the worker has to take orders from a manager, whether they can take work from other sources and the hours they have to work.

Discussion

Are the following characteristics of being employed or of being an independent contractor?

- Set hours of work
- Use own tools or equipment in work
- Regular salary paid
- Holiday taken at time of choice
- Manager directs how work done
- Keep own financial records
- Health and safety training provided
- Tax and pension contributions deducted
- Send out invoices for work completed
- Maternity/paternity leave available
- Can employ workers when required
- Uniform provided
- Have own liability insurance policy
- Have dismissal/redundancy rights
- Provide a contract for services
- Enter a contract of service

Acting in the course of employment

To prove whether an employer is liable, it has to be proved whether the employee committing the tort was acting in the course of employment. This again is a legal test and does not merely cover committing a tort in the workplace.

Acting against orders

If the employee is doing their job but acts against orders in the way they do it, the employer can still be liable for any tort committed by them.

Key case

Limpus v London General (1862)

Facts

The employer instructed its bus drivers not to race other drivers when collecting passengers. One driver caused an accident when racing. The employer was liable as the driver was doing what he was employed to do – even against orders.

Legal principle – an employee may still be acting in the course of employment even if acting against orders.

A more recent example is the case of Rose v Plenty (1976) where a dairy instructed its milkmen not to use child helpers on their milk rounds. One milkman did use a boy to help him but the boy was injured on the round. The dairy was vicariously liable for the milkman's negligence as one judge suggested that the dairy was benefiting from the work done by the boy.

If the employee causes injury by doing something outside their employment, the employer will not be liable. This is shown in Beard v London General Omnibus Company (1900) when a bus conductor, employed only to collect fares, drove a bus injuring the claimant. The employer was not liable as the conductor was doing something outside his employment.

Employee committing a criminal act

If the employee commits a crime during their work, the employer may be liable to the victim of the crime if there is a 'close connection' between the crime and what the employee was employed to do.

Key case

Lister v Hesley Hall (2001)

Facts

The warden of a school for children with emotional difficulties sexually assaulted some of the children. He was convicted of criminal offences. The House of Lords decided that there was a close connection between his job and what he did as the assaults were carried out on the school premises when he was looking after the children.

Legal principle – an employer will be liable for any criminal acts of the employee if there is a close connection between the act and the injury caused to the claimant.

This principle has been confirmed more recently by the Supreme Court.

Key case

Mohamud v Morrison's Supermarkets (2016)

Facts

A man employed at the defendant's petrol station assaulted a customer causing him serious injuries. The Supreme Court considered the job that had been given to the employee and whether there was a sufficient connection between the employee's job and what he did to the customer. They decided that as the employee was acting within the field of his employment – the assault was committed at work and within working hours – the employer was vicariously liable.

Legal principle – an employer will be liable for any criminal acts of the employee if there is a close connection between the act and the injury caused to the claimant.

Employee committing a negligent act

If the employee does a job badly, the employer can be liable for any negligent actions that cause injury to another.

Key case

Century Insurance v Northern Ireland Road Transport Board (1942)

Facts

A petrol tanker driver was delivering petrol to a petrol station when he lit a cigarette and threw a lighted match on the ground. This caused an explosion that destroyed several cars and damaged some houses. The employer was liable to pay compensation as the driver was doing his job, even though he acted negligently.

Legal principle – an employer can be vicariously liable for an employee's negligent actions.

Employee acting on a 'frolic' of their own

If the employee causes injury or damage to another while doing something outside the area or time of their work, the employer will not be liable.

Key case

Hilton v Thomas Burton (Rhodes) Ltd (1961)

Facts

Some employees were working away from their workplace. They took an unauthorised break by driving the firm's van to a café for tea but had an accident on the way back. The employers were not liable to pay compensation to the victim of the accident as the employees were on an unauthorised 'frolic'.

Legal principle – an employer will not be liable if an employee causes injury or damage while doing unauthorised activities during work hours.

If the tort is committed by an employee acting in the course of employment, the employer will be liable to pay compensation to the injured person. By the Civil Liability (Contribution) Act 1978, the employer can recover any compensation paid out from the employee, for example, by deducting from wages.

PAUSE POINT In small groups, consider the justification for vicarious liability.

Hint Compare employed and self-employed status.

Extend What could a business do to ensure that it could not be sued for the actions of an employee?

Assessment practice 7.2

C.P4 C.P5 C.M3 C.D2

Manish comes to your firm as a new client. He tells you he was badly injured in an accident and wants to know whether he can claim compensation.

He was walking across a yard when he was hit by a forklift truck and suffered serious injuries. The yard was originally part of a warehouse complex owned by James. For years, the yard was rarely used and local people used it as a shortcut from a main road to the housing estate where he lives. No one complained or tried to stop Manish or other locals from using the shortcut. Recently, the yard appeared to be used more regularly for brewing beer, and brewing materials and barrels were stored there. Fencing was put up and so were signs warning that the yard was private property. Manish said that recently he had noticed the signs had been blown or torn down, gaps had appeared in the fence and local people, including himself, had been walking across the yard. However, no one had tried to stop Manish or tell him not to use the yard.

Manish said that last week he was crossing the yard when he was hit by a forklift truck driven by Lee. The truck was reversing when it hit Manish, causing him injuries. Manish has found out that Lee was the manager of the site and was employed by James. Lee was an inexperienced forklift truck driver, and he did not look when reversing, hitting Manish.

1 Advise Manish in writing of any rights and remedies he may have against Lee in the tort of occupiers liability and for James' vicarious liability.

2 You decide that, to understand the rules better, you must evaluate the working and impact of the law of occupiers' and vicarious liability. Write up your file notes on this subject.

Plan

- Underline the most important facts or key words in the scenario.
- Identify the relevant areas of the law. What are the relevant statutes or case law?

Do

- I need to consider the possibility of there being more than one set of rules that apply to the scenario.
- I need to structure my answer with headings for each possible type of liability.

Review

- Have I used a relevant case to make each point?
- Have I considered the status of each named person, for example. visitor, trespasser, employer, employee?

Explore liability for private nuisance and Rylands v Fletcher

Private nuisance

Private nuisance is the unlawful interference with a person's use or enjoyment of land coming from neighbouring land. The interference will generally be due to intangible matters causing annoyance to a person, for example, smells, smoke or noise. However, it can sometimes be physical interference, such as tree roots growing onto a neighbour's land.

The person who can take an action in nuisance is the person suffering from the nuisance and they must have an **interest in the land** as an owner or tenant. The person who can be sued is the person causing the problem, whether or not they have an interest in the land.

Private nuisance is all about reasonableness in the use of property. If the court decides that the action is reasonable, they will not find it a nuisance. If they find the action unreasonable, it can be a nuisance.

Key terms

Private nuisance – the unlawful interference with a person's use or enjoyment of land from neighbouring land.

Interest in land – a person has to have a legal stake in the land affected, either as an owner or tenant. A member of the owner's family will not have an interest in the land, unless their name is on the legal documents.

Malice – a deliberate act on the part of the person causing the nuisance.

Factors of reasonableness

In order to decide whether an action causing the nuisance is reasonable or not, the court will take various factors into account (see Figure 7.3):

- Locality and character of the neighbourhood – it was said in Sturges v Bridgeman (1879) that 'what would be a nuisance in Belgrave Square [an exclusive area in central London] would not be so in Bermondsey [a commercial area by the River Thames]'. So, if the problem is occurring in a quiet residential area it may be a nuisance, whereas if it is occurring in a mixed-use area or an industrial area it is less likely to be considered a nuisance.
- The duration of the problem – the longer the action goes on, the more likely it is to be unreasonable. However, in the case Crown River Cruises v Kimbolton Fireworks Ltd (1996), a one-off 20-minute firework display was enough to amount to a nuisance.
- The time of day – if the activity is being carried on in the evening or at night, it is more likely to be a nuisance than if it is being carried on during the day.
- The social utility or usefulness of the action – if the activity causing the nuisance is providing employment or a social benefit in the area, it may be considered to be reasonable. However, in Adams v Ursell (1913) a popular fish and chip shop was found to be causing a nuisance due to smells coming from it and it was forced to close.

Reflect

- Do you think the same result in Adams v Ursell (1913) would be ordered by the court today?
- How could a takeaway shop deal with smells?

- Whether there is any **malice** present – in Christie v Davey (1893) a music teacher complained that her neighbour banged trays on the wall of their terrace house to annoy her and to disrupt her while she was giving piano lessons. His deliberate actions were motivated by bad feelings and the court found them to be unreasonable.

Research

The case of Hollywood Silver Fox Farm v Emmett (1936) is also about malice.

- What were the facts of the case?
- What was the result of the case?

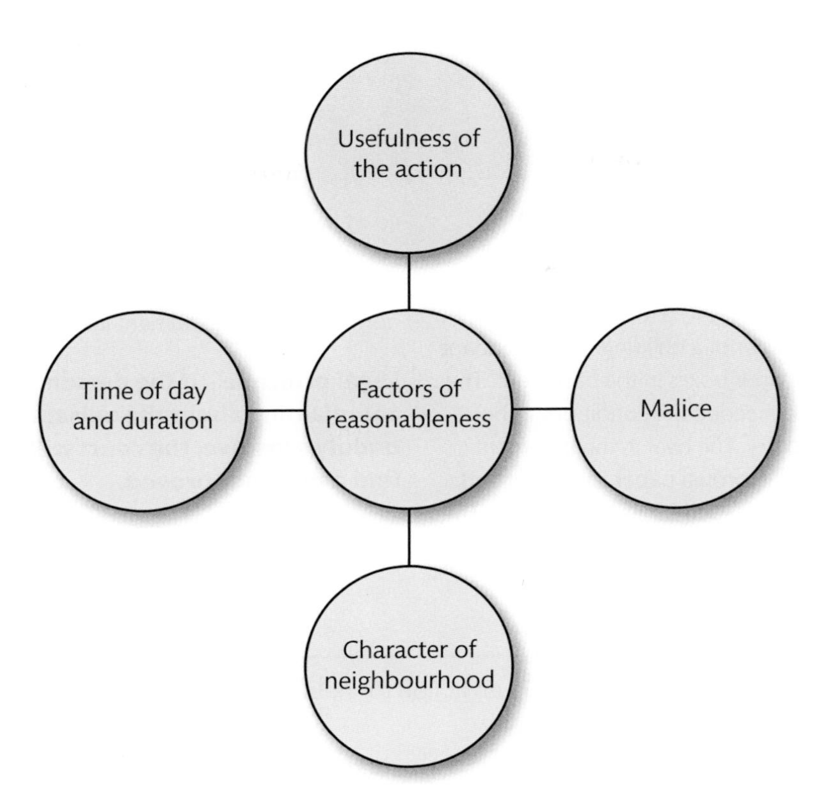

Figure 7.3: Factors that the court will take into account when deciding if an activity is a nuisance

Defences to a nuisance action

- Statutory authority – if permission for the use of the land has been given by the local authority, the action may not be a nuisance. In Allen v Gulf Oil Refinery 1981, the claimant brought an action in nuisance for the smell, noise and vibration created by an oil refinery. Building the oil refinery was authorised by an Act of Parliament. The defendant was not liable as it had a defence of statutory authority.
- **Prescription** may be a defence to an action – if the action has been carrying on for at least 20 years and there has been no complaint between the parties in that time, then the defendant may be said to have a prescriptive right to continue. It has to be between the same parties.
- If the claimant moves into an area where an action has been carried on previously by the defendant without any complaint, then the defendant cannot say that there has been no problem previously and the claimant has only just moved into the area. This can be illustrated in the case of Miller v Jackson (1977).

Key term

Prescription – a defence in nuisance when the activity being complained about has been carried on for at least 20 years.

Research

Research the case of Miller v Jackson (1977) where moving to the area of the nuisance was argued.

- Why were the Millers complaining?
- What did the problem stop them doing?
- What did the club offer to do and was this acceptable to the Millers?
- The Millers came to their house some years after the club had been using their land. Did this matter?
- What was the eventual decision of the majority judges in the Court of Appeal?
- In your opinion, was this a fair result?

- If it can be shown the claimant or their property is particularly sensitive, then the action may not be a nuisance.

Key case

Robinson v Kilvert (1889)

Facts

The claimant stored brown paper on the ground floor of a building. The defendant stored paper boxes in the basement. The claimant needed the conditions to be hot and dry. The heat in the basement caused the brown paper to dry out and the claimant sued for its loss in value. The court decided that the brown paper was particularly delicate and the heat from the basement would not have dried out normal paper. The claimant lost his claim.

Legal principle – if the person complaining about the nuisance is unduly sensitive, the court will not find a nuisance proved.

Research

In Hunter v Canary Wharf (1997), an action for nuisance failed.

- What were the facts of this case?
- What was the problem for the local residents?
- Why did the action fail?

Key term

Injunction – a court order preventing someone from doing an act (prohibitory injunction) or requiring them to do something (mandatory injunction).

Remedies

A person may have to suffer the nuisance for some time before the court will order any remedy. This is particularly so in the case of noise nuisance where the person suffering the problem will have to obtain extensive evidence of the amount and times of the nuisance before the courts will act. If it can be shown that the defendant has been causing a nuisance, the court can order an **injunction** to either stop the problem completely or to partly limit it – for example, to limit the hours when the activity can take place.

Alternative dispute resolution (ADR) as a remedy will often fail or not be possible in a nuisance action as the parties become fixed in their positions as they try to protect their property. Whether the court orders an action to stop or not, the parties will still have to live beside each other and there may well be continued bad feeling between them. Therefore, even a successful legal claim is not a completely practical solution.

Link

See Unit 1 for more information on ADR. The most appropriate methods of ADR for a nuisance action would be negotiation or mediation.

The Supreme Court has recently considered some of the long-established rules of nuisance, as seen in Coventry v Lawrence (2014).

Key case

Coventry v Lawrence (2014)

Facts

The claimant bought a house in 2006, 864 metres from the defendant's motor sport stadium. Planning permission had originally been granted in 1975 for speedway use and subsequently for other motor sport use including stock cars, bangers and motorcross. The claimant brought an action based on noise nuisance requiring an injunction limiting the use of the track but this was refused by the Supreme Court.

Legal principle – the Supreme Court decided that:

- **the rule in Sturges v Bridgeman (1879) regarding the character of neighbourhood still applies, and coming to the nuisance can still be used as a defence**
- **where a claimant builds on their property or changes the use of their property after the defendant has started his use of the activity complained of, then the defence may fail**
- **damages may be considered as a remedy more often in nuisance cases, especially where planning permission has been awarded to the defendant for the use of their land or where the public interest is involved, such as employees losing their jobs if an injunction is awarded.**

Reflect

What is the effect of a civil injunction on a defendant?

Scenario

Do you think the following can be actionable nuisances?

1. Venus holds a noisy party to celebrate her 18th birthday. There was loud music and dancing until 3.00 a.m., which annoyed her neighbours.
   - Would it matter if Venus had told her neighbours about the party and they did not object?
2. The residents of a care home are disturbed by the sound of young children playing in a playground next to the home.
   - Can the residents take action to stop the noise?
3. For more than 15 years, Farmer Giles has kept pigs on his farm. His neighbour Clive eventually objects to the smell.
   - Would it matter if Clive has only recently moved in to his house?
4. Builders are working on Jane's house extension from 8.00 a.m. to 4.00 p.m. every weekday. They are regularly using their drills and mixers to the annoyance of Tim their neighbour who works from home.
   - Would it be different if Tim worked night shifts and was used to sleeping through the day?

PAUSE POINT Produce a poster detailing the ways a nuisance claim can be dealt with both in and out of court.

Hint Look online for ways of dealing with civil cases out of court.

Extend Identify advantages and disadvantages of dealing with a nuisance claim in and out of court.

Rylands v Fletcher liability

If the claimant suffers actual damage to their property, an action in nuisance is unlikely to be appropriate. Instead, an action using the strict liability claim of Rylands v Fletcher could be used as an alternative to claiming in negligence.

Key case

Rylands v Fletcher (1868)

Facts

The defendants instructed builders to build a reservoir so that they could fill this with water to power their mill.

The water was non-naturally occurring, as it was stored for later use. The builders negligently failed to properly cap mineshafts, which flooded when the reservoir was filled causing damage to the mine.

The essentials of this tort are in the following definition given by Blackburn J: 'if a person brings onto his land and keeps there anything likely to do mischief if it escapes, must keep it at his peril and if he does not do so he is liable for all the natural consequence of its escape'

Legal principle – the claimant must show:

- **the storage of a non-naturally occurring material**
- **the material escapes**
- **it causes reasonably foreseeable damage to adjoining property.**

Non-natural use of land

The material stored must be non-naturally occurring and it must be brought onto the land and kept there. For example, neither garden fertiliser nor fireworks are naturally occurring materials and liability for these materials has been found previously. However, in Rickards v Lothian (1913) water for domestic use was considered a naturally occurring substance and the occupier was not liable when the flat below was flooded.

Reflect

In Read v J. Lyons & Company (1947), there was a storage of explosives in a munitions factory. The claimant was injured when there was an explosion in the factory. Her claim in Rylands v Fletcher failed as there was no escape from one property onto another.

- Why do you think she claimed in Rylands v Fletcher?
- In your opinion, why did she not use the tort of negligence?

The nature of escape

There must be a movement of the material from one property onto adjoining property.

Foreseeability of damage

The material that has escaped must cause reasonably foreseeable damage to adjoining property.

Key case

Cambridge Water Company v Eastern Counties Leather (1994)

Facts

There was an escape of solvent from the defendant's leather tanning factory into the claimant's water storage facility. The storage facility was over a mile from the factory. The House of Lords decided that it was not reasonably foreseeable for the water to be contaminated from such a distance and the claim failed.

Legal principle - a claim under Rylands v Fletcher can only be made where the damage caused is reasonably foreseeable.

Rylands v Fletcher, as a strict liability tort, should be easier for a claimant to prove than negligence, particularly where there has been an escape of hazardous material. There is no need to show how and why the material escaped - just the fact that it did and caused damage to adjoining property.

In many areas such as pollution of water, radioactive material and defective products, there is statutory regulation so the need for the tort of Rylands v Fletcher has disappeared. Examples include the Reservoirs Act 1975, when water has been accumulated, and the Nuclear Installations Acts 1965 and 1969, which cover the escape of radioactive substances. These statutory regulations may also allow recovery of damages for personal injury, which cannot be claimed under Rylands v Fletcher.

Reflect

- What are the differences between claiming in negligence and using strict liability?
- What are the advantages to the claimant of using a strict liability action?

Defences

The possible defences to an action in Rylands v Fletcher include:

- an act of a stranger - the material escaped because of an act of a stranger over whom the defendant had no control
- acts of God - natural events such as an earthquake flood or other natural disaster which caused the material to escape, mean the defendant would not be liable
- statutory authority - there is permission given by the local authority for the storage of material
- consent - the claimant was fully or partly at fault for the escape of the material.

When Rylands v Fletcher was decided, there was a view that it was a broad, strict liability action covering both damage to property and personal injury. However, as time went on, the courts took a more restrictive approach as seen in Rickards v Lothian (1913).

There were other factors which make the tort difficult to prove, such as the requirement that there be a non-natural use of land. The simplest way to defeat a claim was to show that the use of land was a natural use. Claimants were encouraged to use the tort of negligence, even though it required proof of fault. In Transco plc v Stockport MBC (2003), the House of Lords rejected the idea of abandoning the tort or that it should be treated as having been absorbed within the general law of negligence. They confirmed that an interest in the land affected by the escaping material is needed and personal injury is not within the scope of a claim.

Scenario

Rufus owned a factory. He stored chemicals used in his production process near to the boundary of the house of his neighbour William. It was found that the chemicals leaked from their storage containers into William's garden, ruining his prize flowers and vegetables. The soil in William's garden was contaminated.

1 Do you think that William would have a claim against Rufus? What would he have to show?
2 Would it matter if it was later seen on CCTV that a burglar had entered Rufus' factory and overturned the storage containers?

Remedies

If the claim is successful the claimant can claim damages for the damage caused to their property. An injunction to prevent further damage may also be appropriate.

Assessment practice 7.3

D.P6 D.M4 D.D3

You are asked by Richard, a partner of your firm, to consider whether Claire, one of his clients, has a possible claim.

Claire lives in a block of flats that was built only a year ago. The land on which the flats were built was formerly wasteland and is close to Adrian's garage business. Claire and the other residents have complained about the noise, smells and general pollution from Adrian's business. When Claire complained directly to Adrian, the noise seemed to increase and it became worse at evenings and weekends.

One day, there was apparently an explosion that seemed to come from the paint shop in Adrian's garage. The explosion caused a film of toxic paint to coat Claire's windows. All of Claire's windows needed to be replaced at a cost of £5,000. Claire has seen a report in the local paper that suggests that the explosion was caused by vandalism.

1 Richard asks you to write a memo, so that he can advise Claire, setting out what rights and remedies Claire may have about the problems with the noise, smell and general pollution, and about the cost of replacing the windows.
2 Richard also asks you to include your thoughts in the memo re. evaluating the effectiveness of liability in private nuisance and Rylands v Fletcher liability.

Plan

- Underline the most important facts or key words in the scenario.
- Identify the relevant areas of the law. What are the relevant factors and case law that have to be taken into account?

Do

- I need to consider the possibility of there being more than one factor and set of rules applying to the scenario
- I need to structure my answer with headings for each possible type of liability.

Review

- Have I used a relevant case to make each point?
- Have I considered the possible outcomes and remedies for each part of in the scenario?

Further reading and resources

Textbooks

Cooke, J. - *Law of Tort*, 12th Edition (Pearson, 2015)

Elliott, C. and Quinn, F. - *Tort Law*, 10th Edition (Pearson, 2015)

Revision guides are less detailed than the textbooks but may give a good guide to the subject:

Bermingham, V. and Watson, S. - *Nutshells Tort*, 10th Edition (Sweet and Maxwell, 2014)

Finch, E. and Fafinski, S. – *Law Express: Tort Law*, 6th Edition (Pearson, 2016)

THINK FUTURE

Patrick Quinn

Chief Executive of an insurance broker

I joined my family's small insurance broking business immediately after leaving school. I had no knowledge of the insurance business at that time, so I had to learn on the job. Over the years I have taken professional qualifications with the Chartered Insurance Institute, and I now encourage all my staff to undertake CPD and to obtain professional qualifications.

When I started, the business was mainly dealing with local clients who required insurance cover; principally this was cover for motor vehicles, but it could also involve cover for premises. Initially, my role was gaining insurance knowledge and applying this to understand and meet my clients' needs. At this time I had a great deal of personal contact with my clients. In recent years, the business has developed to concentrate on the exclusive provision of motor insurance cover. In order to do this we have put in place systems to make us extremely efficient. Our client base has expanded to deal with drivers from all over the country, and much of our contact with clients is through the Internet.

My role within the business has changed to allow me to develop the operation of systems that mean the business can deal with a high volume of enquiries. I now have very little day-to-day contact with clients. I also oversee investigating how the further use of new technology could make the business more efficient while still providing an excellent quality of service to our clients. For example, I am presently working on the development of a phone app and a dedicated YouTube channel.

In the past few years, one technological advance that has proved popular with our clients is having a tracking device installed in their vehicles. This can help a driver prove to an insurance company that they can be considered 'safe'. A client can also monitor their own driving at home, to see what they are doing well and where they could improve. If there is a collision, the tracker allows events leading up to the accident to be reviewed, which may prevent the client from being blamed. Clients who are involved in accidents are referred to their insurance company, who will deal with the legal aspects of a claim. Another benefit is that if a vehicle is stolen it can usually be tracked. In one case, the police accused our client of being a getaway driver in an armed robbery, but he was able to use the tracker to show that he was not involved at all. In another case, a client had an accident in a remote area and was able to use the tracker to call and direct the emergency services to the scene.

Index of key cases

Civil

Criminal

Index

Key terms are highlighted in **bold**

Appendix

District Judges Certificate: FPR 2010.r.7.20(2)(a) **Case No.** MSRB/2017/0021

PRINCIPAL REGISTRY OF THE DIVISION

Between MARY SMITH .... Petitioner
and ROBERT BURTON .... Respondent
and .... Co-respondent

I am satisfied that the requirements of FPR 7.19.7.20 and PD7A have been complied with, and I am satisfied that this is an undefended case within the meaning of FPR 7.1(3)

Dated: 15TH JANUARY 2017 **District Judge:** ....

DISTRICT JUDGES CERTIFICATE

I certify that:
The Petitioner .... has sufficiently proved the contents of the petition herein and is entitled to a decree of (divorce) ~~(judicial separation)~~, the marriage having irretrievably broken down, the facts found proved being

~~(a) the Respondent's .... adultery~~
✓ (b) the Respondent's .... unreasonable behaviour
~~(c) the Respondent's .... 2 years desertion~~
~~(d) 2 years separation with consent~~
~~(e) 5 years separation (no consent required)~~

~~• And to an order that the .... to pay .... the costs of the Petitioner.~~

✓ • and to an order for financial relief as agreed between the petitioner and the Respondent.

~~• and I further certify that I am satisfied that there are no children to whom section 41 of the Matrimonial Causes Act 1973 applies.~~

Delete the boxes which do not apply

Date: 16TH JANUARY 2017 ~~**(Deputy)**~~ **District Judge:** ....

TAKE NOTICE the Court has listed the application on
the 31ST **day of** JANUARY **20**17 **at 10:00am**

for the making of a decree ~~(and of the orders included in the District Judge's Certificate)~~, by a

District Judge sitting at the Principal Registry of the Family Division, First Avenue House, 42-49 High Holborn, London, WC1V 6NP

Please note: *Unless the decree or any of the orders opposed, it is unnecessary for any party to attend Court on the above date; any party who wishes to attend the hearing to make representations on any question as to costs, must serve on every other party, not less than 2 days before the hearing, written notice of their intention to attend the hearing and apply for, or oppose the making of, an order for costs (as the case may be).*

IMPORTANT: If there are children of the family please see overleaf for further details

▶ An example of a divorce certificate (decree nisi)

Identifier: TWL/2012/1111 GRF: 006433

GENDER RECOGNITION CERTIFICATE

1. Name	Katy Belford
2. Date of Birth	12 September 1963
3. Gender	Female
4. Date of Issue	15 March 2012

The above named is, from the date of issue, of the gender shown.

CAUTION: THERE ARE OFFENCES RELATING TO MAKING OR USING A FALSE CERTIFICATE.
***CROWN COPYRIGHT**

WARNING: A CERTIFICATE IS NOT EVIDENCE OF IDENTITY

This certificate is issued in pursuance of the Gender Recognition Act 2004. By section 9 of the Gender Recognition Act, the person to whom this certificate has been issued is for all purposes the gender shown. Valid only if sealed or stamped by an issuing authority under the Gender Recognition Act 2004.

▶ An example of a gender recognition certificate

CERTIFIED COPY OF AN ENTRY OF MARRIAGE

Pursuant to the Marriage Act 1949

Registration District Westminster								
2016 Marriage solemnized at The Register Office in the District of Westminster in the City of Westminster								
Columns:- 1		**2**	**3**	**4**	**5**	**6**	**7**	**8**
No.	**When married**	**Name and surname**	**Age**	**Condition**	**Rank or profession**	**Residence at the time of marriage**	**Father's names and surname**	**Rank or profession of father**
173	Fourth March 2017	Keith Roger MASKELL	48 years	Previous marriage dissolved	Publisher	London, England	Thomas Joseph MASKELL (deceased)	Civil Servant
		Imogen Rose TAYLOR	42 years	Single	Musician	London, England	Timothy Paul TAYLOR	Land Agent

Married in The Register Office **by certificate before me**

This marriage was solemnized between us, { I. Taylor } in the presence of us, { T Maskell } { Alasdair Cuthbert, Superintendent Registrar; M B MacDonald, Deputy Registrar }

Certified to be a true copy of an entry in a register in my custody, ... ***~~Registrar~~/Superintendent Registrar**

Date: 04 . 03 . 2017

▶ An example of an entry of marriage (marriage certificate)

Civil Partnership Act 2004 (c. 33)

NOTICE OF CIVIL PARTNERSHIP

PARTICULARS RELATING TO THE PERSONS FORMING A CIVIL PARTNERSHIP

Name and surname (1)	Date of birth (2)			Sex (3)	Condition (4)	Occupation (5)	Period of registration (6)	Venue in which civil partnership is to be formed (7)	Nationality and registration authority of residence (8)
Edward Henry JONES	25	03	1962	Male	Previous marriage dissolved	Consultant optometrist	More than a month	The Guildhall High Street Windsor	British - The Royal Borough of Windsor and Maidenhead
Daniel John FINNEGAN	25	10	1974	Male	Single	Television producer	More than a month	The Guildhall High Street Windsor	Irish - The Royal Borough of Windsor and Maidenhead

Name and surname (1)	Date of birth (2)			Sex (3)	Condition (4)	Occupation (5)	Period of registration (6)	Venue in which civil partnership is to be formed (7)	Nationality and registration authority of residence (8)
Daniel John FINNEGAN	25	10	1974	Male	Single	Television producer	More than a month	The Guildhall High Street Windsor	Irish - The Royal Borough of Windsor and Maidenhead
Edward Henry JONES	25	03	1962	Male	Previous marriage dissolved	Consultant optometrist	More than a month	The Guildhall High Street Windsor	British - The Royal Borough of Windsor and Maidenhead

To the Registration Authority of The Royal Borough of Windsor and Maidenhead

▶ An example of a notice of civil partnership

Civil Partnership Act 2004 (c. 33)

NOTICE OF MARRIAGE

PARTICULARS RELATING TO THE PERSONS TO BE MARRIED

Name and surname (1)	Date of birth (2)	Sex (3)	Condition (4)	Occupation (5)	Period of registration (6)	Church or building where the marriage is to be solemnized (7)	Nationality and district of residence (8)

To the Superintendent Registrar of the district of ....

I, the above-named .... *(name and surname)*

of .... *(place of residence)*

give you notice that I and .... *(name and surname)*

of .... *(place of residence)*

intend to be married on the authority of certificates within *one month/three months/twelve months from the date of entry of this notice and declare as follows:

1. I believe that there is no impediment of kindred or alliance or other lawful hindrance to the said marriage.
2. I and the person named above have for the period of seven days immediately before giving of this notice had our usual places within the districts named in Column 8 above.
3. In respect of myself, I am eighteen years of age or over.
4. In respect of the said .... *(name and surname)* *he/she is eighteen years of age or over.
5. I further declare that to the best of my knowledge and belief the declarations which I have made above and the particulars relating to the persons to be married are true.
   I understand that if any of the declarations are false I MAYBE LIABLE TO PROSECUTION UNDER THE PERJURY ACT 1911
6. I also understand that if, in fact, there is an impediment of kindred or alliance or other lawful hindrance to intended marriage the marriage may be invalid or void and the contracting of the marriage may render on or both of the parties GUILTY OF A CRIME AND LIABLE TO THE PENALTIES OR BIGAMY OR SUCH OTHER CRIME AS MAY HAVE BEEN COMMITTED.

(Signed) .... **Date** ....

▶ An example of a notice of marriage